John Plamenatz

MAN AND SOCIETY

POLITICAL AND SOCIAL THEORIES FROM MACHIAVELLI TO MARX

VOLUME TWO

From Montesquieu to the
Early Socialists

A New Edition
Revised by M. E. Plamenatz and Robert Wokler

Longman
London and New York

Longman Group UK Limited,
Longman House, Burnt Mill, Harlow,
Essex CM20 2JE, England
and Associated Companies throughout the world.

Published in the United States of America
by Longman Publishing Group, New York

First published 1963
Second edition 1992

British Library Cataloguing in Publication Data
Plamenatz, John
  Man and society: political and social theories
  from Machiavelli to Marx: Vol 2. From Montesquieu
  to the early socialists. – New ed.
  I. Title   II. Plamenatz, M. E.   III. Wokler, Robert
  320.509
  ISBN 0–582–05546–6

Library of Congress Cataloging in Publication Data
Plamenatz, John Petrov.
    Man and society: political and social theories from Machiavelli
  to Marx/John Plamenatz. — A new ed./revised by M. E. Plamenatz
  and Robert Wokler.
      p.   cm.
    Includes indexes.
    Contents: v. 1. From the Middle Ages to Locke — v. 2. From
  Montesquieu to the early socialists — v. 3. Hegel, Marx and Engels,
  and the idea of progress.
      ISBN 0–582–05540–7(v. 1):   — ISBN 0–582–05546–6 (v. 2):
  — ISBN 0–582–05541–5 (v. 3):
      1. Political science—History.   2. Social sciences—History.
  I. Plamenatz, M. E.   II. Wokler, Robert, 1942–   .   III. Title.
  JA83.P53   1991
  3066.2′09—dc20   91–19404
                                                                 CIP

Set by 5 in 10/12pt Bembo Roman
Printed in Malaysia by VVP

To My Father

Contents

Editors' Preface

John Plamenatz first conceived this work in the 1950s, as a set of twenty-eight lectures which he gave at Oxford and then at other universities. Substantially revised and extended over a number of years, these lectures were then recast once again, for publication in two volumes, in 1963. Subject only to occasional minor alteration, *Man and Society* has remained in print, in that form, ever since.

In his original preface Plamenatz observed that his text was 'not a history of political thought', but rather, as his subtitle made clear, a critical examination of some important social and political theories from Machiavelli to Marx. His interpretation of the ideas and assumptions of past thinkers was mainly designed to elucidate significant treatments of central problems in political and social thought which are still pertinent today. It was intended not only as a commentary on the doctrines of important thinkers but equally as a contribution to political theory by way of commentary – that is, through an assessment of the profound insights and fundamental errors of influential thinkers of the past whose ideas have continued to inform the beliefs of persons who reflect upon the nature of society and government. That critical approach was and remains the chief focus of *Man and Society*. In examining the views of others, Plamenatz sought to show why they still matter to us, why propositions put forward at times very different from our own may be judged in the light of their universal application, as their authors themselves so frequently imagined, and often postulated, was the case. Plamenatz believed that while the idiom of discourse of political and social thinkers is always particular and unique, the substance of their arguments, and the truth or falsity of their contentions, do not depend on the local and specific circumstances which give rise to them. Great political thinkers are themselves characteristically critical and innovative. In flouting the political assumptions or linguistic conventions of their age, they aspire to free themselves and their readers from dead dogma. They develop or cross-examine the ideas of pre-eminent thinkers of previous ages and thereby add to or break from traditions of discourse not circumscribed by the lifetime of any single figure. That wider context – indeed the whole of the discipline of political and social theory – is the main subject of Plamenatz's work, to which his critical interpretation of other doctrines itself forms a major contribution.

It would, however, be misleading to read his commentary only in that light. Plamenatz wished to show, to historians, that the meaning of theories was not determined solely by the circumstances that occasioned their production, and, to political scientists, that old theories are often deeper, richer and more lucid than new theories which ignore them. But crucial to both endeavours was the need for accuracy in the interpretation of past thinkers, for familiarity with the varieties of language they employed, for a proper grasp of the meaning they intended to convey through their writings, in so far as it remains accessible. In distinguishing a critical examination of past doctrines from an historical investigation of their origins, Plamenatz was anxious to ensure that he conveyed their sense, as well as their significance, correctly. He was convinced that anachronistic interpretations of ideas were no less discreditable to the political theorist than to the historian, and he went to great lengths to ensure the contextual reliability of his readings. His views on Marx came to be progressively refined by the historical research of other scholars, particularly that which was devoted to Marx's earlier writings, in the years prior to the publication of *Man and Society;* his interpretation of Hobbes, by contrast, was strengthened and reaffirmed in reply to recent scholarship which he regarded as more ingenious than plausible; the best-informed contextual readings of Locke prompted significant revisions of his lecture notes on the subject, especially with regard to the dating of the *Two Treatises of Government* and Locke's connection with the Glorious Revolution.

Over the past twenty-six years or so, readers of *Man and Society* may not have been sufficiently aware of the importance Plamenatz attached to the contextual interpretation of political doctrines, particularly with regard to relatively minor writers who helped more to shape than to transform the conventions and discourse of their age. In his lectures Plamenatz recognized, and indeed emphasized, the historical significance of thinkers who were not so much innovatory as representative, who articulated the widely shared assumptions of their contemporaries but did not seek to undermine them, or whose contributions to political disputations were more polemical than philosophical, more apposite and influential within a particular context, because less abstract. For no other reason than that of sheer lack of space in a work already too long for a two-volume format, Plamenatz was obliged to compress his material, truncating certain chapters and deleting others. Because doctrines most circumscribed by local and contingent interests have less bearing on the aspirations of other thinkers in different cultures, he elected, when required to be more brief, to remove sections which were of more restricted, more exclusively historical, concern. This foreshortening of particular topics, including even the excision of whole periods of debate and controversy, somewhat reduced the breadth and scope of the original lectures. In restoring mainly that material – devoted above all to doctrinal disputes and to the cut and thrust of battles fought in pursuit of power as well as the truth – we have, now in three volumes, sought to rectify this abridgement. More than was possible in the two-volume edition of *Man and Society,* we have followed Plamenatz's initial scheme in joining the peaks of political argument, as he perceived them, not only to each other, but also to the foothills from which they separately rise.

To the original introduction of 1963 we have added a number of lines drawn from his preface to the lectures, which address what Plamenatz took to be the contribution to political theory of minor authors and their polemical writings. We have assembled two lectures on ancient and mediaeval thought, together with fragments of some earlier drafts, to form the new opening chapter in volume I of this edition, including some of the most historically discursive additional material, under the title, 'The Political Thought of the Middle Ages'. Chapter three of volume I, here entitled 'The Reformation and Liberty of Conscience', has been expanded in length by about one-third, embracing fuller discussions of the mediaeval church, the doctrines of Luther and Calvin, and the ideas of their disciples and critics, especially Knox and Castellion. Chapter six of volume I, now bearing the title 'Divine Right, Absolute Monarchy and Early Theories of the Social Contract', has been enlarged by a similar amount, incorporating material from one lecture which Plamenatz offered on contract theory before Hobbes and Locke. In this chapter will be found extended commentaries on Hotman, Mornay, Mariana and Suárez, previously eliminated; the sections on Hotman and Mornay, in particular, initially presented in the form of two much compressed footnotes uncharacteristic of Plamenatz's style, are hereby restored to their originally intended place in this work, more conspicuously, perhaps, than any of our other revisions; we have, moreover, followed the practice of most recent scholarship in attributing the *Vindiciae contra tyrannos* to Mornay rather than Languet. Volume I, chapter seven, entitled 'English Political Theory from the Breach with Rome to the Restoration', comprises material entirely unpublished before, distilled from two lectures in different formats devoted to Elizabethan and Jacobean political thought and to the English Civil War, to which we have appended another lecture on Harrington. In volume II, chapter five, we have incorporated sections from two lectures on Bentham and Philosophical Radicalism and a third on John Stuart Mill, clearly a centrally important figure in modern political thought, whose ideas had already engaged the attention of Plamenatz in his study of *The English Utilitarians,* but who, again on account of lack of space, received only passing mention before in *Man and Society*. In volume II, moreover, we have divided what was originally the longest chapter, on 'The Early Socialists, French and English', into two, now chapters six and seven, adding to each a few pages, where appropriate, drawn from a lecture devoted to the ideas of Saint-Simon. Volume III, embracing the last five chapters of what was volume II, remains largely unaltered, although we have made a number of slight changes to accord with our corrections to the other volumes and have amended the titles of three chapters.

In each case we have tried to shape the new material in a style and order closely approximating the initial format of the published work. Although the lecture variants of several other chapters contain substantial additional and striking differences as well, we have decided not to include any extracts which would have required major alteration to the text of the already printed volumes. In many instances, however, we have changed a term or phrase of the original version, sometimes to accommodate the intercalations, occasionally for the sake of fluency or coherence. We have corrected several passages in the light of evidence of which Plamenatz himself could not have been aware. We have also corrected or identified quotations – in a few cases thanks to the assistance of Dr Terrell Carver, Mr Alistair Edwards or Mr Michael Evans – whose previous citation was inaccurate or incomplete. Since particular themes are raised in the more historically contextual chapters that have great bearing upon the argument of the work as a whole, we have not attempted to reassemble those chapters so that they might incorporate the findings of recent scholarship or the most up-to-date interpretations of old issues and debates. In revising a text originally prepared several decades ago, we felt no duty to speculate on what

Plamenatz might choose to say if he were able to embark upon it now. It is therefore unavoidable that at least some of the material which is published here for the first time must reveal its age. For each chapter, we have, accordingly, appended a list of the most salient contemporary writings on the subject.

We have thus tried to remain faithful both to the published tomes and to the work originally projected, which was of markedly broader conception and more historical in focus. No opportunity arose before his death in 1975 for Plamenatz to make these revisions himself. In attempting to enhance and lend fresh impetus to the most durable and popular of all his writings, our aim has been, not so much to append additional material to an established text, as to impart new breath into old bones and therefore restore the full vigour and vision of *Man and Society*'s original design. We are grateful to Dr Chris Harrison and Mrs Joy Cash of Longmans for all their encouragement and patience; to the British Academy for enabling us, intermittently over a number of years, to meet and sort out the papers we required from a substantial corpus of other unpublished texts; to Dr Janet Coleman and Dr Mark Goldie for their invaluable comments on the new and revised chapters, for which, however, they bear no responsibility and with whose conclusions they do not always concur; and to Mrs Jean Ashton and to Miss Karen Hall for typing them and for their forbearance, in deciphering densely written passages, on demand.

April 1990

Preface

This book is not a history of political thought; it is, as its title implies, a critical examination of a number of important theories. It is not concerned to argue for some interpretations of these theories against others but to examine assumptions, ideas and attitudes.

The book is an expansion of lectures given at various times at three universities, Columbia, Harvard and Oxford. It is hoped that it will prove useful to students of social and political theory whose interest in the subject is more philosophical than historical; and the author has had in mind students in the United States as much as in Britain. He has aimed at lucidity but is aware that some parts of the book make difficult reading.

The most difficult part of all, which treats of Hegel, has been read by Professor H. L. A. Hart and Sir Isaiah Berlin, by Professor Herbert Deane of Columbia University, and by Mr William Weinstein and Mr John Torrance of Nuffield College, and the author is grateful to them for valuable comments and criticisms. He thanks Mr Alan Ryan of Balliol College for making the index. He also thanks his wife for reading the book in manuscript and suggesting improvements of grammar and style.

July 1961   J. P.

Introduction

The artist ploughs his own furrow; the scholar, even in the privacy of his study, cultivates a common field. He is responsible to others for what he does; he feels the need to explain his purpose, to justify his efforts.

There are many things well worth doing not attempted in this book. It is not, for the most part, a history of social and political thought; it does not enquire how one thinker influenced another, and compares them only to make clearer what they said. It scarcely looks at the circumstances in which this or that theory was produced. And it quite neglects several important thinkers. Althusius will get into the index only because he is mentioned on this page, and so too will Vico, who has been greatly and rightly admired. Grotius and Kant are mentioned only in passing. If my purpose had been to produce a history, however brief, of political thought from Machiavelli to Marx, this neglect or scanty treatment would have been without excuse.

Every thinker, even the most abstract, is deeply influenced by the circumstances of his day. To understand why Machiavelli or Hobbes or Rousseau wrote as he did, we must know something of social and political conditions in their day and country and of the controversies then to the fore. But this does not, I hope, mean that whoever discusses their theories must also discuss these conditions and controversies. Is there to be no division of labour? Those conditions and controversies have often been described, and the writer who is primarily concerned with arguments and ideas need not discuss them except to make something clear which might otherwise be misunderstood. He must use his judgement: at times he may need to make a considerable digression, and at other times a passing reference or mere hint will be enough.

Those who say that to understand a theory we must understand the conditions in which it was produced sometimes put their case too strongly. They speak as if, to understand what a man is saying, we must know why he is saying it. But this is not true. We need understand only the sense in which he is using words. To understand Hobbes, we need not know what his purpose was in writing *Leviathan* or how he felt about the rival claims of Royalists and Parliamentarians; but we do need to know what he understood by such words as *law, right, liberty, covenant* and *obligation*. And though it is true that even Hobbes, so 'rare' at definitions, does not always use a word in the sense which he defines, we are more likely to get the sense in which he does use it by a close study of his argument than by looking at the condition of England or at political controversies in his day. These are, of course, well worth looking at on their own account. Nevertheless, we can go a long way in understanding Hobbes's argument and yet know very little about them.

No doubt, Hobbes is a special case. We can get more of his meaning by merely reading what he wrote than we can, say, of Machiavelli's or Montesquieu's or Burke's. It is a matter of degree. But, even in their case, we learn more about their arguments by weighing them over and over again than by extending our knowledge of the circumstances in which they wrote. Hobbes was not less a child of his times than they were. If we want to know why he wrote as he did, or why an argument such as his was produced and found exciting, we have to look at what was happening when he wrote; he was no more independent of his age than was Machiavelli or Burke. Of every really great thinker we can say that, compared with lesser men, he is idiosyncratic; he is, for a time, more liable than they are to be misunderstood because he has more to say that is unfamiliar. He uses the common language but uses it differently. But this is not more true of Hobbes than of Machiavelli. Hobbes belongs as completely to his period as Machiavelli does to his; and if, in order to understand him, we need take less notice of the circumstances in which he wrote, this is because his style and method are different. To understand the argument of *Leviathan* is one thing; to understand the age in which alone it could have been written is another. I do not deny that the second understanding may contribute to the first; I merely doubt whether the contribution is anything like as great as it is sometimes made out to be. Of course, it is of absorbing interest to see a great thinker in the setting of his age. How society and politics are related to political and social theory is as well worth studying as theory itself. Who would deny it? But that is another matter.

Students of society and government make use of ideas and assumptions inherited from the past. In this book I have not been concerned to trace the origins and evolution of these ideas, but rather to examine them critically by considering some of the most familiar and most famous theories which contain them. I have chosen these theories, rather than others, precisely because they are familiar, and because, between them, they contain most of the important ideas and assumptions still used or made, whether by students of society and politics or by persons engaged in political controversies. All these theories, in one way or another, are inadequate; they fail to explain satisfactorily what they set out to explain. They are also – though this is less important – 'out-of-fashion': by which, I am sorry to say, I mean no more than this, that sociologists and political scientists in many places (though not in all) now believe that they have less to learn from them than from one another.

These ideas and assumptions ought to be examined critically; and where can they be so examined to better advantage than in the context of well-known, long discussed and, in some cases, still influential theories? It is sometimes objected that the questions raised by, say, Hobbes or Locke are no longer relevant. But if we discuss social and political matters, we must still speak, as they did, of *law,* of *rights,* of *obligation* and of *consent.* By seeing how they used these words and what arguments they constructed, we learn to use them ourselves. By seeing where their explanations are inadequate, we learn something about what they sought to explain. To treat *right* as absence of obligation (which is what Hobbes did) may do for some purposes, but not for others. By examining critically the argument of *Leviathan* and *De cive,* we learn why this is so. It may be true, as Locke said, that the authority of governments rests in some sense on the consent of the governed; but perhaps it cannot do so unless consent is understood in a sense different from his. By seeing where his argument goes wrong, we are better able to construct another to take its place. If we do not get from Hobbes or Locke answers to the questions we now put, we do, by examining their theories, learn to put our own questions more clearly. And I take Hobbes and Locke for examples deliberately because they are among the most abstract of political theorists. Machiavelli, Bodin, Montesquieu, Hume, Burke, Hegel and Marx all take larger account than they do of history and of the machinery of government.

It is, of course, not only the great thinkers who produce the thought of their age; indeed, they are not even the largest contributors to it. No doubt, they are often the most original, but they are not so always, for they are sometimes only more lively and more vigorous than the rest. The others, the lesser thinkers, enormously outnumber them; and though, as individuals, they may give much less, what they give collectively is much more. What any thinker, however remarkable, has to give is incomparably less than what he takes from others; and the greater part of what he takes does not come from other great thinkers, but from many relatively minor figures, of which most are soon forgotten by posterity. Even in the period of their predominance, the great works do not cover all that is worth noticing. There are important shifts of opinion and outlook not mediated by genius; there are new ideas that find currency and endure, though no Hobbes or Hume has given them a memorable place in his theory.

Much of the political thought of the sixteenth century is to be found in treatises and pamphlets of real interest only to specialists; and yet that thought, taken as a whole, is historically of immense importance. The religious minorities, by pressing their claims against their governments, were not fighting for liberty of conscience but to secure privileges for themselves. Yet, as a result of their struggle, liberty of conscience – perhaps the most precious of all liberties – was eventually established. These minorities made it impossible for the governments of Europe to achieve domestic peace except by conceding religious liberty; and when this concession was eventually made, the greatest moral revolution in modern history was completed. In attempting to follow that revolution in thought and feeling, we must consider such writers not individually but in schools, examining the types of arguments they use and the general conclusions they reach. Our approach in addressing their doctrines must therefore be more historical than may be the case with regard to the pre-eminent thinkers.

The great advantage of these old theories is that they are both rich in content and familiar. If our purpose is to examine ideas used to explain society and government, these theories provide them abundantly, vigorously and attractively. They are a fertile field for the exercise we have in mind. Everyone agrees that students of society and government need to look carefully at the assumptions they make and the ideas they use; that – owing to the nature of their subject – they are especially liable to be the dupes of words. Yet there are now many who question the use of a close study of theories produced long ago in circumstances widely different from our own. It is therefore a point worth making, that such ideas are nowhere better or more economically studied than in these old theories. Nowhere *better* because of the richness and variety they present, and nowhere *more economically* because they have been sifted again and again, so that we can get down quickly to essentials.

The predominant figures in the history of political thought are not great for nothing, or just by chance. They are more original, more profound, than the forgotten or almost forgotten men, who are remembered only by scholars. Their theories are often better constructed; there is usually a greater weight of thought and feeling in their works, and they make a deeper and more lasting impression. Though most of what they offer their readers is taken from others, their powers of selection are unusually fine; they have perception and imagination and an eye for the important, and so their ideas, original to a much smaller extent than appears to the reader who knows little or nothing of their contemporaries, do none the less contain a large part of what is best worth preserving in their age. Most of their contributions to political thought, moreover, are far from dead; they are either still with us – though sometimes in forms we do not immediately recognize – or they are revived among us from time to time when occasion serves. The world is full, not only of Marxists and democrats, but of people who, though they mostly do not know it, are still using the ideas and arguments of Hobbes, or Machiavelli, or Montesquieu, or Hegel or Burke. These thinkers may have originated only a small part of our stock of ideas about human nature and politics, but they gave it the appearance still familiar to us. They mixed only a fraction of the ore, but they refined much of it, put their stamp on it, made it profitable and good currency for our use.

In some circles where the study of these theories is depreciated, there is nevertheless a keen interest taken in the ideas and assumptions used or made by the sociologist or the political scientist. There are sociologists and political scientists who put themselves to great trouble to define the terms they employ and to state their assumptions. They do not always do it well. They wish to be lucid, precise and realistic; they aim at explaining the facts and are in search of a vocabulary adequate to their purpose. It is impossible not to sympathize with them. Yet, for all their efforts, they are often more obscure, or looser in their arguments, or more incoherent, than the makers of the old theories which they neglect on the ground that they are irrelevant. A close study of these theories might be a good discipline for them. Or the social scientist, though he does not know it, repeats what has been said as well, or better, long ago. Ideas very like his own have been used long before his time, and yet he thinks them new because he has coined new words to express them. It is sad to read a book for which it is claimed that it breaks new ground, and to find it thin and stale.

Not for a moment do I suggest that these old theories provide the social scientist with all that he is looking for. They are not a stock of ideas sufficient for his purposes. They are inadequate for all kinds of reasons, some of which are discussed in this book. I suggest only that the study of them is still amply rewarding, and to no one more so than to the student of society who feels that he lacks the ideas needed to explain what he studies. Of course, he will not find the ideas he wants ready-made in these theories, but he will become more adept in the handling of ideas and a better judge of their uses. He will be more discriminating, more scrupulous, and perhaps also more severe with himself and his contemporaries. Bentham said that his purpose in writing *A Fragment on Government* was to teach the student 'to place more confidence in his own strength, and less in the infallibility of great names: – to help him to emancipate his judgement from the shackles of authority'. An admirable purpose. But today, in some intellectual circles, the authority of great names is less oppressive than is fashion, which is an even worse guide. If we neither neglect great names nor defer to them, but seek, to the best of our ability, to take their measure, we are then better placed to take our own.

It is said that, in the past, it was difficult, if not impossible, to study the facts, social and political, whereas now it is much less difficult. There are vastly greater records than there were, more easily accessible; there are methods now used to get at the facts which could not have been used in earlier periods; it is easier than it was to test hypotheses, and we are more sophisticated in making and testing them. The social sciences may have no spectacular achievements to their credit, but then it is not to be expected that they should. It is admitted that they differ greatly from the natural sciences, that there are difficulties peculiar to them, that their conclusions are less precise and more open to question. Such is their nature that – though they call for no less imagination, no less intelligence, no smaller talents from their devotees than other sciences – they afford lesser opportunities; and we are not to expect from them hypotheses as precise, as impressive, as revolutionary and as widely acclaimed as those of, say, Copernicus or Newton or Darwin or Pasteur. And yet it is claimed for them that they do now deserve to be called *sciences*, because those who practise them are seriously concerned to construct theories to explain the facts, and are self-critical and open-minded. As much as the natural scientists, they are imbued with the scientific spirit, even though their methods are more uncertain and their results looser and less well-established. The social scientist is much more apt than the natural scientist to talk nonsense and to make a fool of himself. This is one of the hazards of his occupation. Yet his occupation is science.

But the occupation of the great social and political theorists of the past was not science. They did not study the facts or did so only at random; they did not construct hypotheses and test them. They deduced their conclusions from axioms *a priori* and from definitions, or they relied on what they chose to consider the common sense of mankind. They were not scientific but speculative. What is more, their aim was often less to explain than to justify or to condemn. That they seldom distinguished between their aims is only one further proof that they were not scientists. And so it is sometimes held that their theories are much more impediments than helps to the social scientist, who need not rate his own achievements high to feel that, as compared with them, he is moving in the right direction, given that the object of the journey is to extend knowledge. Hence the need often felt by the social scientist to turn his back on these old and famous theories.

There is nothing arrogant about this attitude, with which it is easy to sympathize.[1] But there can be no real turning of the back on these old theories, whose ideas and assumptions still permeate our thinking about society and government, whether we know it or not. We are not free of them as the natural scientists are of the essences and entelechies of mediaeval and Aristotelian philosophy. We have still to come to terms with these thinkers of the past, to make up our minds about them, if we are to learn to think more clearly than they did.

These theories, moreover, were by no means entirely speculative, nor was their function always primarily to justify or to condemn. They were also, to a greater or a lesser extent, attempts to explain the facts – to explain what the social scientist aims at explaining. To examine them, as is still sometimes done, merely in order to establish how far they are internally consistent, is not an exercise of much use to the social scientist. Nor does it matter to him just which, among several different interpretations of a well-known doctrine, is the nearest to being correct. The enquiry perhaps most useful to him is an enquiry into the adequacy and relevance of these theories. How far do they provide a satisfactory explanation of what they seek to explain? How far are their assumptions and ideas useful for purposes

---

[1] There is more that is arrogant about the disparagement of the social sciences still common in England than about the claims made for them in the United States.

of explanation? Granted that the theories are in many ways inadequate or irrelevant, just why are they so? This book attempts, among other things, to answer these questions – and never more so than when it treats, sometimes at considerable length, of three among the more recent and still widely influential theories, those of Rousseau, Hegel and Marx.

The expositor and critic is bound to give what he honestly believes to be a fair interpretation of the doctrines he discusses. But, if his purpose is not to offer an interpretation which he believes to be an improvement on others, or to pronounce in favour of one among several current versions, he is not bound to argue the case for his interpretation. Since I have been concerned much more to examine the adequacy and relevance of assumptions, ideas and arguments than to establish that Machiavelli or Hume or Marx meant this rather than that, I have refrained from defending my interpretations, except where it has seemed to me that they might strike the reader as unusual or implausible.

Again, I have not considered every aspect of the most important theories; I have considered only those aspects which raised most sharply the issues I wanted to discuss. I have not considered, for example, what Montesquieu has to say about religion and its social functions, though in fact he has a great deal to say about it and says it in the most interesting way. The points I wished to make about religion, and its place in society, I have tried to make in discussing certain beliefs of Machiavelli and of Marx. It may well be that to someone whose field of study is the sociology of religion, Montesquieu has more to offer than either Machiavelli or Marx. Certainly, he treats of religion more elaborately and with greater subtlety than they do. But it seemed to me that their simpler and perhaps cruder treatment served my purposes better.

These theories are more than attempts to explain society and government, and more also than apologies for or attacks upon the established order. They are philosophies of life; and philosophies of this kind are often dismissed as useless or pernicious on the ground that they claim to be more than they really are.

They flourished, it is said, before the scientific study of man, of society and of government had properly begun; they pretended to a knowledge they did not possess. But now that men are beginning to see how to get this knowledge – how to study themselves and society to good purpose – they can do without these pretentious theories. When these theories are not, in the Marxian sense, *ideologies* (when their function is not to defend or challenge the interests of some class or group), they are merely personal statements. They express what somebody feels about man and man's condition in the world. Taken for what they are they may be interesting, but they must not be taken for more.

Certainly, the makers of these theories had illusions about them, and often claimed a knowledge they did not possess. I have already said in their defence that they took some account of the facts and made some attempt to explain them, and I do not suppose that the persons who call their theories 'ideologies' or 'fantasies' or 'mere personal statements' mean to deny this. I believe that these theorists took larger account of the facts and were more seriously concerned to explain them than their critics imply, but that is not what I now want to argue. Nor do I want to argue that the element of class or group *ideology* in these theories is smaller than Marxists have supposed. I want rather to insist that these theories – even when they are not attempts to explain the facts and do not serve to defend or challenge class or group interests – are more than mere personal statements, and that to call them so is grossly misleading. They do more than express personal preferences, even when those are preferences which many share.

Some of these theories are integral parts of a cosmology, of a sometimes elaborate theory about the universe and man's place in it; others are not. Hegel affirms that reality is an infinite Mind or Spirit seeking self-realization, an activity or process passing from level to level, and which is manifest, at its highest levels, in communities of finite selves – that is to say, in communities of men. His social and political theory is rooted in a philosophy which purports to explain everything; or alternatively (and this alternative is perhaps nearer the truth) his philosophy is an attempt to apply to all things ideas which make sense only when applied to human activities and social institutions. Others, as for example the Utilitarians, are more modest. The Utilitarians, for the most part, do not seek to improve upon or to add to the explanations of the physical and biological world offered by science; with rare exceptions they say nothing about divine or immanent purposes. They confine themselves to explaining man and his social behaviour. They take man as they think he is, as a creature of desires who seeks to satisfy them as abundantly as he can at the least cost to himself. They seek to explain his behaviour and all social institutions on this and a few other assumptions about man and his environment; and in support of their assumptions they appeal above all to what they take to be the common sense of mankind. Yet they, too, are concerned to do much more than explain the facts; they too seek to criticize and to persuade. They too have a philosophy of life which is something more than an explanation (however inadequate) of how men actually live.

All these theories, no matter how 'pretentious' or 'modest' they may be, are elaborate philosophies which contain a large element that is not science or conceptual analysis or ideology in the Marxian sense. They are what I venture to call, for want of a better word, practical philosophies or philosophies of man; they are forms of self-expression of which it is lamentably inadequate to say that they are mere personal statements. They are neither mere exercises in psychology – statements about how men feel and think and behave – nor mere excursions into morals. They involve much more than the laying down of ultimate rules (as, for example, the 'greatest happiness' principle or the principle of 'self-realization') or even the construction of elaborate hierarchies of rules.

There is always a close connection between a philosopher's conception of what man is – what is peculiar to him, how he is placed in the world – and his doctrines about how man should behave – what he should strive for, and how society should be constituted. The connection is there, multiple and close, whether the philosopher is a Rousseau or a Hegel, who does not agree with Hume that there is no deriving an *ought* from an *is*, or whether he is Hume himself. For Hume – though he believes that no rule of conduct follows logically from any description of man and his condition in the world – offers to show how man, being the sort of creature he is, comes to accept certain rules. Man and the human condition are, in some respects, everywhere the same, and therefore there are some rules which are everywhere accepted. They are not the only rules which men accept, and are not always in keeping with the other rules. Indeed, these other rules are sometimes preferred to them. Nevertheless, there are some rules which men everywhere accept, or would accept if they understood themselves and their condition; we have, therefore, only to understand what man is and how he is placed in the world to know what those rules are. This way of thinking is not confined to the natural law philosophers and Idealists; it is common to them and to the Utilitarians, and (as we shall see) there is a large dose of it even in Marxism.

In this book I am as much concerned to discuss these theories as *philosophies of life* as I am to examine critically the assumptions they make and the ideas they use in the attempt to explain the facts. And, here again, I confine myself almost entirely to what my authors have to say, attending hardly at all to the origins of their theories or the circumstances in which they were produced. I have already said enough, I hope, to show that this neglect does not come of a failure to appreciate the importance of what I have not tried to do. I have learnt much from many scholars, but the attempt to tread in all their footsteps would be absurd.

Man, as Machiavelli sees him, is self-assertive. He lives, not to seek God's favour or to serve some larger than human purpose, but to satisfy himself; he seeks security and something more; he seeks to make himself felt. He seeks reputation, to make his mark, to create some image of himself which is impressive to others. The stronger he is, the more he is willing to risk security for reputation. Man is both self-preserving and self-assertive; but Machiavelli sympathizes more with the second than the first of these needs. He values above all the two qualities which enable a man to assert himself: courage and intelligence. These are not just preferences which Machiavelli happens to have; they are rooted in his conception of what it is to be a man. Hobbes also sees man as self-assertive but sees him even more as in search of security in a world of self-seeking men; and he puts a high value on prudence and consistency of purpose. Organized society is a discipline which the prudent accept and to which the imprudent must be forced to submit. Rousseau sees man as the victim of society, as a creature who has lost his integrity. Society derives from his needs, develops his faculties, and yet is oppressive to him. As a rational and moral being, man is at once the creature and the victim of society, and can be cured of the ills it produces in him only in a reformed society. Bentham sees man as a subject of desires who, unlike other animals, can compare and foresee; he sees him as a competitor and collaborator with other men in the procuring of what satisfies desires. The proper function of rules and institutions is to ensure that competition and collaboration are as effective as possible – that they help and do not impede men in their efforts to satisfy their desires. Hegel sees man as a creature who becomes rational and moral in the process of coming to understand and master an environment; he sees him transformed and elevated by his own activities. He sees him as changing from age to age, and the course of this change as 'implicit' in his nature, in his capacity to reason and to will. Marx sees man as a creature whose image of himself and the world is a product of what he does to satisfy his basic needs; and yet he also sees him as a creature who comes in the end to know himself and the world, understanding his condition and accepting it, and who thereby attains freedom.

We have here six very different philosophies, even though there are elements common to several of them. And, though we can say of each of them that it was 'the product of its age' – though we can give reasons for its appearing when and where it did – we cannot say of any one of them that it is obsolete or irrelevant. They are ways of looking at man and society which are of perennial interest; we can find traces of them in philosophies much older than the ones which now seem to us to give fullest expression to them. Man and his social condition do change from age to age, but they also remain the same; and the different philosophies which men have produced reflect, not only how they and their condition have changed, but also the diversity of their reactions to what has not changed. Alfred North Whitehead once said that all later philosophies are footnotes to Plato. This may be extravagant but is not absurd, and is least extravagant when applied to Plato's views about man and society. Plato's theory of knowledge and Aristotle's logic have been superseded in a sense in which their political philosophies have not. That is not because epistemology and logic have made progress since their time as the study of man and society has not; it is because political philosophy has always aimed at something more than explanation. One explanation of what is involved in having knowledge or in reasoning may be an improvement on another. But with philosophy, in the sense in which I am now using the word, it is a different matter.

Today, in the social as in other studies, two kinds of enquiry find favour: the aim of one is to explain the facts, and when its methods are (or are held to be) adequate to its aim, it is called science; the aim of the other is to examine the ideas and methods used in explanation and in other forms of discourse, and when those ideas and methods are of wide application, it is sometimes called analytical philosophy. The theories expounded and criticized in this book, though by no means unscientific and unphilosophical in these two senses, are also more than science and analytical philosophy. Moreover (as I have said already, though in different words), as science and analytical philosophy they are often grossly inadequate. Therefore, since science and this kind of philosophy are in favour, these theories, which are often indifferent specimens of both, are in disfavour. And even when it is conceded that there is a large element in them which is neither the one nor the other, this element is written off as an aberration, due to a failure to understand what is the proper business of science or philosophy.

The suggestion is that these theories aim at extending knowledge but do not know how it is to be extended, or that they confuse other things with the extension of knowledge. They have several purposes but fail to distinguish between them, or have purposes so vague that they are not really purposes at all. They aim at explaining the facts or at elucidating ideas or at defining rights and obligations or at persuasion, and move from one aim to the next without knowing that they have done so. They are uncertain of purpose. The present-day critic, coming upon this confusion and trained to make the distinctions these theories too often fail to make, easily concludes that, if they have some purpose beyond explanation, elucidation, definition or persuasion – beyond the purposes familiar to him (and which he does not quarrel with, provided the man who has them knows what he is doing) – that purpose is illusory, rooted in misunderstanding. By all means let a political writer explain or analyse or persuade, but let him know what he is doing. For, if he does not know what he is doing, he will aim at the impossible, or will delude himself into believing he is contributing to knowledge when he is not, or will unconsciously seek to pass off his peculiar preferences as eternal truths.

I have already conceded that most of the great political and social thinkers of the past failed to make certain distinctions now commonly made, and that they were under illusions about their theories. Yet it is a mistake to conclude that, to the extent that they aimed at more than explanation, analysis or persuasion, their efforts were pointless or useless. Their theories have another function besides these, and a function which is not less important than they are.

Sophisticated man has a need to 'place' himself in the world, to come to terms intellectually and emotionally with himself and his environment, to take his own and the world's measure. This need is not met by science. It is not enough for him to have only the knowledge which the sciences and ordinary experience provide. Or perhaps I should say – to avoid misunderstanding – it is not enough for him to have only knowledge; for I do not wish to suggest that what he needs, and science and ordinary experience cannot provide, is knowledge in the same sense as they supply, merely coming to him from another source. Nor is it enough for him to have this knowledge together with a moral code and a set of preferences. He needs a conception of the world and of man's place in it which is not merely scientific – a conception to which his moral code and preferences are closely related. I have here in mind something more than the assumptions on which science and everyday experience themselves rest, assumptions which cannot be verified because they must first be accepted before it makes sense to speak of verification. This need is not felt by all men; and it is felt by some much more strongly than by others; but it is a persistent need. It is a need which can be met for some only by religion, but which for others can be met in other ways (unless any system of beliefs which meets it is to be called a religion). The theories examined in this book are systems of belief of this kind; or, rather, that is one aspect of them, and a very important aspect of some of them.

It would be profoundly misleading to speak of this aspect as if it were no more than a statement of preferences or a laying down of rules or a defining of goals. If it were only that, it would be possible to reduce it to a list, which is not in fact the case. A hostile or perverse critic may say that, as far as he can see, there is nothing more to it than that and a whole lot of verbiage besides, which to him means nothing. If he says this, there may be no arguing with him, beyond pointing out that it is perhaps a kind of verbiage in which he himself indulges when, momentarily, he forgets his opinions about it. When Rousseau or Hegel or Marx tells us what is involved in being a man, he is not – when what he says cannot be verified – either expressing preferences or laying down rules; he is not putting 'imperatives' in the indicative mood; he is not prescribing or persuading under the illusion that he is describing. He is not doing that or else talking nonsense. It might be said that he is telling his reader how he feels about man and the human predicament – or, more adequately and more fairly, that he is expressing some of the feelings that man has about himself and his condition. But he is not describing those feelings or just giving vent to them; he is *expressing* them, and the point to notice is that this expression takes the form of a theory about man and his condition. It could not take any other form. Thus, if it is an expression of feeling, the feeling requires systematic and conceptual expression. Only a self-conscious and rational creature could have such feelings about itself and its condition; and the theories which express these feelings, far from being statements of preference or rules of conduct passed off as if they were something different from what they really are, serve only to give 'meaning' to these statements and rules. Not that they are needed to make the statements and rules intelligible, to make it clear what the preferences are or what is involved in conforming to the rules; nor yet to justify the preferences or rules by pointing to their consequences. They give 'meaning' to them, not by explaining or justifying them, but by expressing an attitude to man and the human condition to which they are 'appropriate'; so that, even when we do not share the attitude, we understand how it is that those who do share it have those preferences and accept those rules. We do not infer the rules from the attitude, nor do we establish, in the manner of the scientist, a constant connection between the attitude and the rules and preferences; our understanding is different in kind from that of the scientist or the logician. It is neither an understanding of how things happen nor that some things follow from others; and yet it is an intellectual enterprise, a rational experience.

Man, being self-conscious and rational, has theories about himself and his social condition which profoundly affect his behaviour: theories which have not been, are not and never will be merely scientific. They will always be more than explanations of how he behaves and how institutions (which are conventional modes of behaviour) function. And they will always be more than statements of preference or assertions of principle and attempts to justify them; they will be more than 'personal statements' and more than exercises in persuasion. I do not say that there cannot be theories about man and society which are merely scientific, nor yet that any social theory which is more than merely scientific must have this particular more to it; I say only that the need for this more is enduring, and is in no way weakened by the spread of the scientific spirit.

But, it may be asked, granted that this is so, is not the study of these old theories, in so far as they do not attempt to explain the facts or do not examine the ideas used in explanation, of merely historical interest? They may once have been persuasive but are not so today, when the issues which inspired them are dead; and, to the extent that they do not seek to persuade but express what you have called attitudes to man and the human condition, our attitudes are no longer what they were. These theories, in this aspect of them, speak for their contemporaries and not for us; they belong to the past, and the study of them is mere history.

To this there are two answers. Issues and attitudes change less than they seem to, for the language used to express them changes more than they do. These theories are products of their age but are also ageless; their diversity shows not only how epochs and countries differ from one another but also the variety of man's attitudes to himself and his condition. It has been said that all men (or is it all thinking men?) are either Platonists or Aristotelians – which, though not literally true, makes a point worth making. So too, in similar style, we can say that in all ages there are Machiavellians and Marxists and Utilitarians, and even men who, like poor Rousseau, despair of the future of mankind while protesting that man is naturally good.

Secondly, man is an object of thought to himself and would not have the capacities peculiar to his kind unless he were such an object. His being a person, his sense of his own identity, his feeling that he has a place in the world, depend on memory – his own and other men's – for he has rational intercourse with them and belongs to enduring communities. Man is more than just the product of his past; he is the product of memory. The past 'lives on' in him, and he would not be what he is unless it did so. Thus, for him, as for no other creature, to lose his past, to lose his memory, is to lose himself, to lose his identity. History is more than the record of how man became what he is; it is involved in man's present conception of what he is; it is the largest element in his self-knowledge.

Man, being rational and capable of self-knowledge, puts to himself two sorts of questions, and science answers only one of them. The sort of question which science answers he puts both of himself and of what is external to him; but the sort which science does not answer he puts only of himself or of creatures whom he believes to be in his own condition. And these questions which science does not answer are also not answered by analytical philosophy. They are questions which have no final answers; for the answers to them differ from age to age and, perhaps even more, from person to person. These questions which science cannot answer are often put in the same form as the questions which science can answer. We may ask, 'What is man?', meaning 'What sort of creature is man?', and look for answers to the biologist, the psychologist and the social scientist. Or we can put the question which Pascal tried to answer in his *Pensées,* which is a different question altogether, though put in the same words. Pascal believed in God; but the need to put that question does not arise from this belief. An atheist may put it and find an answer which satisfies him, and yet remain an atheist. But the answer, whatever it is, is not a mere set of rules. The question, 'What is man?', as Pascal put it – a question which science cannot answer – is not to be reduced to the question, 'How ought man to behave?'.

Political and social theories of the kind discussed in this book are not the only theories, nor even the most important, which attempt answers to that sort of question; and of course they also put questions of other sorts. But this is an important element in them, and still as much worth studying as any other. The putting and answering of questions of this sort is an activity not less rational and not less difficult than scientific enquiry, and neither more nor less useful. These theories have helped to form sophisticated man's image of himself. No doubt, in primitive and illiterate communities men make do without them; but then they also make do without science. To ask, as some have done, 'What is the use of these theories?', is as pointless as to put the same question of science.

CHAPTER ONE
Montesquieu

A lawyer and a man of letters, Montesquieu was for nine years a président à mortier or judge at the *Parlement* of Bordeaux, an office left to him by his uncle, together with other property and the name of Montesquieu. He sold his office in 1725, when he was only thirty-six years old, intending to devote the rest of his life to literature. He had by then already published, in 1721, the *Persian Letters,* supposedly written by two travelling Persians to their friends at home, giving their impressions of France. In 1728 and 1729, he visited Germany, Austria, Italy and Holland, and then, in the company of Lord Chesterfield, came to England, where he stayed another two years. Being well-to-do and well-connected, he was everywhere on his travels received in the best houses, where public affairs were discussed with a knowledge and candour scarcely possible at that time in other places. For the whole of his life Montesquieu remained a traveller in imagination, if not in fact; his curiosity about foreign countries was insatiable. And his was mostly a well-bred curiosity – detached, uncensorious and urbane.

Returning to France, he lived either in his home at La Brède near Bordeaux or in Paris, and devoted his energies chiefly to preparing *The Spirit of the Laws,* though he also found time to write a lesser work, the *Considerations on the Greatness and Decadence of the Romans*, which appeared in 1734. *The Spirit of the Laws* was published anonymously in 1748, and was at once immensely successful.[1] It was accepted as the political masterpiece of the age. Voltaire said harsh things about it and Frederick of Prussia was moderate in his praise, but most of

[1] I have used the Pléiade edition of Montesquieu's works, and the passages quoted are my own translations from the French.

1

the philosophers and princes admired it. Men as different from one another as Hume, Rousseau and Burke paid warm tribute to it as the greatest work of its kind produced in their century. Catherine the Great called it her 'breviary'; she was delighted to find in it the argument that to hold together a large empire requires unlimited power in the ruler. Montesquieu was very much the fashion for about two generations, until it was discovered that his erudition was not always to be trusted, and that no one had ever before been misinformed about as wide a variety of subjects. Early in the next century, Macaulay could treat him almost as a kind of clever fool, assiduously and uncritically collecting every piece of information that came his way.

It is true that Montesquieu was uncritical. He was a considerable traveller when still young and a great reader all his life; he put down on paper a prodigious number of what he took for well-authenticated facts, and had little opportunity to test the accuracy of his sources. He believed whatever the ancient historians told him; all their testimonies were, to him, of almost equal value. He took it for granted that the early history of Rome was more or less as Livy described it; he accepted what he found in Chardin about contemporary Persia, and in Du Halde about China. Having been a traveller himself, observant and truthful, he was ready to believe any other traveller who wrote intelligently and well. He did not distinguish carefully between observation and surmise, and was too little aware how difficult it is for travellers to interpret correctly what they see. For all his scepticism and detachment, he was often credulous. A rationalist who would not believe in miracles, he found it easy to swallow quite tall stories provided they were not told in the interest of religion.

Montesquieu was a master of style and wit, but not of method and exposition. His greatest work is badly planned and loosely put together. It is as if he had taken great care over each part separately, and had afterwards made careless decisions about what order to put them in. *The Spirit of the Laws* is a long book, but not nearly as long as it seems. It is divided into thirty-one books, with anything from twenty to thirty chapters in each book; the chapters are too short, too compact; the longest have seldom more than ten pages, the shortest often less than one. No theme is sufficiently elaborated, and too much is left to the reader's imagination. The style is too brilliant, too concise, too aphoristic. No book so well written, and with so much that is excellent in it, was ever so liable to weary the reader.

How then has Montesquieu acquired his great reputation as a social and political theorist? A gift for satire, a beautiful style, wit and elegance, generalities supported by travellers' tales, examples taken from not always reliable historians: these are not the stuff to make a masterpiece of social and political theory. But Montesquieu had other gifts, less easily noticed but more excellent and rare. He had the kind of imagination that puts new questions and makes new assumptions; he had originality. Yet, like many other original thinkers, he was not himself fully aware of the significance of his own assumptions. He relapsed into the old ways of thinking and speaking; and, when he did so, was sometimes worse than other people. He was often derivative, shoddy and superficial. Though he always wrote well, his thinking was at times commonplace.

It is worth remembering that Montesquieu has had two quite different reputations: the first and more superficial in his own century, as an immensely learned and wise man, whose opinions were respected by absolute monarchs, by parliamentary leaders, by liberal philosophers and by the makers of the American Constitution; and a second and more solid reputation in later times, as the father of sociology, as the inventor of a new method and the framer of new hypotheses, as a man who is important more for what he attempted than for what he achieved. The element common to both reputations is admiration for him as a master of satire and one of the greatest of French prose writers. Macaulay, who did not admire him, caught him, as it were, between reputations, when his learning was already suspect and his wisdom beginning to wear thin, and the novelty of his method and assumptions was not yet recognized.

I. MONTESQUIEU'S CONCEPTION OF SOCIETY

Long before he wrote anything that could properly be called social or political theory, Montesquieu had already proved that he had remarkable gifts as an observer of society – that he was as keenly interested in the social influences forming character as in actual behaviour and motives. He did not take social facts, established usages and opinions, for granted; he felt the need to explain them, to see the connections between them, and to enquire into their origins.

Even as a young man, he had found it easy to look at French society as if he did not belong to it, placing himself in imagination outside it, questioning what had hitherto seemed beyond question. The two Persians in the *Persian Letters* are perhaps not quite true to life. Montesquieu had never been to Persia, and relied on other people's books for what he knew of that country. His Persians are more European than Persian, but they do at least look at France through the eyes of strangers. They know nothing of French ways and have to puzzle them out as they go along. Montesquieu, when he wrote the *Persian Letters,* had chiefly a moral purpose in mind; the book is a satire castigating Frenchmen and Europeans generally. It is not, however, a direct and savage satire in the manner of Swift; for Montesquieu was seldom exasperated by his fellow-men, though he was often sharp and cut deep. The book is much more than satire; it is inspired by curiosity even more than by the desire to expose vice and folly; and it reveals as great an interest in institutions as in men. Some of the letters are no more than witty and malicious, but others are serious discussions of politics, religion and literature as aspects of French life.

The *Considerations on the Greatness and Decadence of the Romans* is an historical essay written by an ardent admirer of Rome and of the Roman historians. Though it accepts uncritically the facts given by those historians, and is therefore full of mistakes, it is not a catalogue of events or a literary portrayal. It is a brief history of Roman institutions, an attempt to explain how they arose, developed and eventually decayed, and it is one of the first serious attempts of its kind. It treats Roman society as a complicated whole, describes the social and political causes of Rome's career of victory and conquest, and explains how these conquests, by forcing the Romans to change their system of government, led inevitably to decay and to final collapse. Montesquieu is concerned to show why the Romans succeeded where others had failed, and how their success so altered the entire structure of their society that it destroyed the very institutions and virtues which made them successful in the first place. The book is short, but its argument is carefully elaborated and always clear. It is much easier to read than his masterpiece, and reveals Montesquieu's peculiar gifts more immediately. *The Spirit of the Laws* is certainly the greater work, but, at a first reading, often baffles more than it enlightens the reader.

Already in the *Persian Letters* and the *Considerations on the Greatness and Decadence of the Romans,* we see how close for Montesquieu is the connection between forms of thought and feeling and social institutions; we already find him enquiring how laws, customs and governments are affected by and affect men's opinions, loyalties and ideas of right and wrong. We already find him looking at a people, not as a multitude of individuals under one government, but as a community distinguishable from others by their manners and institutions. All institutions, political, religious, domestic, economic and artistic, are, in his eyes, intricately related to one another, so that any considerable change in one is bound to affect the others. He did not – as I shall try to explain when I consider his theory of climates – treat any of these influences as paramount, as of its nature always stronger than any of the others. He took them all equally into account, together with their effects on one another and on government. This is not to say that Montesquieu had what is called an 'organic' conception of society. For to have this conception is to have much more than a lively sense of the interdependence of all aspects of social life; it is to assume that society has a self-maintaining structure which determines how it develops. I do not believe that Montesquieu makes that assumption. Nor can we find in Montesquieu a *philosophy of history* of the kind that became popular in France and Germany at the beginning of the next century. What is peculiar to Montesquieu, if we compare him with, say, Hobbes or Locke, is the assumption that government is not to be understood except as one aspect of a people's life intimately bound up with all other aspects. Society, he tells us, is vastly more intricate than we ordinarily have any idea of, and forms our minds in ways unsuspected by us until we begin to study it.

II. MONTESQUIEU'S THEORY OF CLIMATES

After the doctrine of the separation of powers, nothing about Montesquieu is better remembered than his interest in the influence of climate on social institutions. Yet the scope of that interest has been misunderstood.

Montesquieu was interested in much more than climate; he was interested in the physical environment generally, of which climate is only a part. You will find a great deal in *The Spirit of the Laws* about how the quality of the soil, the abundance or scarcity of water, the distribution of mountains, rivers and plains, the nearness or distance of the sea, and the presence or absence of good natural harbours, affect the ways in which men live. To take only one example, no writer before Montesquieu went as far as he did in explaining English institutions and national character as things peculiar to an insular, seafaring and commercial people. This part of Montesquieu's theory has attracted less attention than his discussion of the physiological and social effects of climate, though it is often more plausible and better argued. 'The laws', Montesquieu tells us, 'have a lot to do with the manner in which different peoples procure their subsistence';[1] and of course how peoples procure their subsistence has as much to do with geography as with climate.

It has sometimes been assumed that Montesquieu believed in a kind of climatic or physical determinism analogous to the economic determinism of the Marxists. This assumption usually goes with a failure to understand what economic determinism really amounts to, or at least what it must be taken to amount to if it is to be more than a quite arbitrary decision to treat some kinds of social behaviour as more important than others.

The economic factor is part of the social process; it is a part of the system of human behaviour which constitutes a form of social life. Marx thinks of it as being autonomous in some sense in which the other factors are not; he supposes that how it changes is determined by its own nature and not by other factors. It is continually changing and thereby causing change in all other aspects of social life. It is called fundamental because all, or nearly all, important social changes are supposed to originate in it. It is true that Marx – and Engels even more than Marx – sometimes, in the face of criticism, retreats from this position. Nevertheless, it is the only position that even begins to make sense of their theory; it is the essence of economic determinism.

Montesquieu's position is entirely different. Climate and geography are not parts of the social process; they are only the unchanging physical environment. They cannot therefore stand to social life as, in the Marxist theory, the production of wealth stands to all other social activities. Since climate and geography do not change, they cannot determine the course of social change; they can do no more than set limits to it. They cannot be treated, as Marx could plausibly treat changes in the production and distribution of wealth, as ultimate determinants of all other large social changes. Montesquieu never attempted so to treat them. Indeed, he did not generally conceive of a course of social change – of societies passing through successive stages in a course of development. He was concerned only to compare different types of society, and to explain how they come to be different. The physical environment (including climate) is, he thought, always an important part of the explanation. Not the whole of it, nor even the larger part; for Montesquieu never invites us to believe that the major differences between one society and another all derive from

[1] *Esprit des Lois*, Bk. XVIII, ch. 8.

differences of climate and geography. The physical environment is unchanging and its influence inescapable; it is, of all influences on social behaviour, the most enduring. It is fundamental in that sense alone. There is, I think, no evidence that Montesquieu believed that the physical environment, because it is fundamental in this sense, determines all aspects of social life. The people who have ascribed this belief to him have allowed themselves to be misled by some nineteenth-century social theories, and have interpreted Montesquieu as if he were feeling his way towards an idea which was in fact quite foreign to him: the idea of a single cause (or, rather, causal factor) determining the entire structure of society.

Montesquieu liked to use strong and striking phrases. His words often suggest more than he perhaps meant to convey by them, and it is therefore easy to misinterpret him. He did sometimes lay heavy stress on the influence of climate and geography, but he also made much of other things. I think it fair to say that he believed that the physical environment, decisive in some respects, goes only part of the way in determining how people live. The further people are, so to speak, from nature – or, in other words, the more elaborate and sophisticated their institutions and methods of work and thought – the less these institutions and methods can be explained as effects of climate and geography. This is perhaps the fairest inference from what Montesquieu said, and also very probably true.

His account of the social effects of the physical environment, taken as a whole, makes good enough sense. The examples he gives are not always convincing, but his general conclusion stands. It is what he says about only one part of the physical environment – about climate and its influence on man – which is more open to question, not only in matters of detail, but in principle.

Montesquieu takes account of two kinds of human reaction to climate: how men react to it physiologically and psychologically, which might be called the *primary* reaction; and how they adapt their environment to it – the houses they make to protect themselves from it, the customs and habits they acquire because of it – which might be called the *secondary* reaction. He pays more attention to the primary reaction than to the secondary, although the secondary reaction is probably the more important of the two. He also misconceives the nature of the primary reaction; his account of it is both simple and simple-minded.

Heat, he tells us, expands the ends of our nerve fibres, and cold contracts them, so that people who live in hot climates are apt to be sensitive, lazy and timid, while people who live in cold

7

climates are apt to be tough, brave and hard-working. It is not clear whether Montesquieu believed that the physical and moral qualities thus acquired are passed on by parents to their children or are merely effects of the separate action of heat and cold on each person. We may assume that he knew that black and brown parents have black and brown children, just as white parents have white ones, but whether he believed that distended and contracted nerve fibres are inherited is not to be known. Of natural selection, as Darwin understood it, he had, of course, no inkling. He seems to have taken it for granted that man has been essentially the same at all times and places, though climate has everywhere had a considerable effect on him, especially on his nervous system, and so has made him to some extent different, physically and mentally, in different parts of the world. He did not consider whether climate has affected man directly in other ways than by the action of heat and cold on his nerve fibres and the moral qualities that come of this action.

It would be absurd to blame Montesquieu for not knowing what everyone knows today: that racial differences are not to be explained in this simple way by the direct action of heat and cold on the human body. The process of physiological, or, rather, biological, adaptation to climate is quite different from anything he had in mind. And yet Montesquieu was probably right in believing that the direct action of climate on our bodies and minds is of considerable importance. This we may admit even if we reject his account of the action of heat and cold on our nerve fibres. Heat and cold, dryness and humidity, probably do affect us directly, in mind and in body, quite apart from what we may do to protect ourselves from them or to use them. It would be rash to deny this direct influence or to dismiss it as unimportant. The difficulty is to estimate its importance and to distinguish it from other influences. We know too little about it, though probably enough to incline us *not* to believe most of what Montesquieu tells us about the physical and moral qualities of various peoples.

The secondary influence of climate, which he does not neglect, though he pays less attention to it, is not only more important than the primary in explaining how some peoples differ from others; it is also easier to describe and to measure. It is often easy to see how, in order to protect themselves against heat and cold, wind and rain, or to make the best use of them in supplying their needs, men and women have come to live as they do. The secondary influence of climate Montesquieu could have studied, not unprofitably, even with the information at his disposal, meagre though it was by modern standards and not always reliable. That study, even in his day, would not have been purely speculative. Though, as I have said, he did not neglect it, he did choose to spend more of his time on something less rewarding. And in doing so he was not remarkably ingenious or imaginative. Others before him – among them Bodin – had made large and loose generalizations about the influence of climate on the bodies and minds of different peoples. These precursors had usually taken care to show that climate does most to improve the stuff of human nature in their own part of the world; and Montesquieu, cool and judicious, followed their example, even in this. Indeed, he was less generous to the over-heated peoples of Asia than Bodin was; for Bodin, though he found them sensitive and timid, also ascribed to them greater wisdom and understanding – a larger and more speculative intelligence – than to the Europeans.

III. MONTESQUIEU'S CONCEPTION OF LAW

Of the many chapters of *The Spirit of the Laws,* only six seek to define and classify law; and they are among the worst in the book.[1] It could never be said of Montesquieu, as it was of Hobbes, that he was 'rare at definitions'. He had little talent for the lucid analysis of concepts, and has contributed almost nothing to the abstract theory of law. That is not to say that his conceptions of law are not important; it is to say only that what is important about them is revealed, not in the analytical chapters, but in the rest of the book. These six chapters are snares and delusions. They lead to nothing. They throw no light on what comes after them or on what has gone before; they neither introduce nor summarize.

In the first sentence of his book, Montesquieu defines law as 'necessary relations deriving from the nature of things'. This definition is meant to cover *all* uniformities of behaviour as well as moral rules, customs and civil laws; it therefore treats descriptive and prescriptive laws as if they were of the same general type. This much is clear, though otherwise Montesquieu is so brief and develops his ideas so little, that it is impossible to be sure of his meaning. What did he have in mind, for example, when he said that all laws derive from the nature of things? Did he believe, even of a physical object, that we distinguish its nature from its behaviour, and then infer how it behaves

---

[1] *Esprit des Lois,* Bk. I, chs. 1–3, and Bk. XXVI, chs. 1–3.

from its nature and the natures of other objects which impinge upon it? But we make no such inferences. Some aspects of its behaviour we include in our account of its nature, and the aspects we do not include we discover by observation. Did he believe that we can infer how even a physical object will behave from the qualities belonging to it? No doubt, we often define it partly in terms of its behaviour, and whatever we put into our definition we call its nature. But we do not actually infer its behaviour from its nature; we either include its behaviour in our definition or we discover it by observation. Did Montesquieu believe that we can infer how men *ought* to behave from what they are and from how they do behave? Though he sometimes speaks as if this were what he believed, he never really explains what it is that can be thus inferred – what the rules are which follow logically from man's nature. He seems, in his definitions, often to play with words, but in such a way that it is not possible even to guess at what he is trying to do.

Montesquieu devotes the whole of the second chapter of his book, about one and a half pages, to discussing the laws of nature. Speaking of one of these laws, he assures us that it 'impresses' upon us the idea of a creator and brings us to him; another 'inspires' us to seek food; while a third is the need we have of one another's company, especially when we belong to different sexes. Though this second chapter is as obscure as it is short, we can at least make bold to say that the laws of nature, as Montesquieu here explains them, are not normative rules; they are merely descriptions of how men in fact behave.

In his first chapter, Montesquieu speaks of rules (or, as he puts it, *rapports* or relations) of equity prior to positive law; but he does not call those rules *laws of nature*. These are the examples he gives: that, if there were societies of men, it would be right to conform to their laws; that, if there were intelligent beings who had received a benefit from another being, they ought to be grateful; that, if an intelligent being had created another intelligent being, the creature ought to depend on the creator; that an intelligent being who has hurt another such being deserves to have the same hurt done to himself. Some of these rules, or others like them, have often been called laws of nature, and I do not know why Montesquieu refrained from so calling them. Presumably, he believed them to be laws falling within his general definition of law; he believed them to be 'necessary relations deriving from the nature of things' – the things in question being, of course, in this case, men. Presumably, he believed that these rules derive logically from the nature of man as distinguished from other animals – from the capacities peculiar to man. That would be enough to make them laws of nature in the traditional sense. Presumably, too, Montesquieu believed that these rules are in fact common to all societies, no matter what their customs and civil laws; though this was probably not all that he meant to convey when he said that they were prior to positive law.[1] Yet he refrained from calling them *laws of nature,* preferring to give that name to descriptions of actual behaviour.

I shall not go minutely into Montesquieu's definitions of law or try to weigh carefully what he said about the laws of nature or the rules of equity. He spoke so loosely that his words will bear several different and equally plausible interpretations. And yet it is not this looseness which makes me reluctant to take these parts of his theory seriously. Confusion is often worth unravelling, especially in political and social theory, because the most original and suggestive writers are not always the most lucid. But in this case the attempt is not worthwhile, simply because Montesquieu makes no use, in the body of his work, of his preliminary definitions and classifications. He tells us, for example, that law is human reason, and that the laws and customs of a nation are, or ought to be, applications of this reason to its circumstances.[2] Others besides Montesquieu have spoken in this way; and though the assertion, taken by itself, is too meagre to be clear and cries out for elaboration, it has in fact often been a prelude to important statements about law. With Montesquieu it is not so. This not very lucid utterance commits him to precisely nothing; for he never, in any part of *The Spirit of the Laws,* attempts to show how the laws and customs of any people derive from 'rules of reason' universally accepted. When he discusses what he calls the *spirit* of any system of law, he is never concerned to show how it is connected with universal principles. His general definitions of law lead to nothing, and are probably brought in only out of deference to a traditional theory which he could neither bring himself to discard nor knew how to make use of for the purposes of his own theory.

What Montesquieu calls the *spirit* of the laws is not 'reason' or anything corresponding to the traditional Law of Nature; it is whatever gives to a system of law its distinctive character. It is the way in which the laws that make up the system are related to one another and to the

---

[1] It could be argued that there are some rules implicit in the idea of a social order or community held together by conformity to established norms, no matter what these norms are: as, for instance, the rule of impartiality, that what is required of one person in a given situation should be required of another in a like situation; or the rule that, if some people are exempted from a conformity required of others, there must be a principle to justify the exemption. But this is not what Montesquieu had in mind.

[2] *Esprit des Lois,* Bk. I, ch. 3.

whole complex of institutions which make a distinct community out of the people living in a particular region. Montesquieu is concerned to explain how laws are related to one another, and not how they arise from any supposedly pre-social needs or aspirations of man. We can discover what he understands by law, not from his definitions of it, but from his social theory as a whole. When he uses the word *law* without trying to define it, he says nothing to suggest that there are laws which derive logically from the nature of man. When he uses it in a broad sense, he seems to have in mind any rule of conduct supported by sanctions, any rule the breach of which makes a man liable to punishment or disposes other men to behave in ways likely to deter would-be breakers of the rule. He also uses it in narrower senses, either to mean rules defining rights and obligations which the courts protect or enforce, or rules which those who exercise power must conform to if their acts are to be authoritative. If we compare Montesquieu's *definitions* of law with, say, Hobbes's, we have to admit that he is much the more obscure and inconsistent of the two. But if we see how he uses the concept which he defines so inadequately, we can claim for him that he has a better understanding of the social functions of law. Though, in the fashion of his day, he sometimes calls the laws of nature commands of God, he does not, as does Hobbes, treat all civil laws as commands of a human superior strong enough to enforce the commands. As we shall see later, when we come to consider what he says about political power, he is much nearer than either Hobbes or Locke to recognizing that those who govern are necessarily subject to rules – not merely in the sense that there is a higher law, natural and divine, which they are required to obey, but because government (as distinct from the occasional coercion of some persons by others) is an activity involving procedure, an activity governed by rules and which is effective only because it is so governed. Though Montesquieu does not, any more than Hobbes or Locke, speak of *constitutional laws* or conventions, he takes much larger notice than they do of the fact that government is a systematic and 'public' or official activity. Wherever there is political power there are conventions regulating its use.[1]

---

[1] Montesquieu sometimes loses sight of this fact, especially when he speaks of despotism. And it would be unfair to Hobbes and Locke to suggest that they never took notice of it. Hobbes distinguished the sovereign's public acts from his behaviour as a private person, and this distinction has implications which are inconsistent with some of the things he said about absolute or sovereign power. But then it seldom happens, at least in political theory, that what is obvious to a later age, because it has come to be so much insisted upon, was altogether neglected in earlier periods. Bodin recognized that there were rules, other than God's laws – rules inherent in the French system of government – on which the French king's authority rested.

Writers like Hobbes, Locke or Bentham, who seek (as far as they can) to explain all institutions as instruments to serve human purposes, are much more apt than a writer like Montesquieu to treat civil laws, if not always as commands (for they sometimes retreat from their more extreme positions when they find themselves in difficulties), then at least as effects of power. Indeed, Bentham, who has no use for such concepts as the state of nature and natural law, ordinarily speaks as if rules and institutions were either made deliberately or else emerged to satisfy needs not affected by them. This is his usual assumption, though sometimes he has to admit facts inconsistent with it. But Montesquieu's concern is exclusively with the needs and ambitions of man considered as a social creature. Laws and other institutions are, for him, rules or modes of behaviour seldom deliberately adopted and often not understood by the persons who follow them or to whom they apply. No doubt, society, as he sees it, is entirely human; its institutions and laws are no more than ways in which men actually do or are required to behave. Though only creatures having the capacities of man could be in society together, it is in society alone that men could be as they are. This, I think, is implicit in what Montesquieu says about man in society.

It is easy to pull Montesquieu's theory of law to pieces – not only his definitions, but also his facts and his generalizations from them. It is so vulnerable a theory, and vulnerable at so many points, that the hostile critic, absorbed in the task of destruction, can easily overlook what is true and valuable. If you consider Montesquieu's definitions and some of his favourite conclusions, it is too often obvious that the conclusions are inconsistent with the definitions, and even that both are false. Take a certain line with him, and you reduce him almost to nothing. For the greater part of what is really valuable in his theory of law consists of ideas and assumptions which are not defined or made explicit but are merely used. And, since they have nothing to do with the definitions, they are easily overlooked.

I must, however, take care not to exaggerate Montesquieu's mistakes or the weakness of his arguments. Many of his innumerable 'facts' and conclusions have proved true or close to the truth. Yet he was so often careless that a long list of errors and even absurdities can be reckoned against him. Voltaire, who disliked him, and perhaps disliked his reputation even more, repeatedly found fault with him, and spoke of him almost with contempt. Where he disagreed with Montesquieu, Voltaire was often right; he had more common sense than Montesquieu, and was less easily taken in. But though he did not know it, he also had less insight and less imagination, and so failed to do justice to what was new and important in Montesquieu's treatment of custom and law.

In Rousseau we find a better understanding of Montesquieu, and in Burke a still better. Burke, too, was impressed by the intricacy and variety of laws and customs, by the close connections between them, by their being the slow products of time and experience, by their power to affect our minds, and by our ignorance about them. We cannot do what we like with laws and customs; we cannot easily change them to suit ourselves. What we can do with them is limited by what they are; for they are the context of our lives and purposes, the social environment we are born into, which we take for granted but do not therefore understand. Their spirit is around us and in us, expressed in our habits and our prejudices, in our unthinking responses, in the assumptions we make without even being aware that we make them. We are creatures of law more even than creators of law.

To get a clear notion of Montesquieu's originality, it is not enough to consider his methods and assumptions in a general way, which is all I have done so far. It is better to consider how he treated certain questions often treated before him. He too classified governments, discussed men's motives for obeying them, and enquired how power might be limited. If we see how differently he treated these topics, we can see better just what he contributed to social and political theory.

We must, however, remember this: that a political theorist who has no marked gift for making fine distinctions, for analysing the terms he uses, for clear and rigorous argument, is apt, if he is original, to seem less so than he is. We must remember, too, that a political theorist, if he is brilliant and has a turn for making fine phrases, will often have imputed to him for originality what is not so. There have been political and social theorists who have made reputations for themselves merely by putting old ideas and arguments into a new dress. They too have done useful service, for their admirers might never have had the ideas and arguments brought home to them unless they had come across them in that dress. These people, brilliant but without originality, are often, in the end, seen for what they really are, and their reputations suffer greatly. They come to seem pretentious. And yet probably they were never as pretentious as they come to appear; they only claimed for themselves what they honestly believed was their due, being merely the first to be misled by their own brilliance. Montesquieu was original and brilliant, but his brilliance now serves rather to obscure his originality, often hiding it even from those who are not taken in by his brilliance.

IV. MONTESQUIEU'S CLASSIFICATION OF GOVERNMENTS

Montesquieu distinguished between three main types of government: republics, monarchies and despotisms. He has been criticized for substituting this classification for the older one which derives ultimately from the Greeks – the classification into monarchies, aristocracies and democracies. The principle behind the traditional classification is simple and obvious: it relates to number. It considers whether supreme authority belongs to one person, or to part of the community, or to the whole of it, acting directly or through representatives; or whether it is shared between them in what is called mixed government. These distinctions are important and easy to make. Monarchy really is a different kind of government from aristocracy, and aristocracy from democracy. Nor is it just a question of the number of people who have authority, for from these differences in number follow other more important differences of structure and spirit. The criterion of number is easily applied. What proportion of a community has political authority is something that can be discovered and that people can readily agree about.

Montesquieu's classification appears at first sight less useful, less clear and less easily applied. What, after all, is the difference between monarchy and despotism? Is despotism anything more than monarchy 'misliked', as Hobbes put it? Where supreme authority belongs to the whole community or to a considerable part of it, we have, according to Montesquieu, a republic. But is not this to create confusion by using two criteria, one numerical and the other moral, instead of the traditional single criterion of number? The moral criterion is used to distinguish between despotisms and monarchies; and the numerical to distinguish republics from the other two kinds of government. Montesquieu's classification, by putting democracies and aristocracies together into the same class, seems to imply that the difference between them is less important than how they both differ from monarchy; and that is not at all obvious.

This criticism of Montesquieu fails, I think, to do him justice. No doubt, he was not seldom confused, and it may be that he was so, even when he was distinguishing between the three main types of government. Certainly, in making these distinctions, he sometimes uses a moral criterion, and sometimes does not. The difference he makes between monarchy and despotism is partly a moral difference, whereas the difference between monarchy and a republic is not.

Yet Montesquieu's distinction between monarchy and despotism

15

is not wholly, nor even primarily, moral. Nor is he, when he puts democracies and aristocracies together as forms of republic, neglecting or belittling the great and obvious differences between them. He is merely drawing attention to something important which is common to them, to something obscured by the traditional classification. Admittedly, this is not as plain as it should be. Montesquieu, when he classifies governments, is both using traditional ideas clumsily and pointing to differences neglected before him. His classification, confusing though it may be in some ways, is important because it turns largely on differences in the machinery of government. Let us see how this is so.

Though aristocracy and democracy differ greatly, they have, if we contrast them with monarchy, two things in common: the laws are made by an assembly having elaborate rules of procedure, and there is a clear distinction made between the executive and legislative functions of government, even though there may be some persons who have a share in both. In a monarchy in Montesquieu's sense – in a monarchy as distinguished from a despotism, in (say) eighteenth-century France – the King-in-Council is both the supreme legislature and the supreme executive. It is not just that some people who take executive decisions also belong to the body which makes the law; it is one and the same body which is supreme in both spheres. By contrast, in an aristocracy, as England was in Montesquieu's time, the body that makes executive decisions is clearly separate from the body that makes the law. The King-in-Council is not the King-in-Parliament. It may be that the same persons make executive decisions and also introduce the more important proposals of law; but they do not do so in the same place and in the same way. If the king's ministers could have made laws as they made decisions of policy, without the co-operation of Parliament, the laws that got on to the statute-book in eighteenth-century England would have been very different from what they were.

We must also remember that in England in Montesquieu's time the king's ministers still owed their power as much (and indeed more) to the monarch's confidence in them as to the two Houses. We may think that Montesquieu misunderstood the English system of government, that the legislative and executive powers were not really separate. I believe that he misunderstood the system less than his critics suppose; but that is not the point I now want to make. Whatever the relations between the executive and legislature in England in the early eighteenth century, they were very different from what they were in France, precisely because England had a parliament and France had not. Whether or not they were separate in quite the way imagined by Montesquieu, they were clearly separate in a way in which they were not in France.

A monarch, of course, has official advisers; as lawmaker and supreme executive he acts in council. But his advisers are appointed by him and are his subordinates. A monarch in council, consulting his ministers about the laws he shall make, is not a legislative assembly. When the ultimate legislative power belongs to a deliberative assembly, the machinery of government is essentially different from what it is when that power belongs to one man, even though that one man has advisers. The assembly may include or represent all the citizens, or only a part of them; but it is, in law, an assembly of equals making its decisions by a process of free debate and voting.

England, once an aristocracy and now a democracy, has in both capacities needed a parliament; whereas France, when she became an absolute monarchy, could do without the Estates-General. Montesquieu knew that aristocracy and democracy are very different forms of government, but he was impressed by the fact that the institutions they use, especially in large states and the legislative branch, are broadly similar.

Monarchy is not, for Montesquieu, merely despotism without the more obvious attendant evils. The traditional classification of governments, which would put China and Persia into the same category as eighteenth-century France, seemed to him more misleading than his own. France and England, the one a monarchy and the other an aristocracy tempered by monarchy, seemed to him more alike, even in their forms of government, than France and Persia. Monarchy, according to Montesquieu, is a kind of government where supreme authority, legislative and executive, though it belongs to one man, is exercised in a traditional, public and orderly manner. Where there is monarchy, a careful distinction is made between the ruler as king and the ruler as man. The monarch is a public person, whose acts are attested and whose commands are executed in accordance with a procedure laid down by custom. His decisions are final, but they are accepted only because they are made in the prescribed way. Where there is monarchy, there is a constitution, in the sense of a well-defined body of rules regulating the exercise of power.

If men are to have security, if they are to know what they may and may not do, if their rights and duties are to be exactly defined, the law must be certain and coherent. New laws must be promulgated and registered; they must be carefully devised to fit into the whole body of existing law. And justice must be done, both to criminals and between litigants, by independent courts. Where the law is stable, certain, coherent and administered by independent courts, the ordinary subject, even if he takes no part in government, enjoys a precious liberty. He is a citizen and not a slave. He knows where he stands, both in his relations with his neighbours and with those set in authority over him. He knows his rights and duties, what he can demand of others and others can demand of him. Where such conditions obtain, there reigns the rule of law.

Montesquieu believed that these conditions obtained in France, making that country a monarchy and not a despotism. Under the French king there were subordinate and dependent authorities, long established and with high professional standards. Government was elaborate and regular. The responsibilities of subordinates to their superiors were definite. 'Intermediary, subordinate and dependent powers', says Montesquieu, 'are of the essence of monarchic government, that is to say, of the kind where one person alone governs by means of fundamental laws. . . .These fundamental laws necessarily require channels through which power flows: for, if there is nothing in the state beyond the momentary and capricious will of a single person, nothing can be stable, and therefore there can be no fundamental law'.[1]

One such intermediary power is the nobility, which Montesquieu thinks so necessary to monarchy that he puts forward the maxim, *point de noblesse, point de monarque*. In a monarchy, there are classes whose privileges are so well-established that the king, though his power is sovereign, cannot in practice touch them. Apart from the privileged classes, there must also be what Montesquieu calls *un dépôt de lois,* a depository of laws, 'which is to be found only in political bodies that announce the laws when they are made and call attention to them when they are forgotten'.[2] When he considered his own country, the bodies Montesquieu had principally in mind were the *parlements* or sovereign courts, especially the *Parlement* of Paris, which registered royal edicts and had the right to present remonstrances. Royal edicts did not have the force of law until the *Parlement* of Paris had registered them, and that court had the right to delay registration to give the king time to reconsider his decision. Lastly, where there is monarchy, the king never acts as a judge; justice is enforced by regular courts administering a known law and free from royal interference.

The king's council is not, according to Montesquieu, a suitable depository of law. For it expresses the monarch's momentary and

[1] *Esprit des Lois,* Bk. II, ch. 4.
[2] Ibid.

executive will, not his permanent will which is embodied in the law. Thus, even where there is monarchy, though the supreme executive and legislative powers are in the same hands, they are to some extent differently exercised. They are, in a way, kept separate; their difference is officially recognized. Monarchy is orderly and coherent government; it keeps to well-defined rules which prescribe how it shall function. It is not arbitrary. We can find ideas like these in Bodin, in the distinctions he makes between the different kinds of monarchy. What to Montesquieu is simply 'monarchy' is to Bodin 'monarchy royal and legitimate'. But Bodin habitually confuses a moral distinction with a political one; whereas Montesquieu not only does so much less often but makes the political distinction clearer by relating it to differences in the structure of government. Montesquieu may prefer monarchy to despotism, but his purpose is not just to express this preference. The point he is trying to make is that, while monarchy is a form of constitutional government, despotism is not.

He thinks of despotism as arbitrary government, limited, though loosely and uncertainly, by religion and custom. In a despotism no clear distinction is made between the ruler as a public and as a private person. There are no 'depositories' of law, no professional and independent bodies whose duty is to register the ruler's decisions and to consider how they fit into the whole system of law, and who have a right to appeal publicly to his better judgement. There is no order of nobles whose privileges the ruler cannot touch. The despot can make or break anyone according to his pleasure. The monarch is bound by custom to choose many of his advisers and officers from among the nobility, whose status is secure; he is therefore surrounded by men of independent judgement, whom he has to treat considerately. Though his power is formally absolute, it is limited by the need to retain the confidence of an independent and educated class. But in a despotism no man's social status is secure, and there is, properly speaking, no informed public opinion independent of the despot. The despot, when he so chooses, acts as a judge, or else interferes with the justice dispensed by the courts. In his private relations with other men, he does not submit to law. The courts are not professional bodies learned in the law; they are venal and arbitrary. There is nothing to restrain them except loosely defined custom and the despot's edicts, which they interpret as it suits the momentary interest of the ruler or their own. Only where there is an independent judiciary are there definite canons of interpretation; so that from customs loosely and variously understood, there can emerge a coherent and elaborate body of law, making for adequate, impartial and consistent justice. The despot's power is not unlimited, but it is arbitrary. Even where the despot happens to be just by temperament, the chances are that many of his subordinates will not be so, because the structure of despotic government does not make for impartial justice.

This picture is, of course, overdrawn. Montesquieu could speak well of monarchy because he knew it well; he was a lawyer and a nobleman, and therefore belonged to the two classes whose privileges in fact limited the theoretically absolute power of the French king. About the Eastern world, where what he called 'despotism' flourished, he knew much less. His conception of an almost entirely arbitary power is unrealistic. Political power is essentially regular. Wherever there is government, there is a system of rules in accordance with which power is in fact exercised. The observance of these rules places power in the hands of its possessors, and also limits their power. Completely arbitrary political power is impossible; it is, indeed, a contradiction in terms.

We could, I think, refute Montesquieu out of his own mouth, for there are passages in *The Spirit of the Laws* which imply that all government is to a large extent regular and customary – that before there can be abuse of political power there must be political power, which of its very nature implies status and procedure. The ruler is different from his subjects, not naturally, but conventionally; he is so in virtue of customary distinctions and rules which are in fact obeyed. Government is always, in this minimal sense, the rule of law; it is always to some extent constitutional. As Montesquieu himself admitted, the power of the despot and of his servants is limited by custom and religion. Montesquieu, like other people with a turn for fine phrases, was prone to exaggerate; not so much because his prejudices got the better of him as because he was carried away by his own eloquence. Of the order maintained by despots, he said, 'it is not peace, it is the silence of towns which the enemy is about to occupy'.[1] As if, in countries like China and Persia before they were open to Western influences – countries which he called despotisms – there were no such thing as justice!

Nevertheless, Montesquieu's distinction between monarchy and despotism is important. Where there is a precise and elaborate system of law administered by courts independent of the monarch, where new laws are carefully promulgated and liable to expert and public criticism, where social status is firmly grounded in rights and duties recognized by the courts and by the ruler, the system of government

[1] Ibid., Bk. V, ch. 14.

is very different from what it is where these conditions do not hold or hold much less. There was, in fact, a much greater difference between the French monarchy and, say, the Ottoman Empire than between the French monarchy and the eighteenth-century government of England. France, like England and unlike Turkey, was what the Germans call a *Rechtsstaat*, a constitutional state.

V. THE SPRINGS OF POLITICAL ACTION

Each of the three main types of government has its characteristic motive, its spring of political action, what Montesquieu calls its *principe*. This characteristic motive is not what led to the establishment of the particular type of government; Montesquieu does not explain institutions by their psychological causes. He is not interested in their origins but in how they function. The *principe* of a government explains, not how it arose, but why it works. It is something like what Burke was later to call prejudice; it is what makes people behave as they must if certain institutions are to function properly. As Montesquieu puts it, 'There is this difference between the nature of the government and its *principe,* that its nature makes it what it is, and its *principe* makes it work. The one is the structure peculiar to it, and the other the human passions that cause it to function'.[1]

The characteristic political motive of republics is *virtue,* of monarchies *honour,* and of despotisms *fear.* By virtue Montesquieu means public spirit and patriotism. The virtuous man respects the law and has a deep sense of his duty to the State. By calling virtue the characteristic political motive of republics, Montesquieu does not mean to imply that it cannot be found in monarchies. He means only that it is a motive indispensable to republics, because, unless citizens have it, republican institutions cannot function. He admits that honour and fear are also motives for action in republics, but they are not *characteristic;* they do not explain what keeps republican institutions, as distinguished from other kinds, working properly. Aristocratic republics apparently need virtue less than democracies; they have corporate interests to guard against the unprivileged classes, and this serves to bind the privileged closer together. Moderation is essential to aristocracies or otherwise the masses will rise against them. But democracy is peculiarly dependent on virtue; it cannot survive unless respect for law

[1] Ibid., Bk. III, ch. 1.

is general, and loyalty to the whole community stronger than loyalty to any class or person inside it. 'Virtue', said Montesquieu, 'is love of the republic; it is a sentiment and not a matter of knowledge (*une suite de connaissances*). . . . When once the people have good maxims, they keep hold of them longer than what are called the polite classes (*les honnêtes gens*). It is rare for corruption to begin with them. They often derive from the slenderness of their understanding a stronger attachment to what is established'.[1] Virtue, as Montesquieu conceives of it, is made up of loyalties and sentiments which men acquire in a certain type of society, simply by growing up inside it and learning to do what is expected of them. They learn to behave and to feel as they ought to do if the society is to survive; and to do that they need not understand the society.

The place of virtue, of public spirit, in republics is taken in monarchies by honour, which is a lively sense of what is due to oneself. Honour can inspire actions for the common good, but they are done less for the sake of that good than for the sake of glory or self-esteem or from loyalty to the prince. There can be, and there usually is, a good deal of virtue or public spirit in monarchies, but they can survive without much of it, provided that there is a lively sense of honour among the classes from which the monarch draws his officials and the officers of his army. The man of honour does his duty because it is beneath him to do otherwise; he owes it to himself to do it; if he fails in it he is disgraced in his own and other people's eyes. The man of honour takes care to keep up his position, to do nothing unworthy of himself or of the class or profession he belongs to. He owes allegiance to his king. He is a loyal subject rather than a patriotic citizen. His primary loyalties are to his king, his class and his profession, and not to the State.

When he distinguished monarchies from republics, Montesquieu had in mind ideal types as much as realities. He did not suppose that all governments belong entirely to one or other of his three classes. The government of England (which he greatly admired) was, he thought, partly an aristocracy and partly a monarchy, and he even found a democratic element in it. He would have agreed that virtue and honour were both strong motives of obedience among the English upper classes, and fear, too, especially among the lower classes with no political rights. Mixed governments were not uncommon. Montesquieu's purpose was rather to distinguish between types of institutions and to describe the moral attitudes that go with them,

[1] Ibid., Bk. V, ch. 2.

than to define categories among which all actual governments could be neatly distributed.

Just as he is least plausible when discussing the nature of despotism, so is Montesquieu weakest when describing its characteristic motive. It is, he says, fear. Under the Oriental great king, there are innumerable petty despots, who, because the law is uncertain and control irregular, can – provided they are servile to their superiors – do pretty much what they please to their inferiors. Peculation, corruption and tyranny flourish at all levels of government; there is little security and revolts are frequent. Not only do the common people obey mostly from fear (which is with them a considerable motive even under other types of government), but so too do the great despot's despotic subordinates. They are merely his servants, whose offices and privileges are entirely at his mercy. They have no secure status. They may be raised high at one moment and utterly cast down at another. There is a sense in which all men, under a despot, are equals; but they are equal as servants or slaves, not citizens. The great among them are so only as favourites of the prince; they have no secure social status which gives them prestige and influence independently of his will. They cannot resist him, except as rebels. They are therefore either servile or rebellious, and their motive for being the one or the other is usually fear.

This is obviously too dark a picture. Europeans travelling in Asia, because they did not find there the institutions they were used to at home, were too ready to conclude that everyone (except the most humble, who were beneath notice) was subject to the caprice of a despot; and Montesquieu took his opinions from them. Not all the political virtues are essentially European. Nevertheless, there is such a thing as despotism, and it has many of the qualities ascribed to it by Montesquieu. He chose to take his examples of it from the East; he might have looked nearer home and found what he wanted. He would then have had the advantage of being better able to verify his facts.

The real virtue of Montesquieu's account of the three main types of government, and of the characteristic motives that make them function, lies less in what he has to say about particular matters than in the conception that inspires him. Machiavelli also thought virtue proper to democracy, but he did not consider several types of government and the mental and moral attitudes that go with them. He never made a comprehensive study of institutions, and of the habits and sentiments that make them function. He did not treat all that goes to make up the life of a society, both institutions and prevalent ways of thinking and feeling, as mutually dependent facts. He was concerned with less general, less theoretical, matters: with giving advice to a single-minded ruler willing to unite Italy at whatever cost; with the causes of Roman greatness and Roman decadence; with the virtues of republics. Machiavelli was an acute, and even a profound, observer who liked to draw large conclusions from the study of history and contemporary affairs. Though he liked to call attention to certain connections between different sides of social life, he had no conception of a social system, of a complicated structure of institutions, political and social, so closely bound up with one another that the system is not so much resistant to novelty as pervasive of it, imposing its own character on what is brought into it from outside. Nor did he ever make a comparative study of several types of social system, as Montesquieu tried to do. Montesquieu may have done it crudely and too often carelessly, but he did it deliberately.

He did not, moreover, as others had done before him, consider man primarily as a creator of society, as a bearer of natural rights or a subject of natural needs, devising with other men the means to protect those rights and make easier the satisfaction of those needs; he considered him primarily as a social creature; he considered his customs, laws and institutions, together with the socially induced motives which cause him to conform to them.

VI. MONTESQUIEU ON POWER AND FREEDOM

That is not to say that Montesquieu was interested only in how society functions, in the facts; he also had his own strong preferences which he hardly troubled to disguise. There are indeed two Montesquieus in *The Spirit of the Laws*: there is the unprejudiced, though sometimes credulous and careless, student of society, and there is the lover of freedom insistently pointing to the advantages of the political forms which best preserve freedom. Few writers on politics can match his dispassionate curiosity about institutions which he does not like and his frank approval of the institutions he does like. He is not cold or indifferent, any more than was his compatriot, Montaigne; and he is, like Montaigne, both tolerant and discriminating in his praise. He never undertook to justify his preference for limited government; he merely enquired how freedom could be made secure politically.

It is interesting, in this respect, to compare Montesquieu with Locke. They both care deeply for freedom; they are among the most completely, the most whole-heartedly, liberal of the great political thinkers. Yet their manner of advocating freedom differs greatly. Locke devotes a few paragraphs of his *Treatise* to showing that the legislative and executive powers ought to be kept separate to prevent abuses dangerous to liberty, and he also argues that subjects must not be deprived of any part of their property to help defray the cost of government except with their express consent, mere tacit consent not being enough. But this is almost the full stretch of his concern with practical devices to secure freedom. Much more than in the machinery of liberal government, he is interested in proving that all human authority is held in trust, and that, when the trust is betrayed, subjects may rightfully resist their rulers. But with Montesquieu, this is not so. He takes no notice of the right of resistance, either to assert or deny it. He does not ask what subjects are entitled to do to preserve their freedom; he asks only how government should be organized the better to secure it. How should power be distributed among the persons and bodies that have it, to ensure that the subject is as free as he can be under government?

Montesquieu, in his account of freedom and how it is to be secured, made a false beginning. In *The Spirit of the Laws* he puts forward within a few lines of one another two definitions of freedom: he says that it can consist only in the power to do what one ought to will and not to be constrained to do what one ought not to will, and he also says that it is the right to do all that the laws permit.[1] Since the second of these definitions follows so closely on the first, it is fair to assume that Montesquieu took them to be equivalent. Certainly, he says nothing in this passage to suggest that men might be constrained by law to do what they ought not to will or prevented from doing what they ought to will. If, then, the two definitions are equivalent, it seems to follow that men ought to will what the law requires and ought not to will what the law forbids; and if this is so, Montesquieu's conception is at bottom the same as Hobbes's when he speaks of civil liberty. Judging Montesquieu merely by this chapter, which is the only one in which he is specifically concerned to define freedom, it would seem that, as much as Hobbes, he treats morality and legality as if they were the same thing.

But we have seen already that Montesquieu has little skill in defining his terms. He no more uses the term *freedom* consistently in the sense in which he defines it than he does the term *law*. His account of how the separation of powers makes for freedom suggests that when he speaks of freedom he has more in mind than what Hobbes calls civil

[1] Ibid., Bk. XI, ch. 3.

liberty; it suggests that he has in mind both the power to do what the laws permit, and freedom in some other sense, which he fails to distinguish from that power. This failure to distinguish between two different senses of freedom, both of them involved in his account of how freedom is promoted by the separation of powers, is a fertile source of confusion, as we shall see.

Much more than either Hobbes or Locke, Montesquieu insists that the power of every government is limited in two ways: by the manner in which it is distributed among the persons who exercise it, and by the traditions and beliefs on which authority rests. 'Rome', he tells us, 'was a ship held by two anchors in the storm, religion and *mores*'.[1] Though Montesquieu admired Rome, and especially republican Rome, more even than he admired the England of his day, he did not think that these anchors were peculiar to Rome. Even the power of a despot is limited, and often greatly limited, by religious beliefs and popular conceptions of what is right and proper. Yet in a despotic state men are not free as they were in republican Rome; they do not have either security under the law or freedom in the other sense which Montesquieu fails to distinguish from this security. Men are not free merely because the power of their rulers is limited by religious beliefs and popular ideas about right conduct. It is not so much this limitation as the other – the way in which power is distributed among the persons who exercise it – that makes for freedom. Political power, of course, is always distributed; it is distributed under a despot as much as in a republic. Montesquieu does not deny this. Since all power is limited by the way in which it is organized or distributed, what matters, if there is to be freedom, is that it should be organized or distributed in a certain way. The despot, Montesquieu tells us, actually has less power than the monarch; his power is smaller, but so too is the freedom enjoyed by his subjects. Freedom is not the greater because the ruler's power is small; freedom depends on how power is limited, on how it is distributed, on the rules that govern its use.

This idea – that power, if it is effectively to secure freedom, must not merely be limited (for that it always is) but limited in appropriate ways – is one of the most important and interesting in Montesquieu. Despotism, he thinks, is weak because it is arbitrary, because it is, of all the forms of power, the most uncertainly distributed, the least subject to precise and effective rules. Where power is not exercised according to precise rules, subordinates do not know what is expected of them. In theory they are servants of the despot, obeying him in

---

[1] Ibid., Bk. VIII, ch. 13.

everything; but in practice they can, within uncertain limits, do what they please. They have no rights against the despot, and are therefore perpetually in danger from him; but he, though his authority is in theory unlimited, is also their victim, because he is thwarted at every turn by their clumsiness, dishonesty and stupidity. Since his real power is small, his unlimited authority becomes a cloak for the petty tyrannies of thousands of subordinates. The remedy, which both strengthens government and safeguards liberty, is power exercised under fixed, elaborate and precise rules; it is, to use a modern phrase not used by Montesquieu, *constitutional government.* Strong government is orderly government, and can protect men's rights the more effectively for being itself subject to rules. Political power is like flowing water, which must be properly harnessed before it can exert strong pressure. The first condition of liberty is the rule of law, which can exist under any government except a despotism.

We must remember that Montesquieu, when he spoke of despotism, always had in mind the Oriental kingdoms of his day. That is why he took it for granted that despotism must be weak. We must not confuse despotism as he understood it with the dictatorships, fascist and communist, of our age. We know how immensely strong these dictatorships can be. But they are strong because, structurally and morally, they are quite different from the Asiatic despotisms of the eighteenth century. They are highly elaborate political machines; they require the strictest discipline among the immense political army of persons who exercise power. Power inside them, to the extent that it is arbitrary, is so mostly at the top; and if the power is great, it is so because, everywhere except at the top, it is mostly not arbitrary. And even at the top, it is much less arbitrary than it seems; the dictator must, in practice, conform to the ideology, the social and political faith, which he has built up and on which his power largely rests. The modern dictatorship, fascist or communist, is a *revolutionary state,* even though it uses many institutions and practices first developed in liberal and constitutional countries, but later transformed and put to other uses. It is a form of government that Montesquieu could not imagine, let alone allow for. His ideas about power and its relation to law and custom would need to be considerably modified to allow for it, but would not, I think, need to be changed in essentials.

So far, Montesquieu's position is clear enough. All power is limited. The condition of freedom is not that power should be slight or precarious, but that it should be limited in some ways and not in others. How then should it be limited?

Montesquieu makes a distinction, which he thinks important,

between *laws making for freedom as they relate to the constitution* and *laws making for freedom as they relate to the citizen*.[1] He likes to speak of *free constitutions* as well as of the freedom of citizens; and in one place he utters the paradox that 'a constitution may be free, and the citizen not be so: or the citizen may be free and the constitution not be so'.[2] This paradox is misleading, if not absurd, and I shall have more to say about it in a moment, because it is connected with Montesquieu's definition of freedom as the power to do what the laws permit. But I want first to consider these two kinds of law making for liberty.

About the second kind – the laws making for freedom as they relate to the citizen – there is no special difficulty. Montesquieu discusses them in the twelfth book of *The Spirit of the Laws*. They are the laws and processes ensuring that no one is punished except for a breach of known law; that a citizen is properly indicted, tried and sentenced, in accordance with rules which serve to protect the innocent as much as to discover and condemn the guilty; that he can assert his rights effectively both against other citizens and against the executive branch of government. These laws and processes, if they are to achieve their purpose, require that the courts should be independent of the ruler, in fact if not in name. In short, by the laws making for freedom as they relate to the citizen, Montesquieu means what is usually meant by the phrase *the rule of law*.

The nature of the other kind of laws – the laws that make for freedom as they relate to the constitution – is also easily enough understood. They are the laws prescribing how authority is distributed among those who have it. In other words, they are constitutional laws; and in practice there always are such laws or conventions, even where there is no written constitution. Montesquieu tells us that they do not make effectively for freedom unless they establish a separation of powers.

Clearly, both these kinds of law aim at preventing abuse of authority, and they both prescribe how power shall be exercised. The citizen cannot get a fair trial, cannot make good his rights, unless the courts exercise their powers according to rules established for his protection. It could be argued that all rules governing the use of authority, and thus also the rules which bind the courts, are in the broad sense constitutional. We could therefore say that Montesquieu's two kinds of law making for freedom are both laws making for freedom as they relate to the constitution. Yet the distinction between the two

---

[1] Bks. XI and XII of the *Esprit des Lois* pursue the implications of this distinction.
[2] *Esprit des Lois*, Bk. XII, ch. 1.

kinds of law is real and important. Rules which prescribe how those in authority shall deal with one another – how they shall stand to one another in their official capacities – are different from rules which prescribe how persons in authority shall deal with ordinary citizens. Both these kinds of rules make for freedom, and they make for it in different ways.

So far, so good. The distinction between these two kinds of law is worth making, and has to be made if we are to explain how power is to be organized to preserve freedom. Yet we have to admit that Montesquieu does not make as lucid and good use of it as he might for his purpose. If both kinds of law make for liberty, why say, as Montesquieu does, that the citizens may be free and yet the constitution not be free? What can be meant by calling the constitution free except that it makes for the freedom of the citizen? Strictly speaking, it is only individuals that can be free. To say that a constitution is free is only a roundabout way of saying that it helps to secure freedom to the individual – that political power is so distributed among its possessors as to enable the individual to enjoy the rights which constitute his freedom. Montesquieu really had no freedom in mind except the freedom of the citizen, and when he called the constitution free, he meant only that it was a means to individual freedom.

Why then did he say that the constitution might be free and the citizen not be so? Or that the citizen might be free and the constitution not be so? He was, I think, in the paradoxical and misleading fashion he was too fond of, saying two things: that the separation of powers, though a necessary condition of freedom, is not a sufficient condition; and also that, even where there is no *formal* separation of powers, the citizen can possess a precious kind of freedom – the kind which is the impartial and scrupulous enforcement of a body of carefully formulated laws. France did not have what Montesquieu, following an eighteenth-century fashion, called a free constitution; for in France the legislative, executive and judicial powers all belonged, at least nominally, to the king. Yet Montesquieu believed, albeit with reservations, that, though France lacked a free constitution, Frenchmen enjoyed real freedom – the kind of freedom secured by what he called 'the laws making for freedom as they relate to the citizen'.

These points are worth making, but they do not excuse Montesquieu's paradox, which is grossly misleading. A free constitution, according to him, is one in which the three powers – executive, legislative and judicial – are separate. Now, if Montesquieu's own account of the French system of government is true, France had a constitution which, though nominally unfree, was in reality at least partly free. Though all authority belonged in name to the king, the courts of law were in fact independent of him; and it was because they were independent that in France the laws making for freedom as they relate to the citizen were in practice effective. More than anything else, it was this independence of the courts which made France, in the eyes of Montesquieu, a monarchy and not a despotism. The laws making for liberty as they relate to the citizen are not, of course, the same thing as the independence of the courts; but Montesquieu clearly believed that, unless the courts are independent, there either will not be any such laws or they will be a dead letter.

He ought not to have said that the citizen can be free when the constitution is not free – that is to say, when none of the powers is separate from the others. He ought rather to have said that, though the separation of powers is not in itself enough to make the citizen free, he cannot have freedom unless at least one of the three powers – the judicial power – is separate from the other two, in fact if not in name. That, I take it, is what he meant to say. It is certainly what is implied by what he did say – except, of course, for the unlucky paradox about the citizen's being sometimes free when the constitution is not, and the constitution free when the citizen is not.

If all that is needed to ensure that the laws making for freedom as they relate to the citizen are not a dead letter is that the judicial branch should be independent of the other two, why need the other two branches be independent of one another? Why should the constitution of eighteenth-century England be more 'free' than the constitution of eighteenth-century France? The only freedom in question, the only freedom that could possibly be in question, is the freedom of the citizen, of the individual. Since all that is meant by calling a constitution free is that it makes for the freedom of the citizen, why should a constitution in which all three powers are separate be more free than one in which the judicial power alone is separate from the other two? It is difficult to answer these questions within the limits of Montesquieu's theory. Yet, clearly, he thought the separation of all three powers necessary to the enlargement and security of freedom.

The difficulty arises, I think, from his inadequate definition of freedom as the right to do whatever the laws permit. It is inadequate, not so much because it does not define what most people mean by freedom, as because it does not define what Montesquieu meant by it. If he had really meant by freedom no more than the right to do what the laws permit, he would have been satisfied with no greater separation of powers than sufficed to secure freedom in this sense. He would have been satisfied with the independence of the judiciary, which he thought enough to ensure respect for the laws making for liberty as they relate to the citizen – or, in other words, to ensure the scrupulous and impartial application of the laws to all members of the community. That he was not satisfied with the independence of the judiciary suggests that he had a larger conception of freedom than was covered by his own definition.

It was clear to him that there could be no freedom apart from law, and he could not imagine how there might be freedom against the law. Yet he could not dismiss the possibility that the law itself might be oppressive, even though this assumption does not square with his definition of freedom. If he had been as obstinately logical as Hobbes, if he had had the same respect for his own definitions, he might have been tempted to deny that the laws could be oppressive. But Montesquieu had some of the saving grace of Locke: he would not press a point home when it led him to a conclusion repugnant to common sense. It was clear to him that citizens may be oppressed, not only against the law, but also by means of the law; and he wanted to prevent that oppression, even though, if his own definition of freedom were adequate, there could be no such oppression.

The laws making for liberty as they relate to the citizen clearly do not prevent oppression by means of the law; they prevent only *illegal* oppression. The independence of the courts serves only to make these laws effective. If the laws themselves are not to be oppressive, other precautions must be taken; the executive and legislative powers must be kept separate. The makers of policy must not also be makers of law, or they will make laws to serve their own ambitions. 'Experience has always shown', says Montesquieu, 'that every man who has power is inclined to abuse it; he goes on until he finds limits. . . . That there should be no abuse of power, matters must be so arranged that power checks power'.[1] Abuse of power means, not just unlawful action, but legal oppression as well.

Montesquieu is doubly confusing: because he offers a definition of freedom which does not accord fully with his own conception of it, and because the distinction he makes between the two kinds of law making for freedom is not clearly related to his doctrine of the separation of powers. By saying that the citizen can be free when the constitution is not free, he implies that the laws making for freedom as they relate to the citizen can be effective even where there is no

[1] Ibid., Bk. XI, ch. 4.

separation of powers; whereas his true position seems to be that they require, to make them effective, that at least the judicial branch should be separate, in fact if not in name. And he does not explain, as clearly as he might, why the separation of the other two powers makes for freedom; it does so, not by preventing illegal oppression, but by making legal oppression much less likely than it would otherwise be. And how can law be oppressive except by offending against commonly accepted notions of justice and decency?

Montesquieu puts the separation of all three powers on the same footing, whereas his own general argument requires that he should not do so. The separation of the judiciary from the other two powers does not serve the same purpose as their separation from one another. The independence of the judiciary prevents oppression in contempt of law; while the separation of the executive and legislature greatly discourages, if it does not entirely prevent, oppression by means of the law. Those who make the law, if they do not also administer it, will not be tempted to make oppressive laws for their own benefit. This much is, I think, implied by Montesquieu's distinction between the two kinds of law making for liberty and his doctrine of the separation of powers. The confusion arises because the connection between the separation of powers and these two kinds of law is left obscure; and it is left obscure because Montesquieu's definition of freedom is defective, being both inadequate to the ordinary conception of it and too narrow for his own purpose. If freedom is merely the right to do what the laws permit, there can be no oppressive laws; and if legal oppression is impossible, there is no need for the three powers to be separate. The independence of the judiciary is then enough.

Freedom is primarily a moral rather than a legal notion, and is so, I suspect, as much in primitive societies, where morality and law are not clearly distinguished, as in more sophisticated societies, where they are. Primitive peoples who do not distinguish between the legal and the moral do not use the word law as we use it, and as Montesquieu ordinarily used it, to refer above all to rules enforced by the courts; they use it to refer to any rules to which obedience is required. Law, as they see it, is neither quite what we mean by a moral principle nor quite what we mean by a law; though it is probably closer to the first than to the second. Where the moral and the legal are not distinguished, freedom is perhaps well enough defined as the right to do what the laws permit. But where they are distinguished, as they were in Montesquieu's time, that definition is inadequate. Freedom is then not the right to do what the laws permit, but the right to do what is not wrong. It includes the right to do what the law wrongfully forbids, and the right to refrain from doing what the law wrongfully commands. It implies that rulers have a duty not to make laws which infringe certain moral principles. In primitive societies, where there are neither legislatures nor regular courts, there is not felt the same need to assert freedom against law – to distinguish the moral from the legal. But Montesquieu felt this need, and was therefore at times embarrassed by his own definition of freedom. And yet he failed to provide a better one. He was not tempted to go back to the notion of natural freedom, as we find it in Locke, for the whole spirit of his philosophy is that freedom has no meaning outside society – that is to say, outside the context of laws, customs and manners which make a community what it is. Not being a very clear thinker, he failed to express his belief in the social nature of freedom in a way that made it possible to explain how the law itself could be oppressive.

VII. MONTESQUIEU AND LOCKE ON THE SEPARATION OF POWERS

It has been said that Montesquieu's doctrine of the separation of powers is merely an elaboration of ideas found in the twelfth chapter of Locke's *Second Treatise*. This is not true.

The idea that power ought not to be gathered entire into the hands of one man or body is much older than Locke's *Treatise*. It is traditional; and in the time of Bodin and Hobbes, it was more of a novelty to attack than to uphold it. In England, in Charles I's time, while Parliament had seemed to be merely defending its rights against the King, most sympathies had been with Parliament; but after September 1641 when, led by Pym, Parliament went on to claim a right to control the executive, it lost the support of moderate men, because it seemed to be aiming at a monopoly of power. There was, of course, no systematic theory about the separation of powers; but it had long been taken for granted that the King-in-Parliament, the supreme interpreter of law, was separate from the King-in-Council, who actually governed. Locke was content to repeat the traditional doctrine, making no more of it than had traditionally been made. Though he distinguished between three governmental powers – the legislative, the executive and the federative (by which last he meant the control of relations with other states) – the third is nowadays included in the second; and, in any case, he did not advise that it should be in separate hands. The only separation that seemed to him to matter was between the legislative and the other two powers. Locke did not even mention the judicial power, which he no doubt thought of as part of the executive.

Now, we have seen that, with Montesquieu, it is precisely the power that Locke *did not mention* which it is supremely important to keep separate from the others. It was chiefly because the judicial power was in fact independent in eighteenth-century France, that Montesquieu thought of France as being a monarchy and not a despotism. The rule of law, which is the first condition of freedom, is made possible by that independence.

No doubt, France was not a perfect example of monarchy, as Montesquieu defined it. In a monarchy there is security under the law; and in a country like France, where a man might be deprived of his liberty indefinitely without being brought to trial, if he were arrested on the warrant known as a *lettre de cachet,* there was not full security under the law. Montesquieu approved of *habeas corpus* and regretted its absence in France. The law prescribing its use is an excellent example of what he understood by a 'law making for freedom as it relates to the citizen'. Montesquieu knew that the once formidable *Parlement* of Paris had been humbled by the monarch; he knew also that the nobles, by becoming courtiers, had lost much of their old independence. France, in his day, was not as good an example of monarchy as it had been before the reign of Louis XIV. If we apply Montesquieu's criteria impartially, we have to admit that France in the eighteenth century verged on despotism.

Nevertheless, the institutions which he thought proper to monarchy existed in France, and he was familiar with them in their French forms. There were courts of law with a long tradition of independence and impartiality; there were nobles who were still much more than creatures of the monarch; and there were *dépôts de lois.* France, by the standards of Montesquieu, was not a despotism but a defective monarchy, and perhaps even a monarchy in process of decay. Yet what Montesquieu, when he was defining an ideal type and not describing an actual government, called by the name of monarchy is very like what Bodin dignified by the title of *monarchy royal and legitimate.* And the best example of this form of government, in Bodin's eyes, was the French monarchy – not as it actually was in his day, but as it was entitled to be, as it would be if it were in full possession of its traditional authority.

Though Montesquieu was never, in the same sense as Bodin, a champion of monarchy; though he did not prefer it to all other types of government, reckoning those nations the happiest which were capable of having it, he did find many virtues in it, and his conception of it owes a great deal to the 'idea' of French monarchy as elaborated by Bodin and other fervent royalists. Montesquieu was steeped in the laws and traditions of French monarchy long before he became an admirer of the English political system. I am tempted to make two claims for him: that he understood how England was governed much better than those who accuse him of making a gross mistake about the English system imagine, and that his conceptions and doctrines owe at least as much to French as to English examples. In the sixth chapter of Book XI – the famous chapter describing the English system of government – Montesquieu says, speaking not only of France but of most of the kingdoms of Europe, that in them government is moderate because the prince, though he exercises the executive and legislative powers, does not exercise the third, the judicial power. But in Turkey, where the Sultan exercises all three powers, there is a terrible despotism. Clearly then, the defects of the French government, serious though they are in the eyes of Montesquieu, are not enough to make it a despotism.

For the sake of freedom, he wanted all three powers kept separate; indeed, he insisted more strongly than Locke on the advantages of keeping the legislative and executive powers in different hands; but the separation he thought essential to the rule of law was not so much between the executive and legislative as between them and the judicial power. This doctrine is clearly not the same as Locke's, nor even a development from it. It was suggested to Montesquieu partly by his experience as a French lawyer and judge, and partly by what he saw and heard during his visit to England. Robert Shackleton has shown that Montesquieu's doctrine of the separation of powers is much more like what was being advocated in England by Bolingbroke and his circle than like anything to be found in the writings of Locke. And we know that Montesquieu, while he was in England, saw a good deal of Bolingbroke.[1]

'There is', says Montesquieu in the short chapter serving as an introduction to the long chapter on England, 'a nation in this world the object of whose constitution is political liberty. We shall examine the principles on which it established that liberty. If they are good, liberty will appear there as in a mirror'.[2] And then, in the next chapter,

---

[1] See Shackleton, 'Montesquieu, Bolingbroke and the Separation of Powers', *French Studies,* III (1949), pp. 25–38, and *Montesquieu: A Critical Biography* (Oxford 1961), ch. XII, sect. iv.

[2] *Esprit des Lois,* Bk. XI, ch. 5.

he goes on to show that in England the legislative, executive and judicial powers are separate; that the legislature is divided into two chambers, of which one contains the hereditary nobles (who might otherwise suffer from the envy of their inferiors), and the other is elected by the people generally, except for those whose condition is so low that they are reputed to have no will of their own; that the supreme executive power is vested in a monarch who has the right to veto bills submitted to him; that the legislature has, however, no right to veto executive decisions, but only to call the executive to account for acts done contrary to law; that the popular chamber alone has the initiative in fiscal matters; that it is periodically re-elected; and that certain taxes and also the law allowing the monarch to levy and maintain troops are voted for only one year at a time. These provisions of the constitution are not merely described; they are justified as so many means to liberty. In the English constitution, as Montesquieu described it, there is a separation of powers; but there is also a system of checks and balances, and the separation is not complete. The executive is independent of the legislature, but the legislature has the power in certain cases to call it to account; and the executive in its turn has the power to veto legislation. The three branches are separate, but there are devices enabling two of them to impede one another, even in their own spheres.

Montesquieu wrote the chapter describing the English system of government after he had spent two years in England. He was not an obscure foreigner who saw nothing of men in the highest political circles. On the contrary, he was well received in those circles; and he was also an eager and intelligent observer. We must assume that he knew that nearly all the king's ministers were drawn from one or other of the two Houses of Parliament; it is inconceivable that a man moving for two years in the circles in which he moved, and with his interest in government, should not have known it. And yet he does not mention this fact. 'The executive power must', he says, 'be in the hands of a monarch, because this part of government, which nearly always needs to be expeditious (*qui a presque toujours besoin d'une action momentanée*), is better administered by one person than several'. A few lines further on, he adds that 'if there were no monarch, and the executive power were entrusted to a certain number of persons taken from the legislative body, there would be no more liberty, because the two powers would be united'.[1]

Presumably Montesquieu, like his English hosts, believed that the

[1] Ibid., Bk. XI, ch. 6.

king's ministers, even though most of them were members of one or other of the two Houses, were responsible primarily to the king. They were the king's ministers and not the agents of the legislature. The king exercised the executive power through them, and they were not the less his ministers because it was in practice advisable for the king to govern through men enjoying the confidence of Parliament. As a matter of fact, through the exercise of Crown patronage, it was possible for the king (or whoever exercised that patronage in his name) to provide the government with a substantial following in the House of Commons. It was also generally admitted that the Houses of Parliament ought to co-operate with the king and his ministers, with the executive power. The presence of ministers in the two Houses of Parliament served to make this co-operation easier. But nobody then imagined that, because most ministers belonged to one or other of the Houses, the executive and legislative powers were not in separate hands. It seemed obvious that they were, and Montesquieu probably took for granted what nobody was concerned to deny.

If this is what he did, surely he was right. The king's ministers owed their power to his having chosen them; they were his nominees in fact as well as in name. There was as yet no convention that he had to call upon the leader of the majority party in the House of Commons to exercise this prerogative in his name. It was still truer to say that the king's ministers could get the support of the House of Commons because they were his ministers than that they became ministers because they enjoyed that support. When Montesquieu wrote *The Spirit of the Laws,* relations between the executive and legislature in England were still such that it seemed natural to speak of these two powers as being in separate hands. If it was admitted that the king could not in fact choose his ministers as he pleased, this was seen not as a constitutional so much as a practical limitation on his power. Even the King of France could not choose his ministers as he pleased; even an 'absolute' monarch, if he were to govern effectively, had to look for co-operation and confidence, and the extent to which he got them was apt to depend on his choice of ministers. That a king who was not an absolute monarch should have, in this respect, less freedom than the King of France was only to be expected; but his lesser freedom was not thought to be (and indeed was not in fact) a subordination of the executive to the legislature or a union of the two powers.

Today, when we speak of a separation of powers, we think immediately of the American system of government. There, if anywhere, is a separation of the three powers; there, if anywhere, the doctrine of Montesquieu has been put into practice. And so it comes naturally to us to think of that separation in terms of the most famous system which embodies it. But Montesquieu knew nothing of that system. When he spoke of the separation of the executive and legislative powers, in the sixth chapter of Book XI, he had in mind the English system, and was, no doubt, contrasting it with the French. In England the executive and legislative powers were separate, and in France they were not. Therefore, if we are to discover what he understood by the separation of powers, we must look, not at a system established after his death (even though its founders were to some extent influenced by him), but at the system which he took to be an example of what he had in mind. His description of this system satisfied not only himself; it also satisfied his English contemporaries. It never occurred to them that a distinguished foreigner had misdescribed their form of government, that he had made a great mistake about it. It was not in his own day but many years later that Montesquieu was accused by Englishmen of having seriously misunderstood their political system. By that time, two things had happened: the system had changed, and the United States had come into being.[1]

Where the executive and legislative powers are separate, says Montesquieu, the legislature, though it cannot stop executive action, has the right to satisfy itself that the laws have been duly executed. It has both a legislative and a supervisory power. Montesquieu does not explain either how the supervisory power was in fact exercised in England or how in principle it ought to be exercised; though to assert such a power is clearly to imply that the executive is or ought to be in some way responsible to the legislature. For the legislature cannot exercise its supervisory power effectively unless it can require information about the execution of the laws and can apply some kind of sanction to ensure that its resolutions are not dead letters. Montesquieu says that the legislative body must not have the power to bring to judgement the person 'who executes'. He means, presumably, the chief executive, the monarch, who ought to be, in the old mediaeval sense, above the law, *legibus solutus*. How, then, is the executive to be made accountable to the legislature for the way the laws are executed?

---

[1] As early as 1776, thirteen years before the United States acquired its Constitution, Bentham had argued, in the *Fragment on Government,* that the executive and legislative powers were not separate in England. By their separation, he already understood what the American Fathers were to understand. Yet his understanding of it was not common in England until the next century; and even as late as 1867, Bagehot, in his *English Constitution,* thought it necessary to insist that the executive and legislative powers were not separate in England.

As to how the legislature is to get the information it needs, Montesquieu says absolutely nothing; but he does allude to a right of impeachment, a right of the lower House to bring to judgement before the upper House any citizen who has violated what he calls 'the rights of the people' – who has committed crimes which the ordinary courts cannot, or are unwilling to, punish. Thus we may say of Montesquieu that, while he clearly implies that the executive power ought to be responsible to the legislative for the way it administers the law, he fails to explain how it is to be made so.

Montesquieu's conception of the separation of powers is by no means as clear as those critics take it to be who say that, already at the time when *The Spirit of the Laws* was written, it had ceased (or was ceasing) to apply to the English system. For example, he says that the executive power, since it forms part of the legislative only when it exercises the right of veto, must not take part in debates, and then goes on to say, in the very next line, that it is not necessary that the executive should be able to make proposals of law because it can always reject the proposals made by the legislative.[1] He does not say that the executive, where the powers are separate, *must not* make proposals of law but only that it *need not* be able to do so, which implies that, if it were to make them, this would not of itself annul the separation of powers. Montesquieu says nothing about how the executive would make such proposals. It may be that, in this chapter which deals with the constitution of England, he has in mind the king's acting through ministers taken from the legislature. Certainly, that possibility is not excluded by his saying that the executive power *does not form part* of the legislative. Montesquieu, whenever in this famous chapter he speaks of the executive, seems to mean the chief executive, the monarch. It is the monarch who is outside the legislature, takes no part in debates and has no share of the legislative power, except when he rejects a proposal of law voted by the two Houses. Though he acts through subordinates, his action, no matter who his subordinates may be, originates outside the legislature; it does so even when his subordinates are members of the legislature. This was still the common opinion in the England that Montesquieu knew, and he probably shared it.

I do not wish to suggest that Montesquieu's brief account of the English system of government as it was more than two hundred years ago is altogether correct. He took his opinions about it from the circles in which he moved while he was in England; and no doubt, then as now, there was a wide diversity of opinions. A system of

---

[1] *Esprit des Lois,* Bk. XI, ch. 6.

government is always in process of change, and one of the reasons why it changes is that the persons who work it have certain opinions about it, opinions which vary with their prejudices and interests. Even the fullest and most judicious account is only partial and will soon be out of date. Montesquieu's account is one of the most rapid and most summary, and is by no means precise. But it seemed substantially accurate to his contemporaries, English and French; and it probably was what it seemed. Almost certainly, they read into it more than the actual words would convey to someone who knew nothing of the English system, but that is not to say that they read more into it than Montesquieu intended that they should. A brief account, to those familiar with what it describes, always conveys much more than it literally says; yet later, when what it describes has greatly changed, its brevity makes it the more likely to be misunderstood.

But I must not continue on this tack. To the political theorist, it does not greatly matter how far Montesquieu's account of the English political system in early Hanoverian times is correct. The theorist is more concerned with assumptions and arguments than with historical facts. The criticism of Montesquieu interests him less in its details than for the conclusion drawn from it. Montesquieu, say these critics, maintains that the English owe their freedom to the separation of powers, whereas the truth is that the legislative and executive powers are not separate in England. Therefore, unless we choose to argue that the English are not free (and who would choose to be as perverse as all that?), we must conclude that there can be freedom even where these two powers are not separate.

I do not choose to be perverse, and I do not even deny that a people might be free though the executive and legislative powers were not separate. I venture only to suggest that in England they were separate when Montesquieu wrote *The Spirit of the Laws* and are still separate today. Of course, relations between the executive and legislature in England have changed greatly in the last two hundred years, and are much closer than they were. They are also different in England from what they are in the United States; and if we decide that the two powers are not to be called separate unless they are related to one another as they are in the United States, then it is clear that they are not now separate in England. But, then, as we have seen, it is no less clear that they were not separate in England in Montesquieu's day, for the king could and did choose most of his ministers from the legislature, which the American president is forbidden to do. Yet Montesquieu, who must be supposed to have known how they were chosen, said that the two powers in England were separate. I suggest that in England today these two powers, though no longer related as they were in Montesquieu's time, are still so related that they act as checks on one another.

The King's (or Queen's) ministers are so now only in name; the monarch can no longer help to provide them with a majority in the House of Commons. Their relations with the House of Commons are now vastly different from what they were. Yet the ministers, the men who exercise the executive power which once belonged to the monarch, are no more chosen by the House of Commons than they are by the monarch. The Cabinet and the House of Commons (now much the more important of the two Houses) are not the same body, and neither is anywhere near being the mere tool or agent of the other. They are two separate bodies, of which the smaller is emphatically not a committee of the larger, nor the larger an assembly which merely carries out the wishes of the smaller. That the two bodies are related in ways unforeseen by Montesquieu, and much more intimately than ever the monarch was to Parliament in the days when kings governed and did not merely reign, does not make them one; nor does it ensure that the authority of either comes to it from the other. The House of Commons does not decide who shall belong to the Cabinet or what its powers shall be, and has only a limited control over its exercise of those powers; and the Cabinet, though its control over the House is much greater, is far indeed from being able to do what it likes with it. That the same election normally decides both who shall belong to the House of Commons and who shall be invited to form the executive body does not make these two bodies one or make either the subordinate of the other, though it doubtless helps to make relations between the two very different from what they would be if the executive and legislature were separately elected as they are in the United States.

When Montesquieu spoke of the executive and legislative powers being united in the same hands, he had in mind the sort of situation which existed in his own country. The King of France was the supreme law-maker and the supreme executive; he, with the help of his advisers, exercised both powers. If, having regard to political realities and not to paper constitutions, we were to look today for a country where the legislative and executive powers are united in the same hands as they were in France in Montesquieu's time, we should find it not in England but in Russia. It is there that the same body exercises in fact (though not in name) both the executive and legislative powers, the Supreme Soviet having no other function than to applaud the decisions taken by the real rulers of the country. It is in

Russia, and not in England, that the making of policy and the making of law are the work of the same body. It is true that in England the more important bills are government bills, but before they become law they must be publicly debated and voted on in an assembly where there is strong opposition to the government. And if the government can put pressure on its supporters in the House of Commons to ensure that they vote for its bills, it must also respond to pressure from them; its relations, even with its own supporters, are very different from what they would be if the House of Commons were the same sort of body as the Supreme Soviet.

In England policy is made by one body in one way, while laws are made by another body in another way. Policy is debated in secret, and the decisions reached are made public only when the body that makes them chooses to publish them or takes action which reveals their nature; while proposals of law, no matter where they originate, are publicly debated and publicly opposed, and cannot become law unless they are exposed to discussion and attack. In Russia, both policy and law are made, as they were in eighteenth-century France, by the same body, which takes all its decisions in secret. The difference between the English and Russian systems is not merely that in England elections to the supreme legislature are free while in Russia they are not; it is also that in England there is, in reality and not just on paper, a separation of the executive and legislative powers of a kind unknown in Russia. It is, of course, important that power is acquired in different ways in England and Russia, but it is also important that in the two countries it is differently distributed. The ways in which power comes to its possessors are no more alike in Montesquieu's France and Soviet Russia than they are in Soviet Russia and modern England. If we take old France and new Russia together, what distinguishes them from modern England is not the way in which supreme power is acquired but the way it is distributed.

The chapter on the constitution of England is probably, at least in the English-speaking world, the best known in *The Spirit of the Laws*. More than anything else written by Montesquieu, it influenced writers and jurists in the English colonies and in the mother country. They were so much impressed and flattered by his admiration for English institutions, that they neglected whatever he said about the separation of powers when he was speaking of other institutions. They did not notice that some of his best arguments for an independent judiciary are connected, not with his account of the English constitution, but with the distinction he made between monarchy and despotism. Even in the eleventh book, which is more concerned than any other with the separation of powers, there are eight chapters devoted to ancient Rome. There too, during the period when Roman liberty endured, there was, according to Montesquieu, an effective separation of the three powers. His account of it is even more summary (and at times ambiguous) than his account of the English system of government, but he says enough to make it clear that he did not suppose that in Rome under the Republic the three powers were so distributed that no person or body having a share of one had a share of the others. For example, he says that while the Roman people, jealous of their liberties, contested the legislative rights of the Senate, they did not contest its executive rights.[1] He speaks in a way which suggests that the senate, though it was primarily an executive body, also had some legislative power which the people, for the sake of their liberties, did their best to keep within narrow limits. If, in the eleventh book of *The Spirit of the Laws,* we compare the one long chapter devoted to England with the several shorter ones which treat of the Roman Republic, we may say that, in the two political systems most admired by Montesquieu, there was an effective separation of powers, which was simpler in England than in Rome. And yet in neither system, as he describes it, were the three powers so distributed that no body or person had a share of more than one.[2]

We need not agree with Montesquieu's account of English and Roman institutions to see the force of his doctrine about power and liberty. It may well be that to secure liberty there is no need to distribute the three powers as he thought they were distributed in either England or Rome. For though he leaves too much unexplained, it is clear, even from his own account, that there were great differences in this respect between the constitutions of the two peoples whose political genius he praised. If the English system could differ so much from the Roman and yet make liberty secure, why should not some other system differing greatly from both the Roman and the English do so as well? This we may concede, and yet agree with Montesquieu that, to make liberty secure, the political system must ensure that power checks power. The rules governing the use of power must be such that, whenever some persons having authority

---

[1] Ibid., Bk. XI, ch. 17.
[2] Notice the last words of the eleventh book: 'But one must not always so exhaust a subject that there is nothing left for the reader to do. It is not a question of making him read but of making him think.' It is astonishing how little it takes to exhaust a subject, in the opinion of Montesquieu! He would have done better to write longer chapters on fewer subjects, taking greater care to make his meaning plain. He asks altogether too much of his readers.

are tempted to abuse it, there are others who can, in a quite regular
and legal manner, prevent their doing so. Not only must the courts
be independent of the government, but the supreme executive and
legislative powers must be in different hands, even though they are
distributed in such a way that there are several persons and bodies
having a share of both.

In every community which is political, which has a regular government carried on by persons recognized as holding public office, all who
have authority of any kind exercise it in prescribed ways. So much
is implied by the very notion of a form of government or political
system. In the widest sense of the word, there is a constitution; there
is a body of rules whose general observance by those who govern
makes government possible. Therefore, if this body of rules is such
that abuses of power can be *legally* prevented, it is likely that they
will be so prevented; for the simple reason that all persons and bodies
having a share of authority have one interest in common: that the
rules in virtue of which they have authority shall be respected. Where
others before Montesquieu, for the defence of liberty and against the
abuse of power, had appealed to natural right and natural law; or to
a social contract whose terms oblige both rulers and ruled; or to a
right of popular revolt against governments which break their trust,
he proclaimed the need for constitutional government: for political
power so distributed that anyone having a share of it who is tempted
to abuse it finds others having power able and willing to use it to
prevent or punish him. Liberty does not flourish because men have
natural rights or because they revolt if their rulers press them too
far; it flourishes because power is so distributed and organized that
whoever is tempted to abuse it finds legal restraints in his way.

These restraints will not be effective unless there is a will to use
them – unless the persons who run the system are true to its spirit.
But then the system tends to keep them true to it. Montesquieu does
not belittle the importance of the political emotions, of loyalty to the
constitution and respect for freedom; he merely sees a close connection
between these emotions and the institutions they support. As he sees
it, men do not first conceive of freedom and then set about looking
for the institutions which secure it. Institutions and the sentiments
appropriate to them reinforce one another. Those who are accustomed
to enjoy freedom value it most, and they cannot enjoy it unless they
live in a society whose institutions make it secure. If it is true that
freedom will not survive where it is not valued, where men are not
ready to defend it, it is equally true that they will not set a high value
on it where they have never had, or have long since lost, the means

of defending it. And freedom cannot be defended except where there are some at least of the institutions necessary to its defence. There must already be some freedom, and therefore institutions favourable to freedom, before the love of it can grow strong.

From this it follows that freedom is enlarged slowly; it is the fruit of many victories, and the weapons men use, both to preserve the freedom they have and to add to it, are the institutions they already have. Freedom is an effect of many things which are themselves intimately connected: the laws and habits of a people, their temper and prejudices. It cannot survive, in any large and complex community, unless the rules governing the use of power, while serving to make it effective, also prevent the abuse of it. In England, the oldest home of freedom, government is not weaker than elsewhere, not less able to carry out its will; but its functions are so distributed that those who take part in government are both willing and able to prevent the abuses to which all who have power are liable to be tempted.

Montesquieu's doctrine of the separation of powers is not an effect of an unlucky though excusable mistake about the English system of government; it springs from a deeper understanding of what political power is than we can find in all but a few of his predecessors. Power so organized that it checks power without making government ineffective, a system which is self-regulating because it is so organized that no one who takes part in running it can hope to increase his own share of power by breaking the rules of the system: this idea is to be met with before Montesquieu. It was familiar to Harrington, and there are hints of it in earlier writers. But, as Pascal remarks in *L'Esprit géométrique,* 'All those who say the same things do not possess them in the same way. . . .Therefore we must probe to see how this thought is lodged in its author; in what manner, from what angle, and to what extent he possesses it'.[1] This idea was expounded by Montesquieu with greater insight and elaboration than by anyone before him; he possessed it more fully, saw further into its implications and into the conditions, social and psychological, of its being realized. It is his idea by right of conquest.

★ ★ ★

In this book no social or political theory is studied in all its aspects, but only those parts of it that raise broad issues which cannot be

---

[1] *De l'esprit géométrique,* in *L'Oeuvre de Pascal,* Pléiade edition (Paris 1936), p. 383. The French reads 'Tous ceux qui disent les mêmes choses ne les possèdent pas de la même sorte. . . . Il faut donc sonder comme cette pensée est logée en son auteur; comment, par où, jusqu'où il la possède'.

settled without examining fundamental concepts and assumptions. I have discussed Montesquieu's account of the social effects of man's physical environment and what he does to protect himself from it or to adapt himself to it, his views about the interdependence of institutions and modes of thought and feeling, his conception of the supremacy of law, and his ideas about power and how best to organize it to secure freedom. These are the parts of his theory which call for treatment in a book of this kind. Yet his discussion of them occupies only eleven of the thirty-one books of *The Spirit of the Laws*. There is therefore a great deal left out of account; and, when I say this, I have in mind, not Montesquieu's writings which do not treat primarily of social and political theory, but his best-known work which does. Of the twenty books of *The Spirit of the Laws* that I have not considered, only four deal with matters interesting to jurists; the others are all concerned with what is truly social and political theory. Moreover, they deal, not with small matters, but with great ones. They raise important issues, though not of the kind with which this book is primarily concerned, because to consider them there is no need to examine critically the basic concepts which we use to explain social and political phenomena or to pass judgements upon them. Of course, in every part of *The Spirit of the Laws* – in the parts I have neglected as much as in those I have not – Montesquieu uses these concepts, as any one must do who discusses what he chooses to discuss. He uses the concepts, though not in such a way as to move the reader to examine them critically; it is either clear enough how he uses them or his argument is so meagre or obscure as to make close scrutiny unprofitable.

Yet it is to do less than justice to Montesquieu not to draw the reader's attention to how much this particular discussion of his theories leaves out. He devotes two books to considering slavery, its causes and effects in different societies. In the first, Book XV, he considers what is ordinarily understood by slavery, and in the second, Book XVI, what he calls 'domestic slavery' or the extremer forms of the subjection of women. In these two books, and more particularly in the first, the two dominant passions of Montesquieu the social theorist are both very much to the fore: curiosity and the love of freedom. Though his purpose is to explain slavery, he does not trouble to hide his dislike of it. He treats almost with contempt the arguments used to justify it, and is eager to point out its dangers. Everywhere, except in a despotism, it is dangerous to the established order, for where some men have freedom and others are slaves, the qualities on which the survival of freedom depends are undermined; a state which is not despotic but which allows slavery is in danger of becoming despotic. Though

Montesquieu sometimes calls all the subjects of a despot 'slaves', he is not, when he does so, using that word in the ordinary sense. In the argument we are now considering, he is not saying that, in a country where there are slaves, in the sense of persons bought and sold on the market, all men are in danger of becoming slaves in the same sense; he is saying rather that, where slavery long endures, even those who do not become slaves in this sense cease to have the rights which distinguish the citizen of a republic or even a monarchy from the subject of a despot.

Montesquieu asserts that, if he had to defend the right to make slaves of Negroes, this is what he would say:

> The peoples of Europe, having exterminated those of America, have had to reduce the peoples of Africa to slavery in order to use them to clear so much land. Sugar would be too dear if the plant which produces it were not cultivated by slaves. The people concerned are black from head to foot, and they have noses so squashed that it is almost impossible to pity them. It is not to be imagined that God, who is very wise, would put a soul, and, above all, a good soul, into a body that was all black. . . . We cannot suppose that such folk are men, because, if we suppose them to be men, people might begin to think that we ourselves are not Christians.[1]

Two books treat of religion, and are written, for the most part, much in the spirit of Machiavelli.[2] The reader is immediately warned that the author will examine the religions of the world only to estimate the good that civil society derives from them, and this whether he speaks of the one which has its roots in Heaven or of those which have theirs in the earth. His tone is cool and ironic; sometimes, no doubt, he is genuinely detached and at other times affects to be so. He even disputes some of the conclusions of Bayle, not to defend the truth of any religion (for that is not his business), but to show that it does not have the effects ascribed to it. He is interested primarily in the utility of various religions, and has little to say about their causes or even their effects, other than effects on morals. Islam is, he thinks, better suited to the peoples of Asia, and Christianity to the Europeans, while Protestantism agrees better with the temperament of northern Europeans and Catholicism better with southerners. A new religion accommodates itself to the habits and prejudices of the people among whom it first arises, which makes it unsuited to peoples who differ greatly from them; and this explains why it often begins by making

[1] *Esprit des Lois*, Bk. XV, ch. 5.
[2] They are Bks. XXIV and XXV.

rapid progress over a wide area and then suddenly ceases to spread.

Montesquieu would have governments tolerate religions firmly rooted within their borders, but advises them to discourage new religions on the ground that their adherents are usually intolerant. It is a mistake to use penal laws to force men to believe (or to pretend to believe) what their rulers decide they ought to believe, but it may be necessary, in order to preserve peace and goodwill among men, to discourage the propagation of certain beliefs.[1] Montesquieu does not say what a government should do to discourage such pernicious beliefs. This is yet another among many examples of one of the great faults of *The Spirit of the Laws*: It touches upon too many topics too lightly and rapidly and prompts too many questions which it never attempts to answer.

Montesquieu was no mean economist. Two books of his greatest work are devoted to commerce, and another to money and exchange. In the seventeenth chapter of Book XXII he explains how money has a price like any other commodity, and how that price is determined by the amount of it in circulation and the total quantity of goods actually in trade. In the tenth chapter of the same book he explains how the rates of exchange between different currencies is determined by the balance of indebtedness between holders of these currencies; and in yet another chapter he condemns the laws against usury as restraints on trade. But he was less interested in the economics of trade than its political and other effects. He ascribed the freedom of the English in large part to their being a commercial people.[2]

---

[1] I must take care to do justice to Montesquieu's dislike of intolerance. One of the most moving and eloquent chapters of the *Esprit des Lois* is the thirteenth of Book XXV. It purports to be a humble remonstrance addressed by a Jew to the Inquisitors of Spain and Portugal, inspired by the burning of a Jewish girl at an *auto-da-fé*. It is beautifully done, and is not the less effective because Montesquieu pretends that he is quoting and even appends a footnote criticizing a sentiment expressed in the remonstrance.

[2] Two of the longest chapters of the *Esprit des Lois* treat of the English. The sixth chapter of Book XI I have discussed already. In the twenty-seventh chapter of Book XIX he says (having England in mind) that in a free country there is a natural division between the supporters and opponents of government, their relative strengths varying continually, so that the monarch has to rely first on the one group and then on the other. But, in spite of party conflicts, a free people are not less but more united than others, especially when danger threatens from abroad, and are more willing to make sacrifices and to pay heavy taxes. A free people are tolerant, more given to pride than to vanity, rough in their manners, and in their literature more subtle than delicate. Though in this chapter Montesquieu does not mention the English by name, it is easy to see that he has them in mind. Nor does he merely praise them; like other Frenchmen who have spoken well of the English, he finds them more admirable than attractive. He denies them only one quality which they often boast of possessing, and that is modesty.

Montesquieu gave his masterpiece to the world as a finished work, and we know that he spent a long time in the making and perfecting of it. And yet it has less coherence and less unity even than Pascal's *Pensées*. For the *Pensées,* though never made into a book, are nevertheless the makings of a book; they are pieces brought together by a builder of genius who never completed his building, by a vigorous thinker and artist who knew how to put his thoughts together into a coherent, elaborate and elegant whole. But Montesquieu has left us a vast and shapeless building consisting of innumerable small rooms into which he has put furniture assiduously and abundantly collected over many years. He was, like his compatriot Montaigne, both a collector of facts and opinions and more than a mere collector. He had not only an enquiring but a fertile mind. He was an innovator; he had new ideas and attempted new things. He was, in his own very different way, as much an innovator as Hume. But he was not nearly as lucid and acute as Hume; he had nothing like the same ability to say precisely what he meant. If we could ask Hume what he thought he had attempted and achieved as a writer on society and government, he would probably give us a clear and correct answer; if we could put the same question to Montesquieu, we should almost certainly be disappointed with the content of his answer if not with the style.

Montesquieu was the first to attempt a serious study of forms of government in relation to the entire social structures in which they flourish. His information was less reliable and his ignorance vastly greater than he imagined. For so sophisticated a man, he was at times strangely credulous; if he had something of Aristotle in him, he also had something of Herodotus. It took very little to convince him that he had dealt adequately with any subject he discussed. Perhaps he was the dupe of his style, inclining to believe that whatever he had said well he had said truly. Certainly, he spoke, without misgivings, of matters he knew very little about. Yet he had a considerable knowledge of three very different peoples, the Romans, the English and the French; and, for several of his purposes, they were not a bad sample. His comparative method, applied to them, led to some remarkable results.

Of the great political theorists discussed in this book, only two, Hume and Montesquieu, were much less advocates or critics than observers intent on explaining the facts. They had their preferences, which they did not trouble to hide, but they were quiet preferences. For they lived in quiet times, and did not have, like Rousseau, premonitions of unquiet times to come. They were not eager to defend the established order or to change it. They flourished at a time when men were beginning to believe in progress but had not yet become impatient. They did not believe, as Hobbes and Pascal had done, that all that matters is that there should be an order which nobody challenges. The theories which Locke had attacked were discredited, and there was no need for them to assert that legitimate authority derives from the consent of the governed in order to deny that whoever has it is answerable only to God for how he uses it. They knew nothing of radicals and revolutionaries. They were the least dogmatic and most serene of political thinkers; they wrote in an interval when the sky of politics was unusually clear, and in it a cloud no bigger than a man's hand.

CHAPTER TWO

Hume

Legend has it that a Dutch admiral once tied a broom to the mast of his flagship as a boast or as a warning to his enemies. He meant to convey either that he had swept them from the seas or that he intended to do so; I no longer remember which. If philosophers had emblems, Hume's would surely be a broom. Not that he liked to boast or threaten. He was the most polite as well as the most ruthless of critics; he used his broom deftly and quietly, raising little dust, but he used it vigorously.

As a philosopher – an epistemologist – Hume has received his due, and perhaps more than his due, especially at Oxford. As a social and political theorist, less than justice has been done to him. It is difficult to explain why this should be so, for he spent as much time and thought on political and closely allied moral problems as on the theory of knowledge. Of all his writings, he was proudest of the *Enquiry Concerning the Principles of Morals*. In that work, as in the third book of his *Treastise of Human Nature*, he tries to explain morality entirely as a social phenomenon. Hume is more important perhaps as an eliminator of the obscure, the inadequate and the otiose than as a framer of new ideas and hypotheses. He destroyed more than he created. Yet, to the extent that he was creative, he was more so perhaps as a moralist and political theorist than as a general philosopher. In his theory of knowledge he put nothing really satisfactory in the place of what he took away; whereas his account of justice, though it falls short of the truth, is plausible and suggestive; it is also the heart of his social philosophy.

It is true that Hume's account of justice is not entirely original; almost every part of it can be found, somewhere or other, in writings earlier than his own. What is new about it is less the ideas that go to make it up than the clear, systematic and economical exposition of them. As a moralist, Hume, though not perhaps the equal of an Aristotle or a Kant, is much more than just a discarder of confused or unnecessary ideas.

The same is also true of his more narrowly political theory, though to a lesser extent. There is nothing in his strictly political writings to equal the *Enquiry Concerning the Principles of Morals* or the third part of the *Treatise* in the broad sweep of its argument, in the lucid presentation of an elaborate and well-constructed account of a whole area of human experience. Hume wrote treatises about morals and only essays about politics; but his moral theory is at the same time a theory about society. He is interested not only (nor even primarily) in the analysis of moral judgement; he is also, and even more, interested in the social origins and functions of morality. Man is a moral being, a lover of justice, only in society, and needs government to make justice secure.

I. HUME'S REJECTION OF NATURAL LAW AND THE SOCIAL CONTRACT

Hume rejects the traditional account of natural law and substitutes for it the idea of conventions based on the common experience of mankind. He also rejects the notion of a social contract, not merely on historical grounds, but as a tool of explanation. Scarcely any of the contract theorists had been seriously concerned to argue that contracts had actually been made to set up governments; they had mostly used the notion of contract to explain the duty of obedience and how that duty is limited. They had supposed that we can best understand what government is for, why and to what extent it is our duty to obey it, by seeing what kind of agreement men without government would have to make with one another to establish a government capable of giving them security. This was the assumption of the contract theorists which Filmer and other champions of the theory of divine right denied. Some of them found good arguments to support this denial. But their own theories were as little plausible as the doctrine they attacked; and the conclusions they reached were less popular. Hume's method and purpose are different from theirs. He has no wish to deny the political rights and duties asserted by the contract theorists; he wants only to show that there is no need to postulate a social contract in order to explain them, because there is a better way of accounting for them.

We can get a good idea of Hume's method and purpose by comparing him with Hobbes. In the traditional account of it, natural law sets a limit to all human authority. All government is under that law, so that, where government also makes law, the law it makes is subordinate to a law it does not make. Natural law is the law of God, though not His arbitrary will, because God is entirely reasonable. The law of nature is the law that all men, being God's rational creatures, ought to follow in their dealings with one another. They discover it by reflecting on human nature and on God's purposes for man. Human nature and God's purposes for mankind being what they are, it was supposed that men necessarily have certain duties and rights.

Hobbes had taken this notion of natural law and had quite emasculated it – or, rather, had taken the phrase and given it a new meaning. His law of nature is not properly a moral law; it consists only of rules which experience teaches men it would be to their advantage to follow if they could be sure that other men would follow them too. The laws of nature, as regards their contents, are only maxims of prudence whose general observance would put an end to the war of all against all. Merely as maxims they are not obligatory, but are so only as divine commands; and they are obligatory in a peculiar sense which does not make them what most people call moral laws. They are the commands of an omnipotent God, whom men, when they see that they are powerless before Him, cannot choose but obey. Hobbes's natural laws do not serve to limit the authority of government. It is usually not safe (and therefore not obligatory) to obey them until there is a sovereign to enforce them; and where there is a sovereign they are contained entire in his actual commands. There is no appeal to them to show that what the sovereign commands is, in some higher sense, illegal. Hobbes's method is to take a time-honoured phrase, put a new meaning into it, and incorporate it in a theory whose purpose is to deny precisely what the traditional doctrine of natural law was meant to assert. Hobbes's method is subversive. It uses the letter of an old doctrine to destroy the spirit. It does not reject but undermines and to that extent is of necessity ambiguous.

Hume's method is not subversive but openly critical. There are no eternal moral rules, no laws of nature, which man can discover by the mere use of reason when he contemplates his nature as God created it. There are only conventions which men come to adopt because experience teaches them it is their interest to do so. These conventions are, to begin with, mere maxims of prudence, like Hobbes's laws of nature. Men follow them because it is to their advantage to do so. But they do not remain mere maxims of prudence, for men come to approve the keeping of them and to disapprove the breach of them. It is this approval and disapproval that convert rules of convenience into rules of right. The approval and disapproval are effects of sympathy, of an emotion which is not self-regarding. Though the conventions of morality are rules which it is every man's permanent interest to follow, their moral character does not consist in their utility. It consists in how men feel about them, in feelings men could not have if they were entirely selfish.

The obligation to follow these rules is prior to government. Though Hume rejects the traditional doctrine of natural law, he distinguishes much more clearly than Hobbes does between the moral and the legal. Moral rules are not natural but conventional, and yet man is a moral creature before he is subject to government. What men will put up with from government is limited by the conventions they come to accept as members of society. There are no laws of nature in the sense of universal principles of conduct whose validity is directly apprehended by reason; but there is a law which is not an effect of power and which limits the authority of government – a law which is not command and is prior to the kind of law that is command. Hume, unlike Hobbes, has a good deal of sympathy with the desire to restrain government implicit in the old doctrine of natural law; but he discards the doctrine because he thinks he can express whatever is true and valuable in it in another and better way.

We can see similar differences of method and purpose if we compare the attitudes of Hume and Hobbes to the contract theory. Hume rejects it altogether. Hobbes tries to use it to prove the contrary of what the theory was invented to establish. The terms of the contract were supposed to set limits to the authority of the rules. But Hobbes is bent on showing that it follows from the very nature of a contract capable of ensuring effective government that there can be no such limits. Hume, though he rejects the contract theory, is not concerned to deny that all government rests, in some sense, on the consent of the governed.[1] Power is, he thinks, an effect of obedience. Unless governments were obeyed they would be powerless. The obedience on which power rests must therefore be voluntary.

Yet there is, in spite of these differences, a fundamental similarity between Hobbes and Hume. They agree that no action is right or wrong in itself. It is so only by virtue of some attitude towards it. Hobbes has it that an action is wrong if it is forbidden by someone,

[1] This consent is not agreement or the granting of permission; it is acquiescence, grounded in the knowledge that government is in the public interest.

God or man, strong enough to compel obedience, and right if that someone commands or allows it; while Hume has it that an action is right if generally approved, and wrong if generally disapproved. To explain how it is that there are rules of behaviour among men, both Hobbes and Hume begin by considering what it would be like if there were no such rules. If men were unrestrained in their attempts to satisfy their natural desires, they would repeatedly come into conflict with one another. But conflict is painful and men naturally seek to avoid pain. Reason teaches them, not what is inherently right and inherently wrong, but how they must behave to avoid the pains of conflict. About these rules, as reason discovers them, there is nothing either moral or legal. For reason could as easily discover the means of exacerbating conflict. What gives to the rules which reason discovers the character of law is, Hobbes tells us, that there is someone with the will and the power to compel obedience to them. And Hume tells us that the rules are moral only because men feel as they do about them. In neither case are the rules obligatory because they are rational. The office of reason is not to lay obligations upon us but to discover how we can get what we want. 'Reason is, and ought only to be, the slave of the passions.'[1] The words are Hume's, but the sentiment they express is also the sentiment of Hobbes.

Hume and Hobbes also agree in treating government as a device to ensure that men do not sacrifice their permanent interest to lesser but more immediate advantages. Hobbes is at pains to show that everyone has, on the whole, more to gain than to lose by observing prudential maxims, which he calls – rather perversely – laws of nature, provided other people also observe them. He believes that any reasonable man reflecting on his experience will see this. And yet, though everyone can see it, no one can trust anyone else always to act reasonably. If men were so made that they always preferred their own greatest good to every immediate advantage conflicting with that good, there would be no need for government. For then everyone would follow the maxims of prudence and could reasonably trust everyone else to do so. But unfortunately men are not so made. It is not a defect of reason in them but the strength of their passions which moves them to prefer a lesser immediate good to their greatest good. Thus, if it is to be worth anyone's while to follow the maxims, everyone must be assured that other people will follow them. And there can be this assurance only where there is a power sufficient to

---

[1] *Treatise of Human Nature*, Bk. II, Part III, sect. 3, in *Hume's Moral and Political Philosophy*, ed. Henry Aiken (Darien, Conn. 1970), p. 25.

compel obedience to the maxims and a will to use that power. It is always the sovereign's immediate advantage to compel the obedience which is the condition of social peace, because on the preservation of this peace his power depends. The laws of nature, the maxims of prudence, are necessarily contained in the laws of the sovereign; they are the rules which the sovereign must enforce if he is to retain his sovereign power.

Hume uses what is at bottom the same argument when he says that men must palliate their incurable tendency to prefer a lesser immediate good to a greater but more remote one, by setting up over them some persons whose duty and interest is to compel them, however reluctant they may be, to do what it is in their own long-term interest that they should do. As nearly all men love power, it is easy to find persons willing to undertake the task of government. These persons, whoever they are, will ordinarily be inclined in their own interest to maintain justice, for, unless they do so, their subjects will soon cease to obey them; and justice consists of the rules which it is everyone's permanent interest should be obeyed. Government, as Hume sees it, is not the maintainer of an eternal justice directly apprehended by reason; it is a device which makes it the immediate interest of some persons to promote the permanent interest of everyone.

II. HUME'S ACCOUNT OF JUSTICE AND FIDELITY AS ARTIFICIAL VIRTUES

Justice, or respect for rules of property, and fidelity, or the keeping of promises, Hume calls *artificial virtues*. Since the artificial virtues are the ones on which the stability of society chiefly depends, it is important to discover just what Hume conceives them to be and how they differ from the *natural virtues*. The natural virtues are not natural because they are in keeping with any laws of nature in the traditional sense. All virtues, for Hume, are virtues only because they are generally approved of. What, then, makes a natural virtue natural, and an artificial virtue artificial? Hume says that 'the only difference betwixt the natural virtues and justice lies in this, that the good which results from the former, arises from every single act, and is the object of some natural passion; whereas a single act of justice, considered in itself, may often be contrary to the public good'.[1] We have the gist of the difference here; but Hume's statement is too short

---

[1] Ibid., Bk. III, Part III, sect. 1, p. 135.

to be immediately intelligible. It needs to be elaborated.

Let us consider first the natural virtues, and let us take an example. To help the afflicted is a natural virtue. When we see a fellow human being in distress, the sight of this suffering causes us to suffer. We sympathize with him, and this sympathy, says Hume (and here he differs from Hobbes), is not a refined form of egoism. We suffer at the sight of another man's suffering, and not at the thought of ourselves suffering as he does; though it may be because we ourselves have suffered in the past that we understand his predicament and feel sympathy for him. This sympathy is immediately aroused in us by the sight of his suffering; it is a natural passion that moves us to help him. We help him, not from a sense of duty, but because we feel sympathy for him. And when we see anyone else helping a man in distress, we are pleased by the action. This pleasure is also an effect of sympathy. We are pleased, not because we stand to gain anything ourselves by the action, but because we sympathize with the person in distress and with the person who wants to help him. The pleasure we get from seeing one individual do good to another, and sometimes even to himself, Hume calls approval. Men are so made that, in the absence of motives causing them to feel otherwise, the mere sight of another's pain gives them pain, and the mere sight of another's pleasure gives them pleasure. Men are by nature given to sympathize with one another; they are therefore also given to feel pleasure at the sight of actions that alleviate pain or cause pleasure, and to feel pain at the sight of actions that do the opposite. They are naturally given to approval and disapproval, and it is these feelings alone which make the actions they are directed to virtuous or vicious.

Approval and disapproval, as Hume explains the matter, are directed not so much at external actions as at the motives which inspire them. When we approve of one man relieving the distress of another, what we approve of is the compassion he feels and his readiness to act. But the motives of other people are not directly known to us, and we can infer their motives only from their actions; and so, in practice, it does not much matter whether we say that approval and disapproval are directed at men's actions or at their motives. Approval and disapproval are essentially unselfish; they are always born of sympathy, which is not a self-regarding feeling. They are not always strong feelings; indeed, though stronger in some people than in others, they are commonly weak, if we compare them with such emotions as anger, fear, hatred and love. But they more than make up by their generality for their weakness; they are, as Hume puts it, feelings in which we expect most people to concur with us.

It is easy to see how the natural virtues come to be virtues. The sympathy that moves us to actions which are naturally virtuous is aroused directly by the thought of other people's suffering or their happiness. To some extent, of course, it depends on experience and reflection; as we cannot know directly how other people feel, we must learn what hurts them and what helps them by reflecting on our own experience. But this we learn quickly, and then sympathy moves us to do what is naturally virtuous and to avoid what is naturally vicious – provided, of course, that there are not contrary passions moving us away from virtue and towards vice. The natural virtues are natural, not because they accord with a law of nature directly apprehended by reason, but because it is easy to see how they arise, how sympathy moves us both to practise them and to approve the practice of them.

In what, then, does the artificiality of the artificial virtues, justice and fidelity, consist? It consists in the different motive that impels us to practise them, and in the character of the experience which causes us to desire that they should be practised. Sympathy alone moves us to do what is naturally virtuous, and the experience needed to enlighten us about the sufferings and pleasures of other people is simple and involves not much reflection. But our motive for being just or for keeping a promise is not sympathy but self-love. It is self-love enlightened by much more than knowledge about how we ourselves feel in this or that situation, together with the assumption that other people feel the same in the same situations; it is self-love enlightened by reflection on the remoter consequences of our behaviour towards others and their behaviour towards us. It is self-love enlightened by reflection on our enduring relations with others, or, in other words, by reflection on our social experience.

Hume's account of the artificial virtues does not require us to assume that man is predominantly selfish – that he nearly always cares more for himself than for other people. It assumes no more than that some of his virtues – justice and fidelity – on which the stability of society chiefly depends, arise *in the first place* from self-love. It does not require us to believe that, once society is well-established and justice is generally recognized as a virtue, men are usually just only from enlightened self-love.

Justice and fidelity are not artificial virtues merely because they arise from self-love, but because their root in self-love is less simple and obvious than the root of the natural virtues in sympathy. They are artificial because, compared with the natural virtues, they rest on more subtle reflection; they are artificial because they are sophisticated and also social. Of course, all the virtues and vices, natural and artificial, are the virtues and vices of rational creatures; they all involve some degree of reflection. The peculiarity of the artificial virtues is that they derive from prolonged reflection on what is involved in men's living together permanently. Not every man need go through this process of reflection; he may be taught the artificial virtues by precept; he may practise them on the mere authority of his parents or teachers. But, then again, not everyone can be taught by precept; some must learn by experience, and in fact most people will do so to some extent.

Let us take concrete examples to illustrate Hume's meaning, for it is best to be clear, even at the risk of appearing to labour the obvious. When you see someone in distress, you are quickly moved to sympathy with him, and your first impulse is to help him. But there may be contrary passions at work. If, for example, you are hungry and you see food that someone has set aside for his own use, sympathy will probably not move you to let that food alone. If you take his food, you will cause him pain, and you may sympathize with him on that account; but your sympathy will probably not prevent your taking his food. Hunger will be a more powerful motive with you than sympathy. Not always, of course, but usually. If the food is intended for someone you love, you may prefer to go hungry rather than to cause pain. But love is an emotion you feel for few persons, and will therefore not cause you to respect the property of most people who have what you desire. How, then, does it come about that you do respect their property? You respect it, says Hume, not from sympathy or from fear, but from self-love. For though it is your immediate interest to take from others whatever is useful to yourself, you learn by experience that, in the long run, you have more to gain than to lose by not doing so, provided they in their turn take nothing from you. You learn to do unto others as you would have them do unto you. In other words, you learn to prefer your permanent to your immediate interest; and since other people learn this as well as you, you have good reason to follow the principle you have learnt, even where there is no government to compel you.

Just as enlightened self-love causes you and other people to abstain from one another's possessions, so it causes you to keep your promises. Experience teaches you how useful it is to be able to rely on other people doing what they said they would do, and also that you cannot expect them to do so unless you do likewise. You learn to value mutual confidence and to play your part in maintaining it. The keeping of promises and respect for property are the most important among artificial virtues; they are artificial because they spring from restraints which the self puts upon itself in its own permanent interest. They arise, not from an uninhibited natural passion, but from spontaneous self-love held in check by enlightened self-love.

But it is not self-love that makes respect for property and the keeping of promises virtues, for whatever is virtuous is so because it is generally approved, and approval always proceeds from sympathy and never from self-love. You desire justice from self-love, and you esteem it from sympathy. Justice is not only your interest; it is also the interest of everyone – the general, the public, interest. When, therefore, you see anyone being just, you approve his conduct because you sympathize with the public interest. The moral sentiments are no more self-regarding when they are directed to respect for property and the breach of it – to the keeping and breaking of promises, to the artificial virtues and vices – than when they are directed to the natural virtues and vices.

Since we like being approved of and dislike being disapproved of, we are powerfully and repeatedly influenced by the moral sentiments of other people. These sentiments, though often weak, are also universal. The desire to gain approval and to avoid disapproval is therefore always a strong motive, quite apart from enlightened self-love, to induce people to respect property and to keep their word. That is why justice and fidelity can flourish even in the absence of organized power. Hume has rooted respect for property and the keeping of promises, as Hobbes did before him, in self-love; but he has done so without asserting the universal and invincible selfishness of man, and without concluding that men will not in fact respect property or keep their word unless they are compelled. Though his account of what he calls the artificial virtues still falls short of the truth, it is clearly a great improvement on Hobbes. It does less violence to the facts; it is also more consistent.

So far, I have considered Hume's account of the artificial virtues only in the most general way; I have considered how, in his opinion, men come to conceive of certain rules of behaviour as useful and to desire that people should conform to them, and what it is that makes that behaviour virtuous. I have not yet touched upon Hume's account of the conditions which make the artificial virtues necessary. Would there be such virtues in any conceivable society? Or only in some?

About the conditions of fidelity, Hume says almost nothing. Presumably he believes that, whatever the circumstances of men in society, they would always find it useful to make and keep promises and would therefore set a value on the keeping of them. Respect for property is also everywhere in fact a virtue, because the conditions which make this respect useful in fact hold everywhere. But we can conceive of a society in which these conditions would not hold. We can therefore say that, whereas fidelity is useful in any conceivable society, respect for property is only useful in societies where certain conditions hold. In fact these conditions hold in all societies known to us, and we have no reason to believe that there will ever be a society in which they do not hold. But we can imagine such a society.

Rules of property are needed because men's wants are indefinite and the means of relieving them are scarce, and also because human generosity is confined. If whatever we needed to satisfy our wants were to be had for the taking, and always in a form fit for human consumption; if natural resources were boundless and no labour was required to prepare them for use, we could do without property, without rules governing the use of external goods and their transference from person to person. Nature has dealt less kindly with us than with other animals; we need greater protection than they do from the elements, and we are physically weaker in proportion to our needs. Fortunately, we are also ingenious animals, and can invent better means than nature provides for satisfying our wants. We can work together intelligently for our mutual advantage; and in society our natural infirmities are much more than compensated for. Though in society our needs multiply quickly, our power to satisfy them grows still more quickly. Society originates in our needs, which we cannot adequately provide for except with one another's help; and we cannot, being the sort of creatures we are and having only limited resources at our disposal, help one another successfully unless we have rules of property.

If men were all so generous as to be always willing to part with anything that another person needed more than they did, they might do without rules of property, even in a world where natural resources were limited. But their generosity is too confined for that; and therefore, since in fact there is not enough of everything to satisfy everybody all the time, men must have rules of property if they are to live at peace with one another.

Scarcity of resources and confined generosity: these are the two conditions which make justice, or respect for rules of property, a necessary virtue. Those conditions happen to hold everywhere in our world, and there is no reason why we should suppose that there will ever be a time or place in which they will not hold. Only if the conceivable were also in fact possible, only if men were completely generous or if anything a man wanted were to be had for the taking in exactly the form he needed it, could men live happily together without property.

Hume's account of why we need *some* rules of property is certainly plausible. It is when he sets about explaining why we have the particular rules we do have that his explanation suddenly becomes unconvincing. Indeed the passing from sense to fantasy is so sudden as to be disconcerting. Can the same man who has spoken so much sense still be speaking now?

'That there be a separation or distinction of possessions, and that this separation be steady and constant: this is absolutely required by the interests of society, and hence the origin of justice and property. What possessions are assigned to particular persons, this is, generally speaking, pretty indifferent; and is often determined by very frivolous views and considerations.'[1] We are seriously invited to believe that, though it matters enormously that there should be some rules of property and that they should not change, it does not much matter what they are. Rules of property are like rules of the road; it does not matter whether traffic keeps to the left or to the right, but it does matter that it should keep to the one or the other; it matters that there should be a rule and that everyone should keep to it. True, Hume does not say that it matters not at all what the rules are, provided that there are some and they do not change. 'There are', he admits, 'motives of public interest for most of the rules which determine property; but still I suspect that these rules are principally fixed by the imagination'.[2] He then goes on to mention the five principal rules which establish titles to property: present possession, first possession, long possession or prescription, accession or the rule that the fruit or offspring of what you own is also yours, and succession or inheritance. Hume admits that its utility is enough to explain the first rule, present possession; everyone expects to keep what he has, so that the rule that he should keep it is obviously convenient. But first possession, accession and succession, and perhaps also long possession, arise, he thinks, more from the association of ideas than from convenience. First possession engages the attention most, and we tend to associate things with their first possessors and thus to acquiesce in the rule that whoever first acquires something should keep it. We also associate things with the persons who have long possessed them, and we therefore acquiesce in prescription for the same reason as we do in first possession. 'We are naturally directed', says Hume, 'to consider the son after the parent's

---

[1] *An Enquiry Concerning the Principles of Morals*, Appendix III, ibid., p. 280n.
[2] *Treatise of Human Nature*, Bk. III, Part II, sect. 3, ibid., p. 71n.

decease, and ascribe to him a title to his father's possessions'.[1] A dead man's property must go to some one. How do we decide who it shall go to? The thought of the father brings the son to our minds, and this association of ideas is the root of inheritance. In the *Enquiry*[2] Hume admits that industry is encouraged by property passing to a man's children or near relations, but that, he thinks, is true only of civilized societies, whereas this rule of inheritance is cherished even among barbarians.

When a philosopher gets what he believes is a good idea, he is sometimes tempted to make too much of it. Hume, who had to his own satisfaction used the association of ideas to explain our belief in causality, thought he could also use it to explain how we come by our particular rules of property. His explanation is often pure fantasy. Did it not occur to him that fathers ordinarily want to leave their possessions to their children, and that this is perhaps why it has come to be thought right that they should do so? Why should the association of ideas have anything to do with the matter? A man who has possessed something for a long time expects to keep it, and this is surely enough to explain the rule of prescription without any reference to the imagination. Though Hume, as I have said, did not deny the utility of his five rules, admitting that there are 'motives of public interest' for most rules of property, he did neglect the obvious for the fantastic. He said that titles to property are often determined by 'very frivolous views and considerations'. There is less frivolity about the rules than about his explanations of them.

It was perhaps because he thought it did not much matter what the rules were, provided there were some, that Hume took it for granted that, whatever they are, they ought never to change. If what really matters is that there should be some rules, and it is more or less indifferent what they are, it is unlikely that there will be good reasons for changing them. At the same time, since men's expectations are formed by whatever rules they have, there is always a good reason for *not* changing the rules. Thus we can actually use the 'frivolity' (as Hume puts it) that attends the choice of the rules as an argument for their being, like the laws of the Medes and Persians, unchangeable. The argument is not illogical, but it is odd and unrealistic. I am less moved to refute it than to wonder how it ever came to be made. I feel about it as I should do if someone were to say, 'I am against divorce, because, while it does not much matter whom we marry, it

---

[1] Ibid., pp. 79–80.
[2] *An Enquiry Concerning the Principles of Morals*, Appendix III, p. 281n.

matters enormously that we should marry and stay married'. There are some good arguments against divorce, but I suspect that this is not one of them.

If Hume had looked more carefully at his five rules of property and had tried to discover just what makes them useful, it might have occurred to him to set limits to their utility. He would then have enquired more closely into the conditions which make precisely these five rules (and not just *some* rules) useful; and he might perhaps have concluded that the conditions need not always hold. It might then have occurred to him that, though these five rules are clearly useful in sparsely populated, primitive and agricultural communities, they are not so clearly useful where population is dense or natural resources are scarce or methods of production are elaborate.

Though Hume's account of property is widely different from Locke's, some of the same objections can be made against it. Admittedly, as a general explanation of how there come to be any rules of property, his account is more convincing than Locke's. It makes property not a natural right but a convention arising out of the social experience of mankind. But Hume's explanation of the five rules of property takes as little account of the economic realities of his own day as does Locke's labour theory of property. He takes it for granted that these rules will be much the same in all societies. No more than Locke, does he consider the possibility that the rules may, in the course of time, have undesirable effects – that they may create such large inequalities as to become intolerable to the unfortunate. He admits, of course, that they do lead to great inequalities, but he quietly takes it for granted that the hardships thus created must always be smaller than the hardships that would follow upon any attempt to change the rules.[1] This assumption is groundless. No doubt, any rules, however well conceived, will cause suffering to some people. Hume admits that it is so and seizes upon it to support his conclusion that the rules must never be changed. But it clearly does not follow that, because any rule involves some hardships, it is always better to keep the rules you have than to change them.

By treating property as a matter of convention rather than of natural right, Hume gains, in theory, a great advantage over Locke. Natural right is immutable, whereas what is conventional can change. This theoretical advantage is, however, thrown away in Hume's treatment

---

[1] Compare this with Hobbes's belief that it is always better to bear with the government you have than to take the risks involved in putting another in its place.

of the five rules of property. From eternal right to the association of ideas is a steep descent. The beginnings of the two theories are poles apart, but the conclusion is the same: *Blessed are those that have wealth, because everyone is the better off for not disturbing them in the enjoyment of it.*

Both Hume and Locke speak as if every man produced wealth separately, though later he may exchange his product against another man's. Their theories do not assume that there is no division of labour, but they take no account of several men working together to produce something which is the joint product of them all. They speak as if every man produced external goods primarily for his own and his family's use, and secondarily for purposes of barter. To respect property is essentially to abstain from using what other people have set aside for their own use. But, we may ask, how in a society where there is co-operative production are actual titles to property to be justified by Locke's rule that whoever is first to mix his labour with something has the exclusive right to use it, or by Hume's five rules? That there is a close connection between methods of production and rules of property never occurred to either of them.[1] The connection may not be what Marx and others have thought it was, but it does exist and is close. Hume believed both in economic progress and in unchanging rules of property. To hold these two beliefs together still seemed reasonable in his time; it was not to seem so much longer.

III. OBEDIENCE TO GOVERNMENT

We saw, when we were comparing Hume with Hobbes, that they both treat government as a device to ensure that men follow their permanent interest even when their passions tempt them to do otherwise. It is the immediate interest of those who govern that law and order should be maintained, and this is also the permanent interest of their subjects. Hobbes used the notion of the contract to show how it is all men's interest to have an absolute ruler over them, and also used it to try to prove that it is their duty always to obey their rulers. He wanted to establish the legitimacy of government as well as its utility, though on his own initial assumptions he could do only the second and not the

---

[1] They see, of course, that where there is production and exchange there must be rules of property, but they see no need to alter the rules if methods of production change. Indeed, they take no account of specific methods of production, let alone changes in these methods.

first. By his use of the notion of contract, Hobbes confuses questions of interest with questions of right, and also makes an elaborate and difficult case for absolute sovereignty.

Hume avoids both these mistakes. He never confuses interest with right, and is always ready to admit that the power of governments is and ought to be limited. The notion of contract explains nothing that cannot be better explained without it, and Hume quietly rejects it. Subjects obey their governments, not because they or their ancestors have promised to do so, but because it is their interest that there should be government, which there cannot be unless there is obedience. As with justice, so here, too, we come to approve of what makes for the common interest and to disapprove of what goes against it; and thus obedience becomes a virtue and disobedience a vice.

To try to ground the duty of obedience in contract, in the making of promises, is to offer an elaborate and less plausible explanation where one simpler and more plausible would do. The duty to keep a promise, Hume tells us, is no more easily explained than the duty to obey governments. Promise-keeping is an artificial virtue like respect for property; it is rooted in self-interest and is made a virtue by being commonly approved. Exactly the same can be said of obedience to government, which is also rooted in self-interest and made a virtue by common approval. As soon as we see that the duties of keeping one's promises and obedience to government can both be accounted for in the same way, we are no longer tempted to explain the second by the first. The notion of the social contract, which creates as many problems as it solves, is seen to be superfluous; there is nothing to be gained and much to be lost by holding to it.

Justice is prior to government, according to Hume: 'So far am I from thinking. . .that men are utterly incapable of society without government, that I assert the first rudiments of government to arise from quarrels, not among men of the same society, but among those of different societies.'[1] 'But though it be possible for men to maintain a small uncultivated society without government, it is impossible they should maintain a society of any kind without justice, and the observance of those three fundamental laws concerning the stability of possession, its translation by consent and the performance of promises.'[2] Justice is entirely a social virtue, for the very notion of it, the desire for it, and the esteem in which it is held, arise among men in the course of the experience they gain through living

---

[1] *Treatise of Human Nature*, Bk. III, Part II, sect. 8, p. 102.
[2] Ibid., p. 103.

together. Though society can exist without government, it cannot do so without law, and law is neither 'natural' nor deliberately made, but conventional. Society is held together by common interests and conventional notions of justice; and, unless this were so, government could not arise inside it.

Since Hume thinks it probable that government first arose out of quarrels – not among men in the same society, but among men of different societies – he therefore supposes that it originated to provide military discipline. The chances are that government began as monarchy, because success in war depends on unity of command. The authority of the military commander was found so generally convenient that it soon outlasted the emergency that created it. The commander became the monarch, and his power grew steadily, partly because it was in the public interest that it should grow, and partly because whoever has power tries to increase it. After a time, the defects of monarchy came to be as sharply felt as the advantages, and devices were found to limit the monarch's power, or other forms of government were substituted for monarchy. Hume is as willing as the next man to venture opinions about the probable origins of government; but he does not use these origins to justify authority or to set limits to it. How did government arise?, and What makes it legitimate?, are, for him, distinct questions.

The power of government is limited by the motives of the obedience which makes government possible. Men obey primarily because it is their interest to do so, and when obedience ceases to be their interest, they soon cease to obey. They disapprove of oppression for the same reason as they approve of government – from regard to the public interest. Just as they ordinarily think it their interest and their duty to obey, so, when government becomes oppressive, they come to think it their interest and their duty to refuse obedience or actively to resist. 'The common rule', says Hume, 'requires submission; and it is only in cases of grievous tyranny and oppression that the exception can take place'.[1]

Hume distinguishes the grounds of the general duty of obedience from the grounds of the particular duty to obey the persons who actually rule. Rulers claim the right to govern for all kinds of reasons: they derive their title from long possession, or statute, or treaty, or contract or something else. None of these reasons explains the simple duty of obedience; they explain only the title to rule of some persons in preference to others, the title of those who actually do rule or claim to

---

[1] Ibid., Bk. III, Part II, sect. 10, p. 114.

rule. There may be many people in a country just as capable of ruling it well as the persons who in fact govern it; and if they did govern it, their subjects would have exactly the same interest in obeying them. The general utility of government explains how we come to regard obedience as a virtue; it does not explain why we think some persons have a better title to govern than others. To explain this title, we always resort to some other principle. But we must not substitute this other principle for the grounds of the general duty of obedience; we must not suppose that treaty or contract or election or prescriptive right can make it our duty to obey when it is not the public interest that we should obey. A principle of this kind does not determine the limits of our duty but only the person or persons towards whom we have the duty. It matters much less what the principle is than that we should all be of one mind about it – that we should all agree whom we are to obey. It is usually best to accept whatever principle confirms the authority of those who actually govern. Government should be stable. Prudence and morals require us 'to submit quietly to the government which we find established in the country where we happen to live, without inquiring too curiously into its origin and first establishment'.[1] Hume thought most disputes about legitimacy absurd and harmful. The wise man will accept the existing form of government and rule of succession, and will refrain from contesting the authority of rulers who are not oppressive on the ground that they came by their authority illegally. 'A strict adherence to any general rules, and the rigid loyalty to particular persons and families on which some people set so high a value, are virtues that hold less of reason than of bigotry and superstition.'[2] Clearly, if Hume was a Tory, he was a Tory of a peculiar kind.

In the essay on the 'First Principles of Government', he distinguishes between what he calls 'opinion of *interest*' and 'opinion of *right*'.[3] By the first he means the sense men have that government is to their advantage, and by the second their prejudice in favour of any authority or convention that has existed among them for a long time. Opinion of right is not to be confused with the moral sentiments. The moral sentiments arise from sympathy; we approve of obedience to government, as we do of justice, because we sympathize with whatever is in the public interest, and this obedience is clearly in that interest. Opinion of right arises from habit. It is a prejudice

[1] Ibid., p. 117.
[2] Ibid., p. 120.
[3] 'Of the First Principles of Government', ibid., p. 307.

in favour of what we have long been accustomed to. The longer a form of government has lasted, the stronger our prejudice in its favour. Opinion of right reinforces opinion of interest and the moral sentiments. We obey our rulers partly because we feel it our interest to do so, partly because we approve of what is in the public interest, and partly because we are prejudiced in favour of whatever kind of government we have.

Fear, affection and self-interest (in the narrow sense which conflicts with concern for the public interest) are not, thinks Hume, strong motives for obedience. We only obey from fear when we are tempted to disobey and fear of punishment overcomes the temptation, which is not a frequent condition with most people. We may feel strong affection for our rulers, but ordinarily we do so because they are our rulers or because we think they govern well; so that our affection is more a consequence of the use they make of their power than a motive for the obedience which gives them power. Self-interest in the narrow sense, which is hope of special favours, can inspire obedience in only a few, for most people are in no position to expect such favours. The interest that moves most of us to obedience is therefore not an interest peculiar to ourselves; it is one we share with everyone else. It is the maintenance of law and order, which is the public interest.

Hume is as keen to show that power depends on obedience as Hobbes was to show the opposite. There would be no power worth fearing unless there were motives of obedience other than the fear of power. 'Nothing appears more surprising to those who consider human affairs with a philosophical eye than the easiness with which the many are governed by the few. . . .When we inquire by what means this wonder is effected, we shall find that, as force is always on the side of the governed, the governors have nothing to support them but opinion. It is therefore on opinion only that government is founded, and this maxim extends to the most despotic and most military governments, as well as to the most free and most popular.'[1] The tyrant depends on the opinion of his soldiers; he cannot drive everyone; he must have subordinates who obey him because they wish to do so, because they think it their interest to support him, before he can have power enough to force obedience on the unwilling. This is the sense in which, according to Hume, all government rests on the consent of the governed. Such consent involves no contract, nor anything that could be called a promise. It is at bottom no more than the willing acceptance of what we see is to our advantage or

[1] Ibid.

what we have grown accustomed to. It merely explains what makes government possible; it is not a ground of obligation.

Hume rejects the Tory doctrine of passive obedience just as decidedly as the Whig doctrine that the obligation to obey rests on consent. In his essay on 'Passive Obedience', he argues that, since the duty to respect the law arises from an interest common to all men (i.e., the public interest), law can always be rightly put aside when it endangers that interest. But the danger, he says, must be extraordinary, when public ruin would follow on respect for law or obedience to the established government. Hume is on the side of those who would draw the bonds of allegiance very close, who would justify disobedience only as a last resort in desperate cases. When he moves from explanation to advice, he is always strongly conservative; the advice he gives is in substance the same as Burke's. Yet how different the spirit and the style of the giver! Hume is quite without reverence or admiration; he sees nothing divine or majestic about the State; it is merely a contrivance in the public interest. The more we accept it and the less we tamper with it, the more useful it is likely to be. He thinks nothing 'more preposterous than an anxious care and solicitude in stating all the cases in which resistance may be allowed'.[1] Though his tone is sometimes impatient, it is always the tone of the drawing-room or the lecture-room and not of the pulpit or public meeting.

It may be that Hume's conservatism was greatly strengthened by his belief that power rests ultimately on opinion. He seems to have believed that, as knowledge increases and manners grow milder, government, even when it is absolute, must also grow milder, since its power rests ultimately on opinion. Time and again, we find him repeating that power rests on opinion, and drawing conforting conclusions from this claim and from the growth of knowledge. What he too often forgets is that power does not rest equally or in the same way on the opinion of all the persons subject to it. We cannot assume that, because power rests on opinion, it is scarcely ever used to force unwilling obedience on the majority, or to maintain institutions which most people condemn as unjust. Still less can we assume that, as knowledge increases and manners grow milder, power will belong chiefly to the educated and the mild. But Hume made these assumptions because in his day the people most affected by the growth of knowledge and the spread of more humane

---

[1] 'Of Passive Obedience', in Hume, *Essays Moral, Political and Literary* (Oxford 1963), pp. 475–6.

manners belonged to the privileged classes, who either controlled the government or influenced it. The absolute monarchy of France was, he thought, a mild government because of the influence of these classes.

I suspect that Hume plays down the danger of oppression because he makes a false inference from a quite plausible assumption: that social inequalities rest on conventions which must have been accepted to begin with because they were found generally useful. From this premise, in itself not unsound, he draws the doubtful conclusion that the social order resting on inequality is also useful and generally acceptable. But we cannot conclude that the consequences of what was once useful and acceptable are themselves now acceptable and useful. No doubt, society could not subsist without some rules of property, and no doubt, too, whatever rules there were, some people would always benefit more from them than others. But to show that the first rules probably arose because they were useful and acceptable to most people is not to show that the inequalities they have led to are so as well. Inequality is, of course, very often accepted by many more people than profit by it – by some from habit and by others from fear. Yet it may be that few except those who profit by inequality actually believe that inequality is useful and just. The others may accept existing laws of property because they can imagine no others, or from mere habit, and yet may deplore the inequalities they lead to; or they may condemn existing laws because they believe that there are others more in the public interest. Government will then rest, not on their opinion, but on the opinion of the rich. As far as they are concerned – and they may be the majority – government rests on force rather than opinion. Now, it may be that these not very out-of-the-way ideas sometimes occurred to the ingenious Hume. If they did, he was certainly not moved by them to qualify his assertion that government always rests on opinion much more than on force. True, unless it rested on opinion, it could not use force; but from this it does not follow that it cannot rest on the opinion of a minority and use force against the majority.

I suspect that Hume, if he had seen the simple argument boldly asserted – that the poor consent to the wealth and power of the rich because the rules which enabled the rich to get power and wealth first arose by being generally accepted – would not have been impressed by the logic of it. But, as he never so put it to himself, he was, I suggest, influenced by it without being aware that he was so. Otherwise, I cannot see what inclined him to make so light of the dangers of oppression. That all power rests on opinion is obvious, but no more so than the fact of oppression. Yet Hume (though without quite saying so) would have us believe that because power always rests on opinion, it must somehow rest with the people generally – as if wealth, knowledge and influence, however acquired, give their possessors only a small advantage in pursuing their own interest at other people's expense. He speaks almost as if it followed that, because there can be no power where there is no willing obedience, power can be used only to a slight extent to force unwilling obedience.

The matter is scarcely as simple as that. Not only is force not 'always on the side of the governed', for the obvious reason that it can be so organized as to enable a few people to rule great multitudes against their wills; but also habits and conventions can long survive their usefulness. No doubt, while the poor are contented with their lot, we cannot, if we accept Hume's account of justice, say that they are oppressed. For justice, by that account, is respect for conventions whose social function is to prevent people getting in each other's way as they try to satisfy their actual wants. But as soon as the poor cease being contented with their lot, the conventions which protect the privileges of the rich may cease to be generally useful, even though the poor in their ignorance do not question them. These conventions may stand in the way of the poor getting what they want, and yet the poor may not know this; they may not understand that, if the rules of property were changed, they might, judging by standards which they themselves now accept, be much better off than they are.

Force does not vary directly with number, and is therefore not always, nor even usually, on the side of the governed. Government is a highly organized form of collaboration, and the persons directly engaged in it are collectively much more powerful than the rest of the community. Even if it were true that government and property first arose from a sense of what was needed in the common interest, it would not follow that they always serve that interest, or that, when they change, they change to suit it. Yet Hume, without actually saying that it does follow, ordinarily speaks as if it did; he speaks as if what is to the advantage of the rich were also, at bottom, to the advantage of the poor, and even as if the poor really knew this, though they might at times behave as if they did not know.

IV. PROPERTY AND PARTY

Hume is less ingenious as a critic of institutions than as a critic of ideas. He helps to teach us how to use the language of politics, and warns us against raising unreal problems. In that capacity, he has seldom been equalled and perhaps never surpassed. But he is by no means as happily inspired when he turns his mind to the realities of politics, to how men actually behave and how social facts are related to one another. That is shown, I think, by what we have already considered, and again by what he says about the connection between property and political power. It is also shown in his account of the dangers of party or faction. This account is worth considering; it strikes some fresh notes in political theory, and raises important issues.

Let us first consider what Hume says about the connection between property and power. He accepts Harrington's axiom that the balance of power in the State tends to vary with the balance of property, and then goes on to add a rider which he thinks of fundamental importance but which spoils the axiom. He says that a large property in the hands of one man will give him as much power as several men get from a larger property shared between them. To put the same point another way, the more widely a given amount of property is dispersed, the smaller the political power attached to it – so that one man with £100,000 a year will have more power than a hundred men with £1000 a year each. To illustrate his point, Hume takes for examples Crassus in Rome and the Medici in Florence. The fortune of Crassus, immense though it was, was small indeed compared with the collective wealth of Rome, and yet it was enough to make Crassus, for a time, the equal of Pompey and Caesar, much abler men than he was. The Medici successfully used their wealth to make themselves masters of Florence, although their fortune, as a proportion of the total wealth of the republic, was inconsiderable.

Hume's rider, far from improving on Harrington's axiom, detracts from it. It draws attention to single fortunes rather than to broad categories of wealth. There were special reasons which made it easy for Crassus to use his money to buy influence; if he had lived a hundred years earlier or later, he might have been much richer and yet unable to use his wealth to get power. In general, when we are considering the relations of power to property, it is more important to think, as Harrington does, in terms of classes than individuals.

The distribution of power depends directly on the structure of government. This structure, in turn, depends on all kinds of things – among others, on the distribution of property. To the extent that it depends on that distribution, it is affected, not by every difference in wealth, but only by some. Property and income give status, which in turn gives power; but, clearly, every difference in property and income does not give rise to a difference of status. Where there is a property qualification for the vote, anyone who has the required amount of property gets only one vote, whether he has exactly the amount required or ten times as much. Again, where a certain kind of expensive education is needed to give a man a chance of getting into Parliament or of holding important office, anyone with parents just rich enough to give him that education has that chance. However aristocratic the society, the more stable its social structure and system of government, the less important the differences of wealth inside it which are not connected with differences of status. In a stable aristocratic society, it may matter a great deal that a man should have £2000 a year rather than £200, but much less that he should have £20,000 rather than £2000. Differences of wealth are more important politically because they lead to differences of status than because the richer a man is the more he can spend on buying power; and the more stable a society, the more this is true. Crassus and the Medici could buy power as they did because they lived in troubled times.

Again, a man's political influence often depends as much (or more) on the kind of property he has as on the amount. Privileges, social and political, are usually more attached to some kinds of wealth than to others; say, more to property in land than to liquid capital, or more to inherited wealth than to wealth recently acquired. When a new kind of wealth arises, its possessors may for a long time have little power. The relations between power and property are clearly much less simple than Hume imagined.

What Hume has to say about party or faction is not to be compared, in point of novelty and realism, with the last admirable pages of Burke's *Thoughts on the Cause of the Present Discontents*. Hume sees parties as effects of free government, which cannot be abolished without abolishing freedom. If you want free government, you must put up with parties, just as, if you want children, you must put up with noise. Hume does not see, as Burke was to do, that parties are indispensable to free government, if it is to survive in large countries; that parties are means to freedom, and not just unpleasant but inevitable consequences of it. 'Factions subvert government, render laws impotent, and beget the fiercest animosities among men of the same nation, who ought to give mutual assistance and protection to each other.'[1] This is a more ponderous but not less hostile judgement on parties than Trimmer Halifax's verdict on them, that they are 'conspiracies against the nation'.

[1] 'Of Parties in General', ibid., p. 55. See also 'Of the Coalition of Parties', pp. 484–6.

In spite of this judgement, Hume does not entirely condemn every kind of party. He tries to classify factions and to show that some kinds are less dangerous and more useful than others. Some factions, he says, are held together by loyalty to a person or family, some by common interest, and some by common principles. The last two kinds he calls *real* factions to distinguish them from the first kind, which he calls *personal*. A faction can, of course, be both personal and real; it can be held together by loyalty to a leader or dynasty and also by common interests or common principles. Personal factions arise most easily in small states like the Italian republics or the Greek cities; but real factions often become personal when the interests or principles that give birth to them are forgotten. This classification is useful and, as far as I know, new.

I should quarrel with Hume, not about the criteria he uses for classifying parties, but about his judgements on them. Factions from interest, he thinks, are the most reasonable and excusable of all; for it is clearly reasonable that men should combine to promote common interests. Factions from principle, though sometimes reasonable, are more often absurd and dangerous. It does happen, Hume admits, that the principles proclaimed by a party have practical consequences. If they do, then it makes sense to form the party; for it is always reasonable to work with other people to try to get what you otherwise very likely could not get. To combine from principle is then merely to work with people who agree with you in order to achieve common ends. But most of the principles that factions proclaim have, Hume thinks, no practical consequences; they therefore bring people into conflict, not because they want different and incompatible things, but merely because they have different opinions. People then quarrel only because it is intolerable to them that others should think differently from themselves. This kind of quarrel is as dangerous as it is absurd. For how can it be settled in a way acceptable to both parties to it, since each wants to force its own opinions on the other?

Factions from mere principle, which are the most absurd and dangerous of all, are, Hume tells us, peculiar to the modern world. The Greeks and Romans knew nothing of them; all their factions were either personal or based on common interests. Or, if there were differences of principle, those principles had practical consequences. But in the modern world, there are religious factions, which are factions of mere principle, setting people against one another, not because they want different things in this world, but because they want everyone to share certain of their beliefs. Hume admits that religious factions are factions of interest as they concern the clergy, whose power and good living depend on other people believing what they tell them; but as they concern laymen, they are factions of mere principle. There was a time, Hume tells us, when religion was not divisive, when a religion was only a collection of myths and rites peculiar to this or that nation. It was when religion became philosophical that it grew factious. 'Sects of philosophy, in the ancient world, were more zealous than parties of religion; but, in modern times, parties of religion are more furious and enraged than the most cruel factions that ever arose from interest and ambition.'[1] Or, as we might put it today, there is nothing more absurd or harmful than an ideological conflict, which is that and nothing more.

We can hardly blame Hume for not seeing what was not properly understood until Burke explained it: that parties are not evils inseparable from free government but are necessary to its survival and efficiency. But he might, I think, have looked rather more closely at his own distinction between principles and interests. Principles and interests are much more intimately connected than he supposed. Indeed, interests common to large numbers of people are nearly always put forward in the shape of principles. No party ever deals only in plain demands; it always says more than just 'We want this'; it also always says, 'This ought to be done in the public interest'. If every party did no more than make bare demands for its supporters' benefit, it would find it inordinately difficult to reach satisfactory compromises with other parties. A party's business is not only to make demands but to find arguments in support of them convincing to as wide a public as possible. It must appeal to principles already accepted, or must propagate principles until they are widely accepted. And these principles lead in turn to the putting forward of new demands. Interests arise from principles just as much as principles from interests. If working men now ask for many things they never dreamt of asking for in Hume's time, it is largely because their conceptions of justice – their principles – have changed. The range of permissible demands is not determined only by conventional morality but also by principles evolved by groups actively engaged in the struggle for power. Men acquire new interests largely because they acquire new principles; and their demands are met without bloodshed largely because groups and classes they do not belong to have come to share some of these principles, even when it is not their interest to do so. True, Hume admits that principles sometimes have practical consequences. But he does not see that common interests alone are insufficient to hold

[1] 'Of Parties in General', ibid., p. 61.

a group of men together over a considerable period of time, enabling them to deal effectively and peacefully with other groups.

Nor does he see that it is just as true that men acquire common interests and common principles by belonging to organized groups as that they form such groups because they have common interests or principles. In this respect, he is less a realist than either Burke or Rousseau. The function of a party, as Burke sees it, is not only to bring together men who share the same principles; it is also to maintain a community of interest and principle among them. Every organized group, Rousseau tells us, acquires a general will; it acquires sentiments and interests common to its members. No doubt, unless they had some notion of an interest or principle common to them, men would not come together voluntarily to form a group, but once they have formed it, they influence one another and acquire more precise and elaborate beliefs which distinguish them from others. It is not merely that they reach a compromise in order to be able to work together effectively; they mostly do not (except the unusually thoughtful among them) have clear ideas of what they want before they come together. They get clearer ideas (if they do get them) largely in the process of working together as a group. They also acquire a loyalty to the group, which keeps them tied to it even though, as circumstances change, it modifies its principles and alters its conception of its own and of the public interest. Organized groups often outlive the interests and principles which first united them, and it is useful to the community that they should do so. But they do not, when they outlive these interests and principles, become what Hume calls personal factions; they merely acquire other interests and other principles. And yet there is continuity, for the new interests and principles are not acquired at random but arise out of the old ones and the changing circumstances. There are attitudes of mind which persist despite the change, attitudes not the less precious to those who share them because they ordinarily cannot define them.

Where there are such organized groups, they learn in time to do business with one another; they evolve rules which enable them to reach compromises, and they come to set as much store by the rules as by the interests and principles which divide them. That is why in some societies differences of interest and principle are much less dangerous to domestic peace than in others; they are not less dangerous because they are smaller but because the groups that differ have learnt how to preserve the peace without giving up the principles or interests which divide them. Burke came close to seeing this, whereas Hume did not, largely because he failed to notice that factions, whether it is interest or principle which divides them, learn from experience that they have some interests in common just as much as individuals do.

Hume was wrong in believing that factions whose disputes are inspired by religious differences do not quarrel about practical matters but are concerned only to impose their beliefs upon one another. True, they are concerned that others should share their beliefs. There is an important difference to which Hume rightly directs our attention between beliefs and interests; we want other people to share our beliefs as we do not want them to share our interests. We accept differences of interest more easily than we do differences of belief. Not all beliefs different from ours are difficult to tolerate, but there are often some beliefs necessary to our peace of mind, and it hurts us to hear them openly challenged. We have to learn to be tolerant, and the learning is unusually difficult. In Hume's time these beliefs were mostly religious, whereas in our time they are mostly political. They are apt to cause the most dangerous and the most unprofitable disputes.

To that extent Hume is right. But he is wrong when he suggests that diversity of religious belief does not create differences of interest giving rise to important disputes about practical matters. If his religion means anything to a man, it deeply affects his conception of how he should live;[1] it deeply affects his worldly interests, the claims he makes on his neighbours and on society in general. These claims are no more spurious or absurd for being rooted in religion than if they had some other source. If I want some things rather than others because I am a Catholic or a Protestant or a Jew, my wants may bring me into conflict with other people wanting different things, even though I am not in the least concerned that they should share my religious beliefs. Nor are men necessarily more intolerant about religious than about other beliefs. No doubt, there are principles from which men draw no practical consequences, and about which they quarrel furiously only because they cannot bear it that other people should disagree with them. But I see no reason for believing that religious principles are more liable than others to be thus barren and dangerous.

---

[1] The man without religion is apt to regard the influence of religion as somehow illegitimate or artificial. If the religious man abandoned his beliefs, his wants would be different from what they are now; and the man without religion is inclined to look upon these wants, if they conflict with his own, as arising not from 'genuine' but from fictitious needs. He tends to discount these needs or to dismiss the endeavour to satisfy them as irrational.

V. HUME'S CONCEPTION OF A BALANCED CONSTITUTION

Hume's political scepticism was distasteful to many people less because he came to conclusions unwelcome to solid and respectable citizens than because the arguments he used to support those conclusions were untraditional and unattractive. His real bias was towards the Whig rather than the Tory position. If he has been called a Tory, it is largely because, as a sceptic and a Scotsman, he did not accept the official Whig version of the Revolution of 1688 which drove a Scottish dynasty from the British throne. He also pulled to pieces the political philosophy used to justify that revolution, the philosophy of Locke, which dealt in ideas that he rejected – ideas like the social contract and natural law. But he accepted the consequences of the revolution from conviction, and not, as many a Tory did, because time and habit had reconciled him to them. He approved of them, and found arguments to support them. It was not his conclusions but his political philosophy – the assumptions and arguments he used to establish his entirely respectable conclusions – which were not to the taste of either Whigs or Tories. He lacked reverence and was slow to admire; he liked to show how people did from interest or prejudice or habit what the good Whig or Tory believed ought to be done from better motives. Human nature, seen through his eyes, is somehow diminished, robbed of its dignity, its depth and its pathos. Hobbes had sunk it deeper in self-centredness but had also made it tougher and more formidable, and had used magnificent language to describe it. But the lucid and subtle Hume was also prosaic; he saw society, not as a refuge from terror, but as a kind of market for the more efficient satisfaction of wants. He did not see men, as Hobbes had done, driven to calamity, to the war of all against all, by urgent and restless appetites. His was already the Godless and sinless and calculating world of the Utilitarians and economists, where the great business of life is to get as much comfort as possible at the cost of the least inconvenience.

Hume had a habit that is not endearing. It was one of his favourite occupations to point out that other people's quarrels were unnecessary. In the essay 'Of the Coalition of Parties', he does his best to play down the differences between Whigs and Tories. They both, he says, had good arguments when the quarrel between them began; but the Tories ought now to understand that certain claims to liberty, which were dangerous when they first opposed them because they were then connected with religious fanaticism, are no longer so connected and therefore no longer dangerous. Claims, which they once rightly feared might grow indefinitely till they destroyed the established order, have in fact not been pressed immoderately. Hume warns the Tories that their strongest argument – that what use and practice have established is better than what reason can discover – can now be turned against them; for the system created by the Revolution has endured for several generations. To insist, after so long a time, on recalling a past form of government is to incur the reproach of innovation. The Crown has long since lost many of its rights, and the free constitution we now have does preserve us from evils to which those rights used often to give rise. The impression conveyed by Hume's essay is that the Tories were on the whole nearer being right than the Whigs when first they quarrelled, but that the consequences of the Whig revolution have turned out so much better than anyone could have reasonably expected that the Tories would now be wise to accept them. There is nothing left for the two parties to quarrel about; and the more moderately each puts its case, the more it encourages moderation in the other. The essay is a judicious summing-up in favour of the Whigs by a judge who likes them rather less than he likes their opponents, but feels bound to admit that they are nearer being right, though they are so more by luck than by judgement.

Hume condemned both absolute monarchy and what he called a 'complete republic', meaning thereby pretty much what is today understood by democracy. In his eyes, democracy is close neighbour to anarchy. If there were a 'complete republic' in Britain, the House of Commons would become the whole legislature. It would either make itself perpetual, or, if it were periodically dissolved, there would be a risk of civil war at every election. Representative democracy is better than the direct kind; but, in a country as large as Britain, any kind of democracy is dangerous. Hume thought that the House of Commons was already as powerful as it ought to be. Enjoying popular support and having the power of the purse, it already had the means of making itself virtually omnipotent. If it had not yet done so, it was only because Members of Parliament, as individuals, had so much to gain by placating the Crown, even though collectively they could reduce it to impotence. Crown patronage enabled the king and his ministers to buy the support of individual members of the House of Commons, and this seemed to Hume the only barrier to the otherwise overwhelming power of the lower House. Luckily, human nature being what it is, the barrier was effective. Hume believed that the odds were in favour of the monarchical in the end prevailing over the popular element in the British constitution. Though he wanted neither to get the better of the other, he took comfort in the thought that, if odds there had to be, they should be in favour of monarchy; for democracy was worse than absolute monarchy was ever likely to be in 'civilized' Europe. Hume did not make lucky guesses about the future; he lacked the gift of prophecy.

Perhaps he was also somewhat deficient in imagination. He preferred a representative to a direct democracy, and he knew that the lower House of the British Parliament was a representative chamber. If, then, Britain were ever to become a democracy, it would have to be a representative democracy. The electorate would be enlarged and the House of Commons would gain power at the expense of the monarch and of the upper House. Hume knew this, and yet when he imagined the evils of a future British democracy, he thought of them as being much the same as the evils long attributed to the democracies of antiquity and of Athens in particular. For him, as for so many others in his day, fifth-century Athens was the typical democracy; and he saw British democracy, though he knew that it must have a representative assembly if it were to exist at all, as Athenian democracy many times enlarged and many times worse. He saw only the obvious: that Britain, being much larger than Athens, could never be a direct democracy. He never saw how greatly a large and representative democracy must differ from a small and direct one, both in its institutions and its *ethos*. He did not see, as Montesquieu had done, how intimately the structure and the spirit of government are connected. Though he expressed a preference for a representative assembly over a direct assembly of the people, he had less feeling than either Bentham or Rousseau for the difference between them. Bentham had a keener sense than he had of the advantages of an elected assembly, and Rousseau a keener sense of the disadvantages.

Hume spoke with approval of what he called 'free' government – by which he meant government responsible to the well-to-do and the educated, whom he often referred to, as so many did in his day, as simply *the people*, because he took it for granted that their interests were in line with the true interests of the entire community. He could still take for granted what had seemed obvious to Locke. But later Burke could not take it for granted; he had to argue against democracy and for aristocracy, as Hume never felt the need to do. It was no longer possible in the last decade of the eighteenth century to assume that the House of Commons was a popular House. The radicals and revolutionaries were as much opposed to aristocracy as to monarchy, and it even occured to some of them that kings were better disposed to the people than were the nobly-born or the wealthy.

Hume took it for granted that the classes represented in the House of Commons spoke for the whole nation, that their interests coincided with the public interest. He also believed that the educated and the well-to-do are better judges than the ignorant and the poor of their own and the public interest. It therefore seemed obvious to him that it was best for all classes that government should be responsible only to the educated and the well-to-do. He thought it 'a just political maxim, that every man must be supposed a knave'[1] – that he must be supposed to be out for himself and ready to sacrifice the good of others to his own good – and yet Hume feared no 'sinister interests'. It does not matter, where government is 'free', that those who have an influence on it should be, politically, almost entirely selfish; for their interests are in keeping with the public interest. It is not the interest of all that government should be responsible to all; it is rather their interest that it should be responsible to the enlightened.

Where government is 'free', Hume tells us, authority is effectively limited because those who have power have to seek re-election in order to keep it. Their power is therefore always restrained by public opinion, even where there is as yet no written law but only custom. All government, 'free' or 'unfree', is limited by what Hume calls 'opinion of interest', by the sentiment widespread among the people that it is to their general advantage to obey their rulers. If the rulers weaken this sentiment, they undermine their own authority, which is therefore limited by their need not to use authority in ways that undermine it. But where government is 'free', there is a further limitation on authority; the rulers have a strong motive to avoid using it in ways that reduce the chances that they will be re-elected. Where government is free, public opinion bears on the actual policies of government, and imposes narrower limits on political power than mere opinion of interest could do.

Hume believed that where government is 'free' (or, as we should say, 'responsible'), written law soon takes the place of custom and of popular loose notions of justice. Experience teaches the people that their security is greater if they require their rulers to apply precisely defined rules. Law, therefore, as distinct from custom, arises first under free governments; but its advantages are so obvious that enlightened monarchies soon follow the example of free governments. When Hume opposes government under law to arbitrary government, he is not thinking of constitutional limits on the legislative power; he is thinking of the obligation, either imposed from without or self-imposed, on the executive to govern according to precisely

---

[1] 'Of the Independency of Parliament', in *Essays, Moral and Political*, p. 42.

defined rules. He is thinking in terms of the traditional distinction between the 'government of laws' and the 'government of men'.

According to Hume, the arts and sciences first began to flourish under free governments. Machiavelli had said that they flourish only (or flourish best) under such governments, but Hume makes a smaller claim for political freedom. The arts and sciences are not confined to countries which are politically free, nor are they there necessarily more vigorous and abundant; though political freedom gives birth to them, they can thrive apart from it. But they cannot thrive except where there is personal security, where the individual has well-defined rights which his rulers respect; and personal security is first established where government is 'free' or responsible. Where the individual has personal security, where there is the rule of law, industry and trade flourish. The more secure and prosperous people are, the greater their leisure. They have time to pursue knowledge and to refine upon their pleasures. They become curious, discriminating and delicate. They cultivate the arts and the sciences.

But, though the arts and sciences first grow important under free governments, the taste for them is later acquired by the subjects of other governments. Just as the rule of law, which arises first where there is political freedom and later spreads elsewhere as its advantages come to be appreciated by absolute monarchs, so the arts and sciences, which thrive under that rule, also spread. They thrive under a civilized monarchy, by which Hume means a monarchy where the king, though formally absolute, in fact governs according to law. Indeed, the arts flourish better in civilized monarchies than in countries which are politically free, for a 'strong genius succeeds best in republics, a refined taste in monarchies'. This was also the opinion of Montesquieu, who had said that the English were superior in the sciences and the French in the arts, and had explained this difference as in part an effect of different forms of government. Hume agreed with Montesquieu that the English had greater intellectual vigour and more originality than the French, and the French more taste and subtlety than the English; the first qualities seemed to him, as to Montesquieu, to make for excellence in the sciences, and the second to make for it in the arts. These ideas about science and art and their political conditions were never more prominent than in the eighteenth century, which was also the period when the English and the French, who were then the richest and most powerful peoples in the West, were very much given to bold generalizations often based on nothing better than a comparison between their two countries.

Belief in progress and in the superiority of Western civilization was no doubt less widespread in the eighteenth than in the nineteenth century, but it was perhaps more easy and confident where it was found. Hume shared that belief to the full and with few misgivings. The Benthamites also believed in progress, and so did the early socialists, but they felt it was strenuous and difficult even though it was certain. They saw misery and stupidity close at hand, and felt the need to dissipate them; they saw the light ahead breaking in upon the darkness which surrounded them. They were fighters for progress, eager to bring what civilization had to give within the reach of all classes. But Hume merely contemplated progress and took pleasure at the sight of it. He saw himself already among the most fortunate of mankind. He was in the light, and the light was gaining fast upon the darkness, and he was pleased. He was readier to congratulate his fellow men than to exert himself on their behalf. Knowledge and taste were spreading, and government was growing milder; absolute rulers saw the advantages of the rule of law; and the influence of public opinion, of the articulate, the educated and the refined, was greater than ever it had been. In his essay on 'Civil Liberty', Hume says that there were in his time about two hundred absolute princes in Europe, each reigning on an average about twenty years. In the last two centuries, two thousand such princes had reigned, and yet there could not be found among them tyrants as cruel as Tiberius, Caligula, Nero or Domitian, who were four among only the first twelve Roman Emperors. The sun shone high over Europe, and Europe was the centre of the world.

Hume's preferences were much the same as Montesquieu's; like Montesquieu, he preferred the English system of government to any other, and thought it the best adapted to preserve freedom in large states. He too saw much to admire in the civilized monarchy of France; he too saw many connections between prosperity, the rule of law, and the flowering of the arts and sciences. He believed in what his century had already learnt to call *civilization* – in the kind of life lived by the more thoughtful and refined among the upper classes in England and France. He believed in the enlightened pursuit of happiness; not of the grosser pleasures, which he thought must quickly disgust the pursuer, but of pleasures that give lasting satisfaction, which he took to be the ones that he and his friends happened to care for most. He wanted the kind of society which enables those who are capable of this happiness to get it; a society where property is secure, where the prosperous and the educated form public opinion, where government respects the law, and where there is freedom of thought for the small part of the nation that can value and use it.

He delighted in curiosity, in argument, in new ideas, in good living; he mistrusted zeal and despised obstinacy. He was a friend of the Encyclopaedists of France, more ingenious than they were and less amusing and excitable. He was a very cool customer indeed, except where his vanity was hurt, as it was in his quarrel with Rousseau, when he lost his head a little. Not very much, but just a little – restrained, I suspect, less by a sense of justice than by a desire not to lose face. Though his social philosophy is utilitarian, it is emphatically not the eager and tough radical Utilitarianism of Jeremy Bentham. It is cautious, precise and respectable; unsentimental, unimaginative, sometimes almost unfeeling.

VI. HUME'S IDEAL COMMONWEALTH

Hume was satisfied, on the whole, with English society and English government as he found them. Even if he had not been satisfied, he would probably have been slow to advocate change; for he believed that we cannot reject old forms of government, as we can old engines, in favour of new ones. Men are governed more by authority than by reason, and they attribute authority to what is old and familiar. The wise man will not try experiments upon the credit of mere argument and philosophy, and if he makes improvements will take care to adjust them to what exists.

Yet Hume will not allow that, because innovation is hazardous and ought always to be cautious, there is no use in speculating on what is ideally the best. One of the longest of his essays is deliberately utopian; it is the 'Idea of a Perfect Commonwealth'. Though we must always, when we make changes, take great care how we make them, it can help us to be clearer in our minds what we should do, if we reflect on what would be ideally the best; for we can then strive to bring what exists, gradually and gently, nearer to our ideal, without disturbing society too much.

We have here a conception of reform different from Burke's. Hume does not rule out as harmful and absurd every broad scheme of improvement. Innovation can be large and yet beneficial, provided it is slow and cautious – provided those who undertake it attempt only a little at a time and always take care how their actions affect the people. In Burke's opinion, we understand society so little that to make large schemes for its reformation, however long the time we allow for carrying them out, is patently absurd. Progress is sure because a benevolent God is in control of the universe; but progress, as far as human reason and will are responsible for it, is the cumulative result of many changes, each made by people who can never see far ahead. I do not want to make too much of this difference between Hume and Burke, for Hume did not in fact want great changes made in England and would probably not have trusted any English government of his day to make them. Nevertheless, the essay on the 'Idea of a Perfect Commonwealth' does show that Hume, for all his conservatism, did not think it altogether unreasonable for men to attempt great though gradual changes in their form of government to bring it closer to their ideals.

Of the actual scheme of government imagined by Hume, I need say very little. It owes more to Harrington's *Oceana* than to any earlier model. It is elaborate, ingenious and moderate. Everyone with a modest property has the vote, and there is therefore a large electorate: the voters elect one hundred separate county assemblies which between them have the legislative power; these assemblies elect the county magistrates and also the national Senate, which has the executive power and appoints the Protector, the Secretaries of State and various councils; all proposals of law are debated in the Senate before they are referred to the county assemblies; the representatives or magistrates of any county may send a law to their senator for proposal to the Senate. Hume thinks that all free government should consist of two councils, a smaller and a larger; because the larger, which represents the people directly, would lack wisdom without the smaller (the Senate), and the smaller would lack honesty without the people. The people, through their representatives, must debate the laws and not merely vote on them. If they were to do this in only one large national assembly, there would be confusion. But divide them into many small assemblies, and they can be trusted, properly enlightened by the Senate, to act in the public interest. Hume's scheme is one of checks and balances meant to give some power to all men of property, but much more to the rich and educated than to the rest. Its purpose, to use Hume's own words, is 'to refine the democracy', from the lower sort of people, who merely elect the county representatives, upwards, through these representatives, to the Senate and the higher magistrates, who between them direct the business of the whole State as distinct from the business of the counties.

Hume was undoubtedly a strong conservative. But he did not stand in awe of what is established; he did not see the mark of God upon it. Nor, on the other hand, did he resign himself to it, as a necessary evil, in despair of better things. He accepted it, partly because he thought it more good than evil, and partly because he had little faith in man's capacity to change his social environment greatly for the better. And yet, when he amused himself by devising an ideal system of government, he took for the model to improve on, not what he found in his own country, but a scheme invented a hundred years earlier by a republican opponent of the Stuart monarchy.

CHAPTER THREE
Burke

Burke put forward, against the radicals and revolutionaries, conceptions of society and government meant to show how arrogant and stupid their pretensions were. But these conceptions were not original with him. That society is an intricate and delicate structure imperfectly understood by its members; that men can go only a little way towards adapting it to their principles and purposes; that freedom is an empty notion apart from the institutions which give substance to it; that forms of government are slow growths intimately connected with the traditions and sentiments of particular peoples: all this was as clearly said by Montesquieu as by Burke. And Hume made a clearer and logically more rigorous case than Burke ever did against many of the ideas dearest to the radicals – against natural law and natural right and against the social contract. Montesquieu and Hume were both by temper conservative. The difference between Burke and them was that he alone used the positions common to them to launch an attack on others; he alone of the three engaged in controversies as passionate as they were historically important. Montesquieu was primarily a theorist, a student of manners and institutions; he sought knowledge for its own sake; he was dispassionate though not unprejudiced, for he never troubled to disguise his own strong but calm preferences. Hume was a philosopher, a dissector of ideas, a maker and destroyer of arguments; he was as much a theorist as Montesquieu, though a theorist of a rather different kind. Burke, however, was an orator who wanted to persuade people to act as he thought best. It takes a good deal of thought, and perhaps even some book-learning – some training in philosophy or in social and political theory – to appreciate the qualities of Hume and Montesquieu. Burke is more familiar and more accessible, and also warmer and more colourful.

His principles need to be considered apart from the practical advice he gives on particular occasions. The task of extracting them out of his voluminous speeches, addresses and letters is long but not unpleasant – especially if you like his ornate and diffuse style of oratory, which is too eager and too passionate to be heavy. I can think of no one who can argue a case at such unnecessary length without wearying the reader. Burke's political philosophy is nowhere systematically expounded; it is revealed, sometimes deliberately and sometimes only by implication, in his writings about particular affairs, English, Irish, American and French. To the political theorist the most important of his writings are these: the *Thoughts on the Cause of the Present Discontents* (1770); the great speeches on America, on *American Taxation* (1774) and on *Conciliation with the Colonies* (1775); the long letter to the Sheriffs of Bristol on the *Affairs of America* (1777); and the *Reflections on the Revolution in France* (1790). The last of these, spoilt by excessive passion and also by ignorance of France, makes much the same assumptions about society and government as the others. Burke's temper changed more than his opinions. If he is among the least systematic, he is also among the more consistent, of political philosophers.

I. BURKE ON THE USE OF PARTIES IN FREE GOVERNMENTS

In the eighteenth century the House of Commons was not representative of the people, though it was often called the popular House. Only a small minority of the people had votes, which many of them either sold or used as they were told to do by their social superiors. The great landowners had a preponderance of power, which they exercised less through the House of Lords than because they controlled many of the seats in the Commons. Nevertheless, the electorate was varied; for, though only a small part of the people had the vote, there could be found among them all sorts and conditions of men. This system, which to us seems corrupt and unfair, did not seem so then, even to highly respectable and moral persons. It was thought right and expedient both that somewhere or other in the country every kind of person should have a vote, and that the rich and powerful, the educated and articulate, should have a much greater political influence than the poor and ignorant. England was, consciously and proudly, an aristocracy of the well-born, the rich and the successful – an aristocracy limited, on one side and considerably, by monarchy, and on the other side and much less, by the wants and prejudices of the common people. Burke objected neither to this aristocracy nor to the methods it used. The buying and selling of seats and votes was established practice in eighteenth-century Britain; and so, too, was patronage. Without these expedients it would have been impossible to find stable majorities. Even the continental admirers of the English system of government did not prefer it to their own because they thought it cleaner, but because it seemed to provide, on the whole, better security and more freedom. Burke admired it for precisely the same reasons; he always spoke of it with deep respect and spent many years of his life defending it against what he thought were dangers to it. He defended it first against the king, and afterwards against the radicals.

In Burke's opinion, George III, until the loss of the American colonies reduced his prestige, was dangerous to the constitution because he was using Crown patronage to get more power for himself than he had a right to, than kings of England had possessed since the 'Glorious Revolution'. Now, patronage is a kind of property; it is a power, however acquired, to bestow office or privilege, either by direct appointments and gift or by influence.[1] Patronage, in this sense, exists under every form of government, and is perhaps as necessary to government as lubricating oil to a machine. How much is needed depends on the nature of the machine. In Burke's time, the need for it was generally admitted, and Burke, a great respecter of property, did not object to it. He objected only to what he thought was George III's misuse of it, which upset the balance of power between King and Parliament established by the Revolution of 1688. Crown patronage had always existed, and had always been much greater than the patronage in the hands of any private person, though less than all private patronage put together.

Under the first two Georges, Crown patronage served to strengthen a succession of Whig governments. These governments were not, of course, party governments in our modern sense; they were aristocratic alliances whose leaders used their own patronage and the Crown's to control a majority of seats in the House of Commons. The alliance in power, as a natural consequence of having power, were opposed

[1] Patronage is sometimes acquired with office, as it very largely is today in the United States, or else is inherited or bought. Only when the grant of office or privilege is made for the purpose of increasing the power or influence of the giver or of his friends or associates is it properly an exercise of patronage.

by everyone in Parliament who was not with them. Parliament divided into supporters and opponents of the king's ministers, into 'ins' and 'outs'; but there were no organized parties and no settled party principles. If we use the word *party* in the modern sense, it would perhaps be truer to say that, at least until the younger Pitt became Prime Minister, there were no parties in England, or else that there were a dozen, than that there were only two. When the Whigs began to suspect George III of trying to make himself independent of them by acquiring supporters of his own in the House of Commons, they called these supporters the King's Friends and accused them of being a *party*.

In those days, to call a group of men a party was to suggest that there was something sinister about them. For party was still denounced, in Halifax's phrase, as a 'conspiracy against the nation'. Kings and politicians affected to be above party – to be patriots and not party-men. The king's ministers could not rule without support in Parliament, which was therefore often divided into two parts; but these parts were not parties. They were loose collections or groups of interests, of which one supported the king's ministers and the other did not. This broad division of Parliament into two parts, unknown before the end of the seventeenth century, was accepted only because it worked. No one had evolved a political theory to explain and justify it.[1] It was understood that the king's ministers were responsible not only to the king but to Parliament as well; it was admitted in practice, if not in theory, that Parliament was more than merely a legislature, for its right to criticize policy was allowed as much as its right to make law. But the responsibility of ministers to Parliament, however broadly understood, was not thought to involve anything that could be called party government. *Party* and *faction* were still more or less equivalent terms; they were still mostly used in a pejorative sense, to suggest something narrow, selfish and unpatriotic.

Burke reacted to the King's Friends much as the other Whigs had done. He was as convinced as they were that George III, legally and yet surreptitiously and against the spirit of the constitution, was subverting the English system of government as it had evolved since the 'Glorious Revolution'. The Stuarts had tried to restrain and control Parliament; they had attacked it from without. George III, according to this Whig theory, was undermining its authority from within, though not openly challenging the position it had acquired for

---

[1] Unless we count for a theory a few remarks made by Montesquieu in Bk. XI, ch. 6 of the *Espirit des Lois*.

itself in the seventeenth century. Suspicion of George's motives and resentment at his supposed success caused his political enemies to cry out against party even more loudly than before. What better evidence of the dangers of party than the uses to which George III was putting the King's Friends?

Burke shared the fears of the Whigs, but he was not, as they were, blinded by those fears. Instead of joining in the vulgar outcry against party, he saw in party the only sure defence against royal encroachments. So long as the practice continued of forming governments by striking bargains between aristocratic groups, many of them without settled principles or policies, the king would have an immense advantage over everyone. Disposing of more patronage than anyone else, he could always control the largest single group. The only force strong enough to get the better of him would have to be, not just a temporary coalition of patrons and their political dependants, but a disciplined body held together by common principles and agreed policies. Burke saw no danger at all in the capture of power by a single party, provided that party held power only for a limited period. So long as it could be legally opposed and could be relied upon to give way to a rival when it lost the confidence of Parliament and of the electorate, it would not be a threat to free government, but would strengthen it by making it effective and responsible.

This is the really important message in Burke's *Thoughts on the Cause of the Present Discontents*. Instead of looking upon party as something perhaps impossible to avoid and yet dangerous and potentially evil, or at its best no better than harmless, he welcomed it as a device necessary to responsible government. Instead of treating it, as nearly everyone before him had done, as a 'conspiracy against the nation', he advocated it as something conducive to the public good. To be so conducive, it must be – to use a modern phrase which, though Burke did not use it, does, I think, express his meaning – an *open conspiracy*. Burke was the first to advocate party government as an instrument and preservative of freedom – the first to explain that organizations created for the capture of power are not necessarily obstacles to good and responsible government, but, on the contrary, are means to it, provided they work in the open and respect whatever conventions those who seek or have power are required to respect. Burke did not deplore patronage; he did not suppose that principles and policies alone would hold a party together. He believed in the political ascendancy of the wealthy, well-born and well-educated, and accepted the methods used to maintain that ascendancy. But he did not want the king to beat the Whigs at their own game, because, if he did beat them, parliamentary government, as the eighteenth century knew it, though preserved in appearance, would be destroyed in fact. Burke wanted government truly responsible to the small part of the nation which he considered politically mature. A government ought to be stable and strong while it enjoys the confidence of the politically mature classes; as soon as it loses that confidence, it ought to abandon power and give way to a successor. This was Burke's ideal, which he thought could best be achieved by means of party.

II. BURKE ON AMERICAN AFFAIRS

Burke was an imperialist. Pride of empire, only a little less than concern for freedom, inspires his writings about America. Pride of empire is merely a form of patriotism, and in itself is entirely respectable, though it may sometimes take dangerous or evil forms. It may lead to oppression, or it may be a force making for freedom. It all depends on people's opinions about the best means of holding an empire together. Burke was pro-American, largely because he was an imperialist. He wanted to preserve the empire, though not at any price. He was opposed to George III's American policy for two reasons: because he believed that there were better ways of keeping the Americans loyal to the mother country than the methods the King and his ministers were using; and because he believed that the attempt to coerce the Americans, if it succeeded, would destroy freedom, not only in America, but in England as well.[1]

Though Burke was pro-American, the arguments he used were different from the arguments that excited the colonists. He cared nothing for what he called 'abstract' rights, and could never have composed such a document as the Declaration of Independence. All talk of eternal and inalienable rights was distasteful to him. In his great speech on *American Taxation*, he makes this statement:

> I am not here going into the distinctions of rights, nor attempting to mark their boundaries. I do not enter into these metaphysical distinctions; I hate the very sound of them. Leave the Americans as they anciently stood, and these distinctions, born of our unhappy contest, will die along with it. . . .Be content to bind America by

[1] The war seemed to him a civil war, a war between Englishmen; and also unnecessary and stupid. It was a war that the mother country ought to have been willing to avoid even at great cost, and which she could in fact have avoided at almost no cost.

laws of trade; you have always done it. Let this be your reason for
binding their trade. Do not burden them by taxes; you were not used
to do so from the beginning. Let this be your reason for not taxing.
These are the arguments of states and kingdoms. Leave the rest to the
schools; for there only they may be discussed with safety.[1]

Burke did not object, in principle, to Parliament's sovereignty over
the colonies, and did not even argue that there were legal limits to
that sovereignty. He was willing to vote for the Declaratory Act which
proclaimed in a general way Parliament's supremacy. He could find
no general principle to justify the colonists in their refusal to pay taxes
imposed on them by the British Parliament for purposes of revenue,
since he admitted that they had for generations allowed Parliament to
regulate their trade for the benefit of the mother country; and these
regulations were economically more burdensome by far than the new
taxes. The colonists were not represented in the imperial Parliament,
and yet they had long accepted Britain's rights to make laws that
concerned their most vital interests. The colonists were right, not
because they were defending general principles valid everywhere, but
because they were defending acquired rights. The mother country had
for generations regulated their trade but had not imposed taxes on
them, either internal or external, for purposes of revenue. The colonists
taxed themselves through their own legislatures; they were, in fact,
largely self-governing. It was natural and expedient that they should be
so; it was natural, because they had, as Englishmen, inevitably carried
over with them, into America, English institutions and political ideas;
and it was expedient, because they were separated from England by
three thousand miles of ocean. Massachusetts could not be governed
from London as if it were an English county. Unlimited though
Parliament's sovereignty might be in principle, the English colonies
had inevitably acquired a large measure of independence.

How could the British government or the colonists determine the
proper measure of that independence? Clearly, the government could
not do it by insisting on Parliament's sovereignty, nor the colonists
by asserting the rights of man. Certain relations had arisen during
the last one hundred and fifty years between the mother country
and the colonies – relations not easy to define, still less to justify
in terms of abstract right. But they had in fact proved acceptable to
both parties, and that was their sufficient justification. The ministers
and their supporters in Parliament were trying to alter these relations

[1] *Speech on American Taxation* (19 April 1774), in *The Writings and Speeches of Edmund Burke*, vol. II, ed. Paul Langford (Oxford 1981), p. 458.

against the wishes of the colonists. The measure of independence the colonists had acquired and learnt to value was being threatened. It was absurd, Burke thought, to condemn their resistance on the ground that what was now being asked of them imposed a much smaller sacrifice than, say, the Navigation Acts, whose legitimacy the colonists had never contested. It was no less absurd to try to justify these new taxes on the ground that the money was to be spent for the colonists' benefit. These taxes, light though they might be, seemed to the colonists an innovation, an unprecedented challenge to acquired rights. Just as the English in England valued the rights they had acquired in the course of their history, so, too, did the English in America; and the undisputed enjoyment of these rights was what they understood by freedom. Why restrict that freedom? In order to vindicate the sovereignty of Parliament? But the Americans had never contested that sovereignty while it had not seemed to threaten their rights. To attack colonial liberties was to provoke the colonists to deny Parliament's sovereignty. Why put yourself in a position where you have to impose by force a principle which, if only you had stayed your hand, no one would have wanted to question? If your real purpose is to find a revenue, why impose taxes that are bitterly resented? The expense of raising unpopular taxes is out of all proportion to their yield. If American revenues are needed for American purposes, why not begin by asking American legislatures to vote them?

Burke believed that our ability to understand society and to change it to suit our purposes is slight. In the speech on *Conciliation with the Colonies*, he says,

> When I contemplate these things; when I know that the Colonies in general owe little or nothing to any care of ours, and that they are not squeezed into this happy form by the constraints of watchful and suspicious government, but that, through a wise and salutary neglect, a generous nature has been suffered to take her own way to perfection; when I reflect upon these effects, when I see how profitable they have been to us, I feel all the pride of power sink, and all the presumption in the wisdom of human contrivances melt and die away within me.[1]

The colonies were formed by the Englishmen who went out to found them and not by English governments at home. Nor were they – to interpret Burke's meaning more exactly – formed by the colonists

---

[1] *Conciliation with the Colonies* (22 March 1775), in Burke, *Select Works*, ed. E. J. Payne (Oxford 1904 edition), I.176.

themselves in the sense of being deliberately contrived. The English colonies in America, like all other human societies, were products of the numberless activities of several generations – of a course of events which, taken as a whole, the human mind could scarcely grasp, let alone control. They were products of a 'generous nature', of the natural wealth the colonists found in their new countries, and also of the qualities of character they brought with them.

The colonists, Burke told the House of Commons, had emigrated when English love of freedom was at its strongest. They were 'not only devoted to Liberty, but to Liberty according to English ideas and on English principles'.[1] They were undoubtedly very English societies, but they were also different from the mother country. The colonists were mostly not drawn from the classes dominant in the mother country; and they had now long been separated from that country. Burke found the Americans more self-consciously, more aggressively Protestant than the English, with a passion for liberty both narrower and fiercer. He found them more intractable, more legalistic and suspicious; and he attributed these qualities in them largely to the influence of lawyers, who, as he put it, 'augur misgovernment at a distance; and snuff the approach of tyranny in every tainted breeze'.[2] The colonists had their own peculiar temperament, their own spirit, which the mother country must take into account in all her dealings with them. 'The question is, not whether their spirit deserves praise or blame; but – what, in the name of God, shall we do with it?'[3] It was not a question of asserting rights of sovereignty against the colonists, or of defending the rights of man against George III, but of restoring peace between two English communities which were like each other and yet also unlike. The prejudices and habits of the Americans made them the sort of people they were. The mother country, even in her own interest, must take her colonies for what they were. If she used force to try to gain her end, she would not gain it; for her end was to have loyal colonies attached to her, and loyalty is not won by force. 'Nothing less will content me than *whole America*. . . . I do not choose wholly to break the American spirit; because it is the spirit that has made the country.'[4]

Burke, the defender of American liberties, was a staunch imperialist. And yet, much as he cared for the unity of the empire, he cared even

[1] Ibid., p. 178.
[2] Ibid., p. 183.
[3] Ibid., p. 185.
[4] Ibid., p. 177.

more for liberty, English and American. Better, he thought, that the American spirit, which included a passion for liberty, should not be broken than that the empire should be kept together at the cost of breaking it.

III. BURKE ON THE FRENCH REVOLUTION

Burke was in his forties and at the height of his intellectual powers when civil war broke out between the English in America and in the mother country; he was already sixty when the French Revolution began. His reaction to that revolution was violent and deep. He hated what the French revolutionaries stood for and attacked them more bitterly and contemptuously than ever he had attacked anyone before. The French Revolution taught him nothing; it only made him cling more fiercely and obstinately to opinions long held.

Nevertheless, his *Reflections on the Revolution in France* is a great book. Anyone who reads it for the first time, and who has not read anything else by Burke, will find in it much that is excellent and well put. But what it contains of social and political theory is for the most part not new; for Burke had already published his most perceptive and luminous ideas about society and government before he wrote the *Reflections*. In his speeches, addresses and letters on America we can find nearly all the sentiments and ideas most strongly associated with his name: the distaste for all talk about universal rights; the respect for what is old and national; the insistence that men cannot greatly alter their institutions except for the worse; the belief that prejudice rather than reason holds society together, so that to destroy prejudice is to undermine society.

Yet Burke's speeches on America do not prepare us for his angry denunciation of the French Revolution. The Americans, no less than the French, had appealed to universal principles and universal rights; and Burke, though he had taken little notice of the appeal, had not been offended by it, but had quickly turned his mind to the grievances that lay behind it. He had not troubled to blame the Americans for the 'metaphysical' nonsense about abstract rights to which, in the course of their dispute with George III, they became every bit as addicted as the French. The doctrine of *the rights of man* is as much American as French. Why, then, did Burke object to it so much in the French and so little in the Americans?

The Americans had enjoyed a considerable independence of the mother country. That independence was embodied in institutions, practices and habits of thought and feeling that were products of English and American history. The real concern of the Americans, so Burke thought, had been to defend their independence; until it was threatened, they had not been much interested in the rights of man. Their abstract arguments, little as Burke relished them, were effects of grievances about which he cared very much. Provided that particular claims are just, talk about the rights of man, nonsense though it may be, is not dangerous nonsense. Burke believed in the justice of the American cause and therefore quite properly ignored rather than attacked what he called the 'metaphysical' theories produced in defence of that cause. It would have been, from his point of view, a waste of time, and perhaps even bad politics, to attack the American version of the doctrine of the rights of man.

The French revolutionaries seemed to Burke to be using the doctrine of the rights of man for a quite different purpose: not to justify resistance in defence of a traditional freedom, of acquired rights; nor even to support new claims intended to make that freedom more secure; but to subvert society. They were making claims incompatible with the existing social order, the system of existing rights; they were challenging those rights in the name of such principles as equality and liberty, taken in the abstract.

This challenge, in Burke's opinion, was absurd. Equality and liberty, taken in the abstract, are empty notions. If we want to know what people have in mind when they speak of liberty, we must see what specific claims they are making. Freedom is not everywhere understood in the same way; it does not in all societies include the same rights. We cannot, by considering human nature merely as such, outside any particular social order, decide what rights men ought to have. In all societies men have rights and set store by them. Man is by nature a social and moral creature; and in every society he claims rights for himself and recognizes similar claims made by others. But we cannot discover what claims he makes or ought to make merely by considering his nature, the properties which distinguish him from other creatures. Though it is specifically human to have rights, to make and to recognize claims, there are no *rights of man*; there are only claims which are valid within a particular social order. This, I think, is at least part of what Burke had in mind when he condemned what he called the doctrine of *abstract rights*.

To the doctrine which he condemned Burke opposed another. The best of all titles, he thinks, is prescription; if a claim has long been made and long recognized, the presumption is that it serves an enduring need and is therefore valid. Men have not deduced the claims they make and recognize from abstract principles. Their claims arise out of their needs, and their needs out of the situations in which they find themselves. The persistence of claims is therefore strong evidence that they are useful. Burke calls prescription the most *solid* of all titles.

What are we to understand by this? That the most important rights, the ones most cherished, are prescriptive? Is Burke making no more than what he takes to be a statement of fact? Sometimes it may seem so, but at other times it does not. He is not merely telling us how the most cherished claims arise, or what their social function is; he is not merely putting forward an hypothesis. He is also arguing that prescription is the most valid of all titles. He is not merely saying that, as a matter of fact, among the claims that are made, the most cherished – because they serve the most enduring needs – are prescriptive; he is also saying that prescriptive claims take precedence over all others in the sense that they ought to be preferred to them.

This assertion can be interpreted in two ways. It may be held that, since its age is strong evidence that an old established claim serves a useful purpose, the burden of proof rests always on whoever would abolish or curtail it; or it may be held that its age is sufficient evidence that an old established right does serve such a purpose and that therefore it ought not to be abolished or curtailed. We cannot say that Burke took either of these two positions clearly and consistently. Every reader of the *Reflections* will get his own impression. Mine, for what it is worth, is this: that, though Burke sometimes took the one position and sometimes the other, he inclined more to the second than the first.

He was moved to wonder, to scorn and to anger by the 'arrogance' of the revolutionaries. They pretended, so he thought, to an impossible knowledge; they pretended to know how a free and egalitarian society could be established, and asserted their right to refashion French society to meet that ideal. The doctrine of the rights of man, as they used it (of the rights of man taken in the abstract outside any particular social order) was not only absurd; it was also pernicious. The French revolutionaries seemed to Burke as pretentious as they were fanatical. They could not, he thought, attain their avowed purposes; they could only ruin France in the attempt to attain them. They were like ignorant surgeons preparing to carry out a major operation on a body whose delicate and finely adjusted structure they were scarcely aware of; they could use the knife, but only to damage or to kill what they pretended to cure. Burke was not against men's carrying out minor operations on the body politic; he was only certain that they are never competent to do more. The French revolutionaries were, he thought, even more than usually incompetent; their eagerness to make great changes was itself sure evidence of their folly. 'The fresh ruins of France', he remarked, 'are not the devastation of civil war; they are the sad but instructive monuments of rash and ignorant counsel in time of profound peace'.[1] 'When I hear the simplicity of contrivance aimed at and boasted of in any new political constitutions', he added, 'I am at no loss to decide that the artificers are grossly ignorant of their trade, or totally negligent of their duty'.[2] The wise man knows that society is many-sided and intricate, and that he can do only a little to change it in the way he would have it change. Society is not clay passive to the potter, but a delicate and living whole, more easily damaged than improved.

The French revolutionaries, and the philosophers from whom they took their doctrines, were eager to destroy old prejudices on the ground that they were irrational and obstacles to progress. Burke thought he knew better. 'We know', he said (speaking for himself and also, so he believed, for the English generally), 'that *we* have made no discoveries; and we think that no discoveries are to be made, in morality; nor many in the great principles of government, nor in the ideas of liberty, which were understood long before we were born'.[3] And, he went on, 'Instead of casting away all our old prejudices. . .we cherish them because they are prejudices; and the longer they have lasted, and the more generally they have prevailed, the more we cherish them. We are afraid to put men to live and trade each on his own private stock of reason; because we suspect that this stock in each man is small, and that the individuals would do better to avail themselves of the general bank and capital of nations, and of ages. Many of our men of speculation, instead of exploding general prejudices, employ their sagacity to discover the latent wisdom which prevails in them'.[4]

Prejudice is not irrational. It is not belief that cannot be justified; it is only belief that most people never trouble to justify and are perhaps incapable of justifying for not knowing how to set about doing so. They accept their prejudices on trust, and act confidently on them. They acquire them in the process of growing up and getting ready

[1] *Reflections on the Revolution in France*, in *The Writings and Speeches of Edmund Burke*, vol. III, ed. L. G. Mitchell (Oxford 1989), p. 90.
[2] Ibid., p. 112.
[3] Ibid., p. 137.
[4] Ibid., p. 138.

to take their places in society. All people most of the time, and many people nearly all the time, act on prejudice; they act on beliefs they have never troubled to justify. If they waited to justify them, they could not act. To know how to behave successfully, a man need not understand society in the sense of being able to explain it; but he must know what to do in all the usual situations of life. To know this, he must have the sentiments and beliefs appropriate to his condition. If they are appropriate, he will act successfully; he will want what is within his reach, and will be likely to get it. Of course, he will often have to think for himself, and will sometimes come painfully by new opinions; but among the beliefs he acts on, those he takes on trust will be much more numerous than those he acquires by thinking things out for himself. He will avail himself, as Burke puts it, of 'the general bank and capital of nations, and of ages'.

This 'bank and capital' is not a chance accumulation. It is the fruit of experience and reflection. The beliefs that Burke calls *prejudices* have all, or nearly all, he thinks, been produced by hard thinking; they are beliefs that men have acquired in the past by solving the problems life presented to them. But if every man had to solve all these problems for himself, mankind could never make progress; one of the conditions of progress is that men shall accept ready-made most of the solutions offered to them. They are born into societies whose institutions and beliefs are long established and slow to change. They learn to use the accumulated wisdom of the past much as they learn to put on their clothes; they get the habit of making proper use of what is given to them without troubling their heads about how it came to be what and where it is. Prejudice is not chance or casual opinion; it would never have come into being and been widely accepted if it had not been adapted to men's needs.

Prejudice serves two purposes. It enables the individual to live much better than he could live without it; it enables him to rely on much more than his own wisdom and therefore to satisfy many more wants than he could otherwise do. If the ordinary civilized man lives more commodiously than the savage, it is not so much that his private stock of wisdom is greater as that he has a set of beliefs and habits enabling him to take advantage of the opportunities that civilization offers. Take him out of his environment, and he will be almost as much bewildered, as much lost, as the savage translated from his own society to another quite unlike it. His advantage is that, while he remains in his own civilized community, he can avail himself of an immense stock of wisdom. And he ordinarily does so, not by making it his own in the way that a student does when he understands what he is taught, but merely by acquiring beliefs that he is no more capable of justifying than is the savage capable of justifying his beliefs.

Prejudice also serves to hold society together. Men's prejudices are suited to their institutions. Because of their prejudices, men behave as they must if society is to function properly. Every man plays his appropriate part, not because he understands how that part fits into the whole life of his community, but because he has been taught to play it. There are some prejudices common to all the members of society, and others confined to certain classes, groups or professions. The prejudices of a society, together with its laws, customs, rights and obligations, make it the society it is; they help to give it its peculiar character. They form part of a whole system of beliefs and modes of behaviour, and they help to maintain the system. To destroy them is therefore to damage, if not to destroy, society; it is to deprive men of the motives which cause them – though they may not know it – so to behave that the social order, on which their security and happiness depend, does not disintegrate.

Many English philosophers, according to Burke, instead of exploding prejudices, try to discover the wisdom latent in them. For prejudices, though most people never trouble to justify them, can be justified. They are justified when their social function is explained, when it is shown how they serve to give men security and happiness by preserving the social order. Though Burke praises those 'men of speculation', as he calls them, who make it their business to explain and defend prejudices and not to destroy them, he would much rather have people take them on trust than enquire closely into them. He is not content to say that explanation is a task for which only a few persons have the leisure and the talents, and that most people have no choice but to take society as they find it without hope of ever being able to understand how it functions. He comes at times close to condemning curiosity about it. No doubt, where there are men of speculation bent on exploding salutary prejudices, it is good that there should be other men willing and able to show up their sophistries. The innocent and unreflecting must be protected against those who would argue them out of beliefs necessary to their happiness. But innocence is safer than curiosity, at least for most people. Prejudice is not the enemy of knowledge, but an effect of experience and a substitute for it.

By prejudice, Burke does not mean any belief accepted on trust. We normally accept as true an immense variety of statements which we are in no position to verify: ordinary everyday statements made by our friends and neighbours, expert opinions and scientific hypotheses. Burke, when he speaks of prejudice, has not these things in mind. He has in mind judgements about conduct – that is, beliefs about what is desirable and how men should behave – rather than judgements of fact, though he does not trouble to distinguish between them. When he calls prejudice *latent wisdom*, he does not mean that it is belief capable of verification which most people never verify; he means that it is belief capable of justification which most people never justify. Prejudice is justified when it is shown how it serves to hold society together and to give men security and happiness.

Montesquieu had shown, in *The Spirit of the Laws*, how men's beliefs and sentiments vary with their institutions. He had argued that every type of government has a *principe* or spring of action appropriate to it: virtue in a republic, honour in a monarchy, fear in a despotism. He had seen that, if a type of government is to survive, it matters less that men should understand how it works than that they should have sentiments which move them to behave in the ways that make it work. What he called the *principe* of a type of government is the psychological or subjective factor whose social counterpart is a whole set of institutions; it stands to those institutions in much the same relation as that which Burke called prejudice. Just as prejudice is for Burke more than bare opinion – being opinion backed by emotion – so for Montesquieu virtue and honour are more than bare feelings; they are emotionally charged opinions about how the patriot or the man of honour should behave.

But it is Burke, and not Montesquieu, who gives us much the fuller, the more eloquent and persuasive, explanation and defence of prejudice and prescription, of traditional beliefs and traditional rights. Burke did more than reproduce a theme of Montesquieu's; he breathed upon the bare bones of it and put life into it as Montesquieu had not done.

IV. REFLECTIONS ON BURKE

1. *The Strong Points in Burke's Arguments*

There are admirable things in the social philosophy of Burke – things that are either new or better put by him than by anyone before him. Radicals at all times too often forget them, and were never more disposed to do so than in the latter part of the eighteenth century. For a generation or more before the French Revolution, the iconoclasts had been having it all their own way; they had been writing the books most read and producing the arguments most widely canvassed. It was they who were passionate and aggressive, and the conservative writers who were cool and detached. Burke brought to the defence of the established order passions as strong as any that moved the radicals. He carried the war into their camp. He made conversation articulate as it had never been before; he put into words what many people felt about the French Revolution but did not know how to say. His was not the style of the lecture-room or the intellectual salon. If it was not exactly popular, it was formidable and reassuring. It is doubtful whether his admirers understood him as easily as people inclined to radicalism understood Tom Paine. But at least they got comfort from him; they could feel that here at last was a powerful intellect and an eloquent voice on their side.

Much that Burke says about the French revolutionaries and revolutionaries in general is well founded. It is true that revolutionaries nearly always attempt much more than they can achieve, and that they are bold largely because they are blind. Nowadays we know much more about revolutions than it was possible to know in Burke's time. There have been many small and several great revolutions since then, and they have been carefully studied. Most revolutions lead to results that the people who start them never wanted. Indeed, it is often doubtful whether the makers of revolutions know what they want. They are moved to anger by what they see of the established order, or they want power and hope to get it by using the anger felt by others, or they are moved both by anger and ambition. It is the strength of their feelings, not the depth of their understanding, which moves them to act. Of course, the successful revolutionary leader needs talents that are rare; he is not as foolish and improvident as Burke tried to make him out. In some ways he is less blind than other men; he sees the immediate situation more clearly than they do and is quicker to seize opportunities. Yet the gifts which enable a man to take the lead in troubled times are not the gifts which make the efficient reformer or the deep student of society. It is one thing to know how to get power and quite another to know how to use it to reconstruct society according to plan, and there is no reason to suppose that the two kinds of knowledge need go together. When we say that a revolutionary leader is successful, we ordinarily mean that he succeeds in getting power and keeping it; we seldom mean that he succeeds in changing society to bring it closer to some ideal proclaimed by himself. He may, like Robespierre, have ideas so vague that they cannot be used to estimate how near he comes to getting what he wanted; or he may, like Lenin, have rather more precise ideas, and then it is easier to see how far his achievements fall short of his intention. Indeed, that is putting it too mildly. As Burke saw, it is not that the revolutionary goes only a short way in the direction he wants to go; it is rather that he goes a long way in other directions. He makes great changes, but not the changes he wants to make. He is swept along by events into courses undreamt of before he began. He may reconcile himself to the unforeseen effects of his actions, especially if that is a condition of his keeping power. He may even persuade himself that he has wanted all along what in fact he never foresaw. But the belief that he has reconstructed society according to plan is largely an illusion. All this is borne out by history, and Burke saw it when it was less obvious than it is now.

He was also right in saying that the social order is maintained, not because people know how it functions, but because they act appropriately; and that they do so largely because they accept traditional beliefs and rights and obligations. Men play their parts in society without understanding how those parts fit together to form a whole system of behaviour. They do so, not by chance or because there is a pre-established harmony, but because they have been *conditioned*. They have been moulded by society and so feel at home in it. If their beliefs and their claims get very much out of line with established institutions, the social order is bound to be disrupted. People then ask much more of society than they have been in the habit of getting, and they complain of oppression; they cease to behave in accustomed ways, thereby upsetting other people and themselves. Conditions are chaotic, or are felt to be so; there is frustration and wasted effort, and men seem to have lost their bearings in the social world. It is not that they have ceased to understand what was once intelligible to them, for they mostly never understood it; it is rather that they no longer accept it because their beliefs and ambitions are not adjusted to it.

Again, as Burke said, liberty and equality are differently understood in different societies. We cannot discover what they are, what rights go to make them up, merely by contemplating the 'essential or universal' nature of man. In no society do all men have the same rights; everywhere there are hierarchy and differences of status. When we claim liberty we are not saying that there ought to be no restrictions, just as when we claim equality we are not saying that nobody must have any right which everyone else does not also have. These two claims, if they were interpreted in this way, would be destructive of society: the first because it would deny the need for social discipline, and the second because it would deny that diversity of function entails diversity of right. When we champion liberty or equality, we are putting some rights forward as more important than the rest; we are saying that everyone ought to have them. What, then, gives these rights their special importance, granted that they are not to be derived logically from man's essential or pre-social nature?[1] Since in no society can man do what he pleases, what decides which forms of discipline are tolerable and which are not? What can it be but current ideas about how men should live, ideas which vary from society to society? Thus it is that restrictions felt to be intolerable in one society can be put forward as conditions of freedom in another.

If by freedom and equality are understood rights long established or cherished, there is no danger in them. But if they are used to press new and large claims, which society cannot in fact meet, they are apt to be dangerous to the very classes for whose supposed benefit they are used, and not only to the privileged. Society is well adapted to meet established claims, because these claims are in keeping with what society now is. For that very reason, therefore, it is not well adapted to meeting claims very different from the established ones. By trying to get more out of society than it can give, we risk losing what it has until now given. Or, to use language more like Burke's, by asking for too much freedom we put in jeopardy the freedom that is ours already.

Burke made about as good a case for aristocracy as was made in his time. We may not find it convincing, our assumptions being so different from his, but it is, I think, ingenious. He is right in believing that in every society (except perhaps the most primitive and simple) there must be some kind of social hierarchy and not merely a division of labour; there must be differences of power and station which make men socially unequal. Radicals are no longer concerned to deny this. They part company with Burke, not by saying there need be no hierarchy, but by insisting that it can and ought to be made to rest on differences of ability. They attack, not all superiority of power, income and status, but the superiority which is inherited or otherwise unearned. Many of the arguments they use were devised after Burke's time, and he never met them. His counter-attack on the champions of equality is therefore rather old-fashioned; it is directed against equality as it was understood before the birth of modern socialism. Burke had never seriously to consider the possibility that society might be so organized, and its economy so controlled, as to ensure that differences of income, power and status, correspond fairly closely to differences

---

[1] Unless, of course, that nature is so defined as to include these rights – unless, that is, normative statements are 'disguised' by being put in the form of statements of fact.

of ability measured by standards acceptable to most people. But he did produce arguments for the hereditary principle which are worth considering.

He believed, as Bodin had also done (and the belief is not absurd), that inequalities are often more readily accepted when they rest on birth than on merit. He believed that, in societies where most men expect to die in the class they are born into, they ordinarily do not acquire the ambitions which make them dissatisfied with their lot. Therefore, the less competitive your society, the less envious and the more contented its members are likely to be – from which it follows that to multiply opportunities of rising socially is unlikely to increase happiness. Men feel most secure in stable societies; and the more stable a society, the less movement up and down the social ladder. Burke was not for preventing all movement on it; but he wanted the ascent kept difficult, so as to be beyond the power of all but the most able.[1]

Many people today find this line of argument distasteful and mean; it is against the spirit of our times. But that, though it makes it less persuasive to us, does not weaken it logically. We are not unprejudiced, and for all that we wish it otherwise, it may yet be true that in societies where movement from class to class is difficult, men are less apt to acquire ambitions they cannot satisfy than in societies where such movement is easy. This is an hypothesis not yet tested. Burke may be right.[2]

He believed that the upper classes are the chief repositories of the 'collective wisdom' on which the well-being of the community depends. They are the bearers of civilization; they know how to govern; they enforce the rules that hold society together; they set the tone. This does not mean that the lower orders imitate them in all things, for they too have their own tastes and customs. If they did not, if they were imitators in all things, they would try to assimilate themselves to the upper classes. The upper classes set the tone when, by precept and example, they play the largest part in maintaining the

---

[1] Burke took it for granted that men who rise socially are usually able men, and that society is the better for their success. No doubt, they mostly are able, and owe their success to ability as much as to good fortune. But society may not be the better for their success. The qualities that bring success to the few that have it need not be useful, and may even be harmful, to society at large. This is a possibility which seems not to have occurred to Burke.

[2] There is another argument against easy movement from class to class which Burke does not use. The easier this movement the more are the successful estranged from their families, and the more are people socially 'maladjusted' because they have not acquired in childhood the habits and values needed to put them at their ease in the class into which they have risen.

standards shared by all classes, the standards needed to preserve the social order. The more they respect the rights of their inferiors, the more secure their own position. Their knowing how to govern, their special skill, is not theoretical knowledge; they need not know how the whole system of government works; they need not be political scientists, any more than the good rider need be learned in the anatomy of the horse. They learn how to govern, partly by actually governing, and partly by acquiring – in the process of growing up to be fit members of their class – the manner, the tact and the confidence needed for good government.

The superiority of the upper classes, as Burke conceived of it, is social and not biological. True, he did not believe (as, say, Descartes and Hobbes had believed, or at least had asserted) that men are born with much the same natural abilities, and he did believe that those who rise socially usually owe their success to superior talents. Yet his defence of the privileges of the upper classes does not rest on the assumption that persons born into these classes are better endowed by nature than other people. They owe their superiority less to nature than to social opportunity: by virtue of their position in society, they acquire much the largest share of the wisdom inherited from the past.

It may be objected that Burke's argument is circular. The privileges of the upper classes are justified by a superiority which is itself admitted to be largely, if not entirely, an effect of these privileges. This objection can, I think, be met. First, there is the obvious point that society may not be rich enough to provide these privileges to more than a minority; and yet it may long have ceased to be so simple as not to need the political skills and other qualities which these privileges produce. There is also another argument, subtler and perhaps true, which Burke rather hints at than puts into plain words. He speaks at times as if some of the qualities that make for good government are produced only by a sense of being raised above other people, not by merit, but by birth – as if, even in a society rich enough to educate all its members about as well as the upper classes were educated in his time, these qualities would not exist unless there were an hereditary aristocracy. I may be foisting on Burke an opinion he never had. It is difficult to be quite sure, because he took it for granted that there are in all societies great social inequalities, so that the privileged everywhere owe their privileges more to inheritance than to talent. He never envisaged a society wealthy enough to provide all its members with the amenities and education which the upper classes had in his day, and therefore never really put the question whether even a society of that kind would be the better for having a class with inherited privileges. Nevertheless, my impression is that, if he had put the question, he would have answered it by saying 'Yes'. I suspect that he believed that some of the qualities making for good government are hardly ever to be found except among those who from childhood have been used to thinking of themselves as belonging to a superior class. This belief is peculiarly distasteful to radicals. They often willingly admit that inherited privileges may be desirable in a society lacking the means of providing everyone with a good education and a comfortable living; but the idea that they may be valuable in all societies, no matter how great their resources, is repulsive to them.

2. The Weak Points in Burke's Arguments

I have already conceded that Burke was right in saying that revolutionaries are often reckless and blind. But what exactly is the point of this charge against them? Who is the warning addressed to? Is it to the revolutionaries themselves? If it is, they will certainly not listen; for if they did listen they would not be the stuff that revolutionaries are made of. They are determined to get power, and will not be stopped in their attempt to get it by doubts about their ability to make good use of it. Is the warning then addressed to the people generally? But revolutions happen at times when the people are in no position to choose their rulers. Only when the structure of authority is breaking down do revolutionaries get their chance. They do not create the situations in which they act. They do not make their chances; they only take them. It is less important to expose the reckless folly of revolutionaries than to discover why the structure of authority is breaking down. Yet this is a question to which Burke scarcely puts his mind.

Again, just what is the point of calling revolutions 'destructive'? All social change involves destruction in one sense. It does more than add to what is already there; it also puts an end to some things to make way for others. If what it makes way for is better than what it puts an end to, it is pointless to call it destructive; and this is as true of violent or illegal (that is, revolutionary) change as of legal reform. No doubt, violence is painful; and peaceful change is nearly always to be preferred to violent change. But what if the change can only be made by violence?

If what comes after a revolution is more acceptable to the people generally than what went before, the revolution is more constructive than destructive. And it may be constructive even though revolutionaries are reckless and blind. It may remedy the grievances that gave birth to it; or else it may, without doing this, so change the aspirations and ideas of the people that they come to like what the revolution has produced, though to begin with they neither desired nor imagined it. Let us consider examples.

If we look at the course of events in France from May 1789, when the Estates-General met for the first time since 1614, until Robespierre's fall in July 1794, we see very little consistency of purpose or foresight among the men who ruled the country; we see one group of inexperienced and excited men giving way to another, with scarcely any of them having time and quiet enough to make up their minds what to do; we see far-reaching decisions taken on the spur of the moment; we see France almost as much a prey to reckless violence and blind hatred as she was during the wars of religion in the sixteenth century. Yet the great revolution did for France what the wars of religion never did; it removed long-standing grievances. True, the revolutionaries did not do what Burke said was impossible; they did not reconstruct France as an architect reconstructs an old house, knowing exactly what he is doing and altering it so as to disturb the people inside it as little as possible. But the fact remains that, as a result of what the arrogant and reckless revolutionaries did, the common people got many things they had wanted before the revolution began and still valued after it was over. The task of reconstruction, if reconstruction there were, was left to Napoleon, who reverted in many ways to the methods of the old monarchy. The people were grateful to him for restoring order, but his actual schemes of government meant little to them. What they cared most about, the destruction of old privileges, was the work of the revolution.

Not all revolutions accomplish even this much. Sometimes popular grievances are used to get power, and nothing is done to remedy them. Sometimes, through the actions of reckless and unscrupulous men who never see more than a move or two ahead, society is changed into something that no one foresaw and nobody wanted. But this is not, as Burke would have us believe, the *inevitable* character of every revolution merely because revolutionary leaders, hurried along by a course of events beyond their power to control, are mostly blind, except to the immediate chance. The longer views and the tasks of deliberate reconstruction belong, if to anyone, to the leaders of the post-revolutionary epoch, when a solid apparatus of power exists once more.

The grievances that bring about a revolution may not be remedied, and yet the social order which emerges from it may come to be more generally acceptable than was the social order destroyed by it. A deep and violent revolution, however blind its leaders, in changing society may also change men's ambitions and preferences in such a way that they come to value what the revolution has produced, though they never wanted it before it began. If we look at the dissatisfied classes in Russia in 1917, we can hardly say that the Bolshevik Revolution has remedied their grievances. The peasants wanted to divide the big estates between them; the middle class mostly wanted constitutional government and civil liberties as understood in the West; and the industrial workers wanted to run the factories and share the profits. These classes – between them the great majority of the Russian people in 1917 – never got what they wanted when the revolution was made. Nor did the revolutionaries get what they wanted. True, they got power, but they did not succeed in using it to build the kind of society to which they aspired at the time they took power. Scarcely anyone in 1917 foresaw that Russia would become what she now is; and the few who did foresee it mostly disliked it, condemning the Bolshevik Revolution as premature precisely before they foresaw what it would lead to. Yet it may be that the Russian people of today like what they now have better than the Russians of 1917 liked what they then had. I do not say that it is so; I only say that it may be. Certainly, we cannot prove that it is *not* so merely by showing that the grievances of 1917 have not been remedied and that the men who made the October Revolution had no intention, when they made it, that Russian society should be what it now is. If the Russians are now satisfied with what they have, we can hardly use the arguments of Burke to condemn the Bolshevik Revolution.

Burke attacked the revolutionaries and their friends for being so absurd as to put forward the doctrine of the rights of man. Equality and liberty, taken in the abstract, are empty. In all societies there are some rights which all men have, some respects in which they are equal; and there are rights to which they are strongly attached, and whose loss they would bewail as a loss of freedom.

All this is true, but also, perhaps, beside the point. The revolutionaries were not really concerned to deny it, for it did not affect the claims they were making. They did not demand that everyone, irrespective of age, sex or occupation, should have exactly the same rights; they claimed only that there were some rights which society had not yet granted to all and which all should have. They did not in practice demand unlimited freedom; they understood by freedom some rights which most Frenchmen already enjoyed and some which they did not. As a matter of fact, though Burke did not see it, they wanted to preserve many more rights than they wanted to destroy or to create. Not only conservatives, but radicals and revolutionaries also, are creatures of their age; the plans they make for society are products of their experience in a particular environment. In ways of which they are themselves unconscious, what they can imagine is limited by what they have known. This is even more true of active revolutionaries who catch the ear of the discontented than of utopian dreamers. To conservatives, and perhaps also to themselves, they look like men who aim at reconstructing the entire social order; but their aims are usually narrower than they seem either to their critics or to themselves. Certainly, the aims of the French revolutionaries, especially while Burke was writing the *Reflections* and before the Jacobins came to power, were not nearly as subversive as he made them out to be. The revolutionaries asserted that there were some rights which all men ought to have and which most Frenchmen did not have.

No doubt, they claimed to derive these rights logically from man's nature – his essentially human qualities, his capacity to reason and to make deliberate choices – and therefore called them *the rights of man.* No doubt, too, the securing of these rights entailed larger changes in France than the rebellious Americans had aimed at when they first set up the banner of revolt. But, even if it is true that there are no rights that can be derived logically from man's essentially human qualities, it does not follow that the claims made by the French revolutionaries were invalid. We may reject the arguments used to justify them and still find others to take their place. If there are other arguments in their favour, there is nothing much gained by attacking the particular arguments used by the French to justify them, on the ground that they are 'metaphysical'. Burke's purpose, after all, was to deny that the claims made by the revolutionaries were just; he wanted to do more than merely deny that the arguments used to support those claims by the French revolutionaries were valid. He had himself supported the claims of the American revolutionaries without accepting their arguments.

And what is the point of Burke's objection to *abstract* rights? In what does their *abstractness* consist? In the claim made that they derive logically from man's essential nature or his destiny? But that claim, mistaken though it may be, can be made as easily in favour of established rights as of rights not yet legally recognized; it is not in itself a dangerous claim. Or are rights abstract because they are loosely defined, because it is not made clear precisely what people would get or be allowed to do if they were made legal? If that is a disadvantage, it is easily remedied. New claims are often vague when they first put forward and acquire precision as people set about trying to secure them. It is not their vagueness, moreover, which makes them dangerous. If you confine yourself to saying that everyone should have a living wage, you make a vague and harmless statement. You will probably find rich men agreeing with you as readily as poor men; it is only when you go on to define a living wage as something appreciably more than people are actually getting that your claim begins to frighten the rich and to excite the poor. For centuries before the French Revolution, philosophers had been saying that all men are by nature equal and free. The French revolutionaries were dangerous – or, rather, formidable – precisely because they were not content to repeat these abstract claims, but defined them with at least enough precision to make it clear that, if the claims were to be made good, there would have to be great changes in France. Are we then to call claims *abstract*, however definite they may be, merely because they are claims of a kind not made before? But this would be an abuse of language.

Burke's defence of prescriptive right and prejudice – if we interpret it in the most conservative sense (and that is the sense which his actual words often imply) – forbids, if not all change, then at least most deliberate change. If prescription's being the most solid of titles is taken to mean that old established rights must not be abolished or curtailed, then we may do no more deliberately, by way of legislation, than create new rights which take nothing away from old ones. Old rights may, of course, lapse from disuse, and, as new needs arise, unprecedented claims may come to be made, and, if they are widely recognized, may harden into rights. There can be considerable change though no prescriptive rights and no prejudices are challenged. But not all social change happens in this way. Much of it (except in the most primitive societies) happens because established rights and revered prejudices are openly and deliberately challenged. Wherever there is a legislative function – wherever it is admitted that law can be deliberately made and is not all customary and sacred – prescriptive rights are sometimes abolished or curtailed and prejudices are challenged.

Burke did not exactly deny this. He admitted that reform may be desirable. Nor did he contest the authority of Parliament as it was generally understood in his day. Parliament, in his day as much as in ours, was held to have a prescriptive right to make law; and nobody argued that it lacked any right to make a law which abolished or curtailed long-established rights. No doubt, most people held that Parliament ought to be very reluctant to make such laws, that it ought not to interfere with long-established rights except where it could make a very strong case for doing so. But nobody, not even Burke, denied that Parliament had a prescriptive right to challenge and even to destroy prescriptive rights, and also to aim at goals not compatible with widely received prejudices. We may say, therefore, that Burke's defence of prescriptive right and prejudice, taken literally, is not consistent either with his own admission that reform may be desirable or with the sovereignty of Parliament which he did not contest. If prescription's being the most solid of all titles is taken to mean that it must be preferred to any title created deliberately, then it is not only wrong to abolish or abridge old established rights illegally or unconstitutionally; it is also wrong to abolish or abridge them legally or constitutionally. There can be no prescriptive right to challenge and destroy prescriptive rights, and Parliament, even as Burke knew and cherished it, becomes a body claiming an authority it does not rightfully possess.

According to this strange doctrine, it is always wrong to aim at social change. We must not strive for it, but must only let it happen. It must result, not from legislation, but from what men do when they do not intend to change the social order. As a result of their activities their situation changes. They acquire needs they did not have before, and they cease to have needs they once had. They make new claims, and they cease making old ones. New rights come into being and old ones disappear; but in all this there is no challenging or destroying of prescriptive rights, no conscious or deliberate making of law.

Now, it may be objected that this is an absurd doctrine, and one to which Burke never adhered. That is certainly true. But it is a doctrine which follows from some of his arguments in favour of prescription and prejudice; he did sometimes speak as if a right's being long established were sufficient evidence of its being useful, and as if prejudice were always a better guide to conduct than reasoned argument.

Burke set a moral, not a legal, limit to Parliament's authority. He wanted only moderate reform, and was opposed to any attempt to make a large social or political change. But he was apt to forget that even moderate reform often involves destroying some old-established rights to which those who have them are deeply attached, and challenging some venerable prejudices still widely cherished. The call for even moderate reform finds a response because new needs have arisen and have moved men to make new claims. Being moderate, the reform can be made without interfering with many established rights or challenging many prejudices.

But those who have the prescriptive right (as the king had in France) to make reforms may refuse or neglect to make them. One demand for reform after another may be ignored or refused until nothing less than a drastic change in the entire social system will satisfy any but the privileged classes. If that happens, there is a revolutionary situation which nothing can alleviate except drastic change; and this change, if it is not made according to law, will be made in defiance of it.

It does not really make sense to allow deliberate change when it is moderate, as Burke does, and to forbid it when it is drastic. It would make sense only in a world in which reforms are always made in good time, so that there is never a large volume of pent-up demand to be satisfied. Burke had no good reason to believe that he lived in such a world. It is one thing to say that reform ought to be timely and moderate; it is quite another to forbid drastic reforms in a world in which reform is not always, or even usually, timely and moderate. Burke's defence of prescription and prejudice, if we take it literally, forbids all deliberate reform of the social and political system. But this Burke did not know, and he therefore allowed moderate reform. He did not see that, given that conditions change and that reform is necessary, there is no good reason why reform should always be moderate and never drastic, unless it is always timely – which it very obviously is not.

What is Burke saying in favour of prescriptive rights when he says that age is a proof of their utility? Just what are they useful for? For maintaining the social order? But they are part of that order. To say that they are useful for that purpose is really only to say that if the whole system of rights is to remain what it is, no part of it must be changed. So much is obvious, and nobody will dispute it. It is also irrelevant when the question at issue is: Shall we or shall we not change the system? Or is the proved utility of long-established rights merely their making for happiness or well-being? No doubt, they have seemed worth having to the persons that had them, or else they would not have survived so long. But their long survival does not prove that they ever were, or now are, useful to the whole community – that even those who do not have them are the better off for their existence. They may easily be worse off. Of course, it can often be shown that rights which only a few persons enjoy are useful to everyone; but this cannot be done merely by pointing to their age. When privileges come to be challenged by the unprivileged, why is the challenge not as much evidence that they are harmful to the challengers as their long survival is evidence that they are useful to the privileged? It may well be that in neither case is the evidence sufficient. The unprivileged may sometimes fail to see what they have to gain by the existence of rights which they do not share, just as the privileged may cling from sheer habit to rights they would be better without. But why should we assume that the first situation is more likely than the second?

A man is happy, I take it, when he leads the kind of life he wants to lead. If he cannot lead it, he is unhappy and feels he is getting less than his due or less than is worth having. His conception of a life worth living depends on his standards, moral and aesthetic. If society seems to him so organized as to prevent his getting what he wants, he will want to change it. If that is his mood, it is no good telling him that the rights he already has make for his happiness. They would only make for it if his idea of a worthwhile life were in keeping with his rights. But it is not; and therefore he lacks some of the rights he needs to give him his chance of happiness. It may also be that other people's privileges stand in his way. Perhaps his ancestors, who thought and felt differently, were satisfied with their established rights and were not resentful of privileges they did not share. But what is that to him, and to others like him? If the usefulness of rights is their making for happiness, and if people's happiness depends largely on their living what seems to them a worthwhile life, how can established rights be generally useful if they conflict with many people's conceptions of what is desirable? And does it matter how recently those conceptions have been acquired?

Of course, ideals may be beyond attainment. Society may lack the resources needed to give people what they want, or people may not know how to set about getting what they want. In so far as Burke was saying to radicals and revolutionaries, 'Do not ask for more than it is possible to get!, Be sure you really know what you want and how to get it!, Move carefully, because otherwise you may come to regret the disappearance of many things that now seem worthless or harmful to you, or because you may find that much of what you get is not worth having!', he was giving good advice. But the advice does not stand or fall with the principle that long-established rights, by their mere survival, have proved their utility.

Burke failed to see that ideals and abstract theories have a social function just as much as what he called prejudice. He wanted to discover what makes institutions stable, what moves people to behave in established ways. He found a large part of the answer in prejudice. Though he knew that institutions change, and even believed in progress (and therefore admitted that change can be good), he never tried to explain how change comes about. If he had tried, it might have occurred to him that what he called 'metaphysical' doctrines have an important social function. They can, like prejudice, serve to maintain the existing social order, established institutions and prescriptive rights; they can be conservative. But, unlike prejudice, they can also be used to condemn that order and to justify reform.

It is idle to object to them, as Burke did, on the ground that they are empty or false. These theories are not primarily descriptive but prescriptive; it is less important to discover whether they are true or false than how they arose and what they lead to. No doubt, they ought to be subjected to criticism, and to criticism of two kinds: academic and practical. Since they often claim to be descriptive, it is worthwhile enquiring how much truth there is in them, especially when they have wide currency; because how people think about society affects the claims they make on it. It is also worthwhile investigating these theories for another reason. Social and political theorists have not been the least important among the creators of the current language of politics, and by looking carefully and critically at their theories, we get to understand that language better and to see how far it is adequate to describe political and social facts. But the really important criticism of social theories, when they are influential, is practical. We must ask, What do they require us to do? How far are the demands they make upon us compatible with one another? How far are we able or willing to go towards meeting them? If we try to show that the theories misinterpret the facts, it is largely because we know that the demands they make are intimately connected with the accounts they give of society. By showing that these accounts are false, we can often go a long way towards showing that the demands are unreasonable.

Man is a theorizing as well as a prejudiced animal. Social and political theories, conservative and radical, are an important part of history. Though they are systems with often a great deal of fantasy to them, especially when they are radical, they cannot be dismissed as the aberrations of cranks. Especially not, if we admit, as Burke does, not only that there has been change, but that it has, on the whole, under Divine Providence, been for the better. We must ask: How does social change take place? How are established ways altered? No doubt, as wealth and knowledge accumulate, institutions inevitably change, and so, too, do prejudices. But new prejudices do not arise directly out of institutions without any need for deliberate thought. How can old prejudices be discarded and new ones take their place, if men must rely, as Burke would have them do, on what he calls 'the general bank and capital of nations, and of ages' – if they must rely

117

entirely on established opinions about what is proper behaviour and what claims are allowable?

Burke suggests that progress is made through the remedy of 'proved abuses'. But we cannot get social change merely by the remedy of such abuses. At least not unless a 'proved abuse' is something which does not accord with Burke's account of prejudice and prescription. If a proved abuse does no more than violate established rights or offend against current prejudices, to remedy it is to restore the situation as it was before the abuse emerged. In that case, the more successfully abuses are remedied, the less society changes. It is only if we allow that practices which used not to be considered abuses may come to be so considered because they offend against new standards, that we can explain social change as the cumulative effect of putting an end to abuses.

Burke makes a tacit and doubtful assumption which is at the root of many of his attacks on the French Revolution. Without saying so in so many words, he takes it for granted that the institutions of a great country like France are all compatible with one another and are also in harmony with a mutually consistent set of prejudices. There may be lesser maladjustments, but none that go deep. A great society develops, according to this view of it, much as a physical organism does; its parts change continually but always in ways that leave them about as well adjusted to one another as they were before. Since there can be only lesser social maladjustments, there need be only modest reforms. Over a long period of time there may be great changes, but they are only the sum of many small ones. The small changes are made by men as they deal, one after another, with problems not too large and intricate for them to solve; and the whole course of change is controlled, not by them, but by a God who in His goodness wills the happiness of His creatures.

That the whole course of social change is not controlled by man is, I take it, obvious. No one, I suppose, would want to take issue with Burke here. Whether that course is controlled by God is another matter, which the social theorist is not competent to decide. But Burke's tacit assumption that all things social form an harmonious whole is surely quite gratuitous. He seems to have believed that, because all aspects of social life affect one another and change continuously, they must be well suited to each other, so that no really deep-seated tensions and conflicts can arise in the mere course of social development. Institutions and prejudices grow together and so must be mutually compatible.

But a large society consists of many smaller groups, and each of these, though moved by outside pressures, also changes by reason of what people do inside it. The lesser groups, for all that they continually affect one another, may nevertheless change in ways that bring them into conflict. The mere fact that change is continuous everywhere, and that there is always the pressure of group on group, is not of itself enough to maintain harmony. Yet to Burke it seemed evident that, because the social process is intricate and endless, everything involved in it must be fairly well adjusted to everything else, just as the tides smooth the stones on the beach till they all lie comfortably together. It seemed to him that perpetual interaction between the parts must make the whole harmonious. Yet it clearly need not do so, any more in a large society like France than in a small family. True, all the lesser communities, and all the classes, trades and professions, that make up France would not now be what they are if they had not been connected for centuries in the special ways that make them all parts of a unique community. They are tied to one another by an infinity of bonds, most of them invisible. No country in the world has a stronger individuality than France. Yet France is today, as she was when Burke wrote his *Reflections*, a country divided against herself.

Burke would have us believe that France was divided because of the evil influence on her of the philosophers and revolutionaries, who destroyed venerable prejudices, the cement of French society. But why did anyone listen to them? Why were their theories convincing and their denunciations exciting? What other explanation could there be but that French institutions and prejudices were not all well suited to one another – that there were profound conflicts of interest? When everything works smoothly, most people care little or nothing for what philosophers and theorists have to say; they begin to take notice of them only when things go wrong, and they are looking around for explanations and solutions. It is because there is disharmony, either among institutions or between them and current beliefs about what is desirable, that men are inspired to make social theories and to listen to them. And in their turn, these theories work on their minds, exacerbating the tensions and conflicts that gave birth to them. They undoubtedly cause trouble; Burke was right to that extent. But they are also salutary. Whether or not they go on to condemn the social order, they are attempts to understand it. They do not just make people angry and destructive; they inspire thought and deliberate action.

True, more often than not, they are lamentably inadequate. This inadequacy can be dangerous, but need not be so. If the champions of a single theory get a monopoly of power, they can do great damage, not only by causing much suffering but by doing violence to commonly received notions of justice. If, however, the champions of no one theory engross all power; if all theories are continually challenged and criticized, they need not be dangerous and can do much good. In any but a static or very slowly changing society, social and political theories are indispensable. Not because any one of them explains society adequately or can be used exclusively to control its development, but because between them they help us to understand society and also to formulate the ideals which inspire us to reform it.

Burke treats social and political theories as if they were somehow external to the course of social change – as if the course would be slow and smooth, except for the influence upon it of perverse theories. But these theories are as much a part of the course of social change as anything else involved in it. In Burke's time the world changed more slowly than it does now. Still, if he had cared to look, he could have found examples of rapid change. Invasion and foreign rule, which are always disruptive of established rights and prejudices, were as common then as they are now. Before he attacked the French revolutionaries, Burke had attacked Warren Hastings. Did he never reflect on what was happening in India as a result of the sudden irruption into Indian affairs of Europeans whose prejudices, moral and political, differed so widely from India's? Why was India so easy a prey to the European conqueror? If India had been a well-regulated society, if her institutions and prejudices had been finely adjusted to one another, if she had had an effective system of government, the Europeans might never have got their opportunities. What were the Europeans to do in India? Let her alone? If they had chosen to do that, they would have had to leave. They chose instead to make their power effective, and could do so only by making great and rapid changes in India.

Successful revolutionaries are like an invading army whose easy conquest of a country is due, not to superior numbers or better weapons, but to their victim's being a prey to anarchy. Revolutionaries do not take over a going concern; they cannot use the methods of their predecessors. They are faced with urgent problems that require drastic solutions. If they have not made up their minds beforehand what to do, they must improvise. It is pointless to condemn their lack of deep wisdom and keen foresight; they have grasped power from nerveless hands, and cannot hope to keep it except by making large changes quickly. That is not to say, of course, that they are blameless whatever they do; it is only to say that they cannot be blamed merely for taking large and drastic action.

Even a government which has not seized power by violence may have to take drastic action to prevent revolution – as, for instance, Nehru sought to do in India. Though the English brought Western influences to India, and so created new and tremendous problems for her, there were many great and necessary changes which they probably could not have undertaken (even if they had been willing to do so) merely because they were foreigners. It remains for the Indians themselves to undertake them. If they can take thought beforehand, making the changes rapidly and yet also deliberately and carefully, so much the better for them. But that is an opportunity not given to everyone, and especially not to revolutionaries who get power in a disintegrating society.

Burke's conception of society, as a well-integrated whole with long-established institutions supported by venerable prejudices, made it impossible for him to give a convincing explanation of anarchy and revolution. If his conception is true, it must be wrong for any government, even if it has taken power legally, to attempt rapid and far-reaching change. Burke had no alternative but to set France's troubles down to the influence of false and pretentious theories. France had a history as long as England's; her institutions must therefore have been well suited to her needs, and must have been supported by prejudices worthy of respect. If Burke had allowed that the opposite might be true – that the influence of the philosophers and revolutionaries might be as much an effect as a cause of France's troubles – he would have had to revise his ideas about society and social change. He could not understand the French Revolution; his assumptions forbade his doing so. If what has long existed is thereby proved useful, and if things that have long existed together always form a well-adjusted whole, the French revolutionaries, in their attempt to refashion French society, must have been destroying what was, despite surface appearances, an harmonious social order. On Burke's assumptions, only a revolution of the kind made by the Whigs in 1688, a neat and effective but modest tilting of the balance between long-established powers, is ever desirable – or, indeed, intelligible. Anything else, anything like a deep and rapid transformation of society, cannot be explained – at least not satisfactorily. Burke's account of the French Revolution is in some ways ludicrously inadequate. It is as if we were to say that a ship at sea were storm-tossed because some mutinous sailors on board were troubling the waters. To attribute so much power to the wicked is to do them too much honour. A well-ordered and peaceful France could not have been disturbed so profoundly by nothing but arrogance and ill-will. The revolutionaries were life-sized Frenchmen in a deeply-troubled France; they were not Gullivers moving recklessly across Lilliput.

Society, according to Burke, is the work of God's hands; and so he speaks as if persons who aspire greatly to change society are guilty of impiety. But what is society except the living together of men? If God works on society, He does so, presumably, through men. Revolutionaries and theorists are as much men and members of society as are the conservative and the prejudiced. How could Burke know that they are never instruments of God's will? Or that, if they are, they are so only as scourges?

How different are the theories that different men build on similar foundations! Marx, though an atheist, was as certain as Burke that men do not make society and often scarcely understand it, but are carried along on a course of events beyond their control. He too believed that men acquire their needs, interests and moral prejudices as they grow up to be adult members of society. He too envisaged society as an organic whole, the product of a long evolution. But he described that evolution as a series of conflicts, and put together a theory of social progress which not only allowed for revolution but required it. Far from denouncing philosophers and revolutionaries as disturbers of the peace, moved by envy, vanity and ambition, he explained their activities as a necessary and important part of the historical process.

CHAPTER FOUR

Rousseau

Rousseau was much more than a political theorist; he also wrote about religion and education, and his novel, *La Nouvelle Héloïse*, was received with greater enthusiasm than any other published in the eighteenth century. Yet everything he wrote is, in one way or another, related to his social and political philosophy; he was one of the most self-absorbed and emotional of writers, and his political and social theories are deeply affected by his personal difficulties, by his eccentricities and hatreds. What Rousseau wanted was a world fit for himself to live in, a Heaven fit for himself to go to, and a God worthy of his love. Nobody who spoke so often of man in the abstract gives so strong an impression that he is speaking always of himself. Rousseau thought of himself as the most human of human beings, unique and yet typical, containing in himself, more purely and intensely than other men, the essence of man. In a short essay addressed to his friend Charles Bordes, he remarked, 'Man is naturally good. . .as I have the happiness to feel'.[1]

Rousseau was a *philosophe* and an enemy of philosophy, a rationalist and a romantic, a sensualist and a puritan, an apologist for religion who attacked dogma and denied original sin, an admirer of the natural and uninhibited and the author of an absolutist theory of the State. Goethe is alleged to have said that with Voltaire one epoch ends and with Rousseau another begins. Nobody in the eighteenth century conceived as many ideas and struck as many attitudes that caught on with later generations. His book on education, *Emile*, has been called the best of its kind since Plato's *Republic*. It contains the 'Profession of Faith of the Savoyard Vicar', which, condemned by

---

[1] 'Dernière réponse', in the *Oeuvres complètes de Rousseau*, Pléiade edition (Paris 1959–), vol. III, p. 80n.

Catholic bishops and Protestant pastors, converted many people to an exalted, vague, undogmatic and comfortable religion, much less open than orthodox Christianity to attack from the sceptical philosophers. His *Project of a Constitution for Corsica* and his *Considerations on the Government of Poland* show how moderate, ingenious and practical he could be; they also reveal to us a Rousseau uttering sentiments that might have come from Burke.

I shall confine myself to Rousseau's political philosophy, and even then shall take notice only of its more important aspects. I shall discuss only his account of the state of nature and of the origin of actual societies and states; his belief in man's natural goodness; his conception of a general will; and what he understood by equality. The first is to be found in the *Discourse on Inequality*; the second mostly in *Emile*, though several of his other books and essays throw light upon it; the third in the article on 'Political Economy' published in Diderot's *Encyclopaedia* and in the two drafts of the *Social Contract*; and the fourth in his political writings generally.

I. THE STATE OF NATURE AND THE ORIGIN OF ACTUAL STATES

Rousseau knew how difficult it must be for a man like himself, formed by society, to imagine what a man who had never lived in society might be like. If men ever lived outside society (and Rousseau sometimes seems to take it for granted that they once did so), society must altogether have changed them. He says, in the preface to the *Discourse on Inequality*, that 'like the statue of Glaucus, ravaged by time, the sea and storms, until it looked less like a God than a wild beast, the human soul, altered in the bosom of society by a thousand causes. . .has, so to speak, changed so much that it almost cannot be known'.[1] What he means, of course, is the human soul in its imagined primitive state before society has formed it; that is what cannot be known.

Rousseau begins by admitting that what he would like to discover is not to be certainly known; but he thinks it worthwhile, if we are to understand what society does to man, to try to reconstruct (though the attempt can be no more than plausible conjecture) man's pre-social past. Rousseau says it is absurd to talk (as so many philosophers have done) of man's deliberately creating society in the light of what

[1] *Discours sur l'inégalité*, preface, ibid., p. 122.

have been called 'laws of nature' – principles of conduct supposed
to be known to man by the use of his reason even before he enters
society. Philosophers have always disagreed about these laws; and
their disagreements are evidence that there can be no such laws –
laws supposed to be so simple and obvious that any sane man can
understand them. What the disputing philosophers have proved is
not that there are such laws, but that, if there were any, only the
most subtle reasoners could know them. Men could not have set up
society the better to enforce principles which only a few of them are
capable of understanding even after society has civilized them.

Rousseau's argument is not entirely convincing. There are different
levels of understanding. We are sometimes said to understand something when we can define or describe it correctly, but this is clearly
not the kind of understanding we usually have in mind when we say
that a man understands moral rules. To understand them, he need not
know how to define them; he need only know how to behave. You
cannot prove that there are no principles which have always been
accepted by men, in society and outside it, merely by showing that
philosophers have never ceased arguing about how such principles
should be defined.

But this objection is not really important. What is important
is Rousseau's putting forward an idea commonly ignored by his
predecessors: that man becomes a moral being only in the process of
adapting himself to life in society. Hobbes had, I think, an inkling of
this idea, but no more than that. Hume put it forward as emphatically
as, and more lucidly than, Rousseau; but he understood it differently.

When we say that there is no morality outside society, we may mean
only that men have no rights and duties except against and towards
one another, so that completely solitary men would need to follow
no rules except maxims of prudence; we may mean that there is no
scope for morality, no point to it, except among men who come into
contact with one another. In that sense, Robinson Crusoe, alone on
his island, had no rights or obligations. Or we may mean that it
is only in the process of living together in society that men come
to conceive of themselves as having rights and duties, that they
develop the capacities which make moral persons of them. Hume
and Rousseau meant the second and not merely the first; they believed
that it is by living together in society that men learn to make claims
upon one another and acquire the sentiments which make them respect
these claims. Hume, indeed, kept to this position more consistently
than Rousseau did; for Rousseau also sometimes spoke, as Locke had
done, as if man unformed by society could be moral. Rousseau, as we

shall see, was not quick at drawing the implications of any position he took up. He was attracted by new ideas, and was himself at times an innovator; but he often did not discard old ideas incompatible with the new ones. Since he cared little for logical consistency, he felt no need to do so.

But Rousseau also meant something more than Hume when he said that men become moral in society. Hume meant only that social experience teaches them what kinds of behaviour are beneficial or harmful, and that the habits of approval and disapproval which encourage and discourage this behaviour are acquired in society. He admitted that in society we acquire desires and preferences we would not have outside it; but that is as far as he went. He always spoke of moral rules as if they were rules of efficiency – as if their essential function were to enable us to pursue our ends more successfully than we otherwise could. He did not ask himself to what extent the ends we pursue in society are what they are because they are the ends of moral creatures.

Rousseau spoke of our being 'transformed' by society, of our being so deeply affected by it that it is almost impossible to guess what we should be like outside it. We are altogether different creatures for being social and moral; we pursue ends which it is inconceivable we should pursue unless we were moral. The rules of morality are not mere rules of efficiency; they do not make it easier for us to get what we might want even if they did not exist. As moral beings, as creatures who conceive of rights and duties, who have a sense of values, we are psychologically profoundly different from what we should be without this conception and this sense. Moral rules are not therefore rules which experience teaches us are in the general interest, in the sense that they make it easier for us to get what we want; the ends pursued by a moral being are different in kind from those of that entirely imaginary creature – 'natural' or pre-social man. The happiness of a moral being does not consist in the satisfaction of one appetite or desire after another; it is not what Hobbes understood by felicity. It is living in proper relations with others and with oneself; it is the happiness of a self-conscious creature[1] who does not live

---

[1] Rousseau does not use the words 'self-consciousness' and 'self-conscious' as the German Idealists were to do. He does, however, speak of the feelings that we have for ourselves and for other people as feelings acquired in society. They are feelings that come of our comparing ourselves with others and of our being helped or frustrated by them. They are passions quite different from the natural appetites. They are feelings for or about persons. They involve self-consciousness, and Rousseau sees that they do, though he does not use the word as freely as it came to be used afterwards.

from hand to mouth but feels the need to live a worthwhile life. These proper relations are relations only possible between creatures that are self-conscious and moral. I shall say more later about how Rousseau conceived of them, when I discuss his doctrine that man is by nature good.

Man in the state of nature, potentially rational but making small use of reason, is neither good nor evil. 'Hobbes', said Rousseau – (and Hobbes, like Rousseau, supposed that men in the state of nature were solitary and brutish, i.e. like the other animals) – 'Hobbes did not see that the same cause that prevents savages from using their reason. . .prevents them from abusing their faculties. . . . So that we can say that savages are not evil precisely because they do not know what it is to be good; for it is neither the development of knowledge nor the restraint of law but their calm passions and ignorance of vice that prevent them from doing evil'.[1] Men in the state of nature are not quarrelsome and have no desire to dominate one another; they are solitary, unreflecting and easily satisfied; they have no vanity; they have no self-consciousness and no opinion of themselves, and are therefore not governed in what they do by the desire to be well thought of by others. Jealousy, envy, the desire for vengeance, all the emotions produced by vanity, by the desire to please and be admired, are unknown to the quite primitive and unsocial man. While men are in the state of nature, there is neither education, nor progress, nor speech; the generations succeed one another, and men are no different from their ancestors. There is no enduring inequality, for whatever differences there are between men are without social significance.

It was, suggests Rousseau, probably growth in numbers that first brought men together into society. They could no longer live isolated, meeting only by chance or under the urge of their sexual appetites. Sometime or other, somewhere or other, for reasons that Rousseau admits he cannot know, there were more men than could easily keep themselves alive in the ways common to all wild animals; but precisely because men are not like the other animals but are intelligent and resourceful, they could adapt themselves to their altered condition. They could change their manner of life. At first, they needed to unite their efforts only occasionally; but as their power to satisfy their wants increased, so too did those wants. Men began to live in families; and, gradually, when several families had congregated together, they formed societies. They acquired speech, and with it the power to accumulate knowledge and pass it on to their children. They grew

[1] *Discours sur l'inégalité*, op. cit., p. 154.

affectionate, anxious to please, to be admired, to be thought better or more formidable than other people. They acquired customs and common standards of beauty and merit.

At that stage of man's development, the family was still more or less self-sufficient, producing the greater part of what it needed. Of course, all social intercourse creates other than material needs, making men dependent on one another for company, esteem and affection; but as long as families were largely self-supporting, this kind of dependence did not create social inequalities. What inequalities did exist were not so much between families as inside them, where children depended for survival on the care of their parents. This kind of dependence does not, however, have the harmful social effects of some other kinds, because the members of a family are commonly united, at least while the children are small, by strong affections. This dependence is natural and temporary: natural because children are incapable of fending for themselves, and temporary because it ceases as soon as the incapacity ends.

While the heads of families were hunters and fishermen, they worked together only now and then; most of the time, catching or finding food and other necessities for themselves, their wives and their children, they worked separately and fitfully. Even when they had to work together, their collaboration was simple and required little or no subordination among them. They needed few possessions: their huts and their weapons were enough. This, according to Rousseau, was the happiest period of mankind's social development; for men had by that time acquired language, and their frequent association had sharpened their wits and quickened their hearts. They had no fixed laws but were already creatures of custom; they had common notions of merit and beauty; they were capable of vanity and envy, but also of love, loyalty and the desire to please – feelings unknown to the lonely savage. They had become moral, and their goodness (when they were good) differed in kind from that of natural man. This was the happy age when society already existed but men had not yet become the tools or victims of other men.

It was when they ceased to be hunters and fishermen – when they passed to a predominantly *agricultural economy*, when they learnt to extract metals and to use them – that grown men became, not merely occasionally, but permanently, dependent on one another for much more than the pleasures and affections of society. When land came to be cultivated, it had to be divided; and crops, unlike the produce of the chase, were not quickly perishable. With continuity of possession and the accumulation of wealth, natural differences in strength and intelligence enabled some men to prosper more than others and to pass on their wealth to their children. These inequalities in their turn created greater opportunities for the prosperous than the unprosperous; and the greater the inequality between men, the more the rich sought to dominate the poor and the poor were filled with resentment and envy. Many of the poor consented to become the servants or clients of the rich, while others preferred to live by plundering them. There followed insecurity and violence, dangerous to both rich and poor, though more dangerous to the rich. It was then that some rich man bethought himself of a device from which all men would profit, but the rich more than the poor. He suggested that men should set up over themselves some power to govern them by wise laws, to protect them from each other, and to defend them against their common enemies. His suggestion was universally approved, and political society was at last established. Rousseau agrees with Locke that government was instituted to protect property, but takes care to add: and especially to protect the property of the rich! There is no property, moreover, in the state of nature, because it is only creatures formed by society who can conceive of rights and obligations, and therefore of rules of property.

In a fragment on *The State of War*, probably written at about the same time as the second *Discourse*, Rousseau says that man 'is naturally peaceful and timid; and at the least danger his first impulse is to flee; he only becomes warlike by dint of habit and experience. Honour, interest, prejudice, revenge, all the passions that can make him brave danger and death, are foreign to him in the state of nature. It is only after he has formed a society with some man that he decides to attack another; and he becomes a soldier only after he has been a citizen'.[1] The war of all against all is therefore not, as Hobbes said it was, the condition of man in the state of nature; it is, like the other vices and horrors that Hobbes attributed to solitary and brutish man, a product of society. It is communities and not isolated men that are prone to aggression. The war of all against all, which caused men, so Hobbes tells us, to submit to government in order to put an end to it, is not man's condition outside political society; it is much nearer being the condition of sovereign States in their relations to one another.

The fragment on *The State of War* does not quite square with the *Discourse on Inequality*. In the *Fragment*, Rousseau argues that man is a soldier only because he is a citizen – that war is a relation that can subsist only between organized communities or 'public persons', as

---

[1] 'L'État de guerre', *Oeuvres complètes*, vol. III, pp. 601–2.

he calls them. To claim that one man is at war with another is, he says, strictly speaking, a misuse of language. He is also trying to show how it is that man as a social creature becomes quarrelsome. Though this second argument is different from the first, Rousseau runs the two together. Man, he says, becomes the rival and enemy of other men in society, because it is there that he acquires the passions which incline him to aggression; and he also says that the war of all against all is the condition of sovereign States. The connection between these two statements is not made clear. Are States inclined to war because society makes men quarrelsome? That, perhaps, was what Rousseau meant in *The State of War*. But in the *Discourse on Inequality* he is not thinking of relations between States. He imagines a state of anarchy almost as dreadful as Hobbes's war of all against all. It is not, however, the state of nature, but man's social condition just before the establishment of government; it is an effect of social inequalities, of anxiety and arrogance in the rich, of envy and covetousness in the poor. It is the social relations in which men stand to one another which make them rich and poor, and which also give birth to aggressive passions in them. They then set up the State to protect themselves from these passions.

I shall not criticize in detail Rousseau's account of the state of nature and of man's slow progress, through different forms of society, from solitude to the State. I think it an ingenious theory, a better effort at the imaginative reconstruction of the past than any other made in the eighteenth century. The weakest part of it seems to me the account of how the State was at last established. If the rich were really in danger from the poor, why did they not band together and establish a joint ascendancy over the poor? Where was the need to set up government by deliberate agreement with the poor? Or must we suppose, as Rousseau does, that the rich were as suspicious and aggressive towards each other as the poor were towards them. How, then, did they continue to be rich? To keep his wealth, to secure his property, where there is no government, the rich man must have retainers dependent on him. He and his retainers must, therefore, form some kind of rudimentary society together, in which he is the master. If he is in danger, it must be either from other rich men, who also have their retainers, or from the unrestrained poor, who can only be formidable when banded together. That is to say, there can be no great inequalities unless there are already organized communities of some kind (for example, large households) to protect the rich; and the poor can never be really formidable to the rich unless they, too, are organized. None of these communities, these large households, is established by contract. Why, then, should not the State grow out of them slowly and imperceptibly? Whence the need of a deliberate agreement to set up the State? To bring the contract in this way into a long account of how man became a social animal – an account which up to that point has described a course of development uncontrolled by deliberate human purposes – is a crude device; and it is also unnecessary, for it explains nothing that could not be better explained without it. The essential purpose of the contract in political theory is to explain political obligation. But the contract of the *Discourse on Inequality* has no such purpose. It is altogether out of place. In this respect it is quite different from the contract as elaborated in the *Social Contract*, which is used to explain the rights and duties of citizens.

What conclusions can we draw from what Rousseau tells us in the *Discourse on Inequality* about the state of nature and man's social development? They are, I think, the following: (1) that man, if ever he lived outside society (and Rousseau seems inclined to believe that he once probably did), must have been neither morally good nor bad, but without language, and therefore almost as incapable of sustained thought and reasoning as the other animals, improvident, lazy and unaggressive; (2) that neither his reason (for he had not yet learnt to use it) nor his passions and instincts drew man into society, but that, from some cause unknown to us, it being no longer possible for him to get his subsistence alone, he found himself obliged from time to time to work with other men; (3) that, as this collaboration grew closer, he acquired language, and his understanding and emotions developed until he became at last a rational creature capable of morality; (4) that he did not make society or control its development, but passed from stage to stage without understanding the social process in which he was involved; (5) that natural law and natural right, in the traditional sense of the jurists and philosophers, were unknown to him in the state of nature; (6) that, although society alone has made man moral (that is, a creature having a sense of values and recognizing rights and duties), it has made him more inclined to vice than to virtue, and has thus corrupted him; and (7) that this corruption is largely an effect of social inequality, and takes the form of vanity and aggressiveness.

We are not to suppose that Rousseau, because he says that men in the state of nature know nothing of the law of nature, rejects the traditional conception of that law as a moral law which reason teaches us is incumbent on all rational creatures – that he agrees either with Hobbes or with Hume. That he does not agree with Hobbes is obvious. Hobbes's account of the laws of nature does not make them truly moral laws, and he clearly asserts what Rousseau denies – that man can know these laws even in the state of nature. True, Hobbes, whether he calls the laws of nature mere precepts of reason or insists that they are also commanded by God, says that men in the state of nature do not ordinarily have to obey them; but he also says that they can conceive of them in that state, and indeed that they must do so if they are ever to get out of it. Natural man, man unformed by society, is already for Hobbes a rational creature capable of discovering that it would be prudent to follow certain rules if he could be sure that other people would do the same; whereas Rousseau tells us that natural man has no inkling of such rules, and is therefore no more prudent than moral. Natural man lives from hand to mouth, from day to day, forgetting the past and not minding the future, following momentary impulses and appetites that never, or scarcely ever, bring him into conflict with other men.

I have already said that Rousseau, though he agrees with Hume that it is in society that man develops his reasoning powers and also comes to think of himself as having rights and duties, does not treat moral rules as rules of utility. He insists, as Hume does not, that man's nature is transformed by his social environment. There is also another great difference between Hume and Rousseau. What gives to moral rules their moral character is, according to Hume, only how men feel about them or react to them; whereas for Rousseau, as for Locke, they are rules which men ought to obey because they are men. For Rousseau it follows that man, because he has certain capacities, also has certain rights and duties. Man could not know this in the state of nature, but he can know it in society. These capacities are not yet developed in the state of nature; they are so only in society. But once they are developed, man comes to possess certain rights and duties. Rousseau perhaps never knew of Hume's dictum, that we cannot derive an *ought* from an *is*; at least he took no notice of it. Though he was by no means consistent, much more often than not he agreed with the natural law philosophers that the moral law is a law of reason, in the sense that it consists of rules which can be deduced from our being rational creatures.

There is, of course, an obvious connection, which no moralist denies, between man's being rational and his having duties. Man alone among the animals can compare different courses of action and choose one rather than the others; he alone can discriminate between ends and discover the means to them; he alone can apprehend rules and accept or reject them. Even if actions are virtuous and vicious only because of how we feel about them, these feelings, these moral sentiments, are confined to us alone among animals because we alone are capable of abstract thought and deliberate action. It is common ground to believers in natural law and to moralists like Hume, who call morals an 'experimental science', that justice and reason are intimately connected. The experience which Hume says gives birth to justice is essentially the experience of a self-conscious and rational creature. What Hume and believers in natural law differ about is the nature of the connection. For Hume it is causal. The experience of rational creatures living together in a world in which the resources required to satisfy their needs are limited is such as to cause them to conceive of rules of conduct which it is in the common interest should be obeyed, and to have feelings of approval or disapproval towards those who keep or break these rules. For believers in natural law, the connection is logical; for them, it follows logically that because we are rational we ought to be just. Neither the morality of our actions nor the goodness or evil of the motives that inspire us can be explained in terms of our feelings about them or any other kind of reaction to them.

Rousseau agrees with those who believe in natural law and not with Hume. He thinks that, if we consider what is involved in the rationality of man, in his being a self-conscious, deliberate, purposeful creature recognizing the existence of other creatures like himself, we can know how man ought to behave. Man in the state of nature cannot know it, for he is not then in full possession of his reason. It is only in society that he develops to the full the capacities which distinguish him from other animals, and can know and practise the moral law – a law which is eternally valid for all creatures like himself.

Though this is Rousseau's usual position, not everything that he says is compatible with it. He does not, as we shall see later, succeed in squaring his idea of conscience with his account of the law of nature as a law of reason. He sometimes makes a contrast between conscience and reason, and treats the first as the surer guide to morality.

II. MAN'S NATURAL GOODNESS

Sometimes by man's natural goodness Rousseau means the mere innocence of the state of nature, the condition of man before society has made a moral being of him, which is like the condition of Adam before he ate fruit from the tree of knowledge. In proclaiming man's natural goodness in this sense, Rousseau is denying the doctrine of original sin. That is not the natural goodness I want to discuss.

But there is in Rousseau another, and a much more important

and suggestive, sense of natural goodness, which makes it a moral condition of which social man alone is capable. Many thinkers since Rousseau have used the idea of natural goodness, in this sense, or other ideas closely akin to it. They may not have spoken explicitly of natural goodness; they may have preferred to speak of the fully realized self, of the well-balanced mind, of the integrated personality. All these conceptions have their difficulties. Though there are many versions of them, there is a strong family likeness between them, and they all have a great deal in common with what Rousseau understood by man's natural goodness. If, then, we subject his idea to close scrutiny, we discover some of the difficulties inherent in nearly all versions of it. There is no doubting that the idea, in spite of its obscurity, has been enormously attractive. It has had great vitality; it has had as many heads as the hydra. Moral and political philosophers are more sceptical about it than they once were, but psychologists and sociologists still feel the need to use it. It is an idea as old as the Greeks; it is part of the cultural history of Europe. Rousseau brought it to life again at a time when it had long been moribund; and he also gave it its modern character, which owes almost as much to Christianity as to the philosophies of Plato and Aristotle.

Let me begin with a rough definition of Rousseau's version of it. When Rousseau calls man naturally good in the moral sense, he means that there is a form of development of man's natural capacities and passions which enhances his vitality and sense of well-being, and at the same time disposes him to be benevolent and just in all his dealings with other men. If man develops in this way he not only becomes rational and moral; he also achieves true peace of mind, and stable and satisfying relations with other people. Rousseau also believed that there is in every man an indestructible impulse or feeling urging him towards this desirable condition of himself and deflecting him from courses that prevent his attaining it. This feeling or impulse he called *conscience*. Though conscience is indestructible, it is by no means invincible. Indeed, it is ordinarily too weak to prevent our corruption. But it keeps alive in us the sense that we are 'untrue' to ourselves; it is the 'voice of nature' in us.

Now, if man is thus naturally disposed to some condition of himself which is morally good, it might seem that, unless there is some calamity to prevent his doing so, he must become good. It might seem that men, as soon as they come together in society and their faculties are quickened, must become what it is desirable that they should be. For what is society but the living together of men? If men are by nature disposed to goodness, how can society corrupt them? Must we not suppose a calamity or an intervention of the Devil, something to take the place of the story of the Fall of Adam, to explain how what should have gone right none the less went wrong? But Rousseau will have none of it. Man, he says, is *naturally* good and is yet corrupted by society, though society is no more than the living together of men and what follows from it. We have seen how, in the *Discourse on Inequality*, Rousseau describes a *natural*, in the sense of uncontrolled, course of social development which leads to inequalities that cripple and diminish mankind, morally even more than materially. Men are first brought together by the need to satisfy their natural wants, and this coming together starts a train of events which, through no fault of their own and no calamity, both develops and corrupts their faculties. Society, at least, is not naturally good, even if man is so; there is clearly no natural tendency for society to become what it ought to be if men are to attain natural goodness. This conclusion may seem odd, but we are driven to it by Rousseau's own account of the matter. It is only one of several paradoxes, not to say contradictions, in his social and political theory.

To elucidate Rousseau's admittedly vague conception of natural goodness, it is perhaps best to try to find answers to these five questions: (1) What are the natural passions, and how do the passions acquired in society arise out of them? In other words, what is the genealogy of the passions? (2) What constitutes the goodness of good passions, and the evil of evil ones? (3) What is the impulse which Rousseau calls conscience? (4) What conditions must hold if man is to attain goodness? And lastly, (5) What can be done to create these conditions?

1. The Genealogy of the Passions

Unfortunately, Rousseau does not make it really clear what the natural passions are, nor how the social passions arise from them. He gives several accounts which do not square with one another. To pursue all his inconsistencies would be tedious, and I shall attend only to a few – not so much to show how careless he could be as to illustrate some of the difficulties inherent in the notion of natural goodness.

In the *Discourse on Inequality*, Rousseau says that there are two primitive passions, self-love and pity, from which arise all our civilized virtues and vices. He does not, however, say which of these passions gives birth to the virtues and which to the vices, nor yet how, if both are needed to generate them all, some of the effects come to be good and others evil. In *Emile* he usually treats self-love as if it were the only primitive passion. What does he understand by it? Clearly not an emotion like anger or pity or hatred. He does not suppose that a man who has self-love feels for himself what he would feel for somebody else that he loved. By self-love he very probably means, after the fashion of his day, not a passion of the self directed to the self, but all of a man's desires whose object is to satisfy his own needs and not other people's. Self-love thus consists of desires which even a creature lacking self-consciousness, lacking the idea of itself as the subject of its own desires, could have. In this sense of it, a dog has self-love just as much as a man has it.

How, then, does self-love give birth to other passions? It does so when the desires it consists of are either thwarted or favoured; and they may be thwarted or favoured either by natural events or by what other people do or fail to do. Clearly, it is the second of these influences which is much the more important. The child does not know how to fend for itself; it is looked after by adults; it is provided for and disciplined. It is never more completely dependent on others than during the first months of its life, when it is still as nature made it, unformed by society. As the child begins to take stock of its environment, as it comes to see that its wants are satisfied by those who take care of it, as it comes to feel that it is itself an object of affection, it ceases to be merely a creature of natural appetites. It acquires emotions, directed towards itself and others, which create new needs in it. It comes to feel affection and to need it; it learns to compare itself with others. It comes to attach importance to how it stands in the eyes of others and in its own eyes. This comparison of self with others – this self-consciousness, together with the desire to be loved and well thought of and the capacity to love and admire – gives birth to needs less simple and less easily satisfied than the natural appetites. If the child could remain a mere creature of appetite, it might become independent when it grew up, as most animals do. If, in the process of being looked after by others as a helpless infant, man never acquired any needs beyond those he was born with or which came to him merely with physical maturity, he would never become a truly social and moral creature. He would remain in the state of nature; and adult man, in that state, like other fully grown animals, would be independent. It is chiefly because, while he is looked after by others when he still needs care – and so acquires emotions and wants which are not mere effects of becoming physically mature – that he is still dependent on other men when he becomes an adult.

This is what Rousseau tells us, in the second book of *Emile*, either in so many words or by implication. He tells us that self-love, which prompts us to do what we must do to keep alive and healthy, is natural, and that it is the mother of all the social passions. It is by ministering to our self-love when we are still unable to fend for ourselves that those who look after us awaken in us the capacities and emotions which make social beings of us. In helping us to satisfy the needs we get from Nature, they transform our own nature, creating needs in us which can only be satisfied in social life, even when we are adults and no matter how well-endowed by Nature we may be.

Rousseau, though he often calls self-love the mother of *all* the social passions, sometimes also attributes the virtues to self-love and the vices to vanity. But he clearly does not want us to take vanity for a primitive passion, for he says repeatedly that men come to be vain only in society. Since only self-love is primitive, in the sense of being what it would be even if man were not a social creature, vanity must be born of self-love. What, then, is the point of attributing the virtues to self-love and the vices to vanity? Why call the virtues 'natural' because they issue from self-love, and the vices 'unnatural' because they come from vanity, when vanity itself is born of self-love? Is self-love the 'natural' mother of the virtues and the 'unnatural' grandmother of the vices, having somehow brought forth a monstrous daughter who can bear only deformed children? In the social psychology of Rousseau, self-love stands to vanity as God does to the Devil in certain forms of theology; God creates all things, including the Devil, and then leaves all the dirty work to the Devil while His own hands remain clean.

So far, I have been discussing only what Rousseau says in *Emile*. But even if we combine the doctrines of *Emile* and of the *Discourse on Inequality* – even if we suppose that there are two primitive passions, self-love and pity, and that the virtues and vices come from them in the manner described in *Emile* – we are no better off than before. We are no nearer explaining how what is born of self-love is 'natural' and what is born of vanity is not. For the primitive passions, whether they are one or two or more than two, are all *ex hypothesi* equally part of man's pre-social nature; and it is not clear why what issues from one of them should be more or less natural than what issues from another. Besides, Rousseau never says, or even hints at, anything so improbable as that vanity is born of pity. It is clear that, of his two primitive passions, self-love alone could plausibly be said to give birth to vanity.[1]

---

[1] Only in the first of the *Dialogues*, written towards the end of his life, does Rousseau come near to explaining how vanity arises out of self-love. It is not, he says, the strength of our passions but their weakness which makes us corruptible. Our primitive passions keep us alive and healthy, and do not move

Again in *Emile*, Rousseau distinguishes between two influences working on our primitive passions, the one producing our virtues and the other our vices. The influence that produces vice he calls *external*, but he never makes clear the sense in which he uses that word. If external means 'outside the self', then the influence that makes for virtue must also be external; for Rousseau tells us that it is in society that men become moral beings, which is equivalent to saying that it is in society that they acquire their virtues as well

---

us to harm one another. In the state of nature they are strong enough to maintain life and health. But in society we find more obstacles in our way, and our natural passions, being weak, are diverted from their objects. We are frustrated, and we become more concerned to get rid of the obstacles than to satisfy our natural passions; we become angry, fretful and malevolent. It is then that self-love gives birth to vanity, to the comparison of self with others, and to the desire to avenge and dominate.

Rousseau's description is by no means clear. He means, I think, that men, as they strive to satisfy their natural desires, get in each other's way. They become in the end so taken up with their fears and enmities that they are more anxious to get the better of other people than to make the best of their own lives. They are absorbed in their mutual relations, not from affection and trust and the desire to help one another, but from envy, hatred and fear. They become enemies because they lack the strength to be themselves, to come to terms with life. If their natural passions had been stronger, men would have surmounted or removed the obstacles in their way, or would have had the courage to resign themselves to the inevitable, and would not have wasted their energies in bitterness, ostentation or revenge. The natural passions, self-regarding though they are, do not isolate us from one another. When we are brought together, their inherent tendency, unless they are frustrated, is to give rise to the affections and loyalties that enrich our lives and bind us to each other. Everyone, however strong his nature, needs society to quicken his faculties and to attain true happiness. If he were not corrupted owing to the weakness of his passions, he would develop social affections to sustain and comfort him. His mind would be enlivened by conversation, and the sweetest part of his life would be lived in society with others; for man is so made that he cannot enjoy life to the full, cannot possess himself entirely, except in the society of his own kind.

Rousseau neither affirms nor denies that there are natures so strong as to be incorruptible even in a corrupt society. If he believed that there were such choice souls, he must have thought there were very few of them. And we are not to suppose that he would have counted himself among them. For he tells us in the *Dialogues* that, if he is not corrupt, it is only because, feeling his weakness, he has withdrawn from the world. He is, he says, gentle, compassionate, peaceful, unambitious, neither vain nor modest, easily excited, but lacking in energy, prudence and presence of mind. Clumsy, childlike, lazy and timid, he is soon put out of countenance by anyone more ready and forceful than himself. A lover of virtue, he is too weak to be actively virtuous. He shrinks from evil, lacking the strength to be valiant for good. Over-sensitive and given to dreaming, he avoids action and all unpleasantness. His first movements are lively and pure, but he does not persevere. If he is incorruptible, it is from sheer delicacy of soul. He is not innocent, for he knows evil and has sometimes done it, almost inadvertently and from bewilderment, when life has taken him by surprise. His intentions have always, *always* been good.

as their vices. What are social influences if they are not external to the self? Neither in *Emile* nor elsewhere does he show our virtues emerging out of self-love independently of the influence of other people upon us.

Rousseau says that a good education is essentially *negative*; he often speaks as if the task of the educator were to protect the child from influences which might prevent it developing as it should. He speaks at times as if the moral development of the child were a spontaneous process which must be left to itself if it is not to be vitiated. But this is only a manner of speaking; it is only Rousseau's way of saying that the child must not be taught by precept, so much as left to think things out for itself. The things it has to think out are largely social problems: how it should treat other people, and what it can reasonably expect of them. Emile's tutor is clearly an influence external to Emile; he educates the boy by putting him into situations in which he has to solve problems for himself, and also by seeing to it that he is not faced with problems, intellectual and moral, which he is too young to solve. In short, Emile's tutor educates the boy by creating the right environment, and that environment is, of course, social. Rousseau's saying that the best education is essentially negative therefore detracts nothing from his assertion that it is in society (that is to say, in the process of learning to live with others) that man becomes rational and moral; and by moral he means, in this context, capable of recognizing that there are rules which he ought to obey.

Man becomes moral in society, and it is also society that corrupts him. These two statements, suitably interpreted, do not contradict one another; the first tells us that only social man is capable of virtue and vice, and the second that he inclines more to vice than to virtue. There is no paradox here. But paradox or no paradox, we are still left uncertain why virtue should be more *natural* than vice. There is neither virtue nor vice outside society, and there is no tendency for man to become virtuous rather than vicious in society. Rousseau's account of how the social passions, vicious and virtuous, are produced out of the primitive passions gives us no clue whatever as to why he believed that man is naturally good and is corrupted by society.

It is easy to see what Rousseau means when he says that primitive man – man in the imagined state of nature – is naturally good. He is denying the doctrine of original sin; he is saying that the passions that man is born with or would acquire even outside society, in the mere process of becoming adult, are neither virtuous nor vicious. He is also denying Hobbes's account of the state of nature; for though Hobbes says that man's natural passions are in themselves no sin, he claims that they make man aggressive. Besides these denials, Rousseau further asserts a principle: that man's natural passions serve to keep him alive and healthy. Natural man, having no standards, moral or otherwise, does not praise or blame; but civilized man, contemplating the predicament of natural man, can see that his passions are adequate to his needs, and can approve their being so on the ground that they give him the only happiness of which he is capable. Civilized man can say of natural man: he is neither vicious nor virtuous, and yet it is good that he has the passions he does have. This is the sense in which unsocial man is naturally good.

It is easy to see how Rousseau conceived of such natural goodness. The difficulty is to see how he conceived of the natural goodness which is not innocence, which is not absence of vice as well as virtue, which is not harmlessness – the natural goodness which is a moral condition that only civilized man can imagine and aim at and sometimes attain. It is a condition which, more often than not, he does not attain; but the image of it is always vaguely present to him. When he falls short of it, he is dissatisfied with himself; he is other than he would wish to be, and feels himself to be the victim of his own passions and habits. He expresses this feeling when he says that he is *untrue* to himself. In the *Discourse on Inequality*, Rousseau speaks of man as being *outside* himself. There is a condition of himself which man, as soon as he is capable of understanding it, considers more desirable than any other. That is why, in spite of his wretchedness in the society which has corrupted him, he would not wish to return to the state of nature, if that return were possible.

We have seen that Rousseau's account of the origins of the social passions does not tell us what this condition is, or what makes it more natural to man than the condition which is actually his. We must therefore pass to the next of the five questions we have put, in the hope that by trying to answer them we may discover what Rousseau meant by man's natural goodness. We must ask, What constitutes the goodness of good passions, and the evil of evil ones?

2. *What constitutes the goodness of good passions, and the evil of evil ones?*

Rousseau comes nearer to giving an intelligible answer to this question than to the one we have just considered. The good passions are good because they lead to peace of mind and also to social peace – because they enable us to live without frustration and bitterness, and because they make us well-disposed towards our neighbours. The evil passions are evil because they bring us into conflict with ourselves and with others.

To see how they do this, we must look for a moment at Rousseau's distinction between self-love and vanity, *amour de soi* and *amour-propre*, but this time without troubling our heads about how they are connected. We shall suppose that they are independent of one another. Self-love, you will remember, is in itself neither morally good nor morally evil; it consists of the passions and desires that move us to do what is necessary to keep us alive and healthy. Vanity is always, or nearly always, evil; it is the desire that others should admire us, notice us and take us into account even when justice does not require them to do so. In the fourth book of *Emile*, Rousseau says, 'Self-love, which is concerned only with ourselves, is content when our real needs are satisfied; while vanity, which always compares self with others, is never satisfied and never can be. For this feeling, which makes us prefer ourselves to others, demands as well that others should prefer us to themselves, which is impossible. That is why the tender and gentle passions spring from self-love, and the hateful and angry passions from vanity'.[1] This is an argument immensely important to Rousseau, and he often repeats it. Vanity multiplies our needs, making us depend for our self-esteem on how we appear to others, and creating in us ambitions destructive of their happiness and our own. It makes our neighbours our rivals and enemies, yet binds us to them by chains impossible to break. Vanity makes slaves of us.

The relations between us which arise from what we do to help supply one another's natural wants produce in us affections and needs which draw us more closely together. We are told, also in the fourth book of *Emile*, that 'the child's first sentiment is self-love, and his second, which is derived from it, love of those about him; for in his weakness he is aware of people only through the help and attention he gets from them. To begin with, his affection for his nurse and his governess is mere habit. He calls for them because he needs them and is happy in their presence; it is perception rather than kindly feeling. It takes a long time before he discovers that they are not only useful to him but wish to be so, and that is when he begins to love them'.[2] If we are drawn to other people by the help they give us, or that we give them, we are likely to develop feelings for them which make it easy for us to live at peace with them; but if we come to need them to minister to our vanity, we cannot have easy and pleasant relations

[1] *Émile*, Livre IV, *Oeuvres complètes*, vol. IV, p. 493.
[2] Ibid., p. 492.

with them, for we are bound to ask much more of them than they are willing to give. If the services we expect from others are to satisfy wants which are not rooted in vanity, our demands on them will be modest. They will be willing and able to help us, especially while we are children and most in need of help; and the help given to us will create in us sentiments of gratitude and affection which will make us willing in our turn to help others. Though our affection for others is born of our need of them, it is not a form of self-love. The first persons we love are the persons we most depend on, our parents; but we love them for themselves and not for our own sakes. Love of others springs from self-love, and yet is genuinely altruistic. It enriches life; it enhances the sense of well-being of the person who feels it and of the persons for whom he feels it. When two people are bound together by affection, each needs the other and neither is the mere instrument of the other. Need gives birth to love, which in turn gives birth to other needs; and the needs born of love, as much as the needs that give birth to it, draw men closer together. Self-love is thus doubly 'natural': because the needs it consists of have to be satisfied if man is to keep alive and healthy, and because the passions it gives birth to nourish and strengthen his mind, making him feel that life is worth living.

Vanity, by contrast, is doubly 'unnatural': because the needs it consists of do not have to be satisfied to keep man alive and healthy, and because the passions it gives birth to – jealousy, arrogance, envy, hatred or lust for revenge – are either insatiable or inordinately difficult to satisfy. While these passions are not satisfied they destroy a man's peace of mind; and yet, if they are satisfied, other people must be hurt or humiliated.

A man is 'true to his nature' when his passions are not insatiable, when they can all be satisfied, and when the attempt to satisfy them brings him not enemies but friends. He is then at peace with himself and his neighbours; he is vigorous, free and happy. His freedom is not independence, for he needs his neighbours as much as they need him; it is mutual dependence, cheerfully accepted. Nor is his happiness either the successful pursuit of pleasure or passive contentment with his lot; it is a deep sense that life is worth living, making even the sorrows of life acceptable. The truly happy man is a man of deep feelings, and his peace of mind is not apathy. His kind of happiness is not a happiness to be had outside society, nor one for which society merely provides the means; it is inconceivable except to a social, rational and moral being, a self-conscious person who does not live from day to day but sees life in the round. The lonely savage, the amoral and unsocial man, is not so much happy as free from unhappiness. Anyone who has tasted or even imagined the happiness possible to civilized man could not wish to live from hand to mouth like a savage, whose happiness consists only in his being untroubled by desires beyond his power to satisfy.

Rousseau could have described this condition without calling it *natural goodness*. The name he gave it is misleading, and explains perhaps why he has so often been misunderstood. Natural man, as the eighteenth century spoke of him, is man as he would be if he did not live in society; and the condition we have been discussing is clearly not the condition of pre-social man. True, Rousseau also said that man is good in the state of nature, but the goodness he then had in mind was, as we have seen, quite different from this. And there is, he admitted, no inherent tendency for man to reach that condition in society. On the contrary, his chances of reaching it are small. This, indeed, is the point of Rousseau's dictum that society corrupts man. It is not the condition that man would reach if he were left to develop *naturally*, in the sense of uninfluenced by others, for he can reach it only in society, and to be in society is necessarily to be influenced by others. Nor can it be *natural* in the sense that man alone is capable of reaching it; for it is just as true that he alone is capable of being corrupted by society, and Rousseau did not call that corruption *natural*. In what sense, then, is this condition *natural*? In the sense that man, once the capacities to reason and to will are developed in him by society (and they are capacities that belong just to him), finds life truly worth living only when he has reached it or has hopes of doing so.

I do not say that this obviously desirable condition ought *not* to be called *natural goodness*. The word *natural* has been used in many senses, and there is nothing gained by ruling this one out. But it is only one of several senses in which Rousseau uses the word when he speaks of man's *natural goodness*; and he never clearly distinguishes it from the others, either by definition or by the way he uses it. As often as not, when he calls this condition *natural*, he is speaking of its origins and not of what it is in itself; but what he is then trying to say, I cannot make out.

3. *What does Rousseau understand by Conscience?*

Rousseau ordinarily speaks as if goodness and rightness were qualities in the things called good and the actions called right; he speaks of them, not as sensible qualities, but as qualities apprehended by reason. Reason can therefore tell us what natural goodness is, and can enlighten us about our duties. But reason is not desire; to know the good is not yet to desire it. What makes us desire it – what inclines us to it – even before reason has made it fully clear to us what it is and how we may get it, is conscience. Conscience, indestructible in us but easily defeated, is the feeling that urges us, in spite of contrary passions, towards the two harmonies: the one within our minds and between our passions, and the other within society and between its members. Because we have conscience we are never altogether adrift in society. Conscience is not the strongest impulse in us, but it is always present. It also serves to put us all on a level with one another, because the weakest can appeal to it in the strongest, and the appeal, though often unsuccessful, is always disturbing. However corrupted by power or wealth we may be, either as possessors of them or victims, there is something in us serving to remind us that this corruption is against nature. When Rousseau speaks of conscience, his tone is more proper to the sermon than to the philosophical treatise.

He would not be Rousseau if he left no room for doubt in the minds of his readers. There are times when he seems to be claiming more for conscience than I have just said; there are times when he seems to be claiming so much for it as to set him apart from believers in natural law. He tells us in *Emile*, by the mouth of the Savoyard Vicar, that conscience is 'an innate principle of justice and virtue, whereby. . .we judge our own or other men's actions to be good or evil'.[1] *Principle* does not here mean a general rule; for Rousseau repeatedly says that conscience is not reason, and he also says that its decrees are not judgements but feelings. All this is obscure enough. Perhaps the most plausible interpretation of it is that conscience is a feeling which draws us towards some kinds of behaviour and away from others. This would make the rôle of conscience something like the rôle of what Hume called the 'moral sentiments'; actions would then be right or wrong, not in themselves, but because we were drawn towards or away from them by conscience.

But, though that is the most plausible interpretation of this particular passage (and perhaps several others) in Rousseau, I do not think it gives us his usual position. Morality is not for him, as it was for Hume, ultimately a matter of feeling. It would, of course, be idle to pretend that Rousseau (who seldom dealt with any matter consecutively and at length, but returned to it again and again in different contexts) made clear what he believed to be the relative functions of reason and conscience in the moral life of man. Nevertheless, in spite of ambiguities, it is almost certain that he did not agree with Hume.

[1] Ibid., p. 598.

The moral law, he believed, can be discovered by reason, and its moral character does not consist in how we feel about it. Conscience moves us to right conduct, but the conduct is not right because conscience moves us to it. Rousseau stands here closer to Kant than to Hume.

We have seen that Rousseau calls conscience innate. Yet in the *Discourse on Inequality*, when he describes the imaginary state of nature, he says nothing about conscience. He clearly does not conceive of conscience as an impulse that would move men even outside society; it is not like self-love or pity. Before conscience can move us, we must be self-conscious rational creatures capable of deliberate choice. We must know what it is to be faced by several possible courses of action and to have to choose one in preference to the others. We must also understand what it is to make claims on others and to have them make claims on us. Only in society do we come to have rules of action and standards of excellence. Therefore, only among men who live or have lived in society can conscience have anything to do.

What then is the point of calling conscience innate? If Rousseau had been asked whether we are all born with conscience, he would doubtless have said that we are; but it is not easy to see what he could have meant by saying so. Conscience, he tells us, is an impulse or feeling which is not active in us in the state of nature. If an impulse or feeling is not yet active, it is not there; it does not occur and therefore does not exist. Is it, then, innate because it exists potentially? But that is only to say that, while it does not exist, it may or will do so – that man is the sort of creature who, under certain conditions, will have this impulse or feeling. Exactly as much can be said of vanity, which Rousseau says is not innate.

I do not think that we should take Rousseau literally. Though he would, if challenged, have said that man is born with a conscience, this is probably not what he was most concerned to say when he called conscience 'innate'. What he meant to convey was rather that conscience is the same in all men, whatever the society they belong to – that its office is everywhere to incline them to forms of behaviour which they cannot but recognize to be right, as soon as they see them for what they are. He also, I think, means to deny that conscience arises out of the primitive passions in the way that the social passions do, though he never explains how it does arise. Indeed, he avoids this explanation by saying that conscience is innate, and simply takes it for granted that his meaning is plain.

Rousseau denies that conscience is prejudice or socially induced habit or feeling. He feels the need to do so, because he will not have it that the promptings of conscience could differ from society to society, or in the same society from age to age. Nothing, he thinks, can be right in one place or at one time and wrong in another. If, of two exactly similar actions, one is called right and the other wrong, this is only because a mistake has been made about one or both of them. Conscience is always consistent in the sense that, no matter how often men have to act in a given situation, it will always prompt them to the same action, provided only that they see the situation as it really is. This is what Rousseau means when he says that, though reason is fallible, conscience is incorruptible.

Conscience is a difficult notion, variously understood. However differently we analyse it, we probably all agree that it is closely connected with the feeling we call shame. Was Rousseau, when he said that conscience is incorruptible and is the same in all men, suggesting that everywhere men are ashamed of the same things? Was he denying that men can be made to feel ashamed, within broad limits, of almost anything? Was he denying that there can be misplaced feelings of guilt and false shame, or, as the French put it, *mauvaise honte*? I am not sure how he would have answered these questions. But I cannot help feeling that an account of conscience which does not face them is inadequate.

4. *What conditions must hold if man is to attain goodness?*

To be able to live the good life, to attain the proper balance of their faculties and passions, men must either live in the right kind of society or else be made by education immune from the ravages of corrupt society.

The right kind of society is the society of equals, the society so constituted that men are no longer each other's instruments and victims but are required to obey laws which reason teaches them are just and conscience moves them to obey. This society is described in the *Social Contract*. It is the just society, the only legitimate society, because the only one that conforms to the true nature of man. The laws of this society may thwart some of man's passions; but the better men understand the laws, the weaker the thwarted passions will be. In other words, the better the society, the less its members are tempted to do what they ought not to do. This conception of the just society is the idealist, the Platonic, side of Rousseau's philosophy: it is the idea of a society whose discipline perfects its members. We can discover what that society is by reflecting on the nature of man as a rational and moral being. It is the society in which man is at peace with himself and other men; the society in which he finds it easy to be what he wants to be, and is content to be what he is; the society in which he does not acquire needs and ambitions which move him to live a kind of life that cannot satisfy him and must make him the rival and enemy of other men. Since inequality corrupts man, we have only to discover the social conditions of equality to know what kind of society this should be.

I have said that this conception of the just society is Platonic; and so, essentially, it is. Rousseau, like Plato, assumes that man, by taking thought, can discover the kind of society suited to his nature: a just society very different from the society he lives in.[1] But when Rousseau lays it down that it must be a society of equals, he parts company with Plato and puts us in mind of the utopias of the nineteenth-century socialists.

Men have also another chance of getting virtue and happiness in this world, though only a few can profit by it. A man can be educated to make the best of a bad world; he can be taught to be morally independent of it, not by cutting himself off from it, but by rising superior to its vanities and prejudices. He can be made, by careful education, nearly immune from corruption, and yet truly sociable, just and kindly in all his dealings with other men. They will be the better for his society, and he will be none the worse for theirs. This education is described in *Emile*. It creates a special environment for the child to protect him from the corrupting influences of society until he has grown strong enough, in his reasoning powers and his character, to resist them. What we find in *Emile* may be called the Stoic side of Rousseau's philosophy: it explains how a child, no better endowed by nature than others, can by training acquire so stable and well-balanced a character as to be almost proof against corruption. Not quite incorruptible, but nearly so; and, in any case, better able than others to recover himself when he has temporarily lost balance.

5. *What can be done to create the conditions favourable to the good life?*

This is the easiest to answer of the questions suggested by Rousseau's account of man's natural goodness. For the answer to it is: Not much.

---

[1] Plato and Rousseau agree that the just society, if it is to exist, must be created deliberately. They also agree that, men being what they are, it is unlikely that this society will be created except on the rare occasions when conditions are favourable. Their idealism is tempered by pessimism.

It is obvious that not everyone can get the education given to Emile. Emile has a tutor to himself alone, and Rousseau says that this must be so if he is to be made proof against the corruptions of existing society. A scheme of education which requires as many tutors as there are pupils to teach is altogether too expensive; it goes beyond anything the world has yet known, even in Oxford. Not any tutors, moreover, will do; they must have the wisdom and patience of Emile's tutor, who was none other than Rousseau himself.

If we cannot change society indirectly by the careful education of each separate child, can we change it directly? Can we hope to reform it? How are creatures already corrupt to be induced to set about changing their condition? If they adopt the scheme of government described in the *Social Contract*, they may find themselves unfit to work it. And how can they adopt it? For it can hardly function except in a simple society. Men have all kinds of vested interests in any society, no matter how corrupt it is. They are attached, Rousseau tells us, even to their vices. They may be unhappy; they may be moved by reason and by conscience to alter their social condition and their manner of life. But their vicious appetites are still strong in them, and they lack the will to get the better of them. The transformation of society, even when they acknowledge that it is desirable, is beyond their powers.

In the seventh chapter of Book II of the *Social Contract*, Rousseau says that 'in order that a people. . .should be able to appreciate (*goûter*) healthy political maxims. . .it would be necessary that the effect should become the cause. . .that men should be before they have laws what they are to become as a result of having them'.[1] Or, as we might put it, the wisdom needed to set up or to maintain a good political system is itself the product of that system. Even an uncorrupt people who have never constituted a state, who have never been politically organized, will lack this wisdom. Hence their need of a wise man, a Legislator, to prepare a constitution for them, which they can then freely accept; and the Legislator, unable to use force or to appeal to reason, must use another means of persuasion. He must claim to be divinely inspired. In the *Social Contract*, Rousseau mentions only one people still uncorrupt and 'capable of legislation', the Corsicans. In return for this compliment, he was invited by the Corsicans, then struggling for their independence, to prepare a constitution for them; he was invited to be their Legislator. Let it be

---

[1] *Contrat social*, II.vii, *Oeuvres complètes*, vol. III, p. 383.

Rousseau

said in justice to him that he aspired to persuade only by argument and never claimed divine inspiration.

A man who, believing that there is corruption almost everywhere, offers hope only to the Corsicans and to a few other peoples as uncorrupt as they are, offers little hope to mankind. It is not in the *Project of a Constitution for Corsica*, but several years later and towards the end of his life, in the *Considerations on the Government of Poland*, that Rousseau addresses his mind to the question of how a large and corrupt society, divided into unequal classes, can be brought gradually nearer to the ideal polity described in the *Social Contract*. He advocates a system whereby the Diet or national assembly is elected by provincial assemblies, the executive is appointed by the legislature, and the king has great honour and little power. He wants the serfs emancipated only as they prove their fitness for liberty, because men whose condition has made them servile cannot become citizens overnight. He makes it clear that the Diet, if not the provincial assemblies, must be a representative body, and stipulates only that there be frequent elections and that deputies be closely bound by their instructions. He warns the Poles that their institutions, defective though they are, have made them into a nation distinct from others; they therefore must not hastily get rid of what is old and national but must change it slowly, aiming always at greater equality and freedom.

Roussean's scheme of reform for Poland, brief and incomplete though it is, is ingenious. It embodies few illusions about human nature or social conditions; it is realistic and proves that its author could adapt his ideas to circumstances. Yet the scheme, as Rousseau himself admits, is difficult to apply, requiring rare firmness of purpose, patience and intelligence. Moreover, it is a scheme meant for the Poles, and it is not clear how far other peoples could make use of it.[1]

But there is one thing at least that Rousseau does make clear. The society of equals, the society adapted to the nature of man, the society in which man is satisfied with life as he finds it, does not come into being of itself. It must be deliberately created and deliberately

[1] Rousseau's compliment to the Corsicans came before they asked him for advice, but he did not praise the Poles until after they had asked for it. He was then moved to admire their courage and vigour, because, in the midst of misfortune and anarchy, they had all the fire of youth and dared to aspire to government and to laws as if they were a nation just born (see *Le Gouvernement de Pologne*, ch. I, ibid., p. 954). No doubt it is difficult for the would-be Legislator not to see it as a proof of courage and wisdom in a people that, in adversity, they should turn to him for advice.

preserved. It may be difficult (and at most times and places virtually impossible) to create it. Nevertheless, where it exists, it is an artefact. Nature uncontrolled by man does not produce the society in which man is naturally good.

6. Plato and Rousseau

I have suggested that Rousseau's idea of natural goodness, which differs from brutish innocence, has more than a little in common with what Plato understood by justice. The comparison is worth pursuing for the light it throws on Rousseau's meaning.

In the *Republic*, Plato uses the word justice to refer to two different but closely related things. There is a justice in men's souls and a justice also in society; there is an order and discipline proper to their minds as well as an external order and discipline which both preserve the community and enable its members to live as they ought inside it. For Rousseau, as for Plato, there are two orders and two harmonies, each closely dependent on the other: the order that reigns in the mind and the order that constitutes society. Plato does not say that society corrupts man, nor yet that man corrupts society. He is not concerned to apportion blame or avoid it; he is concerned only to cure men's ills. But to cure those ills he looks to the reform of society as well as of men. Man must be educated into becoming a rational and just creature, and there is a social environment proper to that purpose. Plato's two kinds of justice are inseparable; and both have as much right to be called natural as the goodness of which Rousseau speaks, for it can be said of both of them that they satisfy a creature having the nature of man. This, at least, is the claim that Plato makes for them. Let man but understand his own nature, and he will aspire to them. And again, for Plato as for Rousseau (though Rousseau insists upon it more even than Plato), what is best adapted to man's nature does not come into being of itself; it is not what grows inevitably out of his nature but what is needed to perfect it. Man must discover it, and seek to remould society and himself in its image.

There are obvious similarities between the two theories, as indeed we should expect, seeing how ardently Rousseau admired Plato; but there are differences no less important, though they have been less often noticed. Plato believed that the soul is in good order – that there is justice inside it – when reason controls the passions. But Rousseau, though he sometimes used this Platonic formula or others like it, did not really believe it. He was, after all, a philosopher of the eighteenth century, who had learnt from Pascal and from Hume's French disciples that reason alone cannot move men to action. It can compare the passions and know them; it can discover which are insatiable or in conflict with the others and which can be satisfied; it can know justice but cannot desire it. The Platonic idea that knowledge is virtue, that reason not only enlightens but controls, was no longer accepted by many philosophers; and Rousseau, unfashionable though he might often wish to be, was no doubt influenced by prevailing opinions.[1]

He had also another and stronger motive for playing down the sovereignty of reason. He could not hope to prove that one man's reason is no better than another's, that all men are equally intelligent. Now, if reason controls the passions, and ought to rule, it would seem to follow that, since some men are more reasonable than others, they ought to rule and the others ought to obey them. Again, if to discover justice requires superior reason, which only some men are by nature qualified to attain, it follows that not all men are in the same measure naturally good. These might be conclusions welcome to Plato, but Rousseau, who believed in equality as much as in virtue, could not accept them.

Though Rousseau often spoke of the need to control the passions, he was much less than Plato a lover of discipline. Plato believed that the laws and customs that make society possible also make men good, and that every State, however imperfect, must to some extent impose on its citizens the discipline that makes them virtuous. Rousseau, too, no doubt, believed that every society makes men moral, that life inside it awakens their reason and gives scope to their conscience; but he also said that society corrupts. It makes man capable of virtue and vice, but inclines him much more to vice than to virtue. The restraints it imposes are mostly degrading, and the opportunities it creates mostly occasions of evil. Only a few societies, more similar than most to the ideal society described in the *Social Contract*, are exceptions to this rule; and only a few persons, educated like Emile or born with much more than usual strength of mind, can escape the corruptions of ordinary society. Rousseau believed that most social restraints are imposed on the many for the sake of the few; and also that society mostly restrains men's better feelings while it multiplies and elaborates their

---

[1] But never to the extent of forgetting that the passions of a rational creature are different precisely because he is rational. It is because he is rational that man is self-conscious, that he is a moral being whose happiness depends on how he feels about himself and others. Man needs to feel that he is living in a well-ordered world, and needs self-respect. In many ways, Rousseau was closer to Pascal than to the Encyclopaedists and Hume; he understood, as they did not, man's profound need to feel at home in the world.

evil passions. In the ideal society, men would be very little restrained by the laws, because they would not have the passions which put them at odds with justice, or would get only a mild dose of them. They would not need to put a strong curb on themselves, to be perpetually at war with their baser feelings. They would not, like the Christian hero, have to keep down the devil in their own souls. Man is by nature good. That means, to Rousseau, that when he is as he ought to be, man is internally at peace; he does not have to win one strenuous victory after another over himself.

Rousseau loved freedom; and not all his veneration for Plato, who cared for it so little, could diminish that love. This makes a great difference between their two theories. They both thought evil a kind of anarchy, but Rousseau was more anxious to prevent than to restrain it. The good man is not, in his eyes, the strong man armed with virtue, perpetually on guard over his soul. He did not want a watchful and strict mastery of reason over the passions, any more than the government of the foolish by the wise. He wanted a society where the passions need little or no restraint, where men need few defences against themselves and each other because they live together under such conditions that it comes easily to them to love and help one another – a society where no man is dependent on a superior but only on friends and neighbours, on an entire community, on a society of equals in whose life he takes a full part.

In his book on education, Rousseau makes Emile's tutor his friend and companion, not his master. The tutor does not punish or scold; he does not impose discipline; he merely creates the environment enabling the boy to discipline himself. He teaches the boy to be self-reliant, and cannot succeed unless his lessons are so discreet that the boy scarcely feels them to be lessons. He does for Emile, in a corrupt society, what man's social environment would do for him in a properly constituted State. He makes him a man of goodwill, who freely accepts the rules which must be accepted for the public good.

Though there is an illiberal side to Rousseau's social philosophy, it is his love of freedom, and of equality conceived as a means to freedom, which is more often to the fore. This love he tried to reconcile with the need for order, through his doctrine of the general will; but he also gave simpler and perhaps more attractive expression to it. There are times when Rousseau comes close to Montaigne, who in his *Essays* tells us to let nature take her course, to deal gently with our neighbours and ourselves, not stifling our passions when they hurt us but finding harmless outlets for them. There is a place in nature for everything; let us follow her example and find a place for everything in ourselves.

This, too, is a doctrine congenial to Rousseau, and its influence is often apparent in his writings. Rousseau, like Montaigne, when he finds men trying to impose their preferences on their neighbours, is sometimes moved to ask them by what authority they do so.

III. THE GENERAL WILL

It is in the *Social Contract*, in an early and the final drafts of it, that Rousseau gives us much the longest account of the general will. The *Social Contract* describes the just State, the only State that enables men to live as they should do, in accordance with their nature. The *Social Contract* does not offer to tell us, as for instance Hobbes's *Leviathan* does, why it is men's interest to obey established governments; nor does it seek to explain, as Locke's *Second Treatise of Government* does, what are the limits of political obligation in actual states. Rousseau's *Social Contract*, like Plato's *Republic*, describes an ideal to be aimed at, but does not tell us what we should do, here and now, in the endeavour to attain it. Practical advice we get only in the *Project of a Constitution for Corsica* and the *Considerations on the Government of Poland*; and very cautious and moderate it is.

Rousseau's purpose in the *Social Contract*, as he describes it himself, is to find 'a form of association that will defend, with the whole common force, the person and the goods of each associate, and in which everyone, while uniting with all, still obeys himself alone and remains as free as before'.[1] As soon as we begin to consider these words more closely, we find them obscure. If force has to be used, how can the persons against whom it is used remain as free as before? How can a man in society obey himself alone? When he unites with others to form a society, he either agrees to, or soon discovers he must, obey many more people than himself. His having agreed to obey does not ensure that, when obedience is required of him, he in fact wants to obey. When a man agrees to obey, he may make it his duty to do what other people demand of him, but he cannot undertake always to want what they require.

Rousseau's solution is as obscure as his problem. The social contract, which ensures that everyone obeys himself alone and remains as free as before, is thus described: 'Each one of us puts his person and all his power in common under the supreme direction of the general will, and we as a body receive each member as an inseparable part

[1] *Contrat social*, I.vi, *Oeuvres complètes*, vol. III, p. 360.

of the whole. At that moment, in the place of the particular person of each contracting party, this act of association creates a moral and collective body, made up of as many members as there are voters in the assembly, and receiving from this act its unity, its common self, its life and its will.'[1]

This solution raises more questions than it answers. What is the general will? How does it make a man an *inseparable* part of the society he belongs to? How does it make a collective body out of the persons making the contract? And how can that body take the place of those persons?

If we try to puzzle out Rousseau's statement of his problem and his solution of it, or other equally obscure and famous pronouncements from the *Social Contract*, we shall not make much progress towards discovering what he meant by the general will. It is better, I think, to begin by considering the simpler parts of his description of the ideal democracy. These parts, once we have grasped their significance, may make it easier for us to understand what is more obscure. Rousseau was not a metaphysician with a peculiar and difficult conception of what reality essentially is, and so did not use a technical language derived from any such conception. He was not, like Hegel, impelled to use a special vocabulary created by himself for the express purpose of saying what he thought could not be said adequately in ordinary words. Rousseau was obscure for a simpler reason: because he failed to make his meaning plain. His obscure utterances are, if I may so put it, on the same level of discourse as his simpler ones: they do not deal with what is deeper, or 'more true', or 'more real', in a special language unsuited to the superficialities of ordinary discourse. There is no peculiar logic or metaphysic behind his political philosophy; and that philosophy must therefore, in fairness to him, be treated at the level of ordinary common sense. Rousseau thought the French language, as educated and intelligent men used it, sufficient for all his purposes; he always wanted (though he sometimes failed) to be intelligible to educated men who understand ordinary words in ordinary ways. We can therefore probably get closer to his meaning by interpreting what is obscure in his theory in the light of what is intelligible, than by reading into it ideas suggested to us by what we know of the later philosophies of Kant, Fichte or Hegel. For, though German philosophers were deeply influenced by Rousseau, they were also more systematic than he was, using concepts and making distinctions which meant nothing to him.

[1] Ibid., p. 361.

If we take some of Rousseau's more often quoted statements literally, and try to elicit their meanings, we soon find ourselves caught up in a web of absurdity. Let me give one or two examples of the uselessness of this direct method. In the third chapter of Book II of the *Social Contract*, Rousseau distinguishes 'the will of all' from 'the general will', saying that the first is the 'sum of particular wills', and the second the 'sum of the differences' remaining when the 'pluses' and 'minuses' of the particular wills cancel each other out. Now, this account of the general will, if we take it literally, is sheer nonsense. What can the 'pluses' and 'minuses' of particular wills be except what is peculiar to each of them. Let John's will be $x + a$, Richard's $x + b$, and Thomas's $x + c$, x being what is common to them all, and a, b and c, what is peculiar to each. If the general will is what remains after the 'pluses' and 'minuses' have cancelled each other out, it is x; but if it is the sum of the differences it is $a + b + c$. Whichever it is, it cannot be both; and the second alternative is too absurd to be considered. Beware of political philosophers who use mathematics, no matter how simple, to illustrate their meaning! God will forgive them, for they know what they do, but we shall not understand them.

The first alternative – that the general will is whatever is common to all the particular wills – is not absurd. It makes sense, but it is unrealistic and does not square with Rousseau's account of how that will comes into being. For to discover what is common to particular wills, there is in theory no need for assembly and debate. Each citizen could record his opinion separately, and whatever was found to be common to all opinions could be declared to be the general will. But Rousseau holds that the general will, if it emerges at all, does so in an assembly of equals who freely debate what is of common interest. Even if the general will were a compromise decision reached after a free discussion between people whose opinions differ, it still would not be what was common to those opinions. For in the process of discussion, opinions change in ways impossible to predict, and the eventual compromise is not something that could have been discovered by a calculation based on the opinions that people had before the discussion began.

In the fifteenth chapter of Book III of the *Social Contract*, Rousseau says that sovereignty cannot be represented, because it consists in the general will, and will cannot be represented. He puts this forward as an argument for direct as against representative democracy. The citizens must make their own laws and not choose persons to make them in their place; but they may, and indeed ought, to entrust the executive power to delegates, and not try to exercise it themselves. This statement – that the will cannot be represented – has puzzled several of Rousseau's admirers. They have tried to plumb its depths, taking it for granted that whatever was concealed there must be of the utmost importance. For there is nothing that Rousseau insists on so much as that the people must never surrender the legislative power into other hands. To explain what he means by the will's not being able to be represented is surely to elucidate one of the cardinal maxims of his political philosophy!

It is certainly a good rule to take the theory you are studying seriously; but that, I hope, need not involve trying to get blood out of a stone. Rousseau's dictum, that the will cannot be represented, is either a truism that has nothing to do with the conclusion he derives from it or else is plainly false. If what it means is that nobody can do another person's willing for him, it is true but irrelevant; for it does not follow that nobody can authorize anyone else to make decisions on his behalf. Strictly speaking, it is not wills but persons that are represented; and one person represents another whenever he does what the other has indicated that he desires him to do and what he has the right to do because the other has so indicated his desire. Again, if Rousseau's dictum means that no one has the right or power to appoint someone else to make decisions on his behalf, but only to carry out decisions he has taken for himself, it is plainly false. The dictum is empty or useless or false. Do what you like with it, you will get no pearls of political wisdom out of it. Rousseau, as we shall see, has some strong arguments against representative democracy, but they have nothing to do with anything about the will which makes it incapable of being represented.

Let us deal courteously with Rousseau, but let us not be fascinated by what is obscure and oracular about him. Let us begin by considering what he imagined a free society would be like; let us first take hold of what is plain if not exactly simple. We are told that man, unless he gives up the advantages he gets from society, cannot be independent of all other men; and we know that Rousseau did not wish him to give them up. He believed that man can become moral and rational – can develop his faculties harmoniously – only in society. Since complete independence is not desirable, let alone possible, there must be equal dependence. The free society is a society of equals, where no man is the inferior of another, depending on him in ways in which the other does not in turn depend on him; it is the society where all men depend equally on the community of which they are all active members.

What then, in Rousseau's opinion, is a society of equals? It is a society where, in the first place, every man is entitled to take part in making decisions which all are required to obey; where, secondly, the persons who make these decisions do so as individual citizens and not as members of organized groups smaller than the State; where, thirdly, citizens make the laws themselves and do not elect representatives to do so for them; and where, fourthly and lastly, the body that makes the laws does *not* administer them. If we can discover why Rousseau thought these four conditions indispensable to true equality, we shall be much better able to understand his doctrine of the general will; for it is only in a society of equals that the general will is fully developed.

1. His First Principle

The first condition, *that every man is entitled to take part in making decisions which all are required to obey*, though as important as any, requires the least comment. It is, at bottom, the old doctrine of Locke and the natural law philosophers – that government, to be legitimate, requires the consent of the governed. But Rousseau does not, as Locke and others do, weaken the doctrine by resorting to any such shift as Locke's notion of tacit consent. Sovereign decisions are made by the whole body of citizens.

Notice that the decisions in question are decisions which *all* are required to obey. It is not said that a man is entitled to take part in making any decision which *he* is required to obey. For such a decision might be executive or judicial. A man is not entitled to be a judge in his own case when the law is being applied to him either administratively or judicially; he is entitled only to take part in deciding what the law shall be. He has a right to take part in deciding what shall be required of anyone, including himself, under such and such circumstances. Merely by virtue of being a member of the community, adult, sane and male, you have a right to take part in the making of law; but the right to take any other part in government you can have only if it has been granted to you according to law. The right to apply or enforce the law is a legal right; the right to take part in making the law is a moral right which can be forfeited only by breaking the law. If you break the law, you may be justly punished, and so deprived for a time or for good of your right to take a part in making the law. But if you have not broken the law, you cannot be justly deprived of your right to take part in making it. A decision of the assembly depriving innocent citizens of their legislative rights would not be law but an attack by one part of the community on another; and victims of aggression have no duty to obey decisions made by aggressors. It may be dangerous for them not to obey; but that is another matter.

2. His Second Principle

The second condition, *that the persons making sovereign decisions must do so as citizens and not as members of organized groups smaller than the State, smaller than the entire political community they belong to*, is not so easily explained. It is, of all Rousseau's political principles, perhaps the most completely his own. We are told, in the third chapter of Book II of the *Social Contract*, that 'when factions arise, and partial associations are formed at the expense of the great association, the will of each of them becomes general in relation to its members, and particular in relation to the State: and you can then say that there are no longer as many voters as there are men, but only as many as there are associations. . .there is then no longer a general will, and the opinion that prevails is only particular. It is important, therefore. . .that there should be no partial society in the State, and that every citizen should arrive at his own opinion'.[1]

It was a favourite opinion with Rousseau that men are less divided by private than by organized group interests. The private citizen, who has to rely entirely on himself – on the force of his own arguments – when he tries to get his fellow citizens to adopt some course of action, must speak to them of the common interest. No doubt, he tries to get them to agree to what suits him; he puts forward his own interest as the common interest. But he has no hope of success unless he can persuade them that what he proposes is also in their interest. He has no body of supporters on whom he can rely; he is just one private citizen among others. He neither belongs to an organized group nor is dealing with persons who belong to such groups. He is dealing with a mass of individuals whose private interests are more or less unknown to him; he has a strong motive, therefore, for appealing to the most general interests. The longer he is so placed, and the more he is in the habit of discussing matters of common concern with others placed as he is, the more he accommodates his private interest to the common interest, and the more attached he becomes to the community. He is persuaded by his own arguments devised to appeal to others, and also by the arguments of his fellow-citizens who have the same motives as he has for appealing to general interests.

A private citizen does not ordinarily have his conception of his political interest (of what he wants from the State) ready-made in his mind when he comes to discuss matters of common concern with other citizens; what he wants the State to do for him varies with their

---

[1] *Contrat social*, II.iii, ibid., pp. 371–2.

influence on him. He is usually more persuadable by the others, taken collectively, than they are by him, for he is only one person and they are many. Private citizens who come together to debate public matters and to reach common decisions do not ordinarily have precise and fixed ideas about what should be done; their ideas are mostly fluid and take firmer shape in the course of the debate. It is largely by meeting together to deal with public affairs that they acquire definite political opinions: opinions about what they and others are entitled to ask of the community and what has to be done to meet their claims.

Where a man is in the habit of being concerned with the affairs of his community, he usually has two strong and enduring desires: that the community should flourish, and that he should do well inside it. His idea of what is involved in his doing well will be closely tied up with his idea of what makes the community flourish. The more he takes part, as one citizen among others, in discussing and deciding matters of common concern, the stronger his attachment to the community, and the more his ambitions are in line with the common interest. He will still prefer his own interest to the interest of most other persons, taken individually; but this does no harm when public affairs are being discussed, for it then pays him to advocate some course which reconciles his private interest with what he can persuade others to believe is the common interest. Others are as good judges as he is of that common interest, and, there being no organized group, he has no pull over any section of them. He is so situated that he is insensibly drawn into accommodating his own to the common interest.

But where there are organized groups in the community, the situation is different, because within each group there is at work a process similar to the one which would bind everyone closely to the community if there were no such group inside it. Within each group, citizens acquire loyalties and conscious interests which bind them to the group rather than to the whole community. These loyalties and interests are the stronger for being shared, and for being known to be shared; for it is interests known to be shared which are the most obstinately held to. Men strengthen one another in their common aspirations and resolutions; it is as members of groups, rather than as private citizens, that they make precise and rigid claims on the community. Organized groups are harder, more cynical, more intractable than are private citizens. The process whereby discussion creates a harmony between particular and common interests works much less smoothly where the particular interests are those of organized groups.

Men are most amenable to persuasion when they are least committed, when they are not so placed as to be liable to be accused of inconsistency or disloyalty if they change their minds, and when they cannot count in advance on the support of others. If, then, every citizen comes to the assembly uncommitted, his private interests are less likely to stand in the way of a reasonable and just decision than would a policy, or even mere loyalties and prejudices, shared by people who form an organized group. Rousseau knew, of course, that there are in every community interests which are shared by only some of its members. He was not so absurd as to deny that there are sectional interests, and that they are important. He merely said that the people who have them should not form organized groups to promote them. Or, rather, he said that the ideal, which can be realized only in a small State, is that there should be no such organized groups. But where this ideal cannot be realized, it is better that there should be many such groups rather than only a few.[1]

Though it is in the *Social Contract* that Rousseau tells us that the pursuit of merely private interests is not dangerous to the State, and that he condemns the formation of organized groups in an ideal democracy, some of the points I have been making are better put elsewhere. In some comments written around 1756 on the abbé de Saint-Pierre's *Polysynodie*, he says, speaking of a private citizen trying to persuade his fellow citizens, 'In an assembly all of whose members are clear-sighted and do not have the same interests, each person would seek in vain to bring others over to what suited himself alone: without persuading anyone, he would succeed only in laying himself open to suspicions of corruption and unfaithfulness. No matter how much he may wish to avoid doing his duty, he will not attempt it, or will attempt it in vain, where there are so many to watch him. He will therefore make a virtue of necessity, in openly sacrificing his personal interest to his country's good. . . .For there is then a very strong personal interest, which is concern for his reputation, marching with the public interest'.[2] A few pages further on, speaking of the interests of groups within the State as compared with personal interests, he says that 'they have this added inconvenience, that [a man] takes pride in maintaining, at any cost, the rights and claims of the body he is a

---

[1] Nothing that Rousseau says in the *Social Contract* or elsewhere implies that there should be no parties or pressure groups in the vast democracies known to us. On the contrary, he knew that in large states there must be what he called factions (a term which covers both parties and pressure groups, for he did not distinguish between them); and where there must be factions, he would have people free to form as many as they feel inclined to.

[2] *Écrits sur l'abbé de Saint-Pierre: Polysynodie, Oeuvres complètes*, vol. III, p. 629.

member of; and that the dishonesty of preferring himself to others vanishes in favour of a numerous society he belongs to'.[1]

Apart from these bad effects of group prejudices and policy, there is another danger. Where there are groups active in politics, it is always possible for several of them to make a compromise at the expense of the others. This is what Rousseau has in mind when he speaks of the evils of intrigue. He has a horror of agreements reached behind the scenes by organized groups who then face the assembly with decisions taken outside it and imposed upon it.

We have seen that, where there must be organized groups, Rousseau prefers many small ones to a few large ones. This is presumably because he believes that a coalition of many small groups will be weaker and more unstable than one made up of a few large ones. What he wants to avoid, above all, is the setting up of a permanent majority, whether it consists of one body only or of several bodies firmly allied with one another. For then everyone outside the majority takes no real part in making the decisions of the assembly. He may cast a vote or even speak, but what he does cannot affect the decision. People who feel that they can affect a decision are disposed to accept it as a common decision – a decision of the entire body they belong to – even when they vote against it; but people who do not feel this are not so disposed.

If no citizen belongs to an organized group, every majority is, so to speak, a chance majority. Nobody knows beforehand who will belong to it. The citizens who make up the majority have no more in common than that they happen, on that occasion, to have voted one way; and next time there is a vote, the chances are that the majority will not consist of the same persons. There is no enduring majority to impose its will on the entire community; there are no enduring minorities to combine against one another. No one need feel that he plays an empty part in the affairs of his community. There are no lesser communities inside the great community controlling it for the benefit of some and to the detriment of others.

This is an ideal model, and we cannot be sure how far Rousseau thought it could be realized in practice. Even a small city-state or Swiss canton includes many hundreds, not to say thousands, of citizens. Did Rousseau really believe that an assembly of all the citizens of a State large enough to be self-supporting could function with no organized groups inside it? I do not know. I suspect that he never gave the matter much thought. But, thoughtless though he was in one direction, he

---

[1] *Jugement sur la Polysynodie*, ibid., p. 644.

was thoughtful, and even original, in another. What he says about organized groups, their interests and their loyalties, though only a part of the truth, is yet an important part.

3. His Third Principle

Rousseau's third principle, *that citizens must make their own laws and must not choose deputies to do so for them*, has been condemned as among the more absurd and unrealistic that he put forward; though he was, as a matter of fact, as well aware as any of his critics that in large states the people cannot make the laws themselves. He was against large states, though he knew that the tendency was for states to grow larger. He merely denied that the tendency was good, and the denial is not obviously absurd. Rousseau believed that in large states inequality is inevitable, and truly popular government therefore impossible. It is perhaps more important to see the force of his argument than to condemn him for lack of realism.

It has often been said that the essence of democracy is the making of sovereign decisions by a process of free discussion between the people affected by those decisions. If they do not take part in reaching a decision that affects them, and also in the discussion leading up to it, people may not understand the need for that decision, nor the interests and points of view reconciled by it. The decision is therefore likely to appear to them external and arbitrary. They may get used to acquiescing in such decisions; they may even learn to think of themselves as unfit to take part in making them. But it is when they have themselves had a hand in making a decision that they are most likely to recognize it as just or expedient or, if they find it unjust and inexpedient, that they are best able to consider what should be done to get it reversed.

Where sovereign decisions are taken by an elected body, where the most important business of government – the making of the laws – is done by only a small part of the people, the others (so Rousseau would have us believe) never acquire what deserves to be called a political will. The really important decisions are then taken, not by the people, who may not even understand what is done in their name, but by their deputies, whose responsibility to their electors is, at best, occasional and vague. The people of England, Rousseau tells us, imagine that they are free, but they are so only at long intervals, when they take the trouble to elect representatives. There was no point in his passing this judgement on Englishmen unless he believed that the responsibility of representatives to electors is more apparent than real. The electorate are politically inarticulate; they are mere listeners and voters while the elections last, and afterwards take no part at all in government. They scarcely know what their representatives are doing. Representative democracy is an illusion; it requires the impossible – that the few who make government the business of their lives should be genuinely responsible to a mass of indifferent, if not ignorant, voters. Whenever Rousseau speaks of the people electing deputies to make laws for them, he always speaks as if they were abdicating the most essential of their political rights and duties. When they elect deputies, they are not, as he sees it, taking a real part in the government of their country; they are refusing to take it. They are divesting themselves of a power which they alone can exercise properly. To choose someone to make your laws for you is not to assert your legislative right but to renounce it. It is to refuse the greatest service you owe to your country: the duty to think for it. Rousseau speaks of a people that deliberately gives up the burden of legislation and puts it on other shoulders much as the patriot speaks of the man who refuses to bear arms in his country's defence.

Freedom, says Rousseau, is obedience to a law we prescribe to ourselves.[1] But society cannot subsist if every man makes his own law separately. Therefore all must make the law for all. It is impossible that each of us should say, 'I alone have made the law that I obey'. The most we can hope for is that each should say, 'I obey the law that *we* have made' rather than 'I obey the law that *they* have made'. The ideal is that every citizen should identify himself with the community that makes the law, which, Rousseau thinks, he cannot do unless he is a member, on the same terms as all other citizens, of the sovereign legislature. Rousseau knew that this requires that the sovereign community, the State, should be small. He knew also that it was almost impossible to reduce the size of existing states. They had grown bigger in the past and were likely to continue doing so. He knew that the odds were almost everywhere against the people's sovereignty, against equality, against the institutions which he thought make for freedom and social harmony.

He was as sharply aware as the socialists after him of a process of social change making every man dependent on an always larger number of other men. Society, he knew, was growing faster and more elaborate; the old small, almost self-sufficing, community was fast disappearing. He believed that this increase in the circle of each man's social dependence made inevitably for greater inequality. He

[1] *Contrat social*, I.viii, ibid., p. 365.

therefore condemned the material progress which he thought was the cause of this dependence. It is here that he differs from most, though not all, of the socialists. They disliked inequality as much as he did, but many of them did not see inequality as the inevitable companion of material progress. Conditions, they admitted, might now be growing worse for the poor, but only to grow better afterwards. Rousseau did not share their optimism; he was never tempted to believe that what was wrong with modern society could be put right by workers' co-operatives, or the abolition of certain forms of private property, or the disappearance of the State. He wanted a property-owning democracy. But real democracy, he said, is impossible in vast and intricate societies. Material progress, by enormously complicating the life of society, leads inevitably to great inequalities of wealth and power. Only where society is simple and small can all its members take an active part in managing its affairs; and unless they can do that, they are neither free nor equal. It would, I think, be wrong to call Rousseau a reactionary; he did not want society to revert to what it had been in the past. His ideal society is quite unlike what European society had ever been, except perhaps for short periods of time in a few places. But he was passionately against what the modern world calls *progress*.

Rousseau liked to say that the laws must rule and not men, and he also liked to distinguish between independence and freedom. In the eighth of his *Letters from the Mountain*, for example, he says, 'When everyone does what he pleases, he often does what displeases others; and that is not called a condition of freedom. Liberty consists less in doing what we want than in not being subject to another's will; it also consists in not subjecting another's will to our own'.[1]

Now, it smacks of paradox to say that 'the laws must rule and not men'. Laws are customary or are deliberately made, and in either case are enforced or applied by men. As Hobbes might put it, it is always men that rule, whether they make the law or merely apply it. Rousseau uses this paradox, as it often has been used, as a way of saying that governments must not act arbitrarily but must apply the same rules to all their subjects; but he also uses it to give point to the distinction he makes between independence and freedom. Independence, the power to do as you please, is impossible in society. The most you can hope for is that the laws should not seem to you to be imposed on you by others. But they must seem to be so, Rousseau thinks, unless you take an equal part with others in making them.

[1] *Lettres de la montagne*, VIII, ibid., p. 841.

There is a difference between being made to do what other people have decided you shall do and being obliged to do what you have committed yourself to doing. By taking part, on equal terms with other people, in making a decision, you oblige yourself to accept it, even when you actually vote against it. They do not impose their will on you without taking account of your wishes; nor, conversely, when the vote goes your way, do you impose your will on the minority. The situation, where all take part as equals in making common decisions, is not only morally, but also psychologically, different from some people's imposing their will on others. Not only does it create obligations stronger than would otherwise exist, but people feel differently about the decisions. When they are required to conform to these decisions, they do not feel that they are being subjected to the will of others. Other people are as much bound as they are. To express this need that all should feel an equal dependence on the whole community, Rousseau uses the not altogether happy formula that the 'laws must rule and not men'.[1] The rule of law, in this sense, is realized only in the society of equals, which is necessarily small and simple.

It is, I suggest, beside the point to accuse Rousseau of lacking realism. In the *Social Contract*, his avowed purpose is to describe an ideal community. Far from pretending that it can be easily established, he goes out of his way to assure his readers of the opposite. In the eighth chapter of Book II, he says that many nations are incapable of good laws, and that even those that have them do so only for a time. Nations, like men, become incorrigible as they grow old. If they do not acquire a good constitution at the only time of their lives when they can adapt themselves to it – when they are neither too barbarous nor too fixed in evil ways – they have no hope of freedom. The Russians are lost to freedom forever, because Peter the Great tried to ram civilization down their throats before they were ready for it, and they will therefore never be disciplined. Two chapters later, Rousseau says that the Corsicans are the only people in Europe 'capable of legislation', meaning that they alone can become a properly constituted State. In return for this compliment, they asked him to prepare a constitution for them. In yet another chapter, the eighth of Book III, he goes still further: he implies that there are peoples without even a chance of freedom to miss, if they live in hot countries suited only to despotism or cold ones suited only to barbarism.

---

[1] See especially *Le Gouvernement de Pologne*, ch. I, and Rousseau's letter to Mirabeau of 26 July 1767, ibid., pp. 955 and 1744.

Man is born free and is by nature good. If you happen to be a man, do not rejoice too quickly! You can be free and good only if you live in a society of equals, and there is not much chance of your doing that. There is no question here of religious or racial prejudice. Rousseau does not suggest that there is original sin in you, or that you are born in any way defective, whatever nation or race you belong to. Merely in virtue of your humanity, you are born to freedom. But, unfortunately, you cannot get freedom except in the right social environment, which is not to be had for the asking, but is extraordinarily difficult to create. Those who have it enjoy it more by luck than judgement. I suggest that this is not so much lack of realism as profound pessimism. Rousseau may be wrong about the conditions of freedom; but if he is, we do not prove him so by showing that these conditions can hardly be realized in the modern world. We can refute him only by showing that he mistook the conditions of freedom. This, I think, can be done, though I shall not attempt it here. For the moment, my purpose is only to put the gist of Rousseau's argument as simply, clearly and forcefully as I can. That is worth doing, because Rousseau was the first to give expression to a feeling that many now share: the feeling that man is lost in a social environment too vast and elaborate for him to control.

4. His Fourth Principle

Rousseau's fourth principle, *that the sovereign assembly must not administer the laws it makes*, looks at first sight like a version of the doctrine of the separation of powers. But the point of it is really quite different. Rousseau is not concerned that the executive and the legislative should act as checks on one another; he is concerned rather that the legislative should undertake only what it is fit to do.

Rousseau believed that we are ordinarily much more anxious that justice should be done generally than that it should be done on this or that particular occasion. It matters more to us that the laws should be just than that they should be justly applied to a particular person. When we are considering law in the abstract, as a rule that might apply to anyone, we are not moved by the likes and dislikes which nearly always move us when we are dealing with actual persons. Even in a society of equals, the doing of justice to particular persons must be an activity separate from the making of law. Those who administer this kind of justice have always a limited authority; the procedures they use are laid down by custom and law; they are trained to impartiality by the very nature of their profession, and there is usually a right of appeal from their decisions. Precautions of many kinds are taken to protect citizens against the errors and prejudices of magistrates and officials; but no such precautions can be taken against a sovereign assembly. The proper task of such an assembly is therefore to do what, in a society of equals, it will have no motive for doing badly; and that is to make laws applying to all citizens equally. Provided the assembly consists of all the citizens, that none are excluded, and that the society is simple and homogeneous enough for no section of it to be felt by the others to be alien, inferior or dangerous, then the assembly will have no motive for making unjust laws. It will make mistakes, but it will always desire the good of the entire community.

'Every act of sovereignty', states Rousseau in the fourth chapter of Book II of the *Social Contract*, 'that is to say, every authentic act of the general will, obliges or favours all citizens equally; so that the sovereign takes account only of the body of the nation, and does not distinguish any of the persons that make it up'.[1] In the sixth chapter of the same book, he says, 'When I say that the object of the laws is always general, I mean that the law considers subjects in a body and actions in the abstract, never a man individually nor a particular action. Thus the law may lay it down that there shall be privileges, but can give none to anybody by name'.[2] This is what law must be as an expression of the general will; this is why it assimilates the good of each with the good of all: 'Why is the general will always upright, and why do all continually desire the happiness of each, if it is not that there is no one who does not apply the word *each* to himself, and does not think of himself when voting for [what concerns] all?'[3]

If a law, to be properly so called – to be an expression of the general will – must affect all citizens equally, it seems to follow that there can be very few laws. For the vast majority of what are ordinarily called laws affect some people more than others. Even if we suppose Rousseau to have meant that the makers of law, if what they make is to be genuine law, must not intend to affect some citizens more than others, we are still in difficulties. If the law grants privileges, as Rousseau says it may, to citizens who have deserved well of their country, its purpose is to discriminate. A law that grants benefits to nursing mothers or to widows or to veteran soldiers is not intended to affect all citizens equally. Nor can I, with the best will in the world, when I vote for a law giving benefits to nursing mothers, apply the word *each* to myself.

[1] *Contrat social*, II.iv, ibid., p. 374.
[2] Ibid., II.vi, p. 379.
[3] Ibid., II.iv, p. 373.

If we take Rousseau quite literally, we make nonsense of his arguments, and we also do him less than justice. He was not happily inspired when he said that the law must affect all citizens equally. If, however, we leave out that form of words, we are not left with nothing. For Rousseau also tells us that the law considers subjects in a body and actions in the abstract. In other words, a law is always a general rule of the form: *anyone so and so situated or who has behaved thus and thus shall do this, or not do that, or shall be treated in this way.* When I, as a member of the sovereign assembly, take part in making such a rule, I may know that it can never apply to myself. Yet I know that other rules do apply to me; and I can help make this rule in the same spirit as I would another that did affect me. In an assembly of equals, where all citizens take part in making the rules which apply to whole categories of citizens, each man has an interest in considering every rule as if it applied to himself. The more closely knit and simple the community, and the less inequality inside it, the easier for everyone to act in this spirit.

If I am old, I can never be young again; if I am a man, I can never be in a condition possible only to women, and yet I may take part in making laws that affect only young people or women. If I am poor, I may become rich; if I am rich, I may lose my wealth. There are differences that can never be got over, and others than can. The first are natural, and the second are social. But the natural differences divide men less than the social. It is easier for me, being old, to do justice to the young, or being a man, to do justice to women, than it is for me, being poor, to do justice to the rich, or being rich, to do it to the poor. Family ties are the closest of all, and they bind together persons who differ in sex, in age, in health and in natural ability. These differences, though sometimes divisive, more often serve to bring people closer together. It is much less their natural than their social differences which make it difficult for people to deal justly with one another. It is inequalities of power and wealth and education that weaken the sympathies of human beings for one another, making it more difficult for them to put themselves in each other's shoes. That, at least, is what Rousseau believed.

★　★　★

Bearing these four principles in mind, together with the arguments that Rousseau used in support of them, we may find it easier to discover what is valuable in his doctrine of the general will, and how he came to distinguish between the citizen's *general* and his *particular* will. Let us remember the obvious: that long before Rousseau's time, it had been common practice to speak of groups and communities as if they were individuals; to speak of them as if they had minds and wills of their own. It had also been common practice to speak as if a man could have more than one will. It is often convenient, avoiding clumsy circumlocution, to speak of a class of desires as if they were a will, or of a number of people who want the same or similar things as if they shared a single will. The use of metaphors is not confined to the poet or artist; the scientist or philosopher also needs to use them, though for a different purpose. We need not assume that Rousseau, in speaking of the will as he did, was doing anything more than had often been done before him. We need not assume that he was being literal where others had been metaphorical – that he really wanted us to believe that communities have wills in the way that men do, and that every citizen has two separate wills, a higher and a lower, sharing the first with the other citizens and keeping the second all to himself. The trouble with Rousseau is not that he used metaphors so much as that he sometimes used them inappropriately, to give vent to his feelings rather than to help make his meaning plain.

I would not have political theorists keep their feelings out of their books. That would be asking too much of them. But they can, if they take more trouble than Rousseau took, contrive to be clear and yet also warm and colourful. Certainly, we do not help to make sense of Rousseau by taking literally what had always, before his time, been taken metaphorically. His using these metaphors more often and with greater feeling than they were used before him does not prove that he took them literally; it indicates no more than that he used them to say something he had very much at heart. He was not a logician, or a metaphysician or a psychologist; he was a political theorist using the ordinary language of the educated man, but using it more passionately and less precisely than many earlier political theorists had done.

It is in a manuscript draft of the *Social Contract*, in the second chapter of Book I, in a passage[1] which is not repeated in the final version, that we find the clearest explanation of one, at least, of the senses in which Rousseau used the expression *the general will*. That will is there said to be a set of opinions which a man arrives at when, without being swayed by passion, he reflects on what his neighbours have the right to expect from him, and he from them. The general will is therefore a set of opinions about right conduct. Now, though opinions are not acts of will, Rousseau was not merely careless when he called these particular opinions the general will. He called them *general* because he believed that life in society gives them to nearly all men; and he called

[1] *Contrat social (Première version)*, I.ii, ibid., p. 286.

them a *will* because he believed that men feel so strongly about them that their behaviour is powerfully affected by them. Whenever men live together in a society or work together in a group, then so long as most of them are not mere instruments of the others, so long as they all have a sense of belonging to the society or group, they have these opinions and this feeling. Rousseau believed that a general will, in this sense, exists in every community or association.

No doubt, men can live and work together without a general will common to them all arising among them. In the Nazi extermination camps, the killers and the killed lived and worked together; the victims were not passive in the hands of their tormentors; they received orders and obeyed them; there were forms of intercourse between tormentors and victims possible only among rational beings. But they did not therefore form a community together, and there was no general will common to them. There can be no general will common to a group where some remain with the others only because escape is impossible, and do their bidding only because to obey brings lesser horrors than to disobey. If, however, it is not only force that keeps men together, if they are willing associates, if they all feel they *belong* to one community or group, then, however great the inequalities among them, there does exist a general will common to them. In other words, in every society or group, no part of whose members are the mere victims of another part, there are some common notions of justice and there is a sense of community.

But that is only one meaning of the *general will*. There is, in that sense, a general will in almost every human society; whereas Rousseau also meant by the general will something much more rare than the common loyalties and ideas of justice which help to hold together nearly every group of men living and working with one another. He also meant by it the decisions taken in an assembly of equals from whose deliberations none are excluded, an assembly where every man casts his vote, uncommitted by decisions taken by some smaller group; where the citizen cannot persuade his compatriots to do what suits him unless he can show how it also benefits them; where the very conditions of debate incline him to be public-spirited and to acquire private interests which accord with the common interest. A man's conception of his own interest is always deeply affected by the values and opinions of the social groups he belongs to; Rousseau was concerned that the group having the greatest influence should be the entire political community, and not any class or professional or partial association.

When he speaks of freedom as the creation of the general will, Rousseau means that men, when they take an equal, active and thoughtful part in making the laws, come to desire justice (i.e. that every man should get his due) as much as their own good – to regard it as so constantly the means to their own good that they learn at last to want it for its own sake, and sometimes even to prefer it to their private ends. Equal and active participation in public business makes for virtue, which is the love of justice, and justice is the common good; so that the virtuous man, even though he sometimes has desires incompatible with justice, wants justice to prevail over all such desires. Justice is a supreme value to him, though not all his desires are compatible with it. Where men feel like this, they also feel that the laws which compel them to be just (should they be otherwise inclined), though they force them to do what they may not, at the moment, want to do, also prevent them from becoming what they would rather not be. These laws, being just because they are made by an assembly of equals, keep men – and I use this phrase to express a feeling and not to state a fact – 'true to themselves'.

If society, instead of depraving man, had developed as it should and had made man what he ought to be, the process of development might be described in these words: Men came together in the first place because it was for some reason necessary for them to help one another to satisfy needs which each man could no longer satisfy for himself; they then found that they could not work together unless each of them acted on the assumption that the needs of others were as important to them as his to himself; this co-operation became in time a habit, and men learnt to consider the conditions of it (that is, the behaviour that made it possible) as enjoined upon them, not by maxims of prudence, but by rules of right; and at last, since no great inequalities emerged among them (and we are supposing that they did not), they learnt to prefer justice to the private ends it originally served. They became lovers of virtue, making a difference between the desires and emotions that helped them to live as they wanted to live (that is, as good citizens and virtuous men) and all their other passions. Their general preference for some of their passions over others caused them in time to feel thwarted by the passions which prevented their living as seemed good to them or becoming what they wanted to be; and so it became natural to them to consider the laws that maintained justice, because they satisfied those of their aspirations they valued most, as somehow more truly in accordance with their wills than the temptations to injustice to which they were sometimes liable.

Rousseau never described this process as a whole, but he did, at one time or another, describe and approve all the stages that go to make it up. I have pieced the process together because, in my opinion, it helps us to understand what he very probably meant by the general will; what he meant by the two (or, if you like, three, though the third derives from the second) most important doctrines he variously asserted when he spoke of it: that in every society men have a sense of justice; that they are nevertheless *habitually* just only when they take part as equals in the making of the laws, uninfluenced except by their own principles and by honest and free debate between them; and that, when they are habitually just, they look upon the laws freely made by an assembly of equals as better guides to conduct and more likely to satisfy them than their personal preferences.

Whether or not these doctrines are true is open to dispute, but they are, I think, intelligible; and, though they are not simple, they are free from every taint of mysticism. They are what Rousseau meant – or at least the important part of what he can plausibly be supposed to have meant – by his doctrine of the general will. Together with the four principles discussed earlier (with which they partly overlap), they are the heart of his political philosophy. It would be impertinent to suggest that these doctrines are all that Rousseau intended to mean by the many words he used to describe the general will; I will say no more than that they seem to me to represent nearly all that is important and intelligible which can be fairly extracted from what he actually said.

They help to make clearer his conception of freedom, which appealed so strongly to Kant and the German Idealists. 'Whoever refuses to obey the general will shall be constrained to do so by the whole body: which means nothing but that he will be forced to be free.'[1] How are we to interpret this paradox? How can a man be forced to be free? As Rousseau himself admits, the 'will cannot bind itself'; or, in other words, our wanting something at one time is no warrant that we still want it at another. If we have agreed to something in the past, it does not follow that we now want to abide by the agreement. How, then, when we are forced to abide by it, can it be said that we are 'forced to be free'?

If we take the words literally, they make nonsense. To get sense out of them, we have to interpret them in a larger context, in the light of the whole doctrine of the general will. The general will is the will to justice, the will to treat the good of others as equally important with our own good. We can distinguish between two kinds of desires in ourselves: those in terms of which we create an idea of what is

---

[1] *Contrat social*, I.vii, ibid., p. 364.

desirable in ourselves and others or of a life worth living or of a society worth having, and all our other desires. For example, I covet my neighbour's goods, but I also desire to deal justly by him. There is an important difference between these two desires, for I repudiate one of them and hold fast to the other. I desire to be just, but I do not desire to be covetous, though covetous I am. As a moral person, I am my own judge. The law, if it helps me to behave as I should like to behave, helps me to be the sort of person I want to be; and at the same time it helps to maintain the kind of society I want to live in. This conception of law as a means to moral freedom is not the conception of Hobbes and the Utilitarians, or of Locke and the school of Natural Law; for it does not say that law preserves freedom merely by preventing people getting in each other's way or by protecting their rights.

Freedom, Rousseau tells us, is obedience to a law we prescribe to ourselves. How then does the general will give expression to a law I prescribe to myself? When I vote against a law, I do not literally choose it as a rule to guide my conduct. If, however, I freely take part in the deliberation and the voting; if no combination is formed to impose its will on me; if I have the right to re-open the question provided I do so in the proper way, then I shall probably want the law to be enforced, even though I voted against it. I shall want this, not merely because the enforcement of law makes for my security, but because I want justice done. I shall acquire greater confidence in the wisdom and justice of the community than in my own, and when I find myself differing from the community, I shall think it probable that I am wrong. I shall not think this because the community is more powerful than I am, but because it allows me and everyone else a free and equal part in the making of the laws, taking full account of me and of everyone. It is likely that the laws as a whole – and I will have voted for many of them – will accord with my deepest convictions about how I and other people ought to behave. Though I shall still sometimes be tempted to break a particular law, I shall look upon the laws in general as rules of right. They will accord with the rules I think I ought to obey, with the rules I make my own. They are my own, not because I invented them, or because I deliberately chose each of them in preference to others, but because I now believe that I ought to obey them. Under the spur of passion I may deliberately break a rule which I believe to be a rule of right; but I cannot believe that it is a rule of right without wanting to be the sort of person who obeys the rule. Even when I am deliberately dishonest, I would rather be an honest person than a dishonest one.

But if I take no part in making the laws, if I am merely obliged to obey laws made by others, or to conform to customs I am powerless to change, the less likely it is that the rules I am required to obey will be rules I accept in conscience because they appear to me to be rules of right. When, therefore, I am constrained to obey them, or am punished for disobeying them, I shall be much more inclined to look upon myself as the victim of others.

This is, I think, too simple an account of the matter. Rousseau greatly exaggerates our aversion to laws imposed on us from without, and perhaps also exaggerates our aptness to regard them as just, when we have taken part in making them. To a much greater extent than he was inclined to admit, a man's sense of justice is determined by the laws and customs of his community, even when he takes no part in making them and cannot change them. We acquire our notions of right and wrong much more because we grow used to a discipline which makes us fit for society than because we take a hand in deciding what kind of discipline we shall have.

Yet there is this to be said in Rousseau's favour: as men's attitude to law changes; as they cease to regard it as eternal and as coming to them from a higher than human source; as statute law supersedes custom, they grow less inclined to accept as just rules which they have had no hand in making and have no power to alter. The more they come to distinguish law from justice, the more concerned they are that law should be just; and the greater this concern, the more it matters to them that they should be consulted about the law. The man who has learnt to make a distinction between positive law and justice is disposed to put a high value on moral freedom, on not being obliged to do what he thinks is wrong. For to make this distinction is to imply that there are, or may be, better rules than the ones actually enforced; and the man who thinks this is already well on the way to demanding that what he is required to do shall accord with his sense of what is right.

When men come to look upon law as man-made, then, those among them who have had nothing to do with the making of it are apt to see in it the will of others imposed on themselves. While law still seems to them the will of God, to which their rulers are also subject, though they see themselves as bound by a will external to their own, it is the will of an omnipotent Being to whom they owe everything. Clearly, they are then not free, in Rousseau's sense of freedom, for they are bound by a law *not* prescribed by themselves; and yet they are not aware that they lack this freedom, for the idea that they could be makers of law has not occurred to them. But when they begin to look upon law as made by man, they are tempted to ask, Why should we be bound by the will of other men?

This is the question which all the contract theorists tried to answer; but Rousseau stands out among them as the man who took that question most to heart and made the most uncompromising answer. We must have law, we must be bound, but we must be bound willingly; we must bind ourselves, which we can only do if we actually take part in making the law. 'The law is the will of the community; it is the public will touching on matters of common interest.' This was the formula offered in answer to the question, and it was not invented by Rousseau. He is memorable, not as the inventor of the formula, but as the man who tried valiantly to take it literally. All the contract theorists before him, in one way or another, evaded the issue they claimed to settle; he refused to evade it, and in the uncompromising attempt to settle it put forward, if not a viable scheme of government, at least a new conception of freedom.

For reasons we have already discussed, Rousseau believed that freedom is not to be attained except in small, simple and self-sufficient communities. But history teaches us that the demand for freedom, as Rousseau defines it, has not arisen in such communities but in others which are much larger and more intricate. The small and simple community changes slowly and almost imperceptibly; it is the community where custom reigns and the legislator is looked upon more as an interpreter than a maker of law. Rousseau admired both Athens and Sparta (and Sparta more even than Athens); he admired two communities which never aspired to democracy as he understood it, and never conceived of his kind of freedom. Neither Plato nor Aristotle – the two great apologists of the small and compact community which Rousseau loved – shared his idea of freedom. In the ancient world, it was the Stoics and the Christians who came closest to sharing it, and they flourished in a cosmopolitan and autocratic empire. And in the modern world, where the demand that men should live under laws prescribed by themselves is widely popular, the type of community in which alone, according to Rousseau, this demand can be met, is clearly impossible. What, then, must we conclude: that the demand for freedom arises only where social conditions forbid its achievement, or that he was mistaken about the conditions?

If Rousseau had contemplated these two conclusions, he might have preferred the first to the second. For all that he proclaimed the natural goodness of man, he was also much given to pessimism. And certainly, it would be unreasonable to reject the first conclusion on no better ground than its being depressing. Nevertheless, there are good grounds for preferring the second. Let us not forget that Rousseau is not only concerned that men should take part in making the law; he is concerned also that they should be able to live according to principles which they can critically and willingly accept. He is concerned that they should be (to use an expression which is true to his meaning though he does not himself use it) morally autonomous. He distinguishes, in the second chapter of Book IV of the *Social Contract*, the *constant will* of the members of the community – their will as citizens – from their particular wishes, and he calls this *constant will* their general will. This constant will is the desire for the common good, for justice. It is here spoken of as the desire of every citizen. So the general will, as Rousseau sees it, does not consist merely of those decisions of the assembly which happen to be just; for, if it consisted of them alone, there could conceivably be justice in the State though no one cared for justice for its own sake. Every man might vote from a selfish motive and yet the decision might be just. But Rousseau's doctrine is that, if men are to be free, the general will must be present *in* them; or, in other words, they must have what he calls a constant will. In order to be free, it is not enough that they should take part in making the law; it is also necessary that they should have a constant will in keeping with the law.

Rousseau believes that, unless men take part in making the law, they will not acquire a constant will, and so cannot have freedom. If he is right, then it follows that to take a direct part in the making of law is a necessary, if not a sufficient, condition of freedom. But he is probably mistaken. What matters, if a man is to be free, in Rousseau's sense of freedom, is that he should have a constant will and be able to live in accordance with it, that he should know justice and cherish it, and be able to do what seems just to him and not be forced to do what seems unjust. If the law is contrary to his constant will (or, as we might put it, following Kant, his moral will), he cannot be free; but it is not obvious that he must take part in making the law to ensure that it is in keeping with his moral will, nor yet that, if he does take part, it will be in keeping.

Rousseau is no doubt right in thinking that the constant or moral will is a product of social intercourse, but his belief that that intercourse must be largely political, and political in the way he describes, is mistaken. The man who has a moral will, who is concerned for justice, will want the law to be just, and his ideas of justice will be, at least in part, the fruit of his reflections on established law and custom. Being moral in the sense understood by Rousseau (that is to say, being a man who does not do what is required of him merely from fear or inertia or desire for the good opinion of others), he will necessarily also be critical of himself and of the law. He will want to have his say, he will want to count for something, he will want to be consulted; he will want this, moreover, not for himself alone, but for others also. He will want to live in a community where the makers of law are responsible to those required to obey it. But he will not want only this; he will also want other things not to be had in the small, simple, self-sufficient community in which alone people can make their own laws. Provided the system is one which allows him and others to have their say, either individually or through groups created for the purpose; and provided those who make the laws (and administer them) have a strong motive for taking notice of demands and opinions freely expressed, he may be satisfied. True, he will not believe that all the laws are just, but he may come to believe that the way in which they are made is substantially just: that is to say, about as just as it can be considering how many and how various are the interests that have to be taken into account. Sometimes he will obey the law under protest; he will obey it wishing it were different, and yet he may still obey it because he thinks it right he should do so. He may become, on rational grounds, strongly attached to the political system and think it wrong to weaken it by disobedience even to a law which seems to him unjust, except in extreme cases.

He will not be perfectly free. Indeed, far from it. He would be free only if the laws accorded entirely with his beliefs about justice, which they are never likely to do. Men who think for themselves (and this is what Rousseau wants them to do) are most unlikely to hold exactly the same opinions about what is just. Whoever has a moral will is almost certain to find obstacles to it, not only in himself, but also in established law and convention. But this is as true when he takes a direct part in making the law as when he does not. At least Rousseau provides us with no sufficient reason for thinking otherwise. Even in the small compact community which he imagined, citizens who vote against a decision accept it willingly, much less because they are convinced that, being in the minority, they are probably wrong, than because they believe it is right that decisions should be reached in that way. The virtue of the system is that it inclines men to accommodate their wishes to other people's because they think they ought to do so and not merely because they find they must. It may also be true that, because they are inclined this way, they are the more likely to conclude that when they are in the minority they are wrong; but this (so it seems to me) is more doubtful. They willingly obey because they have been consulted, because their voice has been heard, because the system is such that their wishes and interests count in general for as much as other people's, even though, on this occasion, the decision has gone against them. They willingly obey less because they believe that the law is just than because they believe that it has been justly made.

No doubt, persons accustomed to democracy and who have re-flected upon it may come in time to have strong doubts about their own wisdom as well as other people's. As they look back on their past opinions, they may conclude that they were as much or more mistaken than the persons they disagreed with; they may grow attached to the system because experience has convinced them that the decisions taken under it are, on the whole, wiser and more just for being taken in the way they are. But this reappraisal of past decisions goes on as much among those who voted with the majority as among those who voted the other way. It may well be true that when equals take decisions in common, their confidence in their collective wisdom increases with time; the more experience has taught all of them that they have been unwise and unjust in the past and may be so again in the future, the more considerately they are apt to deal with one another. Free discussion between equals probably does have some, if not all, of the effects imagined by Rousseau; and this, if it is true, is strong evidence in favour of democracy.

But it is not stronger evidence in favour of the direct democracy described in the *Social Contract* than of other kinds. Democracy does not require that everyone should take a direct part in legislation; it requires only that the discussions and negotiations which lead up to the making of law should be spread wide enough to ensure that all important interests and points of view find free expression and are taken into account, and that there should be general confidence that this is so. It requires, not that everyone should take a part in forming the 'political will' of the community, but that those who do take part should speak for all the sorts and conditions of men in the community, and should have the confidence of those they speak for. Provided these conditions hold, it is just as likely as in a direct democracy that the laws will accord with the *constant* or *moral* wills of the citizens. Admittedly, it is not nearly as likely in a representative democracy as Rousseau says it is in the kind of democracy he favours, but then he greatly exaggerates the merits of that kind.

There is another freedom important to sophisticated man besides moral freedom, and Rousseau, where he does not neglect it, disparages it. Man in society acquires, as Rousseau says, a constant will; he acquires moral principles and, to the extent that he takes them seriously, wishes to live up to them. He finds that his passions, natural and acquired, move him to act against his principles, and he therefore aspires to self-discipline. When he curbs his passions so as not to act unjustly, he feels that he is free, not because his passions are in general weaker than his desire to be just, but because he would rather be a just man than a man whose passions make him unjust; he identifies himself with a part of himself against another part. But love of justice is not all that man acquires in society. He also acquires aspirations which are not moral, and are therefore not what Rousseau understands by a constant will, though they are in some ways similar to it. Man desires achievement; he sets up ideals and strives to realize them. These ideals need not be moral, and yet, if a man is to realize them, he will need as much self-discipline as when he aspires to be just or to be a good citizen. No matter what a man sets his heart upon, he must make sacrifices to obtain it, and his passions will sometimes stand in his way. Even if he is self-centred and ambitious, as many artists and men of letters are, reason in him may 'rule' the passions; that is to say, he may succeed in imposing upon himself, deliberately, systematically and over long periods of time, restrictions which serves his ambition. He will be no more a slave to his passions than the just man; for ambition, as much as justice, is possible only in a rational creature who consciously prefers some things to others.

In every society, men aspire to other things besides justice or the common good; they have, to use the idiom of Rousseau and Kant, a rational will which is not merely a constant will or a moral will. They admire other than morally good behaviour; they have standards of excellence which are not moral standards. Though it may be true, as Rousseau tells us, that it is not as a mere creature of appetite, but as a creature capable of rational behaviour and having notions of excellence, that man comes to conceive of freedom and to cherish it, it is not true that he is free only to the extent that he can live in conformity with his constant or moral will. He is free to the extent that he can live as seems *good* to him, and what he thinks good depends on much more than his moral principles. It depends, as the sociologists say, on the *values* he accepts, which are only in part moral; it depends, not only on his ideas about how men ought to behave, but also on his ideas about what is worth doing or having. Man is an artist, an enquirer, and a lover of power and distinction as well as a moralist; and his concern for freedom springs also, and largely, from aspirations which are more properly called aesthetic, intellectual or political than moral. That man has such aspirations Rousseau does not deny, but he has little sympathy for them and takes almost no account of them in his doctrine of freedom.

Since man aspires to much more than justice and virtue, it may be that he cannot be satisfied in the small and compact republic described by Rousseau; it may be that he puts a high value on the much greater opportunities which are to be had only in larger, looser and more varied communities. His attachment to such communities may, of course, be partly due to the causes suggested by Rousseau, to his clinging to vices born of vanity which flourish in such communities, to insatiable desires acquired in a corrupt environment; but it also has other causes not less important. He may have a larger conception of freedom than Rousseau's; he may want what is not to be had in a self-sufficient and simple community small enough to allow all its members to take a direct part in making the laws. If he understands what are the conditions of having what he wants, he comes to accept them; he comes to accept, and even to value, the legal and political system most likely to ensure that the rules of a large community take into account the needs, the moral sentiments, the aspirations and ambitions of their subjects. In that case, modest though his own part in this system may be, he takes it seriously and is a responsible citizen. He is as close to having a rational political will as the citizen of Rousseau's ideal State. He does not obey the law from fear only or inertia or self-interest; he obeys willingly, knowing that by so doing he strengthens a political order which is a condition of the freedom precious to him. Contemplating the State imagined in the *Social Contract*, he might express his feelings about it in these words: 'I can see that men, having only such aspirations as meet with Rousseau's approval, might be happy in such a community. But I aspire to other things, which are not rooted in vanity, and Rousseau has said nothing to show that my aspirations are irrational in the sense that they cannot be reconciled one with another or must bring me into conflict with other people. I could not be happy after the fashion of his citizens unless I ceased to be what I now am and became what I do not wish to be.' He might look upon man's condition in Rousseau's imagined community much as Rousseau says that the citizen of that community looks upon the condition of man in the state of nature. Man, in that state, had only independence and not freedom, and he had the only kind of happiness of which he was capable. Rousseau tells us that, though there was nothing wrong with man in the state of nature, there were things possible to him, which he could not then know, but which, when he came to know them, would make him think himself better off outside it.

It is a neat but misleading phrase that freedom is obedience to a law we prescribe to ourselves. If the law we have in mind is the moral law, it is not literally true that we prescribe it to ourselves. We do not decide that there shall be such a law. It arises out of social intercourse between men; it is an effect of their behaviour towards one another, but they do not decide what it shall be. Even when a man, as the saying goes, 'accepts it inwardly' or 'makes it his own', he does not prescribe it to himself. He is at first compelled to obey, and then acquiescent, and eventually willing. The process whereby men acquire moral principles has very little indeed in common with legislation. If the moral law is a law we prescribe to ourselves, then it is so only in a metaphorical sense.

If the law we have in mind, moreover, is a law deliberately made by men, we cannot define freedom as obedience to it. Though we have ourselves taken part in making it, it does not follow that we willingly obey it whenever we are required to do so. Even though we grant that it is involved in his being a moral creature that man wants to be the sort of person who chooses to act rightly (though in fact he often chooses to act wrongly), and that the law, where it accords with his moral principles, helps him to be that sort of person, we cannot say that his freedom consists in obeying the law. We cannot say it even though he himself took part in making the law. For, at the time that he is required to obey the law, he may not want to obey it. And even if he wants to obey it, his freedom does not consist in his obedience; it consists in his being able to do what he wants. We must not say that obedience to law is freedom, but rather that law promotes freedom to the extent that it makes it easier for men who have aspirations requiring self-discipline (among which the desire to be moral is only one) to achieve what they aspire to. We can say also that law is the more likely to promote freedom in this way for being made by the persons required to obey it or (and here we part company with Rousseau) by persons responsible to them. And, finally, we can agree with Rousseau that it is only as a rational creature capable of self-discipline that man comes to conceive of freedom and to put a high value on it, though we insist against him that man does not discipline himself only, nor even always primarily, in the name of morality.

Yet Rousseau's account of freedom, though it cannot be accepted in the form he gives it, is still the most valuable part of his moral and social theory. In the *Discourse on Inequality*, and in other places, he explains how man, not yet formed by society – man in the state of nature, a mere creature of appetite – easily puts up with the restrictions that nature places on him. If he cannot get what he wants, he soon ceases to want it, unless he needs it to keep him alive. His desires are free of vanity and are unconnected with rational purposes. He is independent, but he is not free. When he is thwarted, he has no sense of being deprived of what is owing to him, of lacking freedom. He has as yet no idea of freedom; he wants, not freedom, but food, drink and shelter. Only as a rational creature, self-conscious and conscious of his relations with others, does man acquire the idea of freedom. But by then he has ceased to be a mere creature of appetite, who seeks to satisfy each of his desires while it is upon him, giving no thought to the future; he is a creature aware of his own preferences and with a more or less stable way of life. He is housed, both his body and his mind; he has seen himself reflected in many mirrors; he has had judgements passed upon him by others and by himself. He is less concerned that he should be able to do whatever is prompted by his appetites than that he should achieve his enduring purposes; and it is then that he claims freedom. But he must live in a community with others, which he cannot do unless he abides by rules which serve their purposes as well as his. He cannot therefore be free unless his purposes are in keeping with the rules; and this they are the more likely to be, the stronger his respect for the rules, and his desire that they should be obeyed by everyone, including himself. For the rules will then inform his purposes. In the social philosophy of Rousseau, justice and freedom are not externally related, as they are for Hobbes or the Utilitarians. Justice is more than a means to freedom, more than a set of rules to prevent our getting too much in each other's way. The law we critically and willingly accept, the law 'we prescribe to ourselves', profoundly affects our conception of a life worth living; and the rights we put a special value on and call freedom are largely determined by that conception.

IV. HOW ROUSSEAU CONCEIVED OF EQUALITY AND WHY HE THOUGHT IT IMPORTANT

In the Middle Ages, it had been the fashion to explain both the institution of property and inequality of wealth as effects of corruption. If men were innocent, they would no more need property than government; there would be neither rich nor poor, neither ruler nor ruled. But for several generations before Rousseau, political thought had been loosening its ties with theology. The idea that property and government are effects of sin and remedies for it had steadily been losing ground. The contract theorists had taught that men first set up government for their own convenience; Locke had treated property as a natural right prior to government, and Hume had explained it as an institution which arose among men because they had found it their interest to have stable rules governing the use and transference of external objects. In the eyes of Locke and Hume, property and inequality were neither effects nor causes of corruption.

In the eighteenth century, as never before, men had come to believe in progress. They were exhilarated by the quick growth of their knowledge, their power over nature and their wealth. Mandeville, Hume and the Utilitarians in Britain, and the Encyclopaedists in France, welcomed this great accumulation of knowledge and wealth. They did not deny that knowledge and wealth, for all that they increased so rapidly, were still confined mostly to the minds and pockets of only a small part of the community; they even admitted sometimes that men were more unequal in their day than they had been in the past. But this inequality did not disturb them, for they believed that all classes gained from the increase in knowledge, wealth and power, though some gained more than others.

Rousseau reversed the mediaeval argument: instead of saying that inequality is an effect of man's corrupted nature, he said that corruption is an effect of inequality. He agreed with Hume that property is a social institution, and with both Hume and Locke, that it is a means to freedom. There was to be private property even in the ideal society described in the *Social Contract*. He agreed also with Locke and Hume that government serves above all to protect property. But he believed, as they did not, that most governments were in fact much more useful to the rich than to the poor. We have seen how, in the *Discourse on Inequality*, he attributed the first establishment of government to a specious argument of the rich, whereby they induced the poor to adopt an expedient from which they stood to gain much more than the poor. That part of the *Discourse* might almost be called an early version of the Marxian doctrine that the prime function of government is to protect the propertied classes against the classes having little or no property. Only in the ideal society – the society of equals – is the defence of property equally the interest of all.

How, according to Rousseau, does inequality corrupt? It magnifies vanity and its evil effects, and it also makes the poor subservient to the rich. It creates such differences between men, exalting some and debasing others, that they are driven to care more for how they stand in relation to one another than for getting what will satisfy them. At the end of the *Discourse on Inequality*, he says that it is 'to the burning desire to have others speak of us, to the passion to distinguish ourselves. . . .that we owe what is best and what is worst among men: . . .that is to say, a multitude of evil things and a small number of good ones'. [1] Sometimes Rousseau gives us to understand that inequality intensifies vanity, and sometimes that it makes vanity more dangerous. Since these assertions do not exclude one another and might both be true, we can assume, there being no evidence to the contrary, that he accepts them both. Inequality adds to our vanity, but, even if it did not – even if we were no vainer as unequals than we would be as equals – inequality would still make our vanity more harmful to others and to ourselves. Therefore, as inequality grows, the evil effects of vanity grow faster even than vanity itself.

Where men are unequal, every man strives to be superior to others and resents being inferior to them. But, since everyone cannot be superior to everyone else, this striving for superiority is mostly unavailing; men do not achieve what they aim at. They are not satisfied, and yet are moved to behave in ways which are hurtful and humiliating. If they were nearer equality, they would be less concerned to establish superiority and to avoid inferiority; they would be less competitive and less envious, and instead of striving for status would strive for what was more likely to satisfy them.

We have seen that Rousseau attributes to vanity some good effects as well as many bad ones. This explains, no doubt, why he devotes so many pages and so much eloquence to the bad effects and so few to the others. But, despite so many and such harsh pronouncements against vanity, Rousseau admits that it is inevitable. Men are without vanity only in the state of nature, where they lack self-consciousness and have no standards of excellence. In society, their happiness always depends greatly on how others think of them, and Rousseau speaks of this concern for reputation as if it were either the same thing as vanity or closely related to it. In his *Project of a Constitution for Corsica*, for example, he says: 'The prime motives which move men to action, if we consider the matter carefully, come down to two, concupiscence (*volupté*) and vanity; moreover, if you take from the first all that belongs to the second, you will find that, in the last analysis, almost everything is reduced to vanity alone. . . . But vanity is the fruit of opinion, is born of it and feeds upon it. Whence it follows that whoever controls the opinions of a people controls their actions. The people strive for things in proportion to the value they place upon them; to show them what they ought to value is to tell them what they ought to do.' [2] He then continues, only a few lines further on, 'Opinion, when it

[1] *Discours sur l'inégalité*, ibid., p. 189.
[2] *Constitution pour la Corse*, ibid., p. 937.

puts a high value on the frivolous, produces vanity, but, when it turns upon what is in itself great and noble, it produces pride'.[1]

Here, as in so many other places, Rousseau fails to make his meaning clear. Are vanity and pride in themselves the same emotion, differing only in their causes? Are they both equally self–esteem, though the first arises from a mistaken judgement while the second does not? Does the vain man take pride in qualities or accomplishments which are worthless? And is the proud man vain of that about himself which really has value? Sometimes, as in the last sentence quoted, Rousseau speaks as if this were what he believed. Yet it goes against the spirit of most of his teaching, for he says in many places that vanity is the root of unhappiness and consists in the desire to be admired by others and to impress them.

We ordinarily speak of pride, when we distinguish it from and prefer it to vanity, in ways which suggest that the proud man has stable principles while the vain man has not. The proud man is above all his own judge; if he falls below his own standards he is ashamed, even though others do not condemn him. Of course, he is not unaffected by their judgements, especially if they share his principles and know the facts. The proud man shrinks from the adverse judgement of his moral peers, of those whose standards are his own, and sometimes his pride will make a coward or a hypocrite of him. But the need to meet his own standards, to avoid the shame of being condemned in his own eyes, may give him courage and sincerity. And he will be little affected by the blame or praise of persons whose judgement he does not respect; he will be independent of them. But the vain man does not have stable principles, or has them so weakly that he fears to abide by them when doing so would make his neighbours blame or despise him. He is, as the proud man is not, the slave of opinion; he is driven to seek admiration by conforming to whatever tastes happen to be fashionable in the circles in which he moves. He is indifferent to other men's judgement only if those men are out of fashion. Both the proud man and the vain man are creatures formed by society; the proud man does not, any more than the vain one, acquire his principles and tastes in solitude. But the proud man is independent in a way in which the vain man is not: he has strength of character and is ready to ignore or to flout opinion which does not conform with his principles. This, I think, is the distinction between pride[2]

---

[1] Ibid., p. 938.

[2] Of course, pride is often condemned, especially by theologians, but I am here considering the sort of pride held to be superior to vanity, and am saying no more about it than seems necessary to explain Rousseau's meaning. It can be (and

and vanity suggested by a common use of those words, and it is also in keeping with Rousseau's account of how society, by exalting men's vanity, corrupts them, producing in them ambitions difficult or impossible to satisfy and making them rivals for admiration.

No doubt, pride (even when it is not arrogance) can be dangerous and vanity harmless. Indeed, the proud man, when he is dangerous, is apt to be more so than the vain one. Pride can be as improper, as misplaced, as any other passion; a man's self-respect may depend on his living up to principles harmful to himself and to others. He may be deeply ashamed of what it would be better that he were not ashamed of. Nevertheless, it may be that pride is necessary to the happiness of a moral being as vanity is not; it may be that society cannot do without it if its members are to find satisfaction in it and to be well disposed to one another. Certainly, Rousseau believed that men, in order to be happy, must have stable principles and tastes and be able to lead a life in keeping with them. He believed that the stronger such principles and tastes in them, the less they are inclined to strive for superiority over others; what is then closest to their hearts is that they should have what they think desirable and be what they think is worth being, and not that they should be preferred to others.

It must be admitted that Rousseau never succeeds in making it clear just what he means by vanity and just why he condemns it. Sometimes he speaks with disfavour of all self-esteem resting on the good opinion of others, while at other times he recognizes that, unless men were moved by the desire to be well thought of, they would not be educable or, as he puts it, perfectible. Man, he tells us, becomes self-conscious in society, acquiring standards of excellence and the desire to excel. If it were not so, he would not be sociable, moral and rational. Though, as we have seen, Rousseau sometimes speaks of Emile's education as if it consisted in his tutor's protecting him from *all* social influences – so that he should reach physical, intellectual and moral maturity in a completely natural way – it really consists in his tutor's protecting him from harmful social influences. Emile does not acquire intellectual and moral independence by being taught to think for himself regardless of the good opinion of others; he desires his tutor's good opinion; he desires to excel by standards which he takes from another, knowing that they come from another. He is concerned for his reputation, and could not become morally and intellectually independent unless he were so. Rousseau both recognizes this, when

---

indeed has been) argued that pride is worse than vanity: the man who defies God or the Church is held to be *proud* rather than *vain*.

he describes Emile's education, and denies it, when he condemns all vanity – all self-esteem resting on the good opinion of others – without qualification. It was seldom his way to weaken the effect of his condemnations by qualifying them at the time he made them. He preferred another method; he preferred to unsay in one place what he had said in another. He sacrificed, at least temporarily, the truth as he saw it to rhetoric. I do not say that he did this deliberately; but he did it often, to the great confusion of his readers. Thus we find him at one time condemning self-esteem as vanity, and at another speaking well of it as pride. Thus too we sometimes find him saying that men must be governed through the control of opinion, and at other times setting great store by independence of mind. And though these beliefs can perhaps be reconciled with one another, Rousseau does not see the need to reconcile them. He either contradicts himself or appears to do so, and seems not to notice the contradictions. Nevertheless, he does sometimes provide us in his own writings with arguments to resolve his paradoxes.[1] What he tells us about the education of Emile does enable us to see how he might have distinguished vanity from pride, if he had ever troubled to do so. For Emile, though without false pride, is certainly not without pride. He is not without self-esteem; he has a proper and firm sense of values, and his self-respect depends upon his living up to standards which he has made his own but which are also products of education.

To ensure that men do have strong and stable principles and taste, Rousseau does not look to education alone; he looks to education and to equality. A proper education teaches men to value what ought to be valued. Children seek to please, to gain approval; they are in their immaturity emulous, having as yet no principles or tastes of their own. We cannot expect them to have independence of judgement until they

---

[1] But I must not create the impression that Rousseau's paradoxes are usually resolved, or that his contradictions are all more apparent than real. In his doctrine of the general will, for example, he insists that every citizen must think for himself and also says that, where there is such a will, it is likely that all will think alike. He wants both independence and uniformity of judgement, and yet does not really explain how the two are to be had together. Again, what he says of public education suggests that he thinks it more important that citizens should think alike than that they should think for themselves, whereas what he says of private education in *Emile* suggests that he cares above all for independence of judgement. True, he describes public education as it ought to be in a properly constituted State, while Emile is to be made incorruptible in a corrupt society. Does he then set store by independence of judgement only in a corrupt society? I do not think so. I suspect that he takes it for granted that, in a just society, citizens will be found to agree about most matters of importance, even though they think for themselves. In his rich, but rather loose and shapeless, social philosophy, there are many things not properly thought out.

grow up, and so, since they cannot help but seek to imitate what they see admired around them; since their self-esteem depends entirely on the approval of others; since they are incapable of being their own judges or of questioning the judgements passed upon them, they have to be moulded by others. To put Rousseau's meaning in other words than his own, we have to use the vanity inevitable in children, and which is harmless if not allowed to get out of control, to create a proper pride in them, a pride which does not make them indifferent to reputation but only to the opinions of those who do not share their principles. Pride, though born of vanity, can serve to reduce vanity and to hold it in check.

But the social order must not be allowed to weaken the effects of a good education. It would be absurd to bring up children to respect principles which they cannot practise except at great cost to themselves. Extremes of poverty and wealth, distinctions of rank unrelated to ability and to services done to the community, magnify vanity and its evil effects. They create temptations difficult for even the properly educated man to resist. Inequality undoes much of the good done by a good education. It does even more; it lowers the quality of education. Children are taught to pay lip service to principles which their elders do not expect them to follow in their conduct; they are taught to be hypocrites. Therefore equality, though not a sufficient, is a necessary, condition of happiness; it is not enough to abolish inequality, for there must also be a good system of education. But these two things go together: where inequality is great, education is unlikely to be good; and where education is not good, men soon acquire passions and tastes which lead to inequality. The well-educated man cares little for wealth; it would seem absurd to him to seek to prove himself superior to others by acquiring greater riches than they have. He is not luxurious and does not advertise himself by a display of his wealth. As Rousseau puts it in the *Considerations on the Government of Poland*, 'So long as the great are luxurious, cupidity will hold sway in all hearts. What the public admires will always be an object of desire to private persons; and if it is necessary to be rich in order to be outstanding, the dominant passion will always be to get rich'. And a few lines later, we are told 'that simplicity of manners and of the trappings of life is less the fruit of law than of education'.[1]

---

[1] *Le Gouvernement de Pologne*, ch. III, op. cit., pp. 964 and 966. As the first passage quoted serves to show, Rousseau, though he puts so high a value on independence of judgement – on not being a slave to opinion – sometimes takes it for granted that most men always will be slaves to it. When he says that what the public admires will always be an object of desire to private persons, the private persons

Equality, in Rousseau's opinion, does not exclude hierarchy or require that no man shall be richer or poorer than another. There must be ranks in society; but men should move from the lower into the higher ranks only as they grow older and more is expected of them, or as their services to the community increase, or when they are elected to a public office. Every citizen should have property of his own and should be, economically, his own master. If men are to be their own masters economically, then some must be richer than others, for some will be abler or more fortunate. Where every farmer owns his own land and lives off it, some farmers will prosper more than others; but this does not matter so long as the rich farmers are not held to be socially superior to the poor ones. So long as distinctions of rank do not spring from differences in wealth but rest on seniority or on services rendered to the community; so long as mere wealth is not held in honour, Rousseau does not object to some men being richer than others. But where wealth is held in honour, men are bound to put a value on what is worthless, on what cannot satisfy; they strive to be as rich as or richer than their neighbours, and they live luxuriously to prove their wealth. Vanity flourishes, and with it all its worst effects.

Apart from magnifying vanity, inequality diminishes independence. In the *Social Contract*, Rousseau says only that no man should be so rich as to be able to buy another, nor any so poor as to be constrained to sell himself;[1] and he has in mind, not the danger of slavery, but of political subservience. Every citizen must be an independent voter in the popular assembly; he must not sell his own vote nor buy that of another. But elsewhere Rousseau launches a more sustained and general attack on inequality as the destroyer of independence. 'Whoever,' he tells us in the *Project of a Constitution for Corsica*, 'depends on another and lacks resources of his own, cannot be free. Alliances, treaties, faith between men – these can all bind the weak to the strong but never bind the strong to the weak'.[2] He says also that 'everywhere where wealth is dominant, power and authority are ordinarily separate, because the means of acquiring

---

he has in mind are adults. He is not speaking here of the education of children. Clearly, he thinks that men can be influenced for their good through their vanity, for he recommends that they be so influenced. He advocates two courses without being aware how different they are: the reduction of vanity and the substitution for it of a proper pride, and the diversion of vanity from the pernicious to the beneficial.

[1] *Contrat social*, II.xi, ibid., pp. 391–2.
[2] *Constitution pour la Corse*, ibid., p. 903.

wealth and the means of coming by authority, not being the same, are rarely used by the same persons. It then appears that power is in the hands of the magistrates, while in reality it is in the hands of the rich. . . . Thus. . .some aspire to authority, to sell the use of it to the rich and so get riches for themselves; while the others, and the greater number, seek wealth directly, knowing that, if they have it, they are sure to have power some day by buying either authority or those in whom it is vested'.[1] In his article on 'Political Economy', Rousseau sets forth in these words what he calls the social compact between the rich and the poor: 'You need me, for I am rich and you are poor; let us then come to an agreement: I will allow you the honour of serving me, on condition that you give me what little remains to you for the trouble I shall take in commanding you.'[2] It proves the perversity of established society, in that the greater a man's needs, the more difficult for him the process of acquisition, and in that it is precisely 'the superfluities of the rich which enable them to despoil the poor of what they need'.[3] No socialist or communist of the next century outdoes Rousseau in denouncing inequality of wealth.

Yet Rousseau was neither a socialist nor a communist. He wanted every citizen to be a man of modest property, a man of independent means; he wanted him to be 'self-employed'. But equality does not maintain itself; and so we are told, in the eleventh chapter of Book II of the *Social Contract*, that 'it is precisely because the force of circumstance tends always to destroy equality that the force of legislation should tend always to maintain it'.[4] How then should it be maintained? Rousseau suggests various devices, not always compatible with one another. In the 'Political Economy', having said that property is the most sacred of all rights, and in a way more important even than liberty because more necessary for the conservation of life, he goes on to say that a man's owning something while he is alive does not give him the right to decide who shall own it after he is dead. Yet he is reluctant to see property pass out of the family, and therefore, instead of drastically limiting the right of bequest, suggests heavy taxes on luxury goods.[5] In the *Project of a Constitution for Corsica*, written some ten years after the 'Political Economy', there is no trace of this earlier reluctance, and we are told that 'the laws concerning inheritance must

---

[1] Ibid., p. 939.
[2] 'Sur l'économie politique', ibid., p. 273.
[3] From a fragment on 'Le luxe, le commerce et les arts', ibid., p. 522.
[4] *Contrat social*, II.xi, ibid., p. 392.
[5] 'Sur l'économie politique', ibid., pp. 262–3 and 271.

always tend to restore equality, so that everyone has something and nobody has too much'.[1] All trade, but especially foreign trade, should be kept within narrow limits to ensure that not only Corsica as a whole remains virtually self-sufficient, but that each district in the island relies as much as possible on its own resources. The Corsicans will be the poorer for it; there will be no rich merchants and bankers among them, and they will have no large towns. Instead, they will have independence, both national and personal. For the man who is his own master, be he farmer or craftsman, though he has needs which cannot be met by the products of his own and his family's labour, can procure the means to satisfy them at the local market, where he is as well placed as his neighbour when it comes to striking a bargain or fixing a price. Where buyers and sellers are for the most part either independent producers or local merchants well known to them, the terms of trade between all parties are more or less equal. There are then no middlemen to control the market and to put producers in a position where they must sell their products on unfavourable terms.[2]

Not only is Rousseau's dislike of inequality as passionate as that of any socialist; it is also justified in much the same way. He agrees with the socialists about the evils which afflict society and about their principal cause, but disagrees with them about the remedy. He does not suggest the abolition of private property in the means of production, distribution and exchange, nor a planned economy, nor co-operative production; he says only that law and government must ensure that all citizens have enough property so that even the poorest of them are independent of the rich. He is not much of an economist, and many of the expeditions he suggests to achieve his purpose are open to serious criticism, even when his purpose is not questioned. Yet he does hold fast to one belief which he expresses time and again: the mass of citizens can be economically independent only in a simple and predominantly agricultural society. Freedom is not secure except among equals, and men are equals, not when they have the same incomes, but when each is economically his own master and no man is more dependent for his livelihood on another than that other on him.

The right to property is as sacred in the eyes of Rousseau as in Locke's eyes. Indeed, it is not Locke but Rousseau who applies the

[1] *Constitution pour la Corse*, ibid., p. 945.
[2] Though I have used here expressions not used by Rousseau, I have endeavoured to be true to his meaning.

191

word *sacred* to this right.[1] Yet the right of property is differently conceived by Rousseau. What every man has a right to is not the product of his labour but as much property as will secure his independence. The sovereign community, whose legislative authority is unlimited, is made up of citizens who are men of independent property. So jealous is Rousseau of the right of property that he favours, both in the 'Political Economy' and the *Project of a Constitution for Corsica* (where he treats of fiscal matters at greater length than in his other writings), the establishment of a public domain whose revenues are to defray the costs of government, This public domain would be worthless unless labour were applied to it, and so he proposes that citizens should be required from time to time to work for it. They should work for the State rather than pay taxes to it. That, he admits, would be an intolerable burden in large states, but in small self-governing communities it has good effects. It leaves the citizen complete master of his estate and yet brings it home to him that he owes service to the community. It preserves independence and enhances patriotism. This is what Rousseau says; though few, perhaps, will accept his reasons for preferring taxes in labour to taxes in money.

We have seen that inequality, in his opinion, is an obstacle to political freedom, because the citizen who depends on another for his livelihood will not follow his own judgement politically; he will speak and vote in the assembly to please whoever he depends on. But there is another reason why inequality stands in the way of freedom; it weakens men's devotion to the community and so makes it less likely that they will want what accords with the general will. Patriotism, we are told in the 'Political Economy', encourages virtue, and 'every man is virtuous when his particular will conforms in all things with the general will, [for] we want what those whom we love want'.[2] In the eyes of Rousseau, the most admirable of all peoples were the Spartans and the Romans, and nothing about them was more to be admired than their patriotism, their devotion to the community. But devotion to the community is devotion to its laws, its institutions, its traditions – to whatever makes it what it is; it differs both from love of our neighbours and from love of justice. A man who is indifferent to most

---

[1] In only one place does Rousseau verge on communism, where he says in the *Project of a Constitution for Corsica* (*Oeuvres complètes*, vol. III, p. 931), 'Far from wishing the State to be poor, I would, on the contrary, have it own everything, and that each person should partake of what belongs to the community in proportion to his services'. There are also other ideas which Rousseau takes up in this way to drop them immediately: they do not affect his general philosophy.

[2] 'Sur l'économie politique', ibid., p. 254.

of his countrymen, taken individually, may yet be deeply attached to his country; a man who is shocked by an injustice done to another man may at that moment be unaffected by patriotism, for the victim of injustice may not be a compatriot. The Englishman shocked by an injustice done to a Jew in Germany may dislike both Jews and Germans. And yet – so Rousseau would have us believe – patriotism deepens our sympathy for our neighbours and our love of justice.

It is as members of a community to which we are devoted that we learn to think of other men as neighbours and that we come to know justice and to put a high value on it. The more equal the members of a community, the deeper their sense of belonging to it; and the deeper that sense, the stronger their love of justice and the quicker their sympathies for their neighbours. But where inequality is great, the rich and the socially exalted look upon the community as their own; they demand justice for themselves and for others placed as they are, but are not much put out by injustice done to inferiors, while the poor feel themselves the victims of the community and their devotion to it is weakened. In a footnote towards the end of the fourth book of *Emile*, Rousseau tells of a splendidly attired stranger in Athens who, when asked what was his country, answered 'I am one of the rich'.[1] This, in Rousseau's opinion, is a very good answer, presumably because it implies that the rich have more in common with one another than with their poor compatriots. In the *Considerations on the Government of Poland*, he compares the vigour and generous instincts of the old Greeks and Romans with what he is pleased to call the feebleness of the French, the Russians, the English and other 'modern' nations. Why, he asks, are we not men like the ancients? He gives several answers, and among them this one: that we lack strong loyalties. The legislators of antiquity, he says, 'looked for the ties which bind citizens to their country and to one another', whereas we are divided from one another by 'our prejudices, our base philosophy and our passionate concern with little things'; we seek, not happiness, but 'the pleasures that separate and isolate men, making them weak'.[2]

The differences between what Rousseau advocated and what the French revolutionaries practised are legion. Yet their motto, 'Liberty, Equality and Fraternity', expresses admirably the spirit of his philosophy, and he might even have been tempted to add (for he liked echoes of sacred texts), 'and the greatest of these is Fraternity'.

[1] *Émile*, manuscrit du Palais-Bourbon, *Oeuvres complètes*, vol. IV, p. 1624 (n. (*b*) to p. 681).
[2] *Le Gouvernement de Pologne*, ch. II, *Oeuvres complètes*, vol. III, pp. 956, 958 and 959.

Patriotism, as he conceives of it, is very closely connected with fraternity; for fraternity is the feeling that men have for one another, not because they are drawn together as individuals, but because they are attached to the group to which they all belong, be it a family or a community or even mankind. Fraternity binds us to one another by ties which are not oppressive, because the community in which we are brothers does not so much lay duties upon us as establish needs which we are eager to provide for. Every enduring community must make large demands on its members; devotion to the community, far from making the demands more burdensome, makes some welcome and others easier to bear.

Rousseau, here as elsewhere, is too extreme. Patriotism can be strong in communities where there are great inequalities. It was so in Rome in republican times and in England in the eighteenth century. It is not true that the more egalitarian a community, the more devoted its members are to it. In a society where class barriers are breaking down, men may become more ambitious, more competitive, more ruthless, more restless and more envious than they were before. An historian could collect, no doubt, much evidence to put against Rousseau's too simple thesis. And the political theorist, without troubling to collect evidence, might put a more general objection; he might say that some inequality is inevitable in any society, even the small agricultural community favoured by Rousseau, and that the degree of inequality which men will tolerate must depend largely on their habits and values. If they are brought up to accept their 'station in society', they may, though that station is inferior, aspire to nothing different and be devoted to the community they belong to. Or if they live in times where ambition is thought good and opportunities are varied – if (for example) they have the tastes and values which most men have today – they cannot get what they aspire to except in large and intricate societies where equality as conceived by Rousseau is impossible, where there must be enormous inequalities of power, if not of income. If they come to understand this, they may come to accept with a good will inequalities condemned by Rousseau and yet be ardent patriots. The idea of equality, of the rights and opportunities which all men should have, varies from society to society. Except when equality is taken to mean a complete identity of rights (and it is hardly ever so taken), it is a concept logically posterior to others, and especially to the idea of justice. If we want to know what at any time is understood by equality, we have to ask what the rights and opportunities are of which it is being said (or denied) that everyone should have them.

Yet there is much to be said in Rousseau's favour. Where men look upon the social order as unchanging and the work of Providence, they put up with inequality readily enough; they are reconciled to their position in society; they accept what God or fate has allotted to them. They are, no doubt, attached to their traditions, and they recognize their obligations to their superiors and may feel loyalty to them. Yet they are usually not patriots; their deepest loyalties are to their families or to their neighbourhood and not to a political community which includes both them and their social superiors. They are not patriots in Rousseau's sense of the word, no matter how attached they may be to that corner of the earth they inhabit and where they and their ancestors were born. A sixteenth-century peasant far from his native Anjou might have longed for it as poignantly as du Bellay exiled in Rome, but the *patrie angevine* of the poet, which was the *patrie* also of the peasant, was no political community. Devotion to a political community – patriotism, as Rousseau speaks of it – is different from acceptance of a social order regarded as the work of Providence and different also from attachment to the ancestral home and region. It may be that devotion to a political community, a State, depends much more than other loyalties on men's feeling that they are, in some important sense, equals. For men are not likely to be devoted to the State they belong to unless they look upon it as a maintainer of justice; and if their idea of equality derives from their idea of justice, then the greater the inequality, the weaker their devotion to the State is apt to be. But this does not mean that devotion to the political community will not be general and strong unless men are equal in Rousseau's sense of equality; it means only that it is likely to be weak unless they are equal in the sense of equality which is in keeping with their notion of justice.

Men, moreover, *become* 'political'; they come to make new claims on their rulers – claims which lead eventually to the emergence of a State, of a solid, intricate, well-defined structure of authority, out of a tribal or feudal society – as their interests and their notions of justice change. There is no State unless there are citizens, unless there are men who take a different, and much more hopeful and demanding, attitude to those in authority over them than is taken in a tribal or feudal society. Where society, in this sense, is *political*, and not tribal or feudal – where there is a State – men do not look upon the social order and the laws as the mere work or will of God; they look upon them as something which it is their right to alter, the better to achieve their own just purposes. While the social order, which puts some men high above the others, is held to be the work of Providence, then even the most lowly placed in that order may find it easy to resign themselves to it and may acquire deep loyalties inside it, if not exactly to it. But where it is held to be something which men may alter for their own and for other men's benefit, then the lowly placed inside it come to question it. Why should it give so much more to some than to others? The demand arises that inequality be justified by being shown to consist of differences in rank or income which are necessary if the community is to do for its members what they require of it, or to be inseparable from freedom or from something else generally valued. It comes to be widely held that, if it cannot be justified, it ought to be abolished. And if it is not abolished, those who look upon themselves as sufferers from it feel that justice has been denied to them. They are, in their own eyes, members of a community which has refused to give them what it owes to them, and their devotion to it is weakened.

All over the world men are becoming, as they never used to be, *citizens*; they are acquiring hopes, fears and loyalties unknown, or little known, to their ancestors. The demand for equality grows ever wider and more insistent, and, though the equality demanded is not precisely what Rousseau understood by the term, it has much in common with it. It is everywhere agreed that men do not get the equality which is a condition of freedom merely by being given the vote; they must also have the security which enables them to use that vote independently and responsibly. If they are to count politically, if they are to have a mind of their own which makers of policy cannot afford to neglect, they must be so placed economically that they are not much more dependent on others than others are on them. They cannot be expected to be devoted to the community if the community takes little account of them. These are principles which liberals and democrats in the West, whose thinking – whatever their party allegiance – has been deeply affected by socialist doctrines, share with Rousseau, who was not a socialist, whose conception of democracy differs greatly from theirs, and who cared nothing for the progress which most of them still believe in. And these principles, despite their generality, are important.

Yet patriotism, as Rousseau often speaks of it, is not attractive to Western eyes, especially the eyes of a democrat who is also a liberal. Not that liberals and democrats lack patriotism; devotion to the political community, to the constitution and to the laws, is probably as widespread and as deep in the liberal democracies as it is anywhere else. Democrats who care for freedom are probably as willing as other men to make great sacrifices in a common cause. But patriotism, as they see it, is something better taken for granted than made much of. Rousseau advocates a cult of the fatherland which to many liberals will seem dangerous to liberty. He praises his heroes, the legislators and other great men of antiquity, because they established national and exclusive forms of worship, encouraged games and exercises to increase men's vigour and self-esteem and to bring them closer together, and provided spectacles to remind them of their country's past. 'A child', he says, 'in opening its eyes, must see the fatherland and must see it alone to the day of its death. Every true republican sucks in love of the fatherland with its mother's milk: that is to say, love of the laws and of liberty'.[1] And he advises the Poles not to leave education to foreigners and to priests but to lay down the matter, the order and the form of it by law. The Poles should establish scholarships for the sons of poor men, gymnasia for physical exercises and games played in common. Public education is better than private, and children are to be accustomed 'to order, equality and fraternity, to compete with one another, to live under the eyes of their fellow-citizens and to desire public approval'.[2] There should be a college of magistrates to control the entire system of education.

Rousseau makes almost a mania of patriotism. It is surely enough that we should love our country, and altogether too much that we should be in love with it and conscious of it every day of our lives. This kind of obsessive patriotism undermines freedom, and so too does a form of education which teaches children what they owe to the community and what it expects of them but does not encourage them to follow their own tastes. An education of that kind differs from the education given to Emile in much more than merely being public while Emile's education was private; it does not seek to do for many children what Emile's tutor sought to do for only one child. Emile was brought up to be a person of independent judgement and a self-disciplined man; he was brought up to be active and free and therefore eventually became a good citizen, since the free man respects in others what he claims for himself. But these Polish children are to be brought up for the State; the direct aim of their education is to make good citizens of them. No doubt, Rousseau, taking it for granted that one who loves his fatherland and its laws is also a lover of freedom, believes that man cannot be a good citizen without also being a free man. Indeed, this is one of the central tenets of his creed. I have argued that there is a sense in which it is true, and that Rousseau, if he does not make this sense altogether clear, comes

[1] *Le Gouvernement de Pologne*, ch. IV, p. 966.
[2] Ibid., p. 968.

at times very close to doing so. The good citizen is also, doubtless, a patriot. We need not deny this. But we must insist, against Rousseau, that the type of public education described in the *Considerations on the Government of Poland* is unlikely to create patriots who are also free men. Admittedly, Rousseau's description is brief and equivocal, and an ingenious advocate might contend that it could be so interpreted as to avoid this conclusion; but this, surely, would be special pleading and not the most natural interpretation of his actual words.

Though for patriotism Rousseau has the deepest admiration, he has nothing but contempt for the desire for national glory and aggrandizement. The too-great size of states is in his view the first and principal cause of the unhappiness of mankind, and he advises the Poles to reduce their frontiers. He is not, in the nineteenth-century sense, a nationalist; he does not put it forward as a principle that all Poles or all Corsicans should be members of the same State. He merely tells the Poles that they ought not to insist on retaining frontiers which bring many foreigners into the same State with them. He takes it for granted that the Corsicans do not want their island divided into several completely independent states, and is therefore content to advise its division into autonomous districts, each with its own popular assembly. Laws affecting only one district should be voted by its assembly, and laws affecting the whole island by all the district assemblies meeting separately. He also supposes that, since all Poles already belong to the same State, they will decide against having a State or states so small that this ceases to be true, and he therefore advocates a federal Poland containing only Poles. But he says nothing to suggest that the Poles, if they were minded to it, would be wrong to form a number of independent Polish states.

On the contrary, he tells the Poles that they have two choices. They can choose to be a great European nation, like several others, or they can make a better choice. If they choose greatness, let them cultivate the sciences, the arts, commerce and industry; let them have regular armies, fortresses and learned academies; let them multiply the use of money and promote luxury. They will then become an avid, ambitious, servile and knavish people, and will be counted among the great Powers; they may even reconquer their lost provinces and perhaps also acquire new ones. They will then be able to say 'like Pyrrhus or like the Russians, that is to say, like children, "When all the world belongs to me, I shall eat sugar"'.[1] But if they make the better choice, they will lead simple lives within even narrower frontiers than

[1] Ibid., ch. XI, p. 1003.

they now have; they will not be admired nor reckoned among the great Powers. But they will have what the wise know is worth having, and the foolish do not envy them for having: they will have justice and liberty. They will even have security, being formidable without being dangerous; for who will be tempted to attack a country offering few spoils and defended to the death by resolute patriots?

V. THE ILLIBERAL LOVE OF FREEDOM

The rhetorical dealer in paradoxes is often the victim of his own eloquence. Rousseau, who proclaimed his love of freedom so loudly, has been accused – and nowhere more than in France – of being an insidious enemy of it. Did he not give to the popular assembly all the powers that Hobbes gave to the sovereign? Did he not leave the citizen helpless against the organized community? Was not what he advocated even worse than the absolute government of Hobbes? For Hobbes admitted that the subject always retains the right to resist the sovereign who threatens his life. Besides, the monarch or the aristocratic senate, however absolute their formal authority, must in practice take account of the people's moods; their power is always smaller than it seems. But Demos is apt to be the worst of tyrants, because there is nothing outside him to restrain him. Rousseau speaks of the 'total surrender of each associate with all his rights to the whole community',[1] and says that 'the sovereign power has no need to give pledges to the subjects, because it is impossible that the body should wish to harm all its members, and we shall see later that it cannot harm any of them. The sovereign, by virtue only of being what it is, is always what it should be'.[2]

It is on the strength of such texts as these that Rousseau is accused of being an enemy of freedom. The accusation, however, rests on a misunderstanding. Rousseau never speaks of the people as Hobbes does of the sovereign; he never says that they have the right to command anything they please. He says only that, provided certain conditions hold in a popular assembly, any law made by the assembly is binding on the entire community for which the assembly legislates.

The people are not sovereign merely by virtue of acting as one body; they are sovereign only while they act as the body created

[1] *Contrat social*, I.vi, ibid., p. 360.
[2] Ibid., I.vii, p. 363.

by the social contract is required to act, only while they act as an assembly of equals with no parties or cliques to prevent free debate and voting. Their sovereignty consists, not in the right to issue any rule, but in the right to make any law; and a law, in Rousseau's sense of the word, is a rule of a special kind. To say that the citizen has no right against the sovereign is therefore not to say that he has no right against the whole body of citizens, when they fail to act in the way which makes their acts sovereign acts.

If that body were to prevent the citizen taking part, on equal terms with everyone else, in its deliberations, its act would be a breach of contract, and therefore by definition not a sovereign act. The body that is sovereign is so *only while it acts like a sovereign*. Rousseau so defines sovereignty that the rights of the individual are included in the definition. The citizen does have inalienable rights: the right to take a full and free part in the making of the laws; the right not to be faced in the assembly by combinations intent on getting their own way; and the right that the law shall not discriminate against him. If we bear all this in mind, the ominous sentence, that 'the sovereign, by virtue only of being what it is, is always what it should be', begins to look harmless. Rousseau is not to be classed either with Hobbes or Hegel; he does not have in mind actual states. Nor does he say that there could be, anywhere in the world, a community such that it would be the duty of its members to do whatever it chose to command; he says only that the decisions of the general will must be obeyed, which is by no means the same thing.

It is largely Rousseau's own fault that his doctrine of obedience has been so often misinterpreted. When he speaks of the sovereign, he uses some of the words and phrases used before him by Hobbes, whose purpose was quite different. Rousseau speaks as if the social contract brought into existence a corporate body against whom the individual has no rights, whatever it may do; whereas what he really means is that the individual has an absolute duty of obedience to that body provided it acts as it should do. The citizen has a right against that body to require, when it claims sovereign authority over him, that it shall indeed act as a sovereign. It is therefore wide of the mark to say, as some of Rousseau's critics have done, that the ideal State imagined by him is *totalitarian*. Rousseau so defines sovereignty that nobody in his ideal State, not even the popular assembly, can stand to the citizen as the government of, say, Fascist Italy or Nazi Germany (to speak only of totalitarian states which exist no longer) stood to its subjects. The popular assembly cannot silence the citizen; he is free to criticize any proposal brought before it, and, if the proposal is made law, is free to propose its repeal. The popular assembly is an organ of discussion and decision, not of propaganda; it does not seek to mould the minds of its members. Their minds are affected by what they hear and say inside it, but its decisions are never beyond question; for, if they were, it would not be sovereign. According to Rousseau, it is the present will of the people which is sovereign; but their present will cannot be known unless they are free to call in question their own past decisions. The sovereign might, perhaps, without ceasing to be sovereign, forbid criticism of its decisions outside the assembly, but it could not do so inside it and still remain sovereign. This is not merely a conclusion which the reader of the *Social Contract* can properly derive from Rousseau's definition of sovereignty; it is a conclusion reached by Rousseau himself, as is shown by his concern that the citizen should be a man of independent judgement. If the general will is to find proper expression, it is important 'that each citizen should come to his own opinion (*n'opine que d'après lui*)'.[1] In Rousseau's State nobody can ever speak for the people except the people, and even they are sovereign only as an assembly of equals whose every member has the right against all the others that they shall not so act as to make his opinion count for nothing. This ideal may be unattainable, but it is not totalitarian.

In several places Rousseau expresses his abhorrence of the doctrine that justice may rightly be denied to the individual to save the community. 'The pretext of the public good is always the most dangerous scourge of the people. What is most necessary in a government, and perhaps most difficult for it, is a strict integrity in rendering justice to all.'[2] He says also that 'the security of the individual is so bound up with the public confederacy that, if it were not that allowance must be made for human weakness, this convention would by right be dissolved if there perished in the State only one citizen who might have been saved, or if only one were kept wrongfully in prison, or if only one lawsuit were lost with obvious injustice'.[3] The law, which is the will of the community, may determine what service or sacrifice may be required of a citizen in an emergency, but every citizen at all times has the right against his compatriots that they shall not sacrifice him in disregard of the law, on the pretext that they do so for the public good.

But we must not go from one extreme to another; we must not call Rousseau a liberal because others have called him a totalitarian.

[1] Ibid., II.iii, p. 372.
[2] 'Sur l'économie politique', ibid., p. 258.
[3] Ibid., p. 256.

There are both liberal and illiberal sides to his philosophy. In the chapter on 'Civil Religion', in the fourth book of the *Social Contract*, he argues that there are certain beliefs which men must have if they are to be reliable citizens: they must believe in a God who is powerful, intelligent, beneficent and provident, in a life to come in which the just will be happy and the wicked punished, and in the sanctity of the social contract and of the laws. Locke, in his *Letter Concerning Toleration*, argues that atheists are not to be trusted and therefore not to be tolerated. For though nobody should be molested merely because he does not share other people's beliefs, no matter how dear those beliefs may be to those that hold them, the community may rightly refuse to tolerate persons whom it is not reasonable to trust; and atheists are not to be trusted because, not believing in God, they lack one of the strongest motives which make men trustworthy. Rousseau is hardly more illiberal in the chapter on 'Civil Religion' than Locke in the *Letter Concerning Toleration*. For though he praises Hobbes for having wanted to unite Church and State, the 'two heads of the eagle', he stipulates that subjects are answerable to the sovereign only for those of their opinions which are important to the community, and then goes on to explain what those opinions are. They consist only of the beliefs contained in what he calls 'a purely civil profession of faith', and amount in practice to little more than the beliefs which a man would need to hold in order not to be an atheist in the eyes of Locke.[1] Both Locke and Rousseau refuse toleration to atheists, and Rousseau differs from Locke merely in proposing that citizens who declare that they hold these minimal beliefs when in fact they do not should be put to death if their lie is discovered.

Yet Rousseau's position, though here scarcely less liberal than Locke's, is certainly less reasonable. Locke does not require subjects to declare publicly their adherence to the beliefs which he thinks necessary to security; he merely says that, if they openly reject them, they ought not to be tolerated. If there are beliefs necessary to security, it is important that people should hold them but not important they should profess them. For if they are to be excluded for not professing them, they are the more likely to profess them when they do not hold them. Rousseau's requirements encourage hypocrisy much more than

---

[1] Belief in a God indifferent to men, a God who neither rewarded the just nor punished the wicked, would hardly strengthen men's motives for acting in ways which make them trustworthy. Locke said nothing about belief in the sanctity of the social contract and the laws, but, given his reasons for not tolerating atheists, we can reasonably conclude what his attitude would have been to persons denying the obligation to keep the contract or to obey the laws.

Locke's do, and not the less so for the terrible punishment he proposes for the hypocrite in the unlikely event of his being found out.

If the just community is as precious to its members as Rousseau says it is, how is it that patriotism and public spirit are not enough to keep citizens faithful to the laws and to justice? It is understandable how someone holding, as Locke does, that government is set up by men for their mutual convenience should want to reinforce their motives for keeping faith with one another by having them believe in God. Prudence, taken merely as a person's sense of what is to his own enduring advantage in this world, may not be enough to afford security: something more may be needed, and it is not surprising that Locke should seek it in the fear of God. But why would Rousseau seek it there, having quite other and deeper views about the social nature of man? That he should himself incline to religion is not surprising, but his belief that it is unlikely that men will be good citizens unless they have faith in God is not in keeping with what he says elsewhere about the bonds which hold men together in a just society. He would have been more consistent had he held that the more unequal and corrupt a community, the greater the need for religion to maintain security.

In the seventh chapter of Book IV of the *Social Contract*, Rousseau discusses censorship without condemning it; he has in mind, not censorship of the press, but the supervision of morals. The censors give, as it were, official utterance to public opinion about private conduct; their purpose is to preserve or to purify morals by passing judgements on conduct for which citizens are not answerable to the courts. Rousseau has in mind the censorship in ancient Rome and perhaps also the practice of the Genevan Consistory. He admits that this kind of public supervision of private morals will be effective only when certain conditions hold, but he implies that it is desirable when they do hold. In his other writings, he often commends the strong pressure of public opinion on the citizen, and he wants Polish children 'to live under the eyes of their fellow-citizens and to desire public approval'.[1] In his *Letter to d'Alembert on the Theatre*,[2] he argues that the opening of a theatre would help to corrupt the morals of the Genevans, and he repeatedly gives utterance to his mistrust of intellect and talent.

---

[1] See p. 197 above.

[2] In this work he fastens on *Le Misanthrope* to show how even the best comedy is corrupting. What he says about it proves his ability to appreciate the merits as a work of art of what he attacks as a bad influence on morals; Rousseau as a critic of Molière is altogether more perceptive than, say, Tolstoy as a critic of Shakespeare.

Rousseau was something of an obscurantist, and every obscurantist is illiberal. He had almost as strong a preference for flatness and the commonplace as John Stuart Mill had for variety and excellence. He praised virtue often and intelligence seldom, and even said that where there is virtue there is no need of talent. Men of talent are, he thought, apt to be heartless, self-centred and vain; and though the world may be the brighter for their presence in it, it is not the happier. For the talented not only often lack virtue; they also undermine it. They hold it in contempt and wither it at the root; they even make men ashamed of it. For the most part, when they moralize, they are sophists who seduce the simple and the sincere, diverting their minds from the truth. They are more than corrupt; they are also corrupters; for society, in its corruption, gives scope to their talents, and they are eager to preserve the conditions which raise them above their fellows. In the greatest of French comedies, the genius of Molière serves only to make virtue, in the person of Alceste, ridiculous.

Rousseau respected passion but was easily put out by gaiety, unless it was simple; he was afraid of the quick-witted, the sophisticated and the elegant. He had sometimes suffered at their hands, and in the labyrinth of his mind their slights echoed again and again. He was deeply moved by his own ideas, and also mortified by his incapacity to put them easily into words. Other men's talents were oppressive to him, and he was silenced by them. He was most articulate when he was alone, in the privacy of his own mind, and yet he needed an audience. Men of talent, it seemed, were not only the natural enemies of virtue, but also of Rousseau, the lover of virtue.

Rousseau spoke slightingly of the arts and sciences. Though he must himself, being one of the great writers of his age, have known the excitement of the artist (an excitement which is in itself quite free of vanity, however vain artists may be), he set no value upon it; he did not see in it, any more than in the excitement of the scientist or discoverer, a moment of excellence in humanity. The dignity of man, seen through his eyes, is entirely moral and not also intellectual and aesthetic. Though he condemned oppression and the manipulation of opinion for private and sectional advantage, he did not condemn it for fear that it should thwart the intellect and the imagination; and it never occurred to him that, even in a society of equals without wealth or ambition or intrigue to corrupt it, public opinion might be oppressive. He took it for granted that superiority is more pernicious than mediocrity; he cared little for idiosyncrasy, for experiment, for adventure. Spiritually, he was parochial; he wanted a tight and cosy world with no room in it for talents great enough to make ordinary men feel small. He wanted a tranquil and unchanging world, a world without mysteries or anxiety because its inhabitants lack curiosity, a world protected by an omniscient and omnipotent God whose creatures are comfortable in their ignorance and their mutual trust.

Rousseau has been called a vain, resentful and small-minded man. No doubt, he was so to some extent, for he sometimes pretended to despise what he secretly envied. Certainly, Voltaire and the Encyclopaedists thought him small-minded; they were offended as much by his being the sort of man he was as by his actions, and they spoke of him contemptuously. They brought out the worst in him, and their ability to do this was as much his fault as theirs. He was vain and resentful, but he was also – and this they did not see – a man who aspired to goodness and who was as profoundly dissatisfied with himself as with the world, even though he blamed the world more than himself. He was deeply unhappy, not because he was small-minded, resentful and vain, but because he was not what he wanted to be and could not, for all his protestations, persuade himself that he was. He was a man who felt that society had made an outcast of him, and who complained bitterly of his lot; he was the 'alienated' man become articulate.

If others brought out the worst in him, he too brought out the worst in them. There is nothing more spiteful and petty in the lives of Diderot and Voltaire than their treatment of Rousseau. They were men of the world, as he was not; they were clever, brilliant and self-confident, as he was not; they were better able to make him look foolish than he them. He was something of a boor, as they were not; and the faults of the boorish, though no worse in themselves, are more painful to contemplate than the faults of the quick and the polished. Envious though Rousseau was, the fact remains that he had talents as great as any that he envied. If he was a moralist, so too, in their different ways, were Voltaire and the Encyclopaedists; and of all the moralists of his age, he was the most eloquent and the most profound. He was accused of plagiarism, rhetoric and sophistry by writers who had less to say that was new and exciting than he had. He suffered from insane suspicions and made false accusations. There was no plot against him of the kind that he imagined. But he had enemies. They were a coterie and he was alone; they supported one another in their dislike and contempt for him. I would not speak as highly of his character as Frederika MacDonald does in a book about him written to defend him against Diderot and his other detractors,[1]

[1] *Jean-Jacques Rousseau: A New Criticism*, 2 vols. (London 1906).

but I agree with her that posterity has seen him largely through their eyes, while most of his contemporaries thought better of him. It is a pity this should be so because, with so personal and passionate a writer, it is difficult to prevent your impression of the man from colouring your estimate of his doctrine.

★ ★ ★

Rousseau's influence on social and political thought has been immense. We invoke his name less often than Marx's because the revolution which he helped to inspire happened so much longer ago and because there are no powerful bodies which profess adherence to his doctrines; but we use his ideas just as much.

We owe to him a deeper sense of what is involved in man's being a social creature. In the *Discourse on Inequality* he describes an imaginary course of social evolution, neither controlled nor understood by man, which makes him a rational and moral being. Man transforms his nature through the activities whose effects are his social environment. In *Emile* Rousseau shows how the child, while its bodily needs are satisfied by those who look after it, acquires feelings towards itself and others which create needs in it different from those it is born with or which arise in the course of mere physical maturation – the emotions and needs of a social, purposeful and moral being. In several of his writings he seeks to show how man can acquire in society passions and needs which society is unable to satisfy – how he can acquire aspirations and needs incompatible with one another and with the social order in which they arise. He turns our minds, as none of the great political and social theorists before him since Aristotle does, to considering how the social order affects the structure of human personality.

We owe to him a conception of freedom not to be found in the writings of Hobbes or Locke or Montesquieu. Man, as a rational and moral creature, aspires not to being able to satisfy as many as possible of his desires but to being able to live well by his own standards. Man cares deeply for freedom, not because he is motivated by appetites, but because he is a moral person having notions of excellence – because he has an idea (albeit vague) of the sort of person he wants to be and of a sort of life which is worth living. He is not the more free the fewer the obstacles to his satisfying his desires; he is the more free the greater his opportunity to be what he wants to be and to live what seems to him a worthwhile life.

We owe to Rousseau an idea of happiness which is intimately

connected with this conception of freedom. To be happy is to be on good terms with yourself and with others, and the terms on which you are with yourself depend largely on the quality of your relations with others, which in turn depend on the social situation. Happiness, as distinct from pleasure, is possible only to a self-conscious and moral being, having aspirations and able to realize them. Man alone can be 'outside himself' – *hors de lui-même* (to use Rousseau's own expression) – and man alone can find happiness by 'finding himself'; or, to speak less metaphorically, man alone can be made wretched by seeing himself impelled by circumstances to be what he would rather not be, and man alone can attain happiness in being what it satisfies him to be.

It was the common opinion of moralists that unhappiness is a consequence of vice. Rousseau was eager to show that vice is an effect of unhappiness, and that men are unhappy because they live in the kind of society which makes them so. He ascribed their ills entirely to their environment and not at all to heredity; he assumed that all men are born with the qualities which would make them capable of happiness in the right kind of society. Mistaken though this assumption may be, it directs the mind towards discovering cures rather than towards the infliction of punishments.

Rousseau was often given to pessimism. Yet his doctrine is not in itself pessimistic. It does not in the least follow that men, because society has 'corrupted' them, cannot find a remedy for their condition; they can, by taking thought, improve society. They can, despite their vices, set about creating an environment suitable to their nature. For, though Rousseau thought it unlikely that they would do so, he merely gave vent to his pessimism without producing evidence to support it. No matter what society has done to them, men can come to know their condition and to imagine a way out of it; they can discover what suits their nature and are by nature inclined to pursue it. This is Rousseau's doctrine. Why, then, should they not strive to attain it? Why should they not make progress towards it? Because, says Rousseau, their vices weaken their will. But, then, reflection on their condition may strengthen their will. Why should it be supposed that what weakens the will must always prevail over what strengthens it? Rousseau provides no reasons; his pessimism is no better grounded in reason than is the optimism of Hegel or Marx.

Rousseau was the first to give passionate expression to man's sense that society has grown too large and too complicated for his own good. Better that the community should be small and stable, with every member a neighbour to all the others, than that it should be

vast, restless and quickly changing, with everyone inside it a stranger
to all but a few. Man's sense of his insignificance and his fear of the
great society which his own activities have produced; his feeling that
he is alone and yet not his own master; his apathy and anxiety in an
environment beyond his understanding and control; his sense of being
lost in an artificial wilderness, man-made but not made for man: these
are sentiments which many have uttered since Rousseau, but none as
eloquently as he did.

   Man, to save himself from society, must refashion society to his
own measure. He must eliminate the inequalities which inevitably
make some men the instruments of others. He must create societies
of equals, which must be small, because there can be equality only
in communities all of whose members can take an active part in the
main business of government, which is the making of law. Equality,
democracy and freedom: to these three words Rousseau gave new
meanings, and meanings which are important because they express
aspirations more and more widely shared since his time. He used old
words to say new things and was more original than he knew.

CHAPTER FIVE
From Bentham to John Stuart Mill

Of the many doctrines put forward by Bentham and his School, I shall discuss only three: his theory of morals, his account of sovereignty and the argument which he and James Mill used in favour of representative democracy. Bentham's account of morality, though in some ways very like Hume's, is also, as I shall try to show, in other ways quite unlike it. I want to make clearer than I have done before how they differ, and to criticize Bentham's views more sympathetically (and I hope also more adequately) than I did in my book *The English Utilitarians*.[1] Bentham's account of supreme power has until recently received less attention than it deserves,[2] since it makes many things clear that Hobbes confused. The Utilitarian argument for democracy, which does not rest on the doctrine of the rights of man, gains certain advantages thereby; but it also has difficulties peculiar to itself because it starts from the assumption that every man is apt to be the best judge of his own interests. The classical economists also made this assumption when they argued for *laissez-faire*. I want to consider both the advantages and the difficulties of the Utilitarian argument.

In this chapter I shall also consider the intellectual legacy of the Benthamite School and the ways in which the Philosophical Radicals, as his disciples were called, have affected our views on society and government. They certainly sought to exercise such influence, and there was never a school of philosophers closer to the world of affairs.

---

[1] *The English Utilitarians* (Oxford 1949). The second edition of 1958 (with further revisions in 1966) includes a chapter devoted to 'Apologies and Corrections', of which certain themes are further developed here.

[2] But see especially Frederick Rosen, *Jeremy Bentham and Representative Democracy* (Oxford 1983), ch. III.

Rousseau and other French thinkers of the eighteenth century brought the *ancien régime* into contempt, but they did not show how, taking the world as it was, men could refashion and improve it. Marx and Engels unravelled present conflicts and predicted others in the future, but they took care to be vague in describing what the world might be like when conflict at last ceased. How wonderfully reticent, how circumspect these prophets of gloom and glory can sometimes be! How unlike the Philosophical Radicals, who were never prophets but were always willing to commit themselves. They were the most practical among abstract political theorists. Living in what was then the most enterprising as well as the freest society in Europe, they could hope to exercise influence without flattery or intrigue. They stood, as I believe no group of thinkers so abstract had ever stood before, at the elbows of an experienced ruling class, thrusting advice, in turn stimulating and annoying, but never seeking to arouse passions against it. They were uncompromising, incisive, untiring critics, but without the least trace of the demagogue.

I shall here try to elucidate as well John Stuart Mill's conceptions of freedom and self-improvement, showing how they can be used to give substance to his notion of progress; and I shall examine his argument for democracy and his fears about it. Mill has acquired a certain reputation for philosophical confusion, and it is notorious that he never shook himself free of the Utilitarian ideas he imbibed from his father and from Bentham, though he often moved away from them without realizing he had done so. I shall not consider just to what extent he was a Utilitarian or try to unravel his confusions of thought; I shall only be concerned to explain what kind of liberal he was. For while Bentham and James Mill were believers in freedom and democracy, and were also individualists, we should, I think, hesitate to call them liberals, because their reasons for putting a value on freedom seem less important to the true liberal than others he would invoke. They are not bad reasons in themselves, and the liberal does not reject them, but rather looks upon them as only a part of the argument, and not the weightier part. Mill's belief in freedom was by contrast exceptionally pure and tenacious: pure because very little mixed up with other beliefs incompatible with it; and tenacious because held in the absence of illusions about human nature. He never shut his eyes to arguments directed against any position he adopted; his was an open-eyed, an intelligent, faith. He believed, not in the inevitability, but in the possibility, of progress; and progress, in terms of his conception of freedom, has a positive meaning.

I. BENTHAM'S THEORY OF MORALS

In his theory of morals, Bentham is engaged in two quite different enterprises without seeing clearly the difference between them. He tries to establish the meanings of such moral terms as *good, right* and *duty*; he defines them entirely in terms of the desires which move men to action and the consequences of those actions. But he also puts forward rules for the attainment of what he says is alone desired for its own sake, namely pleasure. In putting forward these rules he uses such words as *good, right* and *duty*; but he does not use them in the senses he has defined. His definitions make these words merely descriptive, whereas he uses them for other than descriptive purposes. Hence the considerable ambiguity of his doctrines.

There is another source of confusion in his moral theory. He sometimes speaks as if the rules he puts forward, and above all the greatest happiness principle, followed logically from his definitions of *good* and *right*. At other times, he does not seek to derive the greatest happiness principle logically from his definitions, but tries to show that, man being the sort of creature he is, the greatest happiness principle is universally accepted when it is properly understood. This second line of argument has received less notice than it deserves, and neglect of it has led some critics of Bentham into error.

Let us first consider what Bentham says about moral terms when he explains how we use them. If we want to understand what morality is, we must, according to Bentham, begin by seeing that men desire only pleasure and are averse only to pain. 'Take away *pleasures* and *pains*', he says in his *Table of the Springs of Action*, and 'not only *happiness,* but *justice*, and *duty*, and *obligation*. . .are so many empty sounds'.[1] Bentham sometimes speaks as if *good* meant just pleasant, though more often as if it meant either desired for its own sake or universally desired. He usually defines a right action as the action which, under the circumstances, is conducive to the greatest amount of pleasure, or to the greatest excess of pleasure over pain. Bentham's theory therefore requires, not only that pleasures should be measurable, but that pleasure should be commensurable with pain. Yet, when he says that an action is right, Bentham is not just saying that it conduces to the greatest possible amount of pleasure. He is also saying that we ought to do it because it conduces to the greatest pleasure. When he uses the word *right* in this way he is no longer

---

[1] *A Table of the Springs of Action*, in *Deontology*, etc., ed. Amnon Goldworth, *Collected Works of Bentham* (Oxford 1983), p. 89.

using it only descriptively; he is advocating a course of action. But, though he uses the word *right* in two different ways (to say that an action is of a certain type, and to tell us what we ought to do), he never distinguishes between the two uses.

Bentham sometimes speaks as if duty were merely liability to punishment, or, more widely, liability to unpleasant consequences. 'That is my *duty*, to do', he says in the *Fragment on Government*,[1] 'which I am liable to be *punished*, according to law, if I do not do: this is the original, ordinary, and proper sense of the word *duty*'. Elsewhere he broadens the notion of duty to cover any action backed by what he calls sanctions, and by sanctions he usually means any unpleasant consequences to be feared by the person who is considering what to do. There are, he says, four kinds of sanction: natural, legal, religious and moral.[2] A natural sanction is an unpleasant consequence which is not due to the reaction of some other intelligent being. If I knock my head against the wall, I shall hurt myself, and that is a reason for keeping my head away from the wall. Thus it might be said that it is my duty not to knock my head against the wall. There is no need to explain what Bentham means by a legal sanction. By a religious sanction he means a punishment to be expected at the hands of God, and by a moral sanction 'various mortifications resulting from the ill-will of persons uncertain and variable',[3] or, in other words, the blame or other unwelcome reactions of the people you come into contact with. These reactions are not arbitrary; there are habits of praise and blame.

Though Bentham includes natural sanctions along with the others in his list, we can in practice ignore them when we are considering his account of what duty is. Duty, as he explains it, is liability to punishment, and a natural sanction is clearly not a punishment, even in the widest ordinary use of that term. Nor is arbitrary ill-will punishment. Before there can be punishment, there must be some rule of conduct which people are required to obey; and the punishment must consist, not in the fact that a breach of the rule leads to unpleasant consequences, but in people's behaving towards the supposed breaker of the rule in ways likely to discourage the breach of it. Their reaction

[1] *A Fragment on Government* and *An Introduction to the Principles of Morals and Legislation,* ed. Wilfrid Harrison (Oxford 1948), ch. V, p. 107.
[2] Bentham admits that people can be encouraged to act by hope of pleasant consequences as well as discouraged by fear of unpleasant consequences – that there are 'positive' sanctions as well as 'negative' ones. But he does not take the first into account when he is explaining duty; for when a man has a duty, he is said to be obliged, and we do not ordinarily speak of people being obliged to do something when they act from hope of benefit to themselves.
[3] *A Fragment on Government*, ch. V, p. 107 n.1(4).

to him is not punishment, even in the wide sense, unless they react as they do because they believe that he has broken the rule. This is the interpretation fairest to Bentham. He says that the original and proper sense of the word *duty* makes it a man's duty to do what he is liable to be punished, according to law, for not doing. That defines only legal duty; but Bentham clearly supposes that the other notions of duty are, as it were, extensions of this primary notion. There are duties wherever there are rules which people are required to obey, and are liable to punishment for not obeying.

This account of right action and duty is suspect because it leads us immediately into paradox. If the rightness of an action *consists* in its conduciveness to the greatest amount of pleasure possible in the circumstances, and if duty *consists* in liability to punishment for not doing what is required of us, then clearly it may be our duty *not* to do what is right. Bentham was in fact very far from believing that the rules which people are liable to punishment for disobeying (which therefore impose duties by his definition) always make for the greatest happiness. It was precisely because he did not believe this that he wanted to reform the law. Yet it never occurred to him that, if we accept his account of duty and right action, it must sometimes (perhaps even often) be our duty to do what is wrong and to refrain from doing what is right. He took it for granted that it is always our duty to do right and to avoid wrong. Just as he used *rightness* in two senses, to mean conduciveness to pleasure and also to tell us what we ought to do, so he used *duty* in two senses, to mean liability to punishment and also to tell us what to do.[1] In other words, though he defined *rightness* and *duty* as if they meant different things, he often used them as if they were synonyms; but the sense in which he used them, when he used them as synonyms, he never defined. Hence the considerable obscurity of his theory of morals.

Bentham wanted to keep all 'empty' or, as he sometimes put it, all 'metaphysical' notions out of his account of morals. He would not have it that the rightness of an action or the goodness of a motive or condition is some inherent quality not given in sensation but directly apprehended by reason; nor would he allow that there is some special 'moral sense' which perceives the moral qualities. Neither would he admit that moral judgements are no more than expressions of feeling. He wanted to show that there are objective

[1] Thus, in a well-known passage, from the *Fragment on Government* ch. I (p. 51n), Bentham, speaking of Hume, says that he learnt from him 'that the obligation to minister to general happiness, was an obligation paramount to and inclusive of every other'.

moral standards. Speaking of theories other than his own, he says, 'The various systems that have been formed concerning the standard of right and wrong, may all be reduced to the principle of sympathy and antipathy. One account may serve for all of them. They consist all of them in so many contrivances for avoiding the obligation of appealing to any external standard, and for prevailing upon the reader to accept of the author's sentiment or opinion as a reason for itself '.[1] He includes in this general condemnation just as much the moralists who speak of a Law of Nature or a Law of Reason as those who speak of a moral sense. If the moral law is directly apprehended by reason, one man's reason may judge differently from another's; there is no means of deciding the issue between them, and one man's judgement is as good or as bad as another's. It helps nothing to say that reason is the same in all men, if the judgements they make differ, and if there is no agreed method for deciding who is right. Now, from the nature of the case, there can be no such method, it being supposed that reason in every man directly apprehends right and wrong. The appeal to so-called rational intuition is therefore at bottom the same as the appeal to taste or feeling.

Bentham believed that he was providing what he called an external standard by equating goodness with pleasure (or if not with pleasure, with what is desired), and rightness with conduciveness to the greatest amount of pleasure possible in the circumstances. Everybody, he thought, knows what pleasure is, and wants to have it; while statements about conduciveness to pleasure can be verified. If two people disagree about what action is right, they can argue the matter out rationally; each can produce evidence that the action he favours is the more conducive to pleasure, and the one who produces the stronger evidence is likely to convince the other.

Bentham failed to notice that his definitions of *good* and *right* altogether neglect what makes them properly moral terms, and therefore persuasive in argument. If to call something good is only to say it is pleasant or desired for its own sake,[2] then no one who is told that it is *good* will be moved by the statement, unless he himself finds it pleasant or desires it; and in that case he scarcely needs to be told. If *it is good* means merely *it gives pleasure to someone* or *someone desires it for its own sake*, then it always makes sense to ask, Why should anyone who is not to get the pleasure or who does not desire it strive

[1] *An Introduction to the Principles of Morals and Legislation*, ch. II, p. 140.
[2] It is true that Bentham (and other Utilitarians) sometimes mean by good *universally desired*; but this implies only that nothing is good unless it is the kind of thing that everyone desires.

to bring it about? Similarly, if *this action is right* means *it conduces to the greatest amount of pleasure possible under the circumstances*, it always makes sense to ask, Why should anyone who is not to get the pleasure, or who can get more pleasure some other way, do it? Bentham insists that we should aim at the good, no matter whose it is or who desires it, and that we should do what is right even when we could get more pleasure by not doing it. But these rules no more derive logically from his definitions of *good* and *right* than the laws of nature, as they were traditionally conceived, derive logically from the humanity of man, from the capacities peculiar to the species *homo sapiens*.

Bentham wanted to explain what we are doing when we make moral judgements, without recourse to what he called *metaphysics*, without postulating the existence of any qualities not given in sense-experience, any qualities apprehended by reason 'intuitively' or perceived by a special moral sense. He also wanted to provide an external standard of morality involving no appeal to our feelings. If he had had only the first object in view, he might have been content to follow Hume; he might have been willing to say that moral judgements are merely expressions of feeling, of approval and disapproval, whose function is to encourage some kinds of behaviour and to discourage others.

Hume's moral theory is purely explanatory. Its purpose is only to tell us what is involved in the making of moral judgements and how we come to make them as we do; its purpose is emphatically not to improve our behaviour. The primary function of moral judgements, Hume tells us, is to influence behaviour in the ways that make for happiness. We need not know this when we make moral judgements, for we may make them as we do because we have been taught to do so. Yet, if we enquire how men first came to make these judgements, we soon see that there is no satisfactory explanation except that experience taught them what kinds of behaviour ordinarily increase happiness and what kinds ordinarily diminish it. Since men desire happiness for themselves and also sympathize with this desire in others, they come to approve of the types of behaviour which increase it and to disapprove of the types which diminish it. Thus, for Hume, the rules of morality are ordinarily also rules of utility; they help to ensure that, in the pursuit of happiness, we get in each other's way as little as possible. But Hume does not make the morality of an action consist in its utility, its tendency to promote happiness. Its morality consists in how we feel about it, or rather in how we feel about the motives that inspire it. Thus his theory allows us to say that an action is moral even when it is not an action of a type which is ordinarily useful. For that type of action, though it first came to be approved of because it was useful, may now have ceased to be useful and still be approved of, from habit or for some other reason. Hume's theory does not treat morality and utility as the same thing, but merely asserts that the primary function of expressions of approval and disapproval is to encourage useful behaviour and to discourage harmful behaviour. Though he does not, as some philosophers now do, treat moral judgements as disguised imperatives, he does say that they ordinarily serve to control behaviour, and that this explains how men have come to make them.

Bentham cannot follow Hume because he wants to do something that Hume cared little about; he wants to change people's habits of approval and disapproval. He wants to do more than explain what moral judgments are and how we come to make them as we do; he also wants to reform our moral standards. He cannot do this merely by defining *goodness, rightness* and *duty*, as he does define them, because from these definitions nothing follows about how people ought to behave. His definitions reduce these moral terms to mere descriptive epithets. Before he can achieve his purpose, he must get people to accept a fundamental principle which logically has nothing to do with his definitions, though Bentham clearly thinks otherwise. This principle is what he calls the *greatest happiness principle*, or the rule which requires us always so to act as to produce the greatest happiness possible in the circumstances.

Though this rule does not follow logically from Bentham's definitions, it is not altogether surprising that he thought it did. For if we accept the definitions, we are disposed to accept the rule – and this for a simple reason. True, if *good* means merely pleasant or desired for its own sake, it does not follow that we ought to aim at what is good. But then *good* does not mean pleasant or desired for its own sake. To say that something is good is to say, or at least to imply, that we ought to aim at it. That is ordinary usage, and by defining the word contrary to that usage, we do not ensure that we use it in the way we define it. Bentham defines the word *good* in his own way, and his definition is incorrect, because it purports to tell us, not just how he intends to use the word, but how it is ordinarily used; and then, having defined it incorrectly, he goes on to use it correctly, as indeed he can hardly avoid doing. He tells us that *good* means pleasant or desired for its own sake,[1] which is not true, and then goes on to use the word to tell us what we ought to aim at, which is to make a proper use of

---

[1] Good does sometimes mean 'desired' or 'desired for oneself', as when we say of a man that 'he is out for his own good'. But this is not to use the word as a moral term.

it. If, then, we accept his definition, we are disposed to agree that pleasure or what is desired for its own sake (which are, of course, for him the same) is what we ought always to aim at. In the same way, Bentham tells us, falsely, that *right* means conducive to the greatest amount of pleasure possible in the circumstances, and then makes a proper use of the word to urge a line of conduct on us. Once again, if we accept the definition, we are disposed to accept the conclusion, that we ought always to do what conduces to the greatest possible pleasure, even though the conclusion does not follow logically from the definition. There are few more effective methods of persuasion than first to define a word incorrectly and then to go on to use it correctly, provided of course that the definition is plausible. And the method is the more effective for being used, as Bentham used it, unconsciously.

I have said that Bentham, apart from trying to derive his greatest happiness principle from his definitions of moral terms, also produced arguments to show that, since man is the sort of creature he is – egoistic and rational – he always accepts the greatest happiness principle when he understands it properly. I want now to discuss these arguments.

Sometimes, especially when he is deliberately laying down his basic principles, Bentham speaks as though we never desire anything except to enjoy pleasure and to avoid pain. But more often (and more plausibly), in the actual course of his arguments, he says that we desire *for its own sake* nothing except pleasure and the avoidance of pain. I shall assume that the second is his true position; and, for the sake of simplicity, I shall take desire for pleasure to include aversion to pain.

Believing that nothing but pleasure is desired for its own sake, Bentham thought he could persuade everyone that the greatest happiness principle is the one rule which is universally acceptable. Given that, whatever people may desire, they desire it either for the pleasure in it or for the pleasure it will bring, and given that the intensity of their desire varies with the amount of pleasure they expect, you have (thinks Bentham) only to convince them that some things are more pleasant than others, or are likely to bring more pleasure, to get them to desire those things. If, for instance, they approve of one line of conduct rather than another, and this habit of approval prevents them from getting as much happiness as they could get, you have only to point this out to them, and they will cease to approve of that line of conduct. They only came in the first place to approve it because they believed that it promoted happiness. They may have been mistaken from the beginning, or that mode of behaviour, once a means to happiness, may now have become an obstacle to it, without their seeing that it has. They may still be attached to it from habit, and it may be difficult to break the habit, because the breaking of a habit often involves considerable pain. Nevertheless, to break the habit, to get them to cease approving of this mode of behaviour, all you have to do (however difficult it may be) is to persuade them that it never did, or no longer does, promote happiness. This is the way to reform both moral standards and laws.

The only rule that is always accepted when it is properly understood is the greatest happiness principle. Indeed, Bentham seems to have believed that it always is accepted, though not always explicitly, by everyone. He speaks as if his problem were not really to persuade people to accept a principle entirely new to them but to get them to see it clearly and to see its implications. He says, in his *Theory of Legislation*, 'It is not the principle of utility which is new; on the contrary, that principle is necessarily as old as the human race. All the truth there is in morality, all the good there is in the laws, emanate from it; but utility has often been followed by instinct, while it has been combatted by argument'.[1] What is needed, in the sphere of morals, is not to give people new ideas so much as to help them bring the ideas they already have into good order. Because they do not see clearly that the original function of moral rules was to promote happiness, they treat many of these rules as absolute. If they do promote happiness, the mistake is not dangerous; but if they do not, it is. The only rule which is absolute is the greatest happiness principle, because it is the only rule which always of necessity promotes happiness.

We have been so busy criticizing Bentham for the clumsy way in which he tries to derive moral rules from statements of fact – for not seeing that to say that something is universally desired or is alone desired for its own sake is still not to say or to imply that we ought always to aim at it – that we have almost entirely neglected this quite different line of reasoning. The fault, no doubt, is partly Bentham's own. He often mixes up different arguments so much that it is difficult to see that they are different. Yet we must admit that he does say that the greatest happiness principle is the only rule which we can expect people always to accept and to prefer to any other rule which conflicts with it when they clearly understand both rules. There is no question here of deriving moral rules logically from statements of fact. Bentham merely tells us that men, given that they desire only pleasure

---

[1] *The Theory of Legislation*, ed. C. K. Ogden (London 1931), ch. XIII, p. 67.

for its own sake, will always accept the greatest happiness principle, and will always prefer it to any rule which conflicts with it, provided they see clearly the practical consequences of following the two rules. He does not put his position in exactly these words, but they are words which do, I think, put the gist of it without distorting it.

When Bentham says that we desire nothing for its own sake except pleasure, the pleasure he has in mind is nearly always our own. Much of the time, though not all of it, he is a psychological egoist; he holds that it is his own pleasure and not somebody else's that a man desires for its own sake. There may be nothing logically absurd about holding that, while we desire only pleasure for its own sake, we can desire other people's pleasure in this way (that is, for its own sake) as well as our own; but it is a position which few philosophers have taken. Those who have said that only pleasure is desired for its own sake have usually gone on to say that, when we desire other people's pleasure, it is as a means to our own. That is certainly what Bentham believed, at least while he bore in mind his own assertion that pleasure alone is desired for its own sake. Only when he forgot this assertion did he sometimes speak as if we could desire other people's pleasure without any thought of our own.

It has been argued that psychological egoism is incompatible with the greatest happiness principle. If egoism is true, I can accept the greatest happiness principle while the behaviour making for my own happiness also makes for the happiness of other people; but as soon as there is a divergence between what makes for my happiness and what makes for theirs, the greatest happiness principle is unacceptable to me. It is often said that *I ought* implies *I can*. But the word *ought* may be used in such a way that this does not hold. If, for example, *I ought to do this* means only that there is a rule which I ordinarily accept requiring me to do it, or if it means that this is a kind of action generally approved, then it does make sense to say that I ought to do it even though I cannot. No doubt, if I cannot do it, it is no use my saying to myself that I ought to; and no doubt, too, I am not likely to go on saying it if I am convinced that I cannot do it. But that is beside the point. The social function of the rule is to control behaviour, and I can accept it even though it is sometimes impossible for me to obey it. I can desire that there should be such a rule which everyone, including myself, is required to obey. My acceptance of the rule may be merely this desire and the behaviour inspired by it; namely, my appealing to the rule on appropriate occasions when I consider other people's actions or my own. The appeal, of course, will be in vain whenever I see that I have, on the whole, more to gain than to lose by ignoring it. Yet it is still my interest that there should be such a rule generally obeyed, and I therefore accept it. I cannot invoke it against others unless I am prepared to have them invoke it against me; and if I live in a society where the rule is generally respected, I shall soon acquire the habit of invoking it against myself, often effectively, though sometimes in vain.

There is, of course, a rule whose general acceptance is even more my interest than the greatest happiness principle; and that is the rule that everyone should act so as to increase *my* happiness. But, alas, I am not the only egoist in the world; other people are as exclusively concerned with their happiness as I am with mine. They will not accept the rule which is ideally in my best interest. The most I can hope for is that they will accept the greatest happiness principle. I cannot, of course, hope that they will act on it when it is clearly their interest not to do so; but I can hope that, in a world in which the principle is generally accepted, it often will be their interest to act upon it. Among the pleasures that count most with most people is the pleasure of a good reputation, and a good reputation is only to be had by obeying the rules, legal and moral, which are generally accepted. Though it matters enormously to me how other people behave, I cannot control their behaviour in my own exclusive interest, simply because I have not the power to do so. I need the help of others to control it; and I cannot get that help unless I appeal to a common interest. That is why, however selfish men may be, social rules always serve some common interest.

This common interest need not be universal; it may be the interest of a class or profession. No one was more willing to admit this than Bentham. Yet there is at least one interest common to all mankind. It is everyone's interest that other people should recognize that his happiness matters as much to him as theirs to them – that he too should count for one, and that no one should count for more than he does. The rule that serves this universal interest is the greatest happiness principle, which is therefore the universally accepted rule. When we appeal to it, we can expect all mankind to accept the standard we appeal to. Though it may be the interest of some group or class to put forward claims incompatible with the greatest happiness principle, it will never be their interest to repudiate that principle, because they need it to protect themselves against the claims of others. They will take the principle for granted, or else will try to prove that the claims they make on their own behalf are compatible with it. Therefore it will always be possible to appeal to the principle against them.

This argument, as far as it goes, is, I think, sound. There is nothing illogical about holding both that men desire nothing for its own sake except their own pleasure and that the greatest happiness principle is the ultimate moral rule, in the sense of its being the only rule which is always and everywhere accepted when it is properly understood. It is a mistake to argue, as I have done in the past, that egoistic hedonism and Utilitarianism are mutually exclusive doctrines. They may be false or inadequate, but they are not inconsistent with one another.

Yet I am no more inclined than I was to accept either egoism or Utilitarianism, because the arguments against them seem to me as strong as ever they seemed. These arguments have frequently been put, and I propose to say very little about them. Egoism and hedonism (of which Bentham's Utilitarianism is one variety) both rest on rather simple mistakes. When a man gets what he wants, it is often said that he has satisfied himself; even if what he wants is something for someone else, he is said to have satisfied *himself* when he succeeds in his purpose. It is easy to pass from this use of language to the conclusion that the object of all desire is self-satisfaction. But the conclusion is absurd. A man is not satisfied until he has attained the object of his desire; and to say that he is satisfied is only another way of saying that he has attained his object. Similarly, when a man gets what he wants, it is often said that he has pleased himself. This is just another way of saying that he is satisfied, or else it refers to some feeling he has when he gets what he wants, some pleasant feeling which accompanies success. In either case, it is improper to say that his object is pleasure. His object is pleasure only when he wants to procure for himself or for someone else an experience because he believes it to be pleasant.

Bentham took it for granted that the notion of pleasure is simple, and that everyone would understand him when he said that we desire only pleasure for its own sake. But it is not clear whether he thought of pleasure as a feeling about the experiences called pleasant or as a quality inherent in them. His friend and disciple James Mill, who in his *Analysis of the Human Mind* went further into these matters than Bentham did, sometimes spoke as if pleasure were a simple quality, varying in intensity but not in kind, inhering in pleasant sensations; sometimes as if the pleasantness of a sensation consisted merely in our desire to continue having it; and perhaps also sometimes (though rarely) as if pleasure were a separate feeling annexed to the experiences called pleasant, as if we first had an experience and then felt pleased with it. Both Bentham and James Mill, though they say that we desire nothing for its own sake except our own pleasure, and sometimes even that we desire nothing at all except our own pleasure, also say that we can come to desire the means to something as intensely as the thing itself, and can even continue to desire the means when we have forgotten the end. If we can do this, it follows that we can desire for their own sake other things besides our own pleasure, including among these things the pleasures of other people.

But I shall pursue these objections no further. I mention them only to show how confused were the ideas about pleasure and the means to it of two philosphers who were none the less always very certain that nothing is desired for its own sake except pleasure. Nor shall I trouble to consider Bentham's felicific calculus, his elaborate scheme for estimating amounts of pleasure, which assumes that the intensity of a pleasure can be set against its duration, its duration against the likelihood of its being enjoyed, and so on, as if these and other properties were all amenable to a single standard of measurement, and could be multiplied together to get a quantity of happiness, as length, breadth and height are multiplied to get a volume. Suffice it to say that the felicific calculus is useless, not only because we cannot in practice get the required infqrmation, but also because the operations it consists of are logically absurd.

It is, however, possible to substitute for the greatest happiness principle another rule which does not require us to make meaningless calculations. Instead of saying, 'Act so as to produce the largest amount of pleasure possible in the circumstances', we can say, 'Act so as to ensure, as far as you can, that people get what they want, according to their own preferences'. Of course, I have put this rule very roughly; it needs to be qualified in several ways. We need not always take into account everyone likely to be affected by our actions; we are rightly much more concerned to satisfy some people, our friends and relations, than others, Bentham thought so too, and argued that in the long run the general happiness is better promoted if our benevolence is mostly confined to persons close to us, whose wants we know. Again, we must not give people what they want, if by doing so we are likely to harm either them or other people. But this qualification does not detract from our principle, if we hold that they are harmed when something happens to them which they would rather did not happen. By not giving them what they want now we may ensure that, in the long run, more of their desires are satisfied.

Bentham would no doubt say that this rule is at bottom the same as his greatest happiness principle – that it is only a looser way of saying what he wanted to say more precisely. In his eyes, 'Give people as great a sum of pleasures as possible' and 'Give them what they want in the order of their preferences' are equivalent rules. But they are equivalent only if it is true that what men desire is always pleasure, or other things for the sake of pleasure, and if the strength of their desires varies with the amount of pleasure they expect. Since neither of these things is true, the two rules are not equivalent. The first rule really makes no sense because 'a sum of pleasures' (as Bentham defines it) is a logically absurd notion; whereas the second rule does make sense. Bentham accepted both rules, the second as much as the first, and indeed often used the second in place of the first precisely because he believed that the two were equivalent. That is one reason among others why, in spite of his greatest happiness principle, he often spoke the most admirable sense.

This second rule, the rule which does make sense, requires us to help people get what *they* want and not what *we* think is good for them. Nothing could be more in the spirit of Bentham's philosophy. It is not our business to try to make other people better than they are or to try to bring into existence some social order which seems to us the most just or the best suited to the dignity of man. We can discover what we ought to do only by finding out what it is that people in fact want. We must look to their desires and not to any conceptions we may have of a perfected human nature or of rights that belong to men in virtue of their humanity. The Utilitarian argument is that, in any case, these conceptions first emerged because they were useful, because they helped men to control one another's behaviour to prevent their getting too much in each other's way as they strove to satisfy their desires. Ideals and conventions arose out of the need to reconcile desires, and we must see to it that what originally served that need does not now impede it.

This is not to say that we must care nothing for what people are like in themselves – that we must accept all their wants, without venturing to praise or blame them. Some of their wants are frustrating to other people or to themselves; some types of character are harmful and others are helpful. But we must judge characters and wants by their consequences; we must condemn or praise them for the evil or good effects of the actions they inspire.[1] There is nothing ultimately good or evil except people's getting what they want or their failing to get it. We cannot help having our own preferences, being more attracted by some people than by others; but we ought not to interfere with other people except to discourage harmful behaviour or to encourage useful behaviour. It matters what people do rather than what they are; and it matters what they are only to the extent that their being one sort

---

[1] That is, for the pain and frustration or the pleasure and opportunity resulting from those actions.

of person rather than another makes them dangerous or helpful. This is the core of Bentham's doctrine.

Benthamism is optimistic and liberal and also inadequate: inadequate not because of its liberalism and optimism but in spite of them. It is liberal because it invites us to take men as they are, and to aim at giving them what they want and not what we think is good for them; because it forbids our using any notion of duty to God or any conception of human nature or society made perfect as an excuse for bending other people to our will. It is optimistic because it takes for granted that we can, by reforming our laws and institutions, go a long way towards making it easier for people to get what they want.

Bentham's liberalism is, in one way, an improvement on Locke's. It has no truck with the doctrine of natural rights; it does not require us to believe that no government is legitimate unless it rests on the consent of the governed, or that property is inalienable except with the consent of its possessor. It is less rigid than the liberalism of Locke. In general, and quite apart from Locke's version of it, the doctrine of natural rights seems to me either so broad as to amount to little more than the rule, *Act so as to help other people get what they want and not what you think is good for them*, or else leads to conclusions which even the liberal does not in practice always find acceptable. The fundamental rule of the Utilitarians, amended as I have suggested it should be, seems to me preferable to the doctrine of natural rights, because it says what that doctrine has to say more simply and clearly, without using difficult and misleading ideas. True, the amended rule is no longer the greatest happiness principle; yet it deserves to be called Utilitarian because both Bentham and James Mill accepted it, even though they did so under the mistaken belief that it was equivalent to the greatest happiness principle.

I find Bentham's optimism naïve and facile. No doubt, if human wants were limited and unchanging, it would be possible, by taking thought, to make continual progress towards satisfying them completely. Even though we could never ensure that they were always satisfied, we could presumably get indefinitely closer towards satisfying them all. But wants are not unchanging; and by our endeavours to satisfy the wants we have, we create new wants. That does not make it irrational for us to try to satisfy our wants; not does it invalidate the fundamental rule I have just discussed. It merely makes optimism irrelevant. Certainly, it would be absurd to say, *Don't let us bother about our present wants because, in satisfying them, we shall only create new wants.* It is our nature to try to satisfy the wants we have; and if we have them and do nothing about them, we only make ourselves miserable.

Pessimism and quietism are as much out of place here as optimism.

The inadequacy of Bentham's philosophy is that it treats happiness as Hobbes treated felicity – as if it consisted in successfully satisfying one desire after another. But men do not only have desires; they have ideals as well, and we cannot go far towards explaining their desires except in relation to these ideals. What men want depends largely on what they think is worth having, on the kinds of reputation they aspire to, on what they need to believe about themselves in order to have self-respect. These things will vary greatly from community to community, from age to age, from person to person. Man in society is as much a creature of ambitions as of desires; he has a scheme of life. It may be a vague scheme, it may change as he grows older, but it is always there. Whatever it is, however admirable or base, it can never be explained merely as a train or succession of desires. Social man is a moral and aesthetic animal; he is not just a creature of appetites, whose superior reason enables him to foresee what he is likely to want better than other animals, and to take more elaborate precautions to get it. He is a member of a community who is ordinarily much more concerned about how he stands in that community than about pursuing happiness as Bentham understood it. Man is spectator and judge as well as actor, and what he wants to do depends largely on the part he sees himself playing among other men. He is, as the Idealists put it, 'his own end' – with this proviso, that the phrase is not to be taken literally, as the Idealists would have us take it, but metaphorically. It matters enormously to man what he is like, both in his own eyes and in other people's. If that were not so, he would not be the tragic, pathetic and sometimes absurd animal that he is. Bentham treats man much as the economists treat him, as a competitor and collaborator with other men for the satisfaction of one desire after another – with this difference, that Bentham imagines that he has explained all that there is to man, whereas the economists usually admit that they are interested in only a part of his life.

Yet, though his conception of man as a social and moral being is inadequate, Bentham's fundamental rule – that we should aim rather at helping people get what they want than at making them the sort of people we think they should be – may still be acceptable.

II. SUPREME POWER

In the seventeenth century, it had been the fashion to defend absolute power. Hobbes's doctrine of sovereignty, unlike some other parts of his political theory, had been widely attractive. In the eighteenth century, at least in England and France (the two countries whose political writers had the greatest influence in the European world generally), it was much more the virtues of limited government that were extolled. Bolingbroke, Montesquieu, Hume and Burke, each in his own way, were champions of limited monarchy. They were also admirers of the British constitution. Rousseau had claimed for the assembly of the people an authority in some ways more absolute than Hobbes had claimed for the sovereign, but the *Social Contract* was avowedly the description of an ideal state and made no claims on behalf of existing governments.

Bentham was the first to attack the fashionable arguments in favour of the separation of powers. In the course of this attack, which he made in his *Fragment on Government*, he produced a theory of sovereignty different from Hobbes's theory and in many ways more plausible. He freely admitted that political power is always limited and always shared. His account of sovereignty is emphatically not an argument for unconditional obedience; on the contrary, it is combined with a plea for watchful criticism of government and resistance, when resistance is for the public good.

As an expounder and critic of political ideas, Bentham is usually little more than a disciple of either Hobbes or Hume, less formidable than the first and less subtle than the second. He is stronger as a critic of institutions than of ideas. His account of supreme power is, I think, the one important exception to this general verdict upon him, for he gets it neither from Hobbes nor Hume. He rejects, even more completely than Hobbes, the traditional theory of natural law, and also the doctrine of the separation of powers, and yet produces a conception of supreme power very different from Hobbes's conception of it. Bentham makes distinctions that Hobbes never made, and which need to be made to avoid confusion of thought.

Continental exponents of natural law had long insisted that a monarch can be absolute and yet not have unlimited authority. They had repudiated or ignored the argument of Hobbes that the positive law of the sovereign necessarily contains the natural law, or, alternatively, that it is the duty of the subject always to act on the assumption that it does contain it. Hobbes had denied that the subject can be guilty of sin when he obeys a command of his sovereign which is contrary to natural law, for it belongs to the sovereign alone to define that law. Pufendorf, who had a liking for absolute monarchy, nevertheless contradicted Hobbes, saying that a man may sin even when he obeys his lawful sovereign. Yet Pufendorf was reluctant to advise disobedience; he equivocated and in the end almost enjoined complete obedience. Other jurists were bolder than he was: the subject, they said, must refuse obedience, even to an absolute ruler, if he cannot conscientiously do otherwise. The absoluteness of absolute human authority consists, they said, not in its always being the subject's duty to obey whatever that authority may command, but in there being no conventional or statutory limits to it. The ruler's authority is always limited by his duty to respect the natural law and by his subjects' duty to prefer God's law to all human law. Human authority is absolute as long as it is not limited in any other way.

Hobbes wanted to show that men, when they institute a sovereign, leave themselves without rights against him, because the only rights they then have are legal rights, which are grants from the sovereign. At the same time, since his whole theory turned on the argument that men set up the sovereign in the first place for the sake of security, he could not really lay on them an absolute duty of obedience; he had to admit that the subject may disobey when the sovereign seeks to destroy him. Yet, in spite of this admission, which he could not avoid, Hobbes's purpose, when he called the sovereign's power *absolute*, was to do more than say that it is not limited by law, and that therefore the subject has no legal redress; he also wanted to say that, because the subject has no legal redress against the sovereign, he can never have the right to disobey the sovereign, except when the sovereign seeks to destroy him. Hobbes wanted to treat legality and morality as if they were the same, and yet could not avoid sometimes using arguments which mean nothing unless they are different.

Bentham's theory of supreme power, though it completely rejects the traditional conception of natural law, is not open to this objection; it treats supremacy entirely as a political and legal matter. For Bentham, as for Hobbes, there is no law, properly so called, except what the ruler commands. But Bentham does not conclude that the subject has no right to resist the ruler, or has it only when the ruler seeks to destroy him. Bentham's account of morality may be defective, but it does at least enable him to distinguish moral from legal rules. Indeed, he makes this distinction, not only more clearly than Hobbes, but more clearly even than Locke and Pufendorf. He holds that moral rules are not, properly speaking, any kind of law. Law, as he defines it, consists of whatever rules are in fact enforced by those in authority. The rules enforced by mere public opinion are not laws. He distinguishes laws, properly so called, from other rules by the nature of the sanctions attached to them. But he does not, on that account, suppose that rules which are not laws are therefore less effective or inferior.

They serve, alongside the laws, to hold society together; and they serve also to limit the power of governments. Whether law is to be preferred to conventional morality or the other way round depends on circumstances. The proper function of both moral rules and laws is to promote happiness, and when the two conflict, the one to be preferred is that which promotes happiness best. The supreme rule is always to act so as to increase happiness as much as possible. There is not for Bentham, as there was for Hobbes, a direct connection between absolute authority and the duty of obedience. The duty of subjects to their rulers depends on how they govern; only if they govern the better for having absolute power is the duty to obey them thereby increased.

By supreme power Bentham means legislative authority not limited by any express convention. 'Grant', he says, 'that there *are* certain bounds to the *authority* of the legislature: – Of what use is it to say so, when those bounds are what nobody has ever attempted to mark out to any useful purpose; that is, in any such manner whereby it might be known beforehand what description a law must be of to fall *within*, and what to fall *beyond* them?'[1] Bentham wrote the *Fragment on Government* before the American Constitution was made; and he gives – as examples of countries where the powers of the legislature are limited by 'express convention' – the German Empire, the Dutch Provinces, the Swiss Cantons, and the Achaean League.[2] He does not suppose that, in every developed state, there *must* be a supreme legislature; but he does, I think, take it for granted that there will be one unless there are special reasons why there should not be.

Hobbes's sovereign of necessity wields, either directly or through subordinates, every kind of authority, legislative, executive and judicial; he is lawmaker, governor and judge, all in one. Though Hobbes argues that the legislative is the supreme political power, he does not think it enough that the sovereign should be merely the supreme legislator; or, rather, he speaks as if the legislative power, being supreme, carried with it the judicial and executive powers. Bentham does not follow his example. Though he, too, treats the legislative power as supreme, he never speaks as if its being supreme meant that whoever possesses it also has the executive and judicial powers. The executive and judicial powers are exercised according to rules which the sovereign may alter, but this does not of itself make the sovereign's authority more than merely legislative; it does not

[1] *A Fragment on Government*, ch. IV, p. 96.
[2] Ibid., pp. 98–9.

even require that those who have the highest executive and judicial powers should be responsible to the legislature. Because they exercise their powers within limits prescribed by the legislature, they do not therefore exercise them as agents of the legislature. Bentham never suggests, as Hobbes does, what is patently false: that whoever has the right to make laws regulating the executive and judicial powers virtually exercises those powers through subordinates.

According to Bentham's account of the matter, there can be a supreme power even though the highest legislative, executive and judicial powers are in separate hands, even though the executive and the judges are not appointed by or responsible to the legislature. But this does not mean that there can be a supreme power, in Bentham's sense, where there is a separation of powers, as Montesquieu understood it. Montesquieu never asserted the legally unlimited right of the legislature to make law; he never distinguished, as Bentham did, between moral and legal right. The idea of sovereignty, as we find it in Bentham, is entirely absent from his works, just as entirely as the idea of sovereignty which we find in Hobbes. Montesquieu never attributed to the legislature the right to decide how the executive and judicial powers should be organized. He said nothing which suggests that he included in the legislative power the right to make constitutional laws, the right to decide how the community shall be governed. He neither attributed nor denied this right to the supreme legislature. On this matter, where Bentham is explicit, Montesquieu is silent. True, Bentham does not say that it is always desirable that the legislature should have this right (which it must have if it is to be supreme or sovereign in his sense); he is ready to admit that there may be circumstances where it neither has it nor ought to have it, as for example in a federal state. But he does speak as if, except where there are special reasons which make it impossible or undesirable, the legislature probably ought to have this right. Certainly, he sees no threat to liberty in the legally unlimited right to make law.

Though Montesquieu is silent where Bentham is explicit, there are grounds for believing that, had he not been silent, he would have disagreed with Bentham. He did not look upon governments as deliberately set up to achieve definite ends. He thought of them as more or less well adjusted to the communities in which they maintain order; he saw them as the unwilled and unforeseen products of human activities, products which men become attached to from habit. He saw the form of government, or the distribution of power among those possessing it, as a system imperfectly understood by those who govern and understood almost not at all by the vast majority of their subjects. The rules regulating the exercise of authority or, as we might put it, the constitutional rules, are conventional and supported by venerable traditions; and he thought of the separation of powers, where it exists, as resting on custom. He did not have in mind a system in which the authority of each branch of government is defined by a written constitution that the legislature may not alter, nor yet one in which the right of the legislature to make laws is held to include the right to lay down the legal limits of the authority of the other branches. He believed that in practice those who govern have little power to change the structure of government, and said nothing to suggest that he regretted this; he probably took it for granted that, where that structure establishes a separation of powers, the legislature cannot, and ought not to be able to, decide how and within what limits the other two powers are exercised. He believed that it is a condition of liberty, not only that the legislative, executive and judicial powers should be in separate hands, but also that those who exercise the legislative power should not be able to use it to curtail the authority of the other two powers.

Bentham differs from both Hobbes and Montesquieu. He sees that legally unlimited legislative power is not incompatible with a separation of powers, whereas Hobbes says explicitly that it is incompatible, while Montesquieu, though he neither asserts nor denies the incompatibility, seems to take it for granted.

Supreme legislative authority, while without limit in law, is always, according to Bentham, limited in two ways, morally and in fact. It is not true that subjects ought to obey any law which the supreme legislature may choose to make, nor is it true that all its laws are in fact habitually obeyed. To say, therefore, that a legislature is supreme is merely to make a negative statement about it: it is to say that no one has a legal right to set aside or to alter or disobey its laws. It is not to say that it has, in any sense which can deprive subjects of the moral right to resist it, an unlimited right to make what laws it pleases. It has no moral right to legislate as it pleases because it has a moral duty to legislate for the public good; and it has a legal right to do so, only in the sense that all persons within the territory in which its law runs are *legally* obliged to accept whatever laws it makes as valid laws. The legislature also has a moral right to make law, but that right is limited by the nature of the end it ought to pursue. It is supreme only because there are no definite conventions or laws which it has to conform to, no rules which it is someone's legal duty to see that it follows. In that sense, and that sense only, its authority is unlimited. But there is still a right of resistance, which is not confined (as it is with Hobbes) to persons who happen to be in mortal danger from their sovereign, nor justified (as it is with Locke) by an appeal to a higher kind of law. Any subject may resist when, 'according to the best calculation he is able to make, *the probable mischiefs of resistance* (speaking with respect to the community in general) *appear less. . .than the probable mischiefs of submission*'.[1]

Just as Bentham is aware that supreme power does not imply a right to govern as one pleases, so he knows that it does not require that all power should belong to one person or assembly. He admits that the supreme governor's power must, except where it is limited by express convention, be indefinite. How, then, he goes on to ask, can we distinguish between a free and a despotic government? To Hobbes, this distinction could mean nothing, but to Bentham it is important. Does the despot have greater power than a free government? Bentham does not think so: 'The distinction turns upon circumstances of a vastly different complexion: – on the *manner* in which that whole mass of power. . .is, in a free state, *distributed* among the several ranks of persons that are sharers in it: – on the *source* from whence their titles to it are successively derived: – on the frequent and easy *changes* of condition between governors and governed: . . .on the *liberty of the press*. . . .on the *liberty of public association*.'[2] These are all limitations on the power of the supreme legislature and yet take nothing away from its supremacy. Supremacy, thus conceived, does not exclude the division of power; it excludes only the kind of separation of powers that leaves to no person or body of persons the legally unlimited right to make laws. It excludes the separation of powers as the makers of the American Constitution established it, and also, I think, as Montesquieu imagined it.

The British Parliament is legally supreme or sovereign, and yet Britain enjoys a freedom which depends on something more than the limits set to power by popular morality and public opinion; for these limits exist even where there is despotism. Freedom depends, says Bentham, on how the 'whole mass of power' is 'distributed among the several ranks of persons that are sharers in it', 'on the frequent and easy changes of condition between governors and governed', 'on the liberty of the press', and so on. In other words, it depends on how power is organized. Parliament is supreme, and yet has no monopoly of power. It is limited, in all kinds of ways, by the other institutions of the State. Bentham therefore agrees with Montesquieu that, to preserve

[1] Ibid., p. 93.
[2] Ibid., pp. 94–5.

freedom adequately, power must be limited by power, and not just by common morality and public opinion. But he goes further than Montesquieu; he sees that this limitation of power by power need not exclude legal supremacy. Sovereign decisions may be of no effect, not only because they too grossly offend ordinary morals, but because the executive or the courts would not enforce them, even though legally obliged to do so. The supreme legislature's power is limited partly by what people will put up with and partly by the kind of co-operation it can rely on from the other branches of government.

It is the great merit of Bentham's *Fragment on Government* that it makes such matters clearer than they were ever made before. Bentham does not, as some theorists have done, assume that in every well-regulated State there must be a sovereign legislature; nor does he treat sovereignty as monopoly of power. Above all, his account of sovereignty or legislative supremacy is quite distinct from his doctrine of political obligation. We cannot, from his definition of supreme power, predict when he will think it right for subjects to obey or disobey their rulers. Here he improves on Hobbes and anticipates Austin.

III. THE UTILITARIAN ARGUMENT FOR DEMOCRACY

Arguments for democracy have been mostly of two kinds: they have, for the most part, assumed either that all men have certain fundamental rights, or else that every man follows his own 'interest', which he prefers to other people's and of which he is usually the best judge. The first argument assumes an equality of rights, while the second assumes a certain kind of natural equality or similarity. These two arguments do not exclude one another; it is possible, without inconsistency, to use both. For the sake of convenience, I shall call the first liberal and the second Utilitarian.

Neither of the assumptions on which these arguments rest implies that democracy is the only rightful form of government, or even that it is the best. Of course, if man's fundamental rights include the right not to be governed except with his consent, and if the notion of consent is not emasculated until it is left almost without substance, then it does follow that democracy is the only rightful form of government. But it is possible to assert a natural right to freedom without including this right in it. As I have tried to show, when discussing Locke's theory,[1] it does not follow – because every man, in the absence of all government, would have the right to do what he pleased short of harming others – that he cannot rightfully be governed except with his own consent. If there is a natural right to freedom, and if government in fact serves to secure that right, then a man ought to obey government whether or not he has consented to do so. By deriving man's right not to be governed, except with his own consent, from his natural freedom, Locke (and others who thought like him) made a false inference.

Having made the false inference, they then usually avoid the conclusion that only democracy is rightful by emasculating the notion of consent. They neglected to consider what consent must be if government by consent is to be distinguishable from tyranny. We have already seen the consequences of this neglect for Locke's theory, and Locke was by no means the most negligent. On the Continent, there were philosophers and jurists who found it possible to combine a preference for absolute monarchy with the doctrine that man is by nature free and therefore cannot be justly governed except with his consent. They did this by taking such liberties with the notion of consent as to reduce it to insignificance.

The Utilitarians did not believe in natural rights. Yet there is a right entailed both by the *greatest happiness principle* and by the rule which I said might be substituted for it; and that is the right of every man that his happiness or his wants should not count for less than anyone else's. It is the right to equality, which is as fundamental to the Utilitarian philosophy as natural rights are to Locke's – though fundamental in a different sense. The Utilitarian argument for democracy does not proceed merely from this right; it proceeds from it together with certain assumptions about human nature: that every man prefers his own interest to other people's, and that he is usually the best judge of his own interest. Before I consider the Utilitarian argument for democracy, I want to say a few words about *natural* equality and inequality – meaning thereby, not an equality of rights, but of abilities. This is the kind of equality which the Utilitarians assert when they say that every man is usually the best judge of his own interest. It is a kind of equality in wisdom. The claim is not that men are equally wise in all respects, but that they are so in some respect which happens to be relevant.

There was nothing new about their asserting this kind of equality. Hobbes asserted it long before the Utilitarians, and so did other people,

[1] See *Man and Society*, vol. I, ch. 8, pp. 347–9.

many of them believers in absolute monarchy. It never occurred to these people that by asserting this kind of natural equality they might be logically committed to preferring democracy to other forms of government, just as it usually did not occur to people who preferred monarchy to democracy that they might be committed to denying this equality. Indeed, I would hazard the generalization that in the Christian era before the eighteenth century the case against democracy did not rest primarily on the belief that men are unequal, either in virtue or wisdom. I do not suggest that obvious natural inequalities were denied, but only that they were usually ignored, presumably on the ground that they were irrelevant. This is one conspicuous difference between Plato and Aristotle and most of the great political thinkers of the Christian era until quite recent times. Plato argues repeatedly from natural to political inequalities, and so does Aristotle; though Aristotle is also more inclined than Plato to argue from some kinds of natural to some kinds of political equality, as, for example, when he says that all citizens should take part in electing the magistrates because they are on the whole fairly good judges of ability.

How different Plato is from Hobbes! It is unlikely that Hobbes really wanted to deny the obvious: that men differ greatly in intelligence, courage and virtue. Though he explained the virtues as refined forms of egoism, and said that all men are egoists, he never for a moment suggested that all men are equally endowed with virtue. But, for the purposes of his political theory, he assumed that men are pretty much of a muchness, the sovereign being ordinarily no wiser and no more foolish, no better and no worse, than the great mass of his subjects. There is no question of justifying absolute power, as Aristotle justified monarchy, by the superior wisdom and virtue of its possessor. For anything that Hobbes says to the contrary, there might be innumerable persons as fit to have that power as the person (or assembly) that actually has it. It is merely the paramount interest of everybody that only one person or assembly should have it. Absolute government is best, not because the wisest ought to rule or are likely to rule, but because it is everyone's interest that supreme authority should not be divided. This was by no means an opinion peculiar to Hobbes; it was shared by most believers in absolute monarchy, and even by many who believed in the divine right of kings.

Until the eighteenth century, people were more directly concerned with political than social questions; they wanted to justify or condemn forms of government rather than this or that social order. But when they did consider the division of society into classes, they were seldom inclined to justify it on the ground of the natural superiority of the privileged classes. The social teaching of the Christian churches, though often strongly conservative, was not flattering to the rich, the educated and the powerful. It taught that if men were without sin they would live like brothers, without property or power among them. All the institutions making for inequality were supposed to be consequences of Adam's Fall, serving to protect men from one another's evil passions. Hierarchy was necessary to hold society together, and every man ought therefore to accept patiently his lot in life. But this acceptance was by no means held to carry with it respect or admiration for the great of this world or belief in their natural superiority. Though it was commonly admitted that there are substantial natural inequalities between men, it was also commonly held that they have little or nothing to do with differences in power or wealth or worldly esteem.

This Christian tradition was still powerful in the seventeenth century and is nowhere better expressed than in Pascal's *Pensées*. Pascal treats social inequalities as effects of selfishness, force and chance. They are accepted, as most things are by men, from habit and for the sake of peace. It is absurd, Pascal thinks, to contest privilege on the ground that the possessor does not deserve it. 'How wise it is', he says, 'to distinguish men by their outward rather than their inner qualities! Who shall pass first of us two? Who shall give way to the other? The less able? But I am as able as he is, and we must fight it out. But he has four servants, and I have only one. It is for me to give way, and I am a fool if I contest it. Thus there is peace between us, which is the greatest good'.[1]

I do not suggest that this attitude was universal but only that it was common. For reasons not far to seek, champions of aristocracy were more inclined than champions of monarchy to justify social inequalities as effects of natural differences of ability. The privileged classes were never quite rigid castes; it was always possible to rise and to fall in the social hierarchy. That the privileged – in spite of conspicuous examples to the contrary – on the whole deserved their privileges was a not uncommon opinion, at least among the upper classes, before the French Revolution. It was also argued that among these classes natural abilities were strengthened by education. There was room for only a few on the upper levels of society, and those who got there mostly deserved to do so. If getting there enabled them to cultivate their talents, thus artificially widening natural differences of ability, so much the better for society, whose leaders they were.

[1] *Pensées*, in *L'Oeuvre de Pascal*, op. cit., p. 902, § 302.

And yet, in spite of arguments like these, which Burke magnified but did not invent, it never became fashionable before the eighteenth century to justify political and social privileges on the ground that their possessors were abler and better than other people.

The ardour for equality of rights which led to revolution in France and to reform in England was not born of men's at last discovering that they were by nature less unequal than they had hitherto supposed, or that social distinctions bore too little relation to differences of character and talent. It came from the decay of a religion which had taught contempt for worldly distinctions; it came from an increasing determination to make the best of life in this world; it came, above all, from the belief that men could by their own efforts change and improve their political and social environment. It is this belief, this faith, which sets thinkers like the Encyclopaedists in France and the Philosophical Radicals in England apart from the great majority of political and social theorists before them. They were egalitarians because they were optimists. But their optimism did not consist in their asserting human equality in a sense denied before them – in their saying that all men have certain inalienable rights, or that one man's happiness must count for as much as another's, or that every man is apt to be a better judge than other people of his own interest. All this had been said long before they said it. Their optimism consisted in their belief that a great deal could be done, here and now, to improve the lot of all classes in society.

Bentham believed in two kinds of equality long before he became a democrat; he believed that one man's happiness must count for as much as another's, which is an equality of right; and that every man is apt to be the best judge of his own interest, which is a sort of natural equality. He was also, from the beginning of his career, a radical, a severe critic of existing institutions eager to make great changes. In the *Fragment on Government*, which he wrote when he was a young man, he says that the 'motto of a good citizen' is 'to obey punctually; to censure freely', and that censure, 'though ill-founded', serves to promote every useful reform.[1] He was as critical of the political system as of other aspects of social life. Yet it was a long time before it was borne in upon him that that system could be improved by increasing the electorate. Revolutionary France roused neither his enthusiasm nor his anger; he felt for it the benevolent curiosity not unmixed with contempt that radical Englishmen often feel for foreign countries in the throes of revolution.

[1] *A Fragment on Government*, preface, p. 10.

Bentham always believed that government ought to interfere as little as possible with its subjects – that its essential rôle is negative. Given that every man pursues his own interest and is likely to be a better judge of it than other people, it follows, so Bentham thought, that the first duty of government is to ensure that men get in each other's way as little as possible. It is not the business of government to procure happiness for its subjects so much as to remove hindrances to their getting it for themselves. In other words, its function is to keep the peace between them by maintaining laws giving leeway to them all. Government should seek to affect a man's behaviour, not primarily for his benefit, but for the benefit of others. It forbids certain kinds of behaviour and requires or encourages other kinds by attaching sanctions to them – by giving pain to people who do what it forbids or who fail to do what it requires, and by giving pleasure to people who do what it seeks to encourage. Its aim ought to be to promote happiness by indirect means, by removing obstacles to it. Thus the principle of its conduct is, or should be, economy. For practical reasons, the sanctions it uses have to be much more often punishments (or inflictions of pain) than rewards (or bestowals of pleasure). Therefore its chief concern ought to be to get people to behave as it requires at the cost of inflicting as little pain as possible on them.

Until he was well over forty, Bentham was more eager to advise governments how they should act than to discover what conditions must hold before they were likely to take his advice. It was only when he found them uninterested in the reforms and schemes he advocated that it was brought home to him that governments are often indifferent to the good of the governed. He had begun by taking it more or less for granted that governments normally do care for the public good – that it is their own interest, as well as the interest of their subjects, that they should govern efficiently. He took this for granted without assuming that governments are better or wiser than the general run of their subjects, just as Hobbes had supposed that the sovereign, even though in no way superior to his subjects, normally has a selfish interest in maintaining the public good.

It is always the common interest that there should be government; people are always better off with some government than with none. This Bentham never doubted. But in middle life he came to believe much more strongly than he had done hitherto that it mattered greatly that they should have one form of government rather than another. We must not, he thought, assume that a form of government which has lasted for a long time is likely to be the best suited to the people;

we must not assume it, because the interests of rulers and ruled, though they always coincide to some extent, can also greatly diverge. Every man always desires his own greatest happiness, and does not cease to do so when he rules over others. The actual end of every government is therefore the greatest happiness of the governors, whereas its proper end should be *the greatest happiness of the greatest number,* Bentham's formula for the public good. Since the actual and the proper ends do not, unfortunately, always coincide, we must, wherever conditions allow, try to establish a form of government likely to ensure that they do coincide. This form of government is representative democracy, the only kind of democracy possible in any but the simplest societies. Given that every man is apt to be the best judge of his own interests, the people generally will choose representatives keen to promote the public interest, which is merely a sum of individual interests. The representatives will be keen to promote the public interest because they know that, unless they promote it, they risk losing power.

When Bentham decided to move in any direction, he usually went a long way. He wanted much more than manhood suffrage; he wanted votes for women, annual parliaments and the secret ballot; he wanted to get rid eventually of the monarchy, the House of Lords and the Established Church. Members of Parliament should be mere delegates of their electors; the Prime Minister should be chosen by Parliament and should hold office for four years; civil servants should be appointed by competitive examination, and should be invited to put in tenders for doing their work as economically as possible. Since government is a necessary evil, governors should be watched and every device used to ensure that they perform their duties. Though Bentham never became an anarchist, his suspicion of government deepened as he grew older. As his reputation and self-confidence grew, so did his mistrust of the men who, having power, were not willing to take the good advice he gave them. He became, in the end, as fervent a radical as Tom Paine, without ever ceasing to regard the doctrine of the rights of man as so much nonsense. Liberty, he thought, is nothing in itself, and is valuable only as a means to happiness. Leave people alone as much as possible, for then each man will seek his own happiness, of which he is apt to be the best judge. That is the rule of liberty. If decisions have to be made that concern all, then those who make them ought, wherever possible, to be responsible to all, or else they will prefer their own to the public interest, when the two conflict. That is the case for democracy. And equality is merely the rule that no man's happiness is to be preferred to another's unless it is greater or the cost of producing it is less.

James Mill, in an article on 'Government' published in the supplement to the fifth edition of the *Encyclopaedia Britannica* in 1820, puts essentially the same case for democracy, except that he lays more stress on government as a device for protecting men from one another. Since labour is needed to procure most of the means to happiness, it matters greatly that every man should get his proper share of these means. Labour, generally speaking, is troublesome, and trouble is a kind of pain. Most people, more often than not, are averse from labour. They undertake it, not for its own sake, but for what it brings; it is an effort that they would rather not make but which they do make because their desire for what it brings is stronger than their desire to avoid it. If a man gets less by his labour than that labour produces, he suffers more pain than is needed to create the pleasures he gets; or, alternatively, he gets less pleasure than the pain he has undergone produces. A man's proper share of the means to happiness produced by labour is therefore the produce of his own labour or its equivalent. If he gets less than his share, someone else gets more. The general happiness of society is best promoted, says James Mill, by 'insuring to every man the greatest possible quantity of the produce of his [own] labour'.[1] I do not think that this conclusion follows; but I shall not contest it, as the Utilitarian case for democracy does not really depend on it.

The strong, says Mill, will always try to get more than their proper share; they will always, if left to themselves, try to deprive the weak of the produce of their labour. Therefore men must unite and delegate to a few the power needed to protect them all. Government is essentially a device for protecting the produce of every man's labour from the greed of other men – or, in other words, a device for the protection of property.

But government itself makes some men much more powerful than others; it makes it possible for the rulers to plunder the very people they are supposed to protect. How is this plunder to be prevented? Men are so made, Mill tells us, that they always try, if they can, to make the persons and properties of other people subservient to their pleasures. Their lust for power is insatiable. Those who have power will always abuse it unless they are restrained; and they can be effectively restrained only if they get power from the people over whom they exercise it. Just as government is the device that prevents the exploitation of the weak by the strong among private persons, so representative democracy is the device that prevents the

---

[1] 'Government', in *Utilitarian Logic and Politics*, ed. Jack Lively and John Rees (Oxford 1978), p. 57.

exploitation of the governed by their rulers. James Mill did not want representative democracy because he thought it would lead to a redistribution of property in favour of the poor; he wanted it only to prevent misgovernment. In his day there were great inequalities among the classes unrepresented or under-represented in Parliament. He did not condemn these inequalities. He wanted no more than to prevent the classes that dominated Parliament from using it in their own interest to the detriment of other classes. Like most of his contemporaries who favoured parliamentary reform, he took it for granted that there was no serious divergence of interest among the classes for whom he claimed the vote. He even believed that the manual workers, if they got the vote, would follow the lead of the new middle class; and he approved of their doing so because he thought it in the common interest.

Mill did not suppose that men are always good judges of their own interests; he admitted that quite often they are not. But he thought this an effect of lack of education, and therefore curable. A narrow ruling class, no matter how able, will always prefer its own interests to the public good, whenever the two conflict. Ignorance is curable, selfishness is not. Education cannot make a monarch or a privileged class prefer the public good to their own, and it must often happen that the good of one man or one class diverges from the public good. Only democracy can be improved indefinitely by education. It is therefore ideally the best form of government, even though it may not suit all peoples at all times. It can be said for it that it is the form best suited to human nature, in the sense that, where conditions are favourable, it comes nearer than other forms to creating harmony of interests among creatures which are by nature self-regarding. Men can be made fit for democracy, and, when they are fit for it, they are likely to be happier than they would otherwise be.

This is a more modest argument for democracy than the argument of Tom Paine. If Paine is right in thinking that no government is legitimate unless it has the consent of the governed, it follows that democracy alone is legitimate, everywhere and always. That drastic conclusion can be avoided only by cheating – by passing something off as consent which is really not consent. Bentham and James Mill had no need to cheat in this way; they could freely admit that some people's good is better pursued by others than by themselves. That is always true of children, and often so of whole classes of adults, if they are so ignorant as to have more to lose by choosing their governments than by submitting quietly to irresponsible rulers, even though these rulers prefer their own to the public interest when the two conflict.

The Utilitarian argument for representative democracy has, I think, a good deal to be said for it, some of which I have tried to express. But there is one part of that argument which I find puzzling. How, exactly, are we to understand the assertion, that every man is apt to be the best judge of his own interest? There is a sense in which it is obviously true. But is it the sense relevant to the Utilitarian argument? The classical economists also rested their rule of *laissez-faire* on the assumption that every man is the best judge of his own interest. What did they understand by it? That a man is apt to know better than other people what he now wants? Or that he knows better the general pattern of his wants, how frequently they recur and which are the most pressing? In other words, that he is the best judge of his own needs, defined in terms of his own actual and probable desires? For many practical purposes we can accept these assumptions. True, there quite often are people who know more about a man's needs than he does himself; but they are usually close relatives and friends, and not the government and its agents. We can take it as broadly true, at least where social conditions are stable, that men are ordinarily better judges than their governments of their own personal needs. In this sense, which is (unless I am mistaken) what was meant both by the classical economists and Bentham and James Mill, the presumption is that every man is the best judge of his own interest.

But is this sense relevant when we are comparing the merits of different forms of government? Governments do not provide directly for their subjects' personal needs; they do not stand to them as parents do to their children, considering the problems of each in turn and doing what they can to help. They deal with whole groups of people at a time, trying to promote and reconcile group interests. A man's being the best judge of his own interests, in the sense I have already discussed, does not necessarily make him even a passable judge of what policies are likely to reconcile the interests of the group he belongs to with the interests of innumerable other groups; or of whom he can trust to do this work of reconciliation; or of what institutions and political methods are best suited to getting it done. Presumably, people in the countries we call *primitive* know their personal interests as well as we know ours; they know as much about their desires and preferences, actual and probable, as we do; they know as well as we do what they need to make them happy. I do not see that we have any good reason for denying this. When we deny, as we sometimes do, that they are fit for democracy, we are not saying that they know less than we do what they need to make them happy. We are saying only that they do not know what to do to ensure that their rulers promote the common interest, which includes their own. They do not know how to work the institutions whose function is to make it the interest of their rulers to meet their demands as far as possible. That every man is apt to be the best judge of his own needs is not enough to justify even *laissez-faire*, let alone democracy.

If the proper end of government is taken to be to help people get what they need to make them happy, and if they are the best judges of their needs, they must of course be consulted about those needs. But can we discover people's needs by the simple process of counting their votes at elections? Is this not a very clumsy method? Is it not better to ask them, separately and in greater detail, what they need, and then, having got the answers, to set about using limited resources efficiently so as to give them as much as possible of what that happens to be? Is not the *questionnaire* an incomparably better method for this purpose than the general election? If we assume only that each person is the best judge of what he needs to make him happy, we cannot go on to conclude that the policy he votes for is the best suited to give him what he needs, or that the party he favours is the most able or willing to provide it. We cannot argue from such a premise that the policy or party which gets the most votes is the one most likely to give the people as much as possible of what they need to make them happy.

Why, then, should a government's being responsible to the people make it more likely that it acts in the common interest? Where rulers are elected by their subjects, they have a powerful motive for pleasing them. They are likely to take great care not to do what makes the people angry or disgusted or suspicious. But if the people do not know what must be done to enable as many as possible of them to satisfy their needs, there is no ground for believing that the selfish rulers of a community of selfish men will promote the common interest the better for being responsible to their subjects.

I do not say that a logically sound case for representative democracy could not be made on somewhat the same lines as Bentham and James Mill make it.[1] But it would need to be more elaborately and carefully

---

[1] This case, though logically sound, is not necessarily the best case. It is possible to justify democracy on different assumptions from these, and assumptions more generally acceptable. But arguments for democracy of a broadly Utilitarian type have been popular among intellectuals, especially in English-speaking countries. It is therefore worthwhile considering what would be a logically sound argument of this type. Bentham and James Mill would probably accept the argument, but not my comments on it. Let me say, at this point, that intellectuals do not always value things for the reasons they give for valuing them. They prefer some arguments to

argued than they argue their case, and it would reach a more modest conclusion. It would start from different assumptions and arrive at different conclusions; it would be a different argument from theirs. But it would also be in some important respects similar. It would accept one of the basic assumptions of Utilitarianism: that the business of government is to help people get what they ask for and not what their rulers think is good for them.

This amended argument would dispense altogether with the idea that the proper business of government is to make people happy. It would dispense with much more than the obviously untenable conception of happiness as a sum of pleasures; it would dispense with every conception of happiness. For we can hardly ever, when we are comparing whole communities, have good grounds for believing that one is happier than another. Nor yet for believing, of any one community, that people inside it are more or less happy at one time than another. We can hazard a guess, but it will be so uncertain as scarcely to be worth using as a basis for policy. The conditions making for happiness vary from community to community, from person to person; and they also vary with time in ways which are seldom predictable.

No doubt, we have good reason to believe that some conditions nearly always make for unhappiness, and ought therefore to be avoided. Certain minimal needs for food and shelter must be satisfied; certain brutal methods must be used as little as possible. These needs are common to all mankind, and those methods are resented everywhere. We also have reason to believe that people are usually made unhappy when their conditions of life change quickly and in unexpected ways. But the minimal needs that must be satisfied in any society, however poor, are modest indeed. Though the standard of living of the Indian peasant, who is not actually starving, is much lower than that of the English working man, we have little reason to believe that he is less happy. He may even, as his standard of living rises, grow more unhappy; for his idea of what is due to him may change, and he may come to suffer more than he used to do from the knowledge that he lacks many things which other people have. Though we admit that starvation makes for unhappiness, we need not agree that material progress makes for happiness. It may

---

others because they look simpler or less sentimental. The English-speaking peoples, even the intellectuals among them, do not really value democracy primarily on utilitarian grounds, even though, more than other peoples, they have a taste for Utilitarian or quasi-Utilitarian arguments in its favour.

be that democracy encourages people to make greater demands on government than they used to do; it may be that it inflates their ideas of what society owes them. If that is so, we can say that it encourages material progress by perpetually adding to the wants which have to be satisfied to avoid unhappiness; but we cannot say that it makes people happier.

The Utilitarians assumed that the more a man gets what he wants, the happier he is. They also sometimes spoke as if it followed from this that, the more a man wants, the happier he is, provided he gets what he wants. To increase his happiness, he must not only get what he wants; he must also multiply his wants along with his capacity to satisfy them. Material progress is good because it both adds to our wants and to our power to satisfy them. We can, I think, demolish this argument without even troubling to question the notion that happiness is merely the successful pursuit of one satisfaction after another – or, as Bentham would put it, of one pleasure after another. Why should we take it for granted that material progress adds to our wants and to our capacity to satisfy them? It may give us wants we did not have before, merely by depriving us of other wants. It may do little more than multiply in us wants which are difficult to satisfy. Instead of wanting to talk or sit in the sun or sing or dance or take a walk, we may want to go to the cinema or to drive a car or to wear expensive clothes. We may not have more varied or stronger desires; we may have only desires which cost more to satisfy. We may lead as dull or duller lives; the advanced industrial society, though it enormously increases the variety of human occupations, does not therefore ensure that each occupation is less monotonous, or make it easier for a man to choose his occupation or to pass from one to another if he feels he has made a bad choice.

In building up our case for representative democracy, we say nothing about happiness. We do not deny that people make their demands on the government largely in the hope of being the happier for getting what they ask for. We neither deny nor assert it. We merely assume that the proper business of government is to satisfy, as far as may be, the demands made upon it by its subjects, whether or not the satisfaction of these demands increases their happiness.

This assumption needs to be qualified. In its endeavours to satisfy the demands made upon it at any particular time, the government may so act as to make it impossible or much more difficult for it to satisfy future demands. We must therefore qualify our initial assumption, saying that the proper business of government is to satisfy the people's actual and their probable future demands. Government must look ahead, and yet not too far ahead. The further ahead it looks, the more uncertain its predictions about future demands.

Government, in looking ahead, is not acting contrary to the people's will; for no people, however democratic, expect their government to take notice only of their present demands. They expect it to take reasonable precautions on their behalf. They expect more than just to be warned about the harmful consequences of their getting what they ask for; they also expect their demands to be disregarded in their own interest. That is to say, they will blame a government for the harm done to them by its acceding to their demands. This attitude to government seems to me quite reasonable. Sometimes, disrespectfully, it is called capricious; I prefer, more respectfully, to call it feminine, because it is so much like the attitude many sensible women take to their menfolk. They expect to be taken seriously, and they are perfectly well aware of their power. There is nothing servile in their attitude; it is merely a demand that the people whose business it is to look after certain of their interests should use intelligence on their behalf. A trustee, even when he is chosen by the persons for whom he acts, does not carry out his trust effectively if he undertakes to satisfy *all* their demands. When he is chosen by them, the extent to which he can disregard their wishes depends on how far he is able to persuade them after the event that he has acted in their interest.

At this point we must make a second assumption: that government must not be able to decide what demands shall be made upon it. Inevitably, however democratic it is, it will have a large influence on public opinion. But it ought to exercise this influence in competition with others, so that the demands made upon it are not demands which it has decided shall be made. In other words, what is required of government must arise out of negotiations and discussions which those who govern do not control, even though they necessarily take a large part in them.

Our first principle – that the business of government is to meet the demands made upon it by its subjects – would be accepted by Bentham and James Mill. They might think, as I do, that it needs to be qualified, but they would accept it. It would seem to them to follow from the greatest happiness principle together with certain other assumptions; we can disagree with them here and still agree that the proper business of government is to meet the demands made upon it by its subjects.

Our second principle – that government must not be able to decide what demands shall be made upon it – was never actually asserted by the Utilitarians. Yet, clearly, it must be asserted if there is to be a sound case for representative democracy. If all that matters is that the people's demands should be met by the government, then it does not matter how the people come to make the demands which they do make. If those who govern can decide what the people shall demand of them, there is no need for them to be responsible to the people. Our second principle, though it is not put forward by the Utilitarians, would probably be accepted by most of them. But they would accept it more in spite of their Utilitarianism than because of it. For, though they held that freedom is valuable only because it makes for happiness, they were in fact more liberal than they knew. They probably cared for freedom for its own sake, though they did not admit it. That is why they were so ready to believe, without producing good evidence for it, that men must be free if they are to be happy. At least, I suspect that this was so; for where we find people who say that only happiness is desirable for its own sake and then go on to take it for granted – sometimes even against the evidence – that freedom is a means to it, there is reason to suspect that they value for its own sake what they say they value only as a means. Utilitarianism need not, logically, be a liberal doctrine, but most of the Utilitarians were in fact liberals.

On these two principles we can build up a case for representative democracy. We can say that it is the form of government best suited to countries in which there has been great material progress – that is to say, to countries where wants which are difficult to satisfy have greatly multiplied. To put the same point differently, it is the form of government best suited to countries which have become industrial and literate. In such countries, government is extraordinarily active. The work it does or which is done on its behalf or under its control is a large proportion of all the work done in the country. The people expect the government to do much more than just maintain law and order. They do not accept institutions as they find them, asking little more of government than that it should preserve them. They belong to a type of society which stimulates ambitions and ideals not to be satisfied while the social order remains unchanged. In a society of that kind, government, whether or not it is democratic, is likely to be immensely enterprising. But it may be enterprising without doing what its subjects want it to do. To ensure that it does what they want, it must either be able to decide what they want by controlling their opinions and feelings, or it must be responsible to them. Our second assumption forbids the first of these alternatives, and we are thus left only with the second.

It is, in any case, easier to control overt demands than desires. A government in a position to decide what its subjects demand of it is not necessarily in a position to decide what they really want it to do. But I have purposely neglected this point, though it may be important, because I am not sure how important it is. People are very suggestible, and are nowhere more suggestible than in countries where government has always been authoritarian. I would not therefore like to say that, where a government decides what its subjects openly demand of it and then does what they demand, it is much further from doing what they really want it to do than it would be if it were genuinely democratic. That is why I put forward my second assumption as one which needs to be made if we are to have a sound case for representative democracy.

Where representative democracy has lasted for any length of time, there soon arise all kinds of bodies, not controlled by government or by one another, acting as intermediaries between the people and their rulers. The function of these bodies is to formulate popular demands and to put pressure on the government to meet them. This formulation of demands is a creative process, because many of the demands made by these bodies would never have been thought of but for them. As Rousseau only half understood, it is by being organized that the people acquire a political will. These bodies have leaders who are not in the government, but whose business is to watch closely some part or other of what the government does. They learn by experience what can be got out of the government, and they also learn something of the difficulties that face it. They help to multiply and to give precision to popular demands, thus enabling the government to know what the people want it to do for them; and they also teach their clients – the people – to be moderate and realistic, understanding that there are many demands being made on government and only limited means for satisfying them. Representative democracy enlarges and gives precision to popular demands on government, and also evolves methods of satisfying these demands which come to be accepted as substantially just.

By its very operation, representative democracy disposes people to accept our second principle and to attach importance to it. Where government is in fact not able to decide what demands its subjects shall make upon it – where these demands are largely the product of discussions and negotiations between bodies and persons independent both of the government and of one another – it comes to be generally accepted that government ought not to be able to decide what these demands shall be. Representative democracy strengthens the principles used to justify it in the sense that it creates conditions which make people feel more strongly about them than they otherwise would. Yet they are not principles accepted only where there is representative democracy. Wherever there exists a strong tradition that government acts for the benefit of the governed, our second principle is likely to be accepted as soon as it is formulated. Hume, Locke, Burke and Montesquieu would probably all have accepted it, though none of them was a democrat. They did not need to formulate the principle, because in their day much less was demanded of government than is demanded today, and also because government's power to influence opinion was much weaker. It is only when government greatly extends its activities that, in countries with a liberal tradition, a need is felt to put forward this second principle. It is not right that government should be able to decide what its subjects want; its proper business is to help them get what they want.

This principle is unchallenged even in countries which are not democratic but whose rulers pride themselves on being 'progressive'. In the Soviet Union, it is the rulers who decide what popular demands shall be made upon them. They have forced what they call progress on the people, and have perhaps in time succeeded in making the people like it. No age has been as successful as ours in devising methods enabling governments to get their subjects to demand, and even to want, what those in authority have decided to give them. Yet the governments which use these methods successfully do not admit that they use them. They too claim to be responsive to the people's will and not to be in a position to decide what it shall be. We can therefore say that, in countries which are already industrial and literate or else are fast becoming so, our two principles are in fact widely accepted, in the letter if not in the spirit. And there soon will be no other countries but these.

We have seen Bentham arguing that the greatest happiness principle is the one which everyone is disposed to accept when he understands it. He thought that must be so, because man is the sort of creature he is. Instead of appealing, as Bentham did, to psychology, we appeal to history; we say that recent developments all over the world are disposing more and more people to accept the two principles on which we rest our argument for representative democracy.

This argument, though it makes no use of the greatest happiness principle, does make use of the rule which I said the Utilitarians were as willing to accept as the greatest happiness principle, believing mistakenly that they are equivalent: the rule, *Act so as to ensure, as far as you can, that people get what they want, according to their own preferences.* For that reason, and also because it makes no use of such notions as natural right and natural law, I have ventured to call this argument Utilitarian.

IV. THE LEGACY OF PHILOSOPHICAL RADICALISM

1. *The Utilitarians' Use of Language*

In seeking to reformulate the greatest happiness principle so as to make it both more clear and more pertinent, I do not mean to suggest that Bentham and his followers were careless in their use of words. On the contrary, the Philosophical Radicals were preoccupied with the terms they employed; they wanted to be sure that their language was precisely adapted to their purposes, explanatory and prescriptive; and they distinguished, much more carefully than social theorists before them, explanation from exhortation and advice. If they were not the first to teach, they were at least the first to take to heart, the lesson that we must not, in political and social discussion, so define our terms as to reach by inference from them the practical conclusions we happen to favour. They condemned what was, before their time, an almost universal practice among European political philosophers. Indeed, it was the very mark of political philosophy, properly so called, that it derived practical rules from the nature of man or society or law or right – that it so defined these terms as to make it follow that men ought to do this rather than that. This was as much the practice of Hobbes, Locke and Rousseau as of the mediaeval schoolmen. The Philosophical Radicals, Bentham first among them, did more than warn us against this practice; they tried to help us avoid it by constructing a precise and morally neutral political vocabulary. The warning, indeed, was given before they gave it, more clearly and forcefully, by Hume. Following Hume, they tried to set an example which we still think it right to follow, as much as we can, this side of pedantry. Sometimes, as certain lapses of Bentham prove, they did not take their own advice; but they were the first builders of an elaborate social theory who saw and preached the need to take it.

At least in English-speaking countries, it is largely the Utilitarians who have taught us to be more sceptical of suggestive or exciting or comforting words and phrases whose use in explaining our social behaviour is not clear. They did not condemn these words and phrases out of hand; they did not even say that we ought always to avoid using them when our purpose is to explain rather than to counsel or commend; they merely invited us to reflect on what we are doing when we use them. They knew that metaphors are useful even in the description of brute facts – that they enable us to speak more succinctly and to put less strain on the attention. Bentham, the harshest critic of traditional ideas and arguments, was often concerned to do more than expose their vagueness, for he also wanted to discover why such arguments were used, what people were trying to say by means of them. His object in criticizing them was not always, or even usually, to dismiss them as nonsense; it was much more often to show that they were misused, that the sense they were meant to convey could be differently and better put, with greater precision and in a way that did not suggest error. This interest in the use of words; this demand for economy and precision tempered by common sense; this understanding that we should not be led astray by metaphors; this desire to find sense in other theories as well as to expose the nonsense in them; this combination of candour and severity form an important part of our intellectual heritage. The Utilitarians were seldom sloppy, either in feeling or in thought.

If we compare, for a moment, the attitudes of Burke and Bentham to the ideas and arguments of the French revolutionaries, we find in Bentham the assumptions and dogmas of the revolutionaries ruthlessly dissected; we find the myth of the social contract and the doctrine of the natural and inalienable rights of man clearly and firmly repudiated. In Burke we find no less severe criticism of such doctrines, together with an angry condemnation of everything the revolutionaries wanted to do. But Bentham does not condemn all their intentions, nor blame them for trying to change their country's institutions. The difference between him and Burke is that he knows, as Burke does not, exactly what he wants to accept or reject, as much in the theory as in the practice of the revolutionaries. He knows where he stands; he is cool and can discriminate. Much the same can be said of his attitude towards reformers of schools other than his own in England. He is at once a more devastating and more generous critic than Burke; when he strikes at the theoretical foundations of popular radicalism, he cuts deeper because he understands what he is striking at. But he also shares, as Burke does not, some of the aspirations of the people whose theories he rejects. I do not mean to praise Bentham at Burke's expense, for I willingly admit that Burke had gifts of imagination which Bentham lacked; I am only trying to show some of the advantages of systematic and rigorous thought.

Most of the powerful myths and dogmas that now stand in the way of clear thinking about social and political matters are quite different; many are the products of German Idealism and of Marxism. Large conclusions about what we ought to do are nowadays drawn, not from definitions of man and society, so much as from theories about the course of history. These theories have, I think, been both less attractive and less repulsive to intellectuals in the English-speaking world than elsewhere; they have had a powerful influence, and yet have never been swallowed whole by more than a few people. They have been received with greater scepticism and subjected to closer and more dispassionate analysis than in the countries of their origin. They have been assimilated slowly and only in part, and yet there have always been people willing to take them seriously, people willing to ask: How much truth is there to this doctrine? How must we rephrase it to make what truth there is stand out more clearly? Have we made sure that we are putting the right questions, that we know what we are asking, and how to set about trying to find an answer? It is, I suggest, largely the Philosophical Radicals who have taught us to take these now elementary precautions when we embark on political and social theory, either to criticize the views of others or to put forward our own.

I am not suggesting that these precautions are ignored outside the English-speaking world, but only that the first to make a habit of taking them and to explain why they ought to be taken were the Utilitarians. Of concepts and theories, as much as of institutions, they asked, What is the use of them? Do they help us to understand our social environment? Or do they serve chiefly to condemn or praise that environment, to make people want to change or preserve it? At least they saw clearly, as many others have not seen, that the tasks of explanation and reform are separate. That is why, in spite of their many inadequacies, they excelled both as theorists and as reformers. Of course, they were inadequate. For all their coolness and candour, and their desire to sift the sense from the nonsense in other people's theories, they lacked imagination. They quite often failed to see what was valuable in the views they criticized. But their intention was nearly always to discriminate and reformulate rather than repudiate or condemn outright.

2. *The Practical Nature of their Radical Philosophy*

The Philosophical Radicals or Utilitarians rejected the doctrine of natural rights, the traditional conceptions of freedom and equality. But they were as much believers in equality and freedom as were the upholders of the doctrine they rejected, though they conceived of them differently. They believed nothing more strongly than that it is for every man to make what he wants of his life, provided he respects the same right in others and does not refuse his share of the burden which society must lay on its members if it is to subsist. They believed in man's capacity to improve his condition indefinitely; they believed also that it is the duty of government to release men's energies. Yet, with them, belief in the autonomy of the individual was supported, not by the assertion of fundamental rights, but by a theory about the social origins and functions of morality. For them, all rules of conduct, and therefore all rights and duties, emerge to suit men's convenience; and the essence of man, what distinguishes him from all other animals, is that he is inventive and aspiring, always eager to improve his lot.

It was Hume who first explained that we cannot infer men's rights or duties from their nature. Moral rules do not follow logically from statements of fact, and if they appear to do so, it is only because what are taken for mere statements of fact are moral rules disguised. But Hume, though he said this, also said, quite consistently, that rules which come to be accepted by men are determined by their needs, their capacities and their environment. Because they have the appetites they do and can learn from experience, and because they live in a world in which they have to work, and even to work together, men come to accept certain rules in their behaviour towards one another, in order to get the wherewithal to satisfy their appetites. The rules of morality are therefore practical solutions to a practical problem: How can we all get what we want with the least friction? They have nothing to do with God's purposes for man or with any conception of a perfected human nature. They are rules of efficiency, at least in origin. Hume, of course, did not say that what makes them moral rules is their being rules of efficiency; on the contrary, as we have seen, he held that what makes them moral is men's feeling about them as they do. But he took it for granted that the current rules, whatever they were, did perform their function. It is here that the Philosophical Radicals differed from him. Essentially, their theory of morals was much the same as his, though sometimes cruder and more confused. What made them radicals, while he remained a conservative, was their troubling to ask whether existing rules of conduct, moral and legal, really were rules of efficiency. The first rules came into existence, as Hume had explained, to serve all men's needs; but it did not follow that existing rules now served them. For circumstances change, and in organized society power is unequally distributed: the rules that now exist may serve some people's needs to the detriment of others. And so the Philosophical Radicals were not only moral theorists, venturing to explain what morality is; they were also moralists who wanted to tell their fellow men what to do. In producing a code of conduct with one overriding rule, which they called the *greatest happiness principle*, they invoked this rule, not only to tell ordinary folk what to do, but above all to advise legislators and educators, the makers of rules and those who teach them. Here at last was a worldly social philosophy, entirely free of theology and metaphysics.

It is often said of Bentham and his School that in promoting this philosophy they were superficial, that they neglected history, that they had too simple ideas about why men behave as they do. Leslie Stephen[1] accused them of setting up an artificial person, a standard or average man, and then using arguments that hold only if most men are like this person, which they very likely are not in societies different from those familiar to the Philosophical Radicals. Elie Halévy said that their method was too deductive.[2]

These charges contain some truth, but they are often made out of place. No doubt, the psychological theories of Bentham and James Mill were superficial – as when they tried to reduce the social affections to refined forms of egoism, or treated happiness as a sum of pleasures, or religion as an effect of fear and ignorance, or neglected patriotism and other group loyalties. They were perhaps not superficial by the standards of their own day, but today their explanations often seem inadequate. There is a great deal about men and society not dreamt of in their philosophy. Yet their practical rules – their rules for dealing with men – suffer much less from this inadequacy than is often supposed. If we want to control or influence other people's behaviour, it is important to distinguish, as Bentham would have us do, between men's motives and their intentions; and between the various consequences of an action, how it affects its agent, or the person or persons he means to affect by it, or other persons; and also between the immediate and remoter consequences. These rules of method hold, no matter what people's motives or intentions, no matter how they come by them, no matter what their social circumstances. So, too, the rules of evidence and of debate must be largely the same in any society, if the object is to get at the truth without too much waste of time, or to reach decisions quickly after as full and relevant a discussion as time permits. Such technical rules are of first-class importance, and, the better we understand them, the more successfully we can adapt our institutions to our purposes. Democratic politics is the art of reaching decisions that are generally acceptable; and it was to this that the Philosophical Radicals, above all other political theorists, addressed their minds. Not to practise it themselves, but to discover general rules. Now, to elaborate and explain these rules,

[1] See *The English Utilitarians*, 3 vols. (London 1900), vol. I, pp. 270–1 and 299–301.
[2] See *The Growth of Philosophic Radicalism* (London 1928), pp. 493–8.

we do not need to be historians or psychologists; nor can we rely on mere common sense. We must have a very uncommon capacity for clear thought and rigorous argument. We must know just what assumptions we are making and what follows from them; we must be good at abstraction and deduction.

In their explanations of society, and of man as a social and moral creature, the Philosophical Radicals often fall short of the truth. They also have almost nothing to tell us about that part of our lives which concerns only ourselves and the persons closest to us. Their abstract and practical philosophy is essentially, if I may so put it, commercial; it provides us with rules for our transactions with other people as competitors and collaborators for the satisfaction of needs; it deals with what is, in the widest sense of the word, the business side of life. What belongs to the inner life or the inner circle – what concerns all those relations between men which are much more than transactions – lies outside its sphere. But within that sphere, it has, as a practical philosophy, much to be said for it, even today; it is still alive, still relevant.

The Philosophical Radicals, as no social theorists before them, were interested in the tools of their trade, in the vocabulary of politics; they were moralists of a new kind; and they also put forward arguments for democracy especially well adapted to modern conditions. They were hard-headed and practical, not in spite of their love of abstract principles, precision of language and rigorous argument, but very largely because of it. For the use of logic, even in the study of politics, is not to take us away from the facts, but to help us deal with them.

3. Their Relation to Modern Liberalism

John Stuart Mill, in claiming that it matters what men are like as much as what they do, manifestly departed from the creed of the older Philosophical Radicals; and the modern liberal would agree with him rather than them. Yet the practical consequences of the two creeds are much the same. For Mill and the modern liberal would agree with Bentham that it is not for other people to decide what manner of person a man should be. It is for him to try to live up to an ideal or pattern of life he has chosen for himself. The overriding rule of Bentham still holds: So act that people, as far as possible, get what *they* want. This rule is by no means all that there is to the creed of the modern liberal, but it is an essential part of it. It is the rule which he thinks matters most in all our dealings with other adults, although there may be other rules as important to him in our dealings with ourselves or with children. I do not say that this rule cannot be found in any writer who lived and wrote before the Philosophical Radicals, or that everyone who now accepts it has got it, directly or indirectly, from them. All kinds of influences lead to the widespread acceptance of a fundamental moral rule. But it was the Philosophical Radicals who first put the rule forward, boldly and simply, as a moral rule free from traditional doctrines of natural law and natural right – doctrines as difficult to interpret as to apply. They extracted the rule from its metaphysical setting, and used it neither to justify society nor to condemn it wholesale, but to help make careful plans to reform it.

No liberal today believes – or at least dares to say with Bentham – that push-pin is as good as poetry.[1] The modern liberal often speaks instead, as Bentham never did, of 'self-fulfilment' and of the 'well-balanced personality' which is not at odds with itself because it has come to terms with society. These ideas go back at least as far as Rousseau, and no doubt (in rather different forms) much further. They are difficult ideas. Unless we take care how we use them, we easily lapse into nonsense or else reach conclusions that every liberal must reject. Yet the modern liberal, though not quite at home with these ideas, feels that there is much to be said for them. He realizes, as Bentham and James Mill did not, that a man's happiness does not consist in continual or frequent success in satisfying one desire after another, but in his being able to live a kind of life that seems worthwhile to himself and respectable to his neighbours. He realizes, much more fully than the Philosophical Radicals, how deeply a man's desires and ambitions are determined by the moral and aesthetic standards of the communities and groups he belongs to; how, in terms of these standards, he builds up an image of himself as he thinks he is or would like to be; and how much his happiness depends upon his confidence that he really is as he would have himself be and is accepted by others more or less at his own valuation. The liberal is as apt to explain men's wants in terms of their morals as their morals in terms of their wants. In all this he differs greatly from

---

[1] The expression is John Stuart Mill's rather than Bentham's (see *Mill on Bentham and Coleridge*, ed. F. R. Leavis [London 1950], 'Bentham', p. 95). It is, however, based on a passage from Book III, ch. 1 of Bentham's *Rationale of Reward* (see *The Works of Bentham*, ed. John Bowring [Edinburgh 1843], II.253, col. 2): 'Prejudice apart, the game of push-pin is of equal value with the arts and sciences of music and poetry. If the game of push-pin furnish more pleasure, it is more valuable than either.'

the Philosophical Radical. Yet he can still, though he holds all these beliefs, accept their overriding principle: 'So act as to enable people, as far as possible, to get what they want', with the corollary, 'Never oblige them to do something merely because you think they will thereby be better persons'.

It may be objected that I have made the Philosophical Radicals out to be more liberal than they in fact were, and also that I have left out of account what liberals today think a good education should achieve. For they are concerned to do more than give children useful information and teach them so to behave that people get what they want as much as possible; they also want to prepare them to lead as good a life as they can aspire to, making them better or more admirable persons in themselves.

It is certainly true that the Philosophical Radicals were not liberals in the usual sense of the word. They delighted to speak of the duty to maximize happiness rather than of the right to live as one pleases. If it could have been proved to them that happiness could be more increased by interfering with people than by letting them alone, they would have been logically committed to accept the interference, no matter how great. True, their theoretical position is different from that of the liberal; for the liberal does not justify freedom as a means to happiness. But, as we have already seen, their account of desire and volition, mistaken though it was, did lead them to believe that happiness is in fact maximized by enabling people, as far as possible, to live as they please. They assumed that we must always begin by taking people's wants as we find them – in effect, that the problem is always to fit supply to demand. It never occurred to them that it might be easier to get men to want what is easily provided than to provide what they actually want. If we can mould men's desires in such a way as to make it easier to satisfy them, why should we not do so? The Philosophical Radicals, to be logical, would have to say that we should. This, from the point of view of the liberal, is the Achilles' heel of their theory. It might, given the appropriate circumstances, justify the methods of Plato's guardians or of the Communists. The practical liberalism of the Philosophical Radicals rests on an assumption that does not necessarily always hold: that it is easier to give people what they want than to make them want what you can easily give. The true liberal need not make this assumption; his principles forbid our moulding other people to suit ourselves, even when it is easier to change their wants than to satisfy them as they are.

We can scarcely blame the Philosophical Radicals, however, for not having even noticed an assumption which was much nearer holding in their day than it is in ours, when the arts of the propagandist and manipulator are so much more developed. It may even be that, if they had noticed it, they would have come to doubt the greatest happiness principle. I suspect that they were more liberal in feeling than in doctrine. Their bias was always towards leaving people alone, even when it was far from obvious that to do so would make them happier.

The modern liberal also objects that education ought to do more for children than give them useful information and teach them not to interfere with other people and to be helpful – that it ought to form their tastes and preferences, as much to improve the quality of their own lives as to make them more tolerant and helpful to others. If the modern liberal believes this, and surely he does, he parts company with the Philosophical Radical. No doubt the liberal looks askance at attempts to form the tastes and preferences of grown-up persons – at adults setting themselves up as mentors to other adults. But he does so, surely, because adults are set in their ways and their tastes, while children are malleable. It is no good thrusting poetry on a grown man who prefers push-pin; we risk annoying him or perhaps even shaming him into pretending that he likes what he does not like. It is difficult, and usually not worthwhile, trying to change the characters and tastes of grown-up persons; the most that can usefully be done is to control their conduct, to prevent their doing harm to others or themselves, or to oblige them to carry out their duties as citizens. With children it is different; we can form their characters and their tastes, and we ought to do so, not only to make them happier, but also to improve the quality of their lives.

The modern liberal differs here in principle from the Philosophical Radical, in that he cares for something more than happiness and satisfying actual wants, and he aims directly at getting it. Yet we must not exaggerate the difference even where it is greatest, in the sphere of education. Though the liberal wants children taught to become more than successful journeymen in the pursuit of happiness, though he wants them to acquire worthwhile tastes and ambitions, he looks upon this part of education as being more guidance than discipline. He wants the child to be taught to appreciate as much as possible what society has to offer; he wants to extend the range of choice open to him; he wants to make sure that the child who has it in him to enjoy poetry and to prefer it to push-pin gets the chance to do so. But he also insists that children are not to be forced against their natural inclinations; and that among adults, those whose characters, occupations or tastes are the most admired – those who look upon themselves and are admitted by others to be more admirable – have no right to impose their preferences on others.

Thus the moralities of the Philosophical Radical and the twentieth-century liberal, in spite of considerable differences in their basic assumptions, are in practice much alike. They exclude the setting up of an historic mission, of a duty supposed to be laid on a nation or class or party or élite by its place in history, or of obligations to the State or any other community, above men's duties to one another simply as creatures pursuing whatever ends seem good to themselves. Philosophical Radicalism, like liberalism, excludes the double standard in morality. As Bentham put it in his *Theory of Legislation*, 'That which is politically good cannot be morally bad, unless we suppose that the rules of arithmetic, true for large numbers, are false for small ones'.[1] In public life, as in private, we are always dealing only with individual men and women; and our prime duty to them is to ensure that we do not prevent them from living – and, when we can, to aim even to help them to live – as they want, according to their own notions of what makes a good life.

Now, it might be asked, was this not also the position of Locke? Why, then, speak of it as part of the legacy of the Philosophical Radicals? Why speak as if we owed this belief more to them than to Locke? Far be it from me to be less generous to Locke than Bentham would have been. For Bentham liked to say that the great moralists of the past really agreed with him, though they might not appear to do so – that their opinions, as far as there was sense in them, were much the same as his. He fancied himself less as a discoverer than a liberator of true principles; less as putting them forward for the first time than as setting them loose from clinging error. We all subscribe, he thought, to the greatest happiness principle, though we too often also cherish other beliefs that prevent our attaining happiness. I should not want to put it quite this way. Yet I do say for the Philosophical Radicals that they put their principles to much larger use than Locke did his. Though Locke condemned despotic monarchy in his day, he otherwise took society much as he found it; he was quite satisfied with an aristocratic England, for all his belief that men are by nature free and equal. The doctrine of natural rights, in the hands of many of its advocates, was a bludgeon to be used occasionally against tyrants, whereas Bentham and his disciples used their doctrines as surgeons use their knives, to cut deeply and with a sure hand. Since the surgeon's knife and not the bludgeon was their weapon, they looked long and

[1] *The Theory of Legislation*, ch. V, p. 16.

closely at what they wanted to operate on; they were intensely curious about the actual workings of society.

V. THE CONTRIBUTION OF JOHN STUART MILL

Bentham is said to have wished that he could awake once in a century and witness how the world had progressed in happiness because it had embraced his principles. A more modest man might have expressed such a wish differently. Bentham thought that happiness is just a sum of pleasures; but, unfortunately, it is a sum that no one, under any imaginable circumstances, could add up. However often Bentham reappeared, he could never have good reason for believing that men were happier, or indeed less happy, in his sense of happiness, at one time than at another. If Providence were to grant Bentham his wish, he would be condemned to perpetual frustration, an altogether too heavy punishment for philosophical error. Bentham believed that progress is possible if not inevitable, and he supposed that such progress comprised a measurable advance of happiness. But the truth is that progress in happiness is an empty notion, since the conditions of happiness differ from man to man, and from age to age. There are no permanent and universal conditions of happiness, enabling us to say that the more we provide of these conditions the happier people will be. Of course all ideas of progress are, in a sense, arbitrary, for they depend in the last resort on assumptions not amenable to proof. But among arbitrary notions, some have their uses and others not; the idea of progress as happiness is one of the least plausible notions.

John Stuart Mill put foward a conception of progress as well, and his idea has at least one great advantage over Bentham's, in making it possible for us to decide whether one people are more advanced than another, or more advanced at one time than at another. His conception was essentially one of progress in terms of self-realization or self-fulfilment, not unlike the view of the German Idealists. Of course Mill was no Idealist; his logic and his theory of knowledge are altogether different from theirs. But his moral theory has at times a certain affinity with theirs, even if the differences are more obvious. The Idealists were, by and large, better psychologists than the Utilitarians, and it is therefore to Mill's credit that, in spite of the bias of his earlier principles, he was able in some matters to think as they did. He never went very far in their direction; he was never attracted by their theory of the State. But he did speak as they did of self-realization; and though he did not mean by it quite what they meant, his notion and theirs have something in common. To Mill, self-realization – or self-improvement, as he preferred to put it – matters more than happiness as the older Utilitarians defined it. No doubt Mill did try to relate self-improvement to happiness in the Benthamite sense; he could not bring himself to reject what he had been brought up to believe. But he never succeeded in establishing the relation, and though he was still caught up in their doctrines even when he was breaking away from them, it is the non-Utilitarian part of his philosophy which is the more interesting and the more his own – not, perhaps, in the sense of having been invented by him, but closest to his heart.

I must, however, take care not to make too little of the younger Mill's Utilitarianism. Though he was much else besides, he was indeed a Utilitarian. And to his Utilitarianism he owed one great merit. He was never tempted to exaggerate the importance of social influences, nor was he drawn to anything remotely like the worship of the State we find in many Continental writers of his age. He took into account many matters unknown to the older Utilitarians or neglected by them: the conservative philosophy of Coleridge, inspired by Burke and by half-assimilated doctrines taken from Germany; the sociology of Comte; and the earlier socialist theories, English and French. These were all theories resting on assumptions different from those made by the Utilitarians. They were much less individualist. In the light of what he learnt from them, Mill qualified – or, rather, transformed – the individualism he inherited from the older Utilitarians; but he was always careful not to concede too much, not to allow the State to make too many claims on the individual.

1. Freedom and Self-Improvement

Many political theorists have been exponents of what is rather loosely called *individualism*. Locke was one, Bentham another, and Mill a third. But Mill's individualism was not quite theirs. He did not reject what they taught; rather, he took up their ideas in his own doctrine and went beyond them. For Locke and for Bentham, government at bottom is no more than a contrivance whose authority is limited by the purpose it serves. Its function, Locke tells us, is to defend rights which it does not create, and, according to Bentham, it exists to promote men's interests. For both Bentham and Locke, the individual is prior to organized society in the sense that government is only a means to serve ends that would exist even if there were no government to serve them. And these ends belong to individuals – not to society, but to the persons who make up society. In this respect, the individualism of Locke is the same as that of Bentham, even though he believes in natural rights while Bentham does not. The individual's purposes are his own, and government has no right to interfere with him, except to prevent harm to others. The order maintained by government serves, not to make people what they ought to be, but to induce them to let one another alone.

Mill does not so much disagree with Locke and Bentham as go beyond them. For him, too, all ends are individual, and the function of government is to make it easier for individuals to attain their ends. But the best ends, he supposed, are not known to uncivilized man. Organized society does much more than enable men to get what they want; it causes them to want what they could never have wanted outside it. It quickens their faculties, it enlarges their personalities, it raises them above their natural selves, it gives them ideals and opportunities. Such a doctrine, of course, had already been developed by Rousseau and Hegel; and, though less obviously, it is no less the doctrine of John Stuart Mill. It is implied by his saying that it is better to be Socrates dissatisfied than a pig satisfied.[1] For Socrates was a highly civilized man, and if he was better than his fellow Athenians (which Mill clearly thought he was), it was because he understood better than they did what man could make of himself in society. Mill believed in education for more than prudential reasons; he believed in the good effects of voluntary co-operation, in self-government as a means of moral improvement, in virtue as a constituent of happiness. It matters, says Mill, 'not only what men do, but also what manner of men they are that do it'.[2] They must be free; they must pursue ends which seem to them worthy of pursuit; they must not be driven; they must not be used for ends that seem good to others. They must do what they please, but it is important that they should please to do some things rather than others. Not that they should all do the same things, but that each should have an ideal chosen by himself, which he strives to live up to: 'What more or better can be said of any condition of human affairs than that it brings human beings themselves nearer to the best thing they can be?'[3] A man who can put a question like this has moved very far indeed from Utilitarian philosophy, and no less far from the philosophy of natural right.

---

[1] *Utilitarianism*, ch. 2, in J. S. Mill, *Utilitarianism, Liberty, Representative Government* (Everyman's Library 1972 edition), p. 10.
[2] *On Liberty*, ch. 3, ibid., p. 127.
[3] Ibid., p. 132.

From Mill's remarks on moral obligation in *Utilitarianism*, we can see how thoroughly he believed that morality is a product of a social life which shapes and transforms minds that are amenable to its influence. Moral obligation is not for him, as it was for his father, a fear aroused in us by an experience teaching us that some kinds of action, or indeed inaction, prompt unpleasant responses from others. It is a very complex feeling compounded, for instance, of sympathy, love, fear, self-esteem and religious emotions. It is a product of a life lived in close association with others, in dependence on them for much more than the satisfaction of material needs. Mill believed that we cannot live for ourselves alone, though he sometimes found it necessary, in deference to the Utilitarianism he professed, to speak otherwise.

One argument used by him, to reconcile a doctrine he adds to the parent creed of Utilitarianism, shows how much more he cares for that doctrine than for the creed. Virtue, he says, is a means to happiness, and comes to be desired in the first place only because it is so. In time, however, men come to want it for its own sake; and so virtue becomes a part of happiness. And this, Mill thinks, quite reconciles his account of virtue with Utilitarianism. 'Whatever', he says, 'may be the opinion of utilitarian moralists as to the original conditions by which virtue is made virtue; however they may believe (as they do) that actions and dispositions are only virtuous because they promote another end than virtue; yet this being granted. . .they not only place virtue at the very head of the things which are good as a means to the ultimate end, but they also recognise as a psychological fact the possibility of its being, to the individual, a good in itself, without looking to any end beyond it; and hold, that the mind is not in a right state. . .not in the state conducive to the general happiness, unless it does love virtue in this manner – as a thing desirable in itself'.[1] In other words, unless men love virtue above all things, even above happiness, they cannot be truly happy; and yet this is compatible with nothing being ultimately valuable except happiness, because, as Mill goes on to say, virtue, when it comes to be desired for its own sake, becomes a part of happiness.

In certain respects this seems a curious argument, since it does not follow that virtue, when it comes to be desired for its own sake, becomes a part of happiness in the Utilitarian sense, unless to be desired for its own sake means the same as to be pleasant. Mill sometimes speaks as if it does, but he much more often assumes the

[1] *Utilitarianism*, ch. 4, ibid., p. 37.

contrary. He does not really think that to say that nothing but pleasure is desired for its own sake is to utter the tautology that nothing but what is desired for its own sake is desired for its own sake. As we have already seen, a Utilitarian such as Bentham, or anyone anxious (as Mill was) to pass himself off as one, simply cannot treat 'pleasant' and 'desired for its own sake' as synonyms: for if he does, he can hardly treat pleasure as an end, which his philosophy requires him to do. If pleasure is an end, and to be pleasant is to be desired for its own sake, then to desire pleasure is to desire to desire something for its own sake. This is not an impossible situation, for men can wish to desire something and not merely to have it; but I doubt whether the Utilitarians had anything so sophisticated in mind. Pleasure for them is not desire but the object of desire. And virtue, whatever it may be, is not pleasure, though it may be true that men are, on the whole, the happier for being virtuous, and sometimes even find the practice of virtue pleasant.

I must not linger over the ambiguities and errors of Mill's account of the connection between virtue and happiness. He quite often got into difficulties that his father and Bentham avoided, precisely because he was nearer the truth. Men do desire virtue for its own sake, and it is as social creatures that they come to desire it. They desire not merely justice but to be just. Hume had called justice an artificial virtue and had explained how men learn to set a value on it. Experience gained in the process of living together teaches men that it is to the advantage of everyone that there should be rules of conduct which all accept. They come to desire these rules, and to disapprove of the breach of them; they come to desire justice and to approve it. But to desire justice is merely to want people to conform to certain rules. To want to be just is to want to be the sort of person who acts justly. Mill, when he says that virtue is desirable for its own sake, is passing beyond the point in the argument reached by Hume. He is saying more than that men learn in society to approve and disapprove of conduct they could not otherwise conceive; he is also saying that in society they learn to care about *what they are* as much as about *what they do*. He does not say this in so many words, in the essay on *Utilitarianism*, when he explains how virtue comes to be desired for its own sake; but he does, I think, imply it. For, otherwise, what would be the point of insisting that 'the mind is not in a right state' unless it loves virtue for its own sake? Hume also spoke of motives and dispositions, saying that some are approved of and others disapproved, but he took it for granted that men care about them only because they care about their consequences – about the effects, in terms of pain and pleasure, of the actions inspired by them. It did not matter to Hume, as it did to Mill, that the mind should be 'in [the] right state'; and it would not be at all in the spirit of his philosophy to say, as Mill said in *On Liberty*, that 'It really is of importance, not only what men do, but also what manner of men they are that do it'.

What manner of men? There are infinite possibilities. Who is to decide, among the many things that a man could be, what he ought to be? It is not enough to say, as Mill does, that it really matters what men are, and to leave it at that. For Mill does not make it sufficiently clear why, if it matters what men are like, it should also matter that they should be free. Free for what purposes, and to what extent?

The idea that it is what men are like, as much as what they do, that is important, is at least as old as Plato, who cared little for freedom. But for Mill, as is evident from the essay *On Liberty*, freedom is all important. It matters as much that men should be free as it does what manner of men they are. He insists as much on the one point as on the other. How, then, are they to be reconciled? How must we conceive of freedom if we are to make it as wide as possible and yet contrive that the men who are free are not also base? It is, I think because his idea of freedom is too simple – too much like that of his father and Bentham – that he is unable to answer such a question satisfactorily.

Hegel proposed an answer to this question which, though not sufficient, is strong precisely where Mill's is weak. According to Hegel, it is as a member of society, as a creature standing in determinate relations to his fellows, that man becomes a purposive and moral being, that he acquires the conception of himself as a person having stable interests and ideals. He feels the need of freedom, not because he is the subject of a random succession of desires, but because he is a moral person with a whole life to live according to standards that seem good to him. It is within society, which is a moral order, that the individual becomes a moral person, and it is because he is such a person that freedom comes to be precious to him. Therefore, says Hegel, the individual has no right against this moral order, and no right against the State, which is the highest expression of it.

There is nothing in this answer of Hegel's that Mill – as a believer both in freedom and self-improvement – need object to, except the conclusion that the individual has no right against the State. For that conclusion was intended to have practical consequences of a kind which Mill could not accept; it was meant to suggest, without saying it in so many words, that subjects have a duty of absolute obedience to the laws. Such a suggestion, of course, is not meaningless; it is merely a conclusion that does not follow from what has gone before. Because it is only in society, under the discipline of custom and law, that man becomes moral, it does not in the least follow that he has no right to disobey custom and law. And to say that the citizen has no right against the State – if the State is thought of as the moral order (which is how Hegel ordinarily thinks of it) – is just plain nonsense. All rights are held against persons, and a moral order is not a person. It is not possible either to have a duty to it or a right against it. When we say we have a duty to obey the State, we are (or ought to be) speaking, not of a moral order, but of persons who have a right to command because of the special position they occupy in that order. In any sense of the word *State* that allows us to have duties to it, we can also have rights against it.

What manner of man is it that Mill would have his fellow-creatures be? Why is it important that they should be free? Why is it better to be Socrates dissatisfied than a contented pig? Mill's answer is that men should be creatures who strive to live up to some ideal they have freely chosen for themselves. If they are free, they may live up to no such ideal; they may not care what manner of men they are. But unless they are free, they cannot live up to it. What is supremely important is not that they should be made into what others think is good for them to be, but that they themselves should strive to attain their own chosen end. They will not, of course, choose their ends at random; they will, as social animals, be powerfully influenced by the moral order they are born into. Mill knew that this must be so. There is, however, a world of difference between just conforming to the standards and tastes of the society or class one belongs to and acquiring principles and tastes of one's own. The more people there are who choose to live as seems good to them, and who respect this right in others, the greater the variety and depth of human experience. Life is thereby enriched and enlarged. Men have wider opportunities and are more intensely alive. 'He who lets the world, or his own portion of it, choose his plan of life for him, has no need of any other faculty than the ape-like one of imitation. He who chooses his plan for himself, employs all his faculties.'[1] And a little later, Mill continues, 'Among the works of man, which human life is rightly employed in perfecting and beautifying, the first in importance surely is man himself'.[2] The implication is clear: by choosing your own plan of life, you employ all your faculties, and you perfect yourself. Mill would not deny that it is only as a social creature that one can make such a choice, or even

[1] *On Liberty*, ch. 3, ibid., p. 126.
[2] Ibid., p. 127.

understand the possibility of it, but he is more concerned to insist that a man must be free.

Unfortunately, Mill's conception of freedom is inadequate to his idea of the end he means it to serve. He has often been criticized for saying that 'the only part of the conduct of any one, for which he is answerable to society, is that which concerns others. In the part which merely concerns himself, his independence is, of right, absolute'.[1] His critics have pointed out that there is no kind of action which is not liable to concern others, and that therefore Mill's criterion is useless. Such hoary criticism really amounts to very little. Of course, any kind of action is liable to concern others, but this does not mean that there are not innumerable occasions when a man's actions affect other people not at all, or very much less than they affect himself. If Mill's criterion were useless, it would be impossible ever to have good reason for saying that a man was minding his own business. The distinction between self-regarding and other-regarding actions is one of the commonest we make. The fault of Mill's criterion is not that it cannot be used but that it has no obvious connection with his own idea of the good life. He admits that children ought to be prevented from doing harm to themselves as well as to others. Why? Because it is our duty to bring them up to be free and responsible persons. Men are not born but are made free.

Mill, of course, knew this. Immediately after proclaiming the rule of freedom, he proceeds to exclude, not only children, but what he calls 'backward states of society', that is to say, primitive peoples. 'Liberty, as a principle', he says, 'has no application to any state of things anterior to the time when mankind have been capable of being improved by free and equal discussion'[2]. In other words, freedom is desirable only among people capable of self-improvement. We cannot, of course, force people to improve themselves, to try to live up to some ideal they freely accept. We cannot force them to be morally responsible, for that would be a contradiction in terms. But we can educate them for freedom; and while we are doing so, we have to prevent them injuring themselves as well as others. In a sense, we impose our own ideal on them; we try to make them what we would have them be; but our aim is that they should be free, that they should be able to make a plan of life for themselves and pursue it responsibly, without trying to deprive other people of the same opportunity.

[1] Ibid., ch. 1, p. 78.
[2] Ibid., p. 79.

This is Mill's ideal, and it also, I think, lies at the heart of what we in the West call liberalism. It is an intelligible doctrine, and we can measure progress in terms of it. And that, after all, is more than we can do with happiness. For Bentham and James Mill, freedom is only a means. They take it for granted that every man is, on the whole, the best judge of his own interest, of what makes for his own happiness; and they go on to argue that the general happiness will be most rapidly increased if, within broad limits, everyone is allowed to pursue his own ends without interference. But what they take for granted is not at all obvious. What if men in their business (a skill so much admired by the Utilitarians) found their happiness generally frustrated? What if someone should come along with a prescription for converting them into satisfied pigs at the cost of depriving them of their freedom? If the prescription proved effective, Bentham and James Mill could not logically forbid its use. But from self-improvement as the younger Mill conceived it, freedom is inseparable. It does make sense to aim at freedom as John Stuart Mill portrayed it: to aim at giving everyone a chance to follow a self-chosen course, to fashion for himself his own manner of life, to become the sort of person he would like to be. Such freedom, like any other, has to be limited, but it is, as an object of policy, intelligible and practical. Far more so, at least, than the pursuit of happiness. Many societies have been blind to this freedom; others have denied it; some have praised and tried fitfully to achieve it. If it is taken for desirable, it makes sense to speak of progress towards it, and to judge societies and governments by reference to it. To make this assumption, without qualifying it in ways that destroy it, is to have the faith called liberalism.

I put in the proviso about not qualifying the assumption destructively in order to guard against misunderstanding. Hegel believed in self-realization and in moral freedom in a way that Plato, for instance, did not, but his peculiar notion of the State and his cult of authority and hierarchy make it impossible to call him a true liberal. Rousseau's love of freedom was less equivocal than Hegel's, but it, too, was not pure. The simple life, as he preached it, excludes too much that is good and liberating in civilized society. No one, he thought, who had known what his ideal community has to offer, would prefer the sophisticated trappings of the contemporary world. His own argument, however, could be turned against him: many people who have enjoyed the refinements – material and spiritual – which he rejected would find his ideal narrow and restrictive. He wanted freedom passionately for himself, and therefore clamoured that everyone should have it; but he also wanted everyone to want what he wanted. He was an unhappy and unadventurous soul seeking a refuge. Mill's love of freedom was bolder and more pure.

2. Mill on Representative Government

We have already seen that Bentham and the older Mill, thinking that men are, on the whole, the best judges of their own interest, concluded that representative democracy is the best form of government. They were not as absolute in their conclusion as is sometimes supposed. They did not in fact believe that all peoples everywhere would be forthwith the better for adopting representative democracy. Nor did they enquire particularly what made a people fit or unfit for it. They were content to argue that it is the best form of government because, more than any other, it ensures that those who govern seek their own good in ways that also promote the good of their subjects. It creates a more perfect harmony of self-regarding interests than could exist without it, and therefore increases the sum of human happiness.

Here, as elsewhere, the younger Mill did not reject their argument, but fitted it into a larger whole which almost dwarfs it. Representative government is, for him, ideally the best because it improves the quality of the people who exercise it, rather than because it creates a harmony of selfish interests. As he put it, 'The most important point of excellence which any form of government can possess is to promote the virtue and intelligence of the people themselves'.[1] Representative government makes men more responsible as well as more critical – more public-spirited as well as more self-reliant. It takes them out of themselves, out of the narrow circle of personal and family interests; it broadens their minds and their sympathies. In a representative democracy, the great majority of the people can take only a small part in the government of their country, but that small part is important, and it matters greatly that they should take it. People whom others control, because they think them unfit to control themselves, are mentally and morally diminished. 'Wherever the sphere of action of human beings is artificially circumscribed, their sentiments are narrowed and dwarfed in the same proportion. . . . In a despotism there is at most but one patriot, the despot himself.'[2]

Representative democracy, Mill thought, is not suited to all peoples at all times. It is absurd to force it on those who know nothing of

---

[1] *Representative Government*, ch. 2, ibid., p. 207.
[2] Ibid., ch. 3, pp. 219–20.

it and do not want it. And even when they do want it, it may not be suited to them – either because they do not care for it enough to be willing to make real sacrifices to preserve it, or because they have not acquired the habits of thought and feeling that make it possible for them to work its institutions. To be capable of self-government, a people must first learn to respect the law; and they will not learn to respect it unless they have been subject to a discipline imposed from above. Savages are often improvident, and slavery may be deemed good for them because it gets them accustomed to regular work. Primitive peoples may be the better for being subject to conquerors more civilized than themselves. A monarch aiming at despotism, by destroying the independence of feudal lords and even by putting down local autonomies, can help prepare a great people for self-government. The habit of obedience to a remote but powerful authority controlling a large territory accustoms millions of people to think of themselves as one nation. It was irresponsible monarchy and not representative government that created the large, civilized and active nations of the West. Despotism has many dangers; it can easily corrupt both the despot and his subjects. It is, nevertheless, often a necessary form of government; and nations are created and made capable of freedom by passing through the discipline it imposes. The belief that democracy is the only kind of government really compatible with the moral dignity of self-reliant and public-spirited men; willing admission that all peoples at many stages of their development are unsuited to democracy; adherence to the view that both individuals and communities are made fit for freedom by social discipline; a keen scent for whatever corrupts the body politic – all this Mill shares with Rousseau, who was far indeed from being a Utilitarian. But whereas Rousseau was a pessimist, believing that most peoples can never become capable of freedom, Mill did not suggest that any people are perpetually excluded, by history or by race, from the blessings of free government. However backward or corrupt they may be, it is always possible for them to make progress, by their own efforts or by the efforts of their rulers, domestic or foreign.

Mill was realistic in his appraisal of the limitations of democracy, even under ideal conditions. No popular assembly, direct or representative, is fit to make the laws, let alone administer them. Lawmaking is a task for experts, for every new law must fit into a complicated structure of already existing law. The most that an assembly can do is to examine the bills put before it, and to accept or reject them. It is important that it should do this, but it is equally important that it should acknowledge its incapacity to do more. The proper task of a popular assembly is to deliberate, to criticize, to lend support to government, and also to oppose it. It is 'the nation's Committee of Grievances, and its Congress of Opinions. . .where every person in the country may count upon finding somebody who speaks his mind, as well or better than he could speak it himself'.[1]

Mill believed that the best form of government is a bureaucracy responsible to a popular assembly. The Roman Republic owed its greatness, not just to being an aristocracy, but to being an aristocracy of public officials. The Senate consisted entirely of men who had held great offices of state; and in Venice, too, the real business of government was in the hands of governors by profession. In Rome, there was also, as there was not in Venice, a popular element; and Mill, who thought Rome and Venice the greatest of aristocracies, preferred the Roman to the Venetian system of government. The disease of bureaucracy is routine; a bureaucracy always tends to become what Mill calls a 'pedantocracy'.[2] It can be saved from degeneration only by being made responsible to a popular assembly. Democracy keeps bureaucracy vigorous and enterprising, and bureaucracy makes democracy prudent and efficient. Mill had no love for the kind of aristocracy that rests chiefly on birth and wealth and hardly at all on talent and public service.

His conception of liberty is not tied, as Rousseau's was, to the small and simple community; it takes full account of the size and complexity of the modern State, and of the institutions which that State cannot do without. His liberalism requires democracy, but does not make an idol of it. And it is not incompatible with imperialism, if by imperialism is meant the deliberate and persistent endeavour of a wealthy and self-governing people to fit other people to govern themselves in the ways that enlarge individual freedom. Whether Mill's principles could justify any empire that exists today, is another question; but they certainly do not exclude every form of imperialism. Here, as with a good deal else, Mill seems a kind of mirror of his age, reflecting much that is best in it with the least distortion. He is a typical, a representative, thinker, not because there were many like him – for his breadth of sympathy and understanding were quite out of the ordinary – but because he is the most comprehensive: the one who absorbed in the largest measure what his age had to offer. It is perhaps in this sense that John Stuart Mill was at once the most characteristic and most remarkable Victorian philosopher, economist and political theorist.

[1] Ibid., ch. 5, pp. 258–9.
[2] Ibid., ch. 6, p. 266.

CHAPTER SIX

The Early Socialists, French and English I

I. THEIR PREDOMINANT INTERESTS

The French economist, Bastiat, writing before the world had heard of Marx, called the socialists 'grandchildren of Rousseau'. Presumably Bastiat had in mind the early French socialists rather than the English ones, for his remark seems to apply more readily to them. Not that the French socialists thought of themselves as being descended, morally and intellectually, from Rousseau. Many of them, as we shall see, spoke contemptuously of what seemed important to him and cherished hopes which he would have thought absurd. Yet the early socialists, English and French, held two beliefs which we associate more with Rousseau than with anyone else, because he was by far the most eloquent exponent of them: the belief that man in his wretchedness is the victim of society, and the belief that freedom is impossible except in a community of equals. No doubt, most of the great political thinkers before Rousseau had proclaimed a belief in equality, in one form or another; but equality, as they conceived of it, consisted in all men's having certain rights, prior to government – rights held to be realized in existing society or to require only an extension of the franchise for their realization. They did not hold, as Rousseau did, that equality, and therefore freedom as well, is impossible except in communities profoundly different, socially as much as politically, from any that existed.

Society is evil, irrational and corrupting because it allows of great inequalities unconnected with differences of ability or merit. This is one of the two recurrent themes of Rousseau's philosophy; the other is that freedom is grounded in an equality consisting in much more than everyone's enjoying the sort of rights which had interested

Locke or the Levellers. These are themes as central to socialism as to the philosophy of Rousseau. The early socialists were indeed, in a limited but important sense, though most of them did not know it, 'grandchildren of Rousseau'. For Rousseau was the most revolutionary of all critics of the established order. Revolutionary, not in calling for its destruction by force – for that he never did – but in expressing a horror of it so profound and persuasive as to make it seem hateful to many who might otherwise have resigned themselves to it, as Christians had long been taught to do. And yet his disgust with the world was in many ways in the Christian tradition, though his message was addressed to his own and to succeeding generations, to men who (like himself) mostly could not find in their hopes of the next world compensation for their anxieties in this one. Like the early Christians, he made the world distasteful to men but, unlike them, he did so without reconciling them to their lot and without giving them hopes for the future. He was a great disturber of souls, an enthusiast who was also a pessimist.

1. *Their Difference from Rousseau*

It is here that the early socialists differ the most obviously from him. They were all hopeful men; they all believed in progress, as he did not. They also differed from him in other ways, which I propose to discuss because these serve to bring out sharply some of the essentials of nineteenth-century socialism. The early socialists nearly all believed in the salutary effects of the extension of knowledge; they were most of them either suspicious of the State or uninterested in it; there was little or nothing Stoic or ascetic about their creeds; and several of them were ardent feminists. Bastiat might just as truly have called them 'grandchildren of Hume and the Encyclopaedists', for they had at least as much in common with them as with Rousseau. And yet it is natural that he should have been more struck by their community with Rousseau. He himself, as a disciple of the classical economists, was a 'grandchild' of the Encyclopaedists, just as he was a critic of the socialists; he was therefore less impressed by what he had in common with them than by what made them seem so different. If they had not seen man as the victim of society – if they had not condemned inequalities rooted in the social system which the economists took for granted – they would not have been socialists. This was obvious to Bastiat. What was not obvious to him was that they could hardly have been socialists unless they had been hopeful of the future, and that their hopes rested on convictions and arguments which they held in common with the *philosophes* of the previous century with whom Rousseau had quarrelled, not only because he was temperamentally unsuited to them, but because his whole attitude to life was different.

Admittedly, the vision of man as at once the maker and the victim of society, whose institutions arise out of his efforts and yet are imperfectly understood and scarcely controlled by him, is less elaborate, less profound, less deeply felt in the early socialists than in Rousseau. We can scarcely find in their writings, as we can in Hegel's and in Marx's, the conception of *alienation*; and it is this conception, perhaps more than any other common to these two thinkers, which brings them closest in thought and feeling to Rousseau. The sense in which, for the early socialists, man is the victim of society is relatively simple. Man has a variety of illusions about himself and his environment which prevent his attaining happiness; he is a victim of ignorance. He sees the world and himself as different from what they really are, and, because he is thus mistaken, he behaves from motives which would not be so strong in him if he knew the truth – motives which bring misery to himself and to others. As seen by the early socialists (and by Condorcet), mankind has suffered from an ignorance which has been, until recently, inevitable, because it takes time for men to accumulate and to organize the knowledge required to give them a true picture of the world. To begin with, they scarcely know how to correct their mistakes; they are incapable of distinguishing knowledge from fantasy. In order to have scientific or solid and systematic knowledge, they must come to understand and to criticize the methods whereby they accumulate what they take to be knowledge; they must learn to be philosophical, to doubt and to test assumptions hitherto unchallenged. While they are ignorant, they do not understand and cannot control the social effects of their own activities. They create, without knowing how they do it, an environment in which, being the sort of creatures they are, it is only natural that they should act as they do. In this sense, they are the victims of a social order which they and their ancestors have made without having desired to make it. Within that social order there arises a variety of what Bentham would call 'sinister interests', so that it becomes the advantage of certain privileged groups to perpetuate a system which is harmful to the community as a whole.

Now, it is possible to believe all this – and many of the early socialists believed it – without having any notion (even though by another name) of what Hegel and Marx understood by *alienation*. To make my point clearer, let me compare this conception with the difference between the state of nature and the social state as Hobbes imagined it. In the state of nature man is more suspicious, more treacherous, more aggressive than in the social state; he, too, can be said to be a victim of his environment. He is in a situation in which he is impelled to behave in ways which make others, and himself also, insecure and unhappy. In the social state, he is no longer impelled to act in these ways; he can afford behaviour which reconciles his own permanent interest with other people's. Passions which were strong in him in the state of nature are much weaker in the social state, and other passions which were weak are much stronger. But man, essentially, remains always the same. His nature is not transformed by the social discipline to which he is subjected. This is what Hobbes usually gives us to understand, though there are times when his words suggest that he knows better.

Of course, for Hobbes, man is not the victim of society; it is society which is the saviour of man. Nor does Hobbes envisage a long process whereby man acquires the knowledge enabling him to create the environment which makes for his happiness in the place of the one which leads to misery. The state of nature, the wretched state, is the condition into which man is born before he has used his reason to get out of it; it is not, as is the society of which man is the victim in the eyes of the socialists, itself the outcome of a long process of evolution. There are no illusions and no sinister interests in the state of nature to stand between mankind and the enlightenment which is to bring happiness. Two centuries of speculation and scholarship separate the early socialists from Hobbes; they belong to different intellectual worlds. Yet the socialists come scarcely any closer than he does to believing that man, if he is to escape misery and find happiness, must himself be profoundly changed in the process which transforms his environment. There is in Rousseau a conception, rich though confused, of *alienated* man, of man deeply disturbed, psychologically and morally, by the pressure of society on him, of man 'outside himself' (*hors de lui-même*) driven by his environment to seek satisfaction where it is not to be had; there is this same conception in Hegel and in Marx, together with the idea of man made whole again, 'restored to himself', gradually and painfully by his own endeavours, to become master of himself and his environment. These are the conceptions lacking, except for occasional hints, in the writings of the early socialists, and whose absence makes the idea of progress characteristically so much more shallow and less exciting in their writings than in those of Hegel or Marx.

Similarly, in deploring the ill effects of inequality, the early socialists merely see men as driven to crime and violence by poverty and ignorance. Because men are situated as they are, they are exposed to great temptations. The difference between them in their degradation and as they would be in the just society is seen almost entirely as a difference between external situations. Change their situation and they will behave differently, not so much because this change will lead eventually to a psychological and moral transformation, as because what once seemed worth doing will no longer seem so. The early socialists do not follow Rousseau in seeing man as deeply corrupted by excessive poverty or excessive wealth; they see him rather as deprived of opportunities which he otherwise would have, or as exposed to temptations from which he would otherwise be free. They do not see him in the grip of contrary passions produced in him by his environment; they do not see him driven by these passions into courses which create frustration and self-loathing because they infringe principles which are themselves products of social life. They do not see man as half accepting and half rejecting these principles; they do not see him at war with himself, an unwilling hypocrite, a creature impelled by desires which make him what he does not want to be. Or, if they do see him in this way, it is only fitfully and almost unconsciously, as persons unaware of what their own thoughts imply. Teach the poor what they do not know, give them what they do not have, and the evil effects of poverty and ignorance will quickly vanish. This is the gist of what Owen, Saint-Simon, Fourier and Proudhon all tell us, and they were the most influential socialists before Marx. But Marx, though less impressive as an observer of the psychology of social man than either Rousseau or Hegel, says more than this, no doubt because of what he has learnt from Hegel; he imagines a long and difficult advance towards equality, an advance in which man, as he gradually transforms society, also transforms himself, both intellectually and at a deeper level than the intellect.

The conception of man as at war with himself, as in need of internal peace, is also Christian, and can perhaps be found in other religions. Mankind did not need to wait for Rousseau to become aware of the spiritual conflict expressed by St Paul to the Romans in the words, 'For the good which I would, I do not; but the evil which I would not, that I do'. But Christianity does not see this conflict as an effect of man's social environment; it does not see natural man as innocent, without reason or morality, becoming rational and moral only as he becomes social; it does not see him as creating, through activities whose remoter consequences are unforeseen by him, both the moral rules which bind him inwardly and the excessive and disorderly passions which move him to break the rules; nor does it imagine a worldly, a social, order, in which man would be free of this conflict. Rousseau was deeply affected by Christian thought, and was also caught up in moral crises of which Christianity takes large account, although it offers only a theological explanation of them. The explanation which Rousseau attempted, however, was sociological and psychological.

2. *Their Interest in History*

Though most of the early socialists were not, in any serious sense, historians, they had what may be called a sense of history. They were believers in progress, and they knew that progress in the past had been slow. They knew that the society which they hoped to transform had been different in the past from what it was in their time, and they were aware that the pace of change was increasing. They were therefore very conscious, as for example Hobbes and Locke had not been, of having a place in history. There is little evidence that either Hobbes or Locke thought of their doctrines as being products of an age, as being conceivable and persuasive only in a period which was unique because it was a particular stage in an unceasing course of social change, a course whose every stage differed from the one before it. But the socialists believed that their doctrines had come in the fullness of time, as incidents in a long process of social evolution which was at once economic, political and intellectual. History had prepared their audience for them, and they expected to be listened to because they were convinced that their message was timely.

Of all the early socialists, Saint-Simon was the most interested in history. As much as Hegel or Marx, he had what is called a 'philosophy of history', which we shall examine later; he had a fairly well-defined and elaborate theory about how European society had changed since the eleventh century, and he claimed to be able to use this theory to predict, in broad outline, the course of future change. Actually, his interest in the future was limited; he was mostly concerned with the immediate future. But he did claim to base his predictions, not merely on observations of the present and the recent past, but on a number of general propositions about the course of history over a period of eight hundred years. And, though he had little to say about events outside that period and outside Europe, he believed that he had discovered a law of change which applied to all societies and all epochs.[1]

---

[1] I do not believe that he ever succeeded in formulating this law clearly enough to make it worthwhile discussing it; he never got even as far as Marx did in the Preface to his *Contribution to the Critique of Political Economy*. He believed,

Fourier's philosophy of history is much less interesting than Saint-Simon's. Saint-Simon was deeply excited by history; he was no exact scholar, but he was bold and perceptive. His account of the course of change in the West from the eleventh to the nineteenth centuries is brilliant and suggestive; or, rather, his various though broadly similar accounts are so, for he quite often changed his mind about details. His conception of the course of history, moreover, is closely connected with his views about how society should be transformed. With Fourier it is quite different. To understand why he wanted society transformed in the way he did, there is really no need to know anything about the pattern of social change as he imagined it. He had a passion for tidy elaboration. Where Saint-Simon confines himself almost entirely to describing in considerable detail just two stages of social evolution and how the earlier passes into the later one, giving only the vaguest indication of what any other stage might be like, Fourier asserts that mankind must pass through thirty-six different periods, though he offers to describe only the first eight, the others being so far in the future that we cannot imagine them. The West, as he knows it, is in the fifth period, which he calls *civilization*. Indeed, the West has been, he thinks, in the third phase of the fifth period for nearly one hundred years, though it shows signs of having passed, in some respects, into the fourth and last phase of that period, and even into the sixth period; for a society can, he tells us, be more advanced in some respects than others. The period he is most concerned with – the period he describes in loving detail as being the best that we can now imagine and foresee – is the eighth, which he calls *harmonism* or *composite association*. It is the period when the social order ceases to frustrate man, when it is in keeping with his natural passions, allowing them full and harmless expression. But Fourier, though he deals with the past with a tidiness and self-confidence which never desert him, deals with it scantily and with little insight. It is not his brief survey of the past but his condemnation of the present and his detailed hopes for the future that reveal what he knows of human nature and the influence upon it of the social environment. And yet it would be misleading to say that he lacks a sense of history. He gives little evidence of having understood the past or how the present has

presumably, that any society similar to Western Europe in the eleventh century would develop more or less as Western Europe had done; and he also believed, presumably, that mediaeval Europe had developed out of an older type of society much as any other society would have developed. But he never described this older type, nor attempted to show how mediaeval Europe arose out of it. In practice, he was interested only in how mediaeval Europe had developed into the Europe of his day.

emerged out of it, but he is very much aware that the present, which he condemns, and the future, which he foresees and approves of, are products of a long course of gradual change. He is aware also, though less certainly, that the times must be ripe if ideas like his own are to catch on.[1]

Proudhon can hardly be said to have a philosophy of history; he has no developed theory about what causes society to evolve and he puts forward no set pattern of social change. Sometimes he speaks as if progress were inevitable and sometimes as if it were not. Since man is rational, he can come to see that, in the long run, equality is the only rule acceptable to all creatures like himself. Man, being free and rational, is faced with problems which he is able to solve, and by solving them he changes his situation and enlarges his understanding. Progress is therefore possible, and, to the extent that it happens, it brings men closer to the society of equals; but it is not inevitable. This is, I believe, the gist of Proudhon's doctrine of progress as it is expounded in *De la Justice dans la Révolution et dans l'Église*, published in 1858, a work which, in the opinion of many, is his greatest. It is probable that when he was younger he believed that progress was inevitable and that later he changed his mind. It is difficult with a writer so much given to paradox, so much excited by ideas and with so little intellectual discipline, to be quite sure of his meaning. But, whatever his views about progress, he certainly believed that it was only in his time that the workers were acquiring the capacity to understand and carry out proposals such as his. For all his confusions and paradoxes, Proudhon was as much steeped in history as Marx, and as much aware that the times must be ripe for them if social theories calling for great changes are to be received.

Of the four most famous socialists before Marx, Owen was perhaps the least interested in history; and yet even he was aware that he lived in an age unlike any other before it and that he therefore had unprecedented opportunities. He believed that hitherto men had been educated on false principles, and that it could hardly have been otherwise, for they were ignorant and prejudiced. Only recently had they become enlightened enough to receive the truth offered to them

---

[1] I say 'less certainly' because Fourier once said that his discoveries might have been made two thousand years earlier, and mankind could thereby have been spared much suffering. This is a curious statement for a man to make who insists that progress is made by stages and that the passage from stage to stage is *necessary*. Even if we allow, as Fourier does, that some sides of social life are well in advance of others, this *necessity* implies that every side of it must pass through every stage. Whether this was clear to Fourier, I do not know.

by Owen. As he put it, 'The time is *now* arrived when the public mind of this country and the general state of the world call imperatively for the introduction of this all–pervading principle, not only in *theory* but into *practice*. Nor can any human power now impede its rapid progress'.[1] The 'all–pervading' principle is that 'any general character, from the best to the worst. . .may be given to any community. . .by the application of proper means; which means are to a great extent at the command. . .of those who have influence in the affairs of men'.[2] Nobody believed more firmly than Owen that there had been and would be progress; that it had been slower in the past and would be quicker in the future because the obstacles to it were breaking down; and that he was himself in the van of progress, because he had a message peculiarly suited to the times. And this belief was shared by most of the early socialists in France and England, even those among them least interested in history.

Marx and Engels called the early socialists utopian. If they meant by this that the early socialists took no account of the state of society at the time they wrote – of what Marxists like to call 'the objective conditions' – the charge they make is grossly exaggerated. No doubt, the early socialists were too sanguine, too little impressed by the difficulties that stood in their way. But most of them thought they had good reason to believe that, society and the intellectual climate having become what they were, they would find a ready audience for their doctrines, an audience made ready for them by the 'march of events'. Some of them, indeed, gave little thought to the matter, but others gave a great deal. Owen, for example, comes much closer to being a utopian, in this particular sense, than does Saint-Simon. Owen is content to say scarcely more than that progress has now reached the point when the world, or at least the small part of it known to him, is ready to accept and to apply the great principle preached by him. He produces no arguments to support this assertion, any more than he produces evidence to support the principle about which he makes it. And he says, time and again, that whoever understands his principle cannot but accept it and be moved to act upon it; he takes little notice of the fact that men may have interests which close their minds to the principle, or which move them not to apply it even when they have understood and accepted it. But Saint-Simon does produce arguments tending to show that his doctrines are likely to be accepted by the class to which they are addressed because they are in line with the 'true'

---

[1] *A New View of Society* (Penguin Books 1970 edition), First Essay, p. 102.
[2] Ibid., p. 101.

interests of that class; he claims that his insight into the course of social change has taught him what those interests are and how they can be promoted. He produces what he takes to be good evidence that this class is already so placed in society that it has power enough to do what he urges upon it. His arguments, no doubt, were not as sound as he thought them, but then neither were Marx's when he discussed the 'true' interests and future destiny of the proletariat. That is not to my present point, however, which is merely that Saint-Simon's attitude to the *industriels*, the class whose cause he espoused, was essentially the same as Marx's to the proletariat. He, too, thought that he was taking large and sufficient account of 'objective conditions'. We may therefore say that, in at least one sense, he was no more utopian than Marx. I shall say more later of the mistakes made by the early socialists about the success likely to attend their efforts, and how their mistakes compare with Marx's.

3. *Their Dislike of the State*

The early socialists were almost all of one mind in predicting that, as a result of the reforms they advocated, the use of force to maintain order would greatly diminish. Society had hitherto enabled a small privileged class to exploit the rest of the community; it had been divided into rich and poor, and the rich had needed to defend their property. Though this exploitation and that division could now be shown to be necessary at a particular stage of social evolution – though they could now be justified retrospectively as essential parts of a process leading to a desirable end – they had had to be maintained by force. They were practices and institutions made necessary by the ignorance of mankind, and therefore capable of rational justification. While that ignorance lasted, while they were justifiable, force was necessary to maintain them, because the ignorant could not otherwise be induced to accept them; but as soon as the ignorance was dispelled, they ceased to be justifiable. If the unprivileged and the poor had been enlightened enough to understand their necessity, they would already have ceased to be necessary. Seen as elements in an unavoidable process, exploitation and inequality can be justified rationally, but by the time that most men are capable of appreciating these reasons the need for exploitation and inequality has disappeared. Force to maintain order is necessary and therefore reasonable only while reason in most men is still defective, because not sufficiently educated. In the societies of the future, as imagined by the socialists, men will see that the rules they are expected to obey, whether customary or deliberately made, are in the common interest, and they will therefore want to obey them. They will be societies where, for the first time, every man's interest will be in keeping with the common interest, and everyone will be enlightened enough to see that it is so. Temptations to disobey the rules, though they will arise, will do so much less frequently than they do now, and will ordinarily be much weaker. Therefore the mere pressure of public opinion will be enough to maintain social discipline.

We need not suppose that even the most sanguine of the early socialists believed that in the future society of equals (and each of them conceived of it in his own way[1]) nobody would ever be unreasonable or violent. The use of force to maintain order ceases to be necessary, not where everyone is always reasonable and pacific, but where there is so little to be gained by violence, and so much to be lost, even in the short run, that whoever is violent, as soon as he begins to calm down, sees that he has made a mistake. His anger, and the violence it leads to, isolate him morally, and this isolation must be painful to him unless he is an *enemy of society* – that is to say, unless he has been so treated by society as to reject the values it upholds. But this, in the just society as the socialists imagined it, never happens; no man is an enemy of society. And the painful moral isolation ceases as soon as the offender sees the error of his ways. There may be some violence, and therefore a need for those directly exposed to it to use force to defend themselves; but there is no need for the use of organized force, no need for the infliction of punishment by a regular process in the name of the community. This is an extreme position which only some of the socialists took up fully, though many of them were attracted by it.

Rousseau also believed that in his ideal society, which he thought of as a community of equals, rules would be in the common interest and citizens would ordinarily see that they were so. He also believed that, where there is equality, there are no enemies of society. And yet he did not say that in the society of equals there would be no need of organized force to maintain social discipline. Why was Rousseau so much less hopeful than Saint-Simon or Fourier?

---

[1] Saint-Simon attacked the dogma of equality as Rousseau preached it; he did not want all men taking part in the making of the laws; he welcomed hierarchy and was willing to tolerate considerable inequalities of wealth. As much can be said of his disciples, except that they went further than he did in condemning private inheritance. It would be misleading to say that Saint-Simon and his disciples wanted a society of equals, since they did not want what was ordinarily understood by that term. But they did believe in equality of opportunity, preaching the doctrine, *from each according to his ability, and to each according to his work.*

No doubt, Rousseau never supposed that citizens can discover the common interest merely by getting at the facts and reflecting upon them, nor did he believe that they will come to desire it merely by getting to know it. He believed that citizens acquire knowledge of the common interest and the desire to promote it by taking an active part in managing the affairs of the community. If I have understood his doctrine of the general will rightly, Rousseau did not imagine that the common interest can be discovered by a mere process of calculation, by finding out how best to reconcile particular interests. He believed, rather, that a common interest and particular interests in keeping with it emerge together in the process of men's living among one another as equals, which they can do only if they all take part in the making of law. Rousseau did not admit that the common interest can be discovered by experts, precisely because he did not see it as something which can be determined by anyone who knows the facts and whose logic is sound. Nor did he allow that it can emerge from the mere interplay of particular interests, as some of the classical economists thought. Nobody was further than he was from believing in a natural harmony of interests. There is no harmony of interests until men have acquired notions of justice and the desire to be just – until they have become moral persons, so that even their particular interests are the interests of moral persons. But, we may ask, could not Rousseau have insisted on all this (and therefore on much that the early socialists took no notice of) and yet have allowed that in the just society there would be no need of organized force to maintain social discipline?

Certainly, if he had allowed it, he would not have been guilty of inconsistency. Why, then, did he not allow it? Was it merely that he was less hopeful than the socialists, less inclined to believe that – in the just society – the passions moving men to injustice would be much weaker than they were in his day? This would, I think, be too simple an explanation. Rousseau did believe that the motives to injustice would be weaker in a society of equals, but it was not only because he differed from the socialists about the extent to which they would be weakened that he never imagined the just society without organized force. In Rousseau's just society, man is free and also just because he has an internal censor who agrees with the external judge. His freedom does not consist in the absence of passions moving him to break the law; it consists in his wanting to be law-abiding because he sees that the law is just, even though his passions sometimes tempt him to break it. Admittedly, the more just a man is, the weaker in him the passions making for injustice. As I remarked earlier, Rousseau does not see the just man as a moral hero gaining one hard victory after another over his evil passions. But neither does he see him as giving free play to all his passions because they are all either harmless or good; he sees him as a moral or self-disciplined person, and he sees this self-discipline as intimately bound up with a law imposed by all upon each. Where there is no internal censor there is no moral freedom, which is the only kind of freedom that a social being can achieve fully, even in ideal conditions (the conditions described in the *Social Contract*); and there is no internal censor where there is no external judge. What is wrong ought to be *punishable*, not because these two terms are synonymous, but because where men are not liable to punishment the sense of wrong is weakened in them. Discipline is needed because men's unjust passions are strong. That is true. But it is also true that discipline weakens those passions. To be happy, man needs a discipline which he is convinced is just, and can have it only in a society so constructed that the internal censor agrees with the external judge. This is an idea not dreamt of in the philosophies of the early socialists.

The doctrine that, in society, rationally organized government is supplanted by administration will always be associated with Saint-Simon.[1] If he was not the first to expound it, he invented the formula which gives neatest expression to it. Government gives way to administration; the prime function of those who control society ceases to be the maintenance of order by the organized use of force and becomes the management of the resources of the community to ensure that they are used to its best advantage. And the work of management is to be done by experts, by the persons who have proved their ability to undertake it. To begin with, Saint-Simon accepted the parliamentary system, though without noticeable enthusiasm and without pressing for extensions of the franchise. But, eventually, he came to reject political democracy and the parliamentary system on the ground that they attribute to the people a competence which the people lack. The people generally do not decide who is to practise medicine or be an engineer; it is important to them that doctors and engineers should be competent, but they are unable to act as judge of their competence. Of this they are aware, and therefore do not claim the right to make these decisions. The management of the community's resources is no less a matter for experts than medicine or engineering. The people will come in time to know this and will

---

[1] See especially his *Système industriel*, tomes I and III in the *Oeuvres de Saint-Simon et Enfantin* (Paris 1869), XXI.177–8 and XXIII.91.

not want to undertake what they are incompetent to do; they will not want to damage themselves.

In the sixth letter of *L'Organisateur*, Saint-Simon describes how he thinks this management should be constituted; it is not the only scheme of its kind which he put forward, but it serves as well as any to illustrate his conception of what management is and how it should be carried on. He puts forward a plan of administration by three chambers, of which the first, the chamber of invention, is to consist of artists and engineers whose function is to make plans and to explain them; the second, the chamber of examination, is to consist of scientists who examine the plans made by the first chamber and who also control education; while the third, the chamber of execution, or deputies, is to consist of the heads of business enterprises who will alone approve and put into effect plans proposed by the first chamber and examined by the second. It is not made clear how these three chambers are to be recruited, but, since they are chambers of experts and Saint-Simon is contemptuous of political democracy as the French revolutionaries conceived of it, it is clear that they are not to be elected by the people generally. The name of the third chamber, the *Chamber of Deputies*, does, however, suggest that Saint-Simon thought it might be elected by much the same persons as elected the lower chamber under the restored monarchy. That electorate was narrow and consisted for the most part of the better-to-do members of what Saint-Simon called the industrial class. In that class he included everyone who worked and whose work was useful to society; he included in it both entrepreneurs and wage-labourers, as well as scientists and artists. But he insisted that the natural leaders of that class were the entrepreneurs, and especially the more substantial among them – those who came to be called the 'captains of industry'. Saint-Simon thought them the men best suited to control an 'industrial society'; his complaint against them was not that they lacked capacity but that they were too diffident. He thought it his mission in life to persuade them to assume the over-all control of production, which was precisely what he meant by the administration of society as distinct from its government.

The 'industrial society' (whose prophet he thought he was) would be a society of equals, and yet it would be hierarchical. The ablest would rule, and everyone would be rewarded according to the contribution he made to the community. True equality consists, according to Saint-Simon, not in everyone's taking an equal part in the management of common affairs (which, in any case, is impossible as well as undesirable); nor in everyone's getting the same income no matter how little useful the work he does; but in everyone's having the chance to contribute as much as he is by nature capable of doing and being rewarded according to his contribution. If every man's position in society depends on his usefulness to it, and if all men are sufficiently educated to see that it is so, then hierarchy is acceptable to all and there can be effective authority with almost no use of force. Saint-Simon does not forbid the use of organized force or even predict its complete disappearance; he is content to say that the longer 'industrial society' endures the less the need for such force, and that those who apply it perform only a subordinate function.

Of the early socialists, only Saint-Simon pays much attention to the problem of political (or, as he might prefer to put it, *administrative*) organization on a large scale. The others, for the most part, confine themselves to explaining how the small communities they advocate should be run (either taking the established political system for granted or else passing severe judgements upon it without troubling to say how it should be reformed); or they wish for and foretell the disappearance of the 'bureaucratic state'; or they accept it and lay new functions upon it, demanding only that it be made democratic.

Fourier's ideal community – the *phalanx*, lodged in what he terms a *phalanstery* – is to consist of about 1600 persons; it is to be so organized that everyone will want to do what it is in the common interest that he should do, and so there will be no coercion. There will be officials to organize the work of the community, and Fourier foresees that they will be elected. Though each phalanx will be largely self-sufficient, it cannot be so entirely; there will be movements of persons and goods from phalanx to phalanx. Fourier does not see mankind in the future divided into innumerable small communities shut off from one another; and, certainly, there is no reason for supposing that co-operative production, even by groups of only about 1600 persons, makes administration on a large scale less necessary than the productive system of France as he knew it. Yet Fourier, who goes minutely into the organization of the phalanx, touches but lightly upon problems insoluble inside it; indeed, he is scarcely aware that there are such problems. He does not suggest that there will be no need for administration outside the phalanx when all men shall have become members of one, but he thinks it enough that there should be a loose federal structure which leaves almost intact the autonomy of the small community in which alone he delights.

Owen and Thompson also produced schemes for co-operative production, and they both took it for granted that these co-operatives would be run democratically by their members. The prime function of such communities would be, not to keep the peace, but to organize labour efficiently and to distribute its fruits justly; it would be, in the language of Saint-Simon, *administration* rather than *government*. Owen supposed that the communities would be formed by persuading workers to join them, getting well-to-do men of goodwill to put up the money needed to launch them, and even by enlisting the government's support. Thompson, much less inclined to believe in the goodwill of the rich and the powerful, expected the workers to provide most of the money needed to found the communities and hoped that the trade unions might take the initiative in founding them. Owen was not much interested in strictly political questions. Presumably he accepted the parliamentary system as he found it in his own country; at least he did not attack it, and seems to have believed that some form of national government would always be needed to see to the defence of the country and to look after its external affairs, and might eventually carry out certain economic functions; but he never made it clear what those functions would be.

Thompson, as might be expected of a disciple of Bentham, was a more convinced democrat. He favoured a system of provincial, state and national legislatures elected by the people grouped in communes. Every law voted by a higher legislature must also receive the assent of a majority of the legislatures inside the region subject to it. He proposed many other devices to ensure that laws would, as far as possible, be acceptable to the persons required to obey them; he advocated the referendum and the recall. He also favoured the popular election of all officials, including judges. But Thompson, despite his much greater interest in government and his much stronger devotion to democracy, was no more interested than Owen in the control of production and exchange outside the co-operatives. Neither of them thought in terms of a national economy to be managed to the greatest advantage of a vast community numbering millions of souls. Therefore they never put the question first raised by Saint-Simon: What is the structure of authority appropriate to a vast economy centrally controlled, an economy whose resources are used as efficiently as possible to satisfy the wants of millions of persons, most of whom are strangers to one another? This question meant no more to them than to Fourier, even though they accepted industrialism much more whole-heartedly than he did, and refrained, as he did not, from disparaging the parliamentary type of democracy dear to the radicals.

Louis Blanc wanted the State to control all the banks, the factories, the railways, the insurance companies and the larger commercial enterprises; and he also wanted manhood suffrage. Small businesses should remain in private hands. Like many social democrats in the West today, he called for an economy divided into a 'private' and a 'public sector', over which the State should exercise a general control. But he never really went into the question of how the State should manage the economy and the public sector, and how this management could be reconciled with effective democracy. He also neglected the question put by Saint-Simon: What is the structure of authority appropriate to a large-scale economy, centrally controlled?

Proudhon is much the most difficult to understand of all the early socialists. Bouglé, speaking of one of his earlier works, called it 'a hasty and apparently feverish self-examination of an autodidact with too many ideas'.[1] This could be said almost as truly of his later works, including even the best of them, *De la Justice dans la Révolution et dans l'Église*. Proudhon sees the course of history as a slow process whereby men acquire an ever deeper understanding of justice and of other 'eternal' ideas. If anyone could grasp these ideas intuitively, he could show men how to get peace and absolute justice. But all men are children of their times, and the wisest are only a little wiser than their own generation. Mankind have therefore come slowly and painfully by the knowledge which brings peace and justice. This peace and this justice, when men come to possess them fully, will not be an order maintained by force or rules made by a government and applied, albeit impartially, to its subjects. There will be neither organized force nor laws made by a central authority controlling the lives of millions of persons, an authority whose very size ensures that it can never be truly responsible to those required to accept its decisions. In the place of legislation, Proudhon puts contract or agreement. Guided by common principles of justice, individuals will form groups by mutual consent, and neither individuals nor groups will be bound by anything apart from the principles of justice and agreements freely accepted. There will be no authority above the contracting parties to enforce their contracts, to decide how they are to be understood, or to set limits to them. This, at least, is how I interpret a passage from Proudhon, which seems to put his position more clearly than many others.[2]

He does not explain what is to happen when some contracts are

---

[1] Célestin Bouglé, *La Sociologie de Proudhon* (Paris 1911), p. 86.
[2] See Proudhon's *General Idea of the Revolution in the Nineteenth Century (Idée générale de la Révolution au XIX siècle)* of 1851 (London 1923 edition), Fourth Study, p. 112: '*Commutative justice*, the *reign of contract*, the *industrial* or *economic system*, such are the different synonyms for the idea which by its accession must do away with the old systems of *distributive justice*, the *reign of law*, or in more concrete terms, *feudal, governmental* or *military* rule. The future hope of humanity lies in this substitution.'

found to be incompatible with others; or when a contract made by two individuals or groups is deemed by third parties to be injurious to them; or when the parties to a contract disagree about how it is to be interpreted and cannot agree on an arbitrator. Does he imagine that such things will not occur in a society in which certain necessarily rather abstract principles of justice are shared by everyone? It seems to have escaped his notice that in every society, even when there are bitter disputes inside it, there are many principles of justice shared in common.

The system whereby contract takes the place of law Proudhon called *mutualist*, and admitted that it could work well only on a small scale. He therefore favoured loose federations of small communities or associations. But he never undertook to show how these federations can hold together if the associations inside them differ strongly on matters of policy. Yet he did not deplore the increasing division of labour or the use of machinery on a large scale; he did not want to confine men to methods of production which make it easy and natural for them to form small and almost self-sufficient communities. He was blind where Rousseau's vision was clear; he did not see that it is impossible to have a highly industrial society of small communities loosely federated.

Sometimes the Marxian doctrine of the *withering away* of the State is traced back to Saint-Simon and to the distinction he made between government and administration. Certainly, Engels also made this distinction and understood it in part as Saint-Simon had done. The formula is that the *government* of *persons* will give way to the *administration of things*; and this is taken to mean that there will be some form of social control of production but no force used by a hierarchy of officials to maintain obedience to the law. Yet the Marxian doctrine of the withering away of the State is more than another way of saying what had already been said by Saint-Simon. It is also a prediction that in the classless society there will be no bureaucracy, no elaborate and highly centralized administration. There is implicit in it Proudhon's promise that, in the society of equals, contract will take the place of legislation. The 'withering away' of the State implies more than the disappearance of organized force; it also carries with it the suggestion that there will be no law as we know it, no rules made to control the actions of millions of persons by sovereign legislatures, no professional courts to settle disputes about how the rules apply to particular cases, no vast executive hierarchy to carry out policies made by a handful of leaders on behalf of an immense community. But all this, though quite in the spirit of Proudhon, is not at all in the spirit of Saint-Simon.

Clearly, we cannot say that the early socialists neglected political questions. We have seen that two of the most important of them, Saint-Simon and Proudhon, had a great deal to say about government in the ordinary broad sense of the word and not only in the narrow sense peculiar to the socialists who distinguished it from administration. They reflected about government, its uses in the contemporary world and its place in the better world predicted by them. We have seen that some of them paid great attention to it, and yet their theories are not, for the most past, impressive.[1] They were misled by their hopes and their fears. Because they disliked the use of force to maintain order, they easily persuaded themselves that force would no longer be needed when all men were educated and production was rationally organized. It seemed to them that they had plenty of evidence that force was used in the present, and had been used in the past, by the idle rich, the privileged and the secure, to keep the ignorant, the exploited and the insecure subservient to them, and so they concluded that in a society without ignorance, exploitation and insecurity there would be no need for organized force. But, even if we suppose that all the facts they pointed to in support of their argument were well established (and they mostly were), the conclusion they wanted to reach does not follow. For these are not the only relevant facts. It may be true that where there is no organized force there cannot be unearned privilege and regular exploitation of the poor by the rich, but it does not follow that where there is no privilege and no exploitation there is no need for force. They were so intent on showing that the force they abominated served purposes which it could not serve in a society of equals that they never stopped to enquire what other purposes it served.

Some of the early socialists went much further than to condemn force; they were suspicious of all authority. They disliked the modern State as much for being an elaborate and immensely powerful hierarchy – a vast administrative machine – as for being an organ of force and an instrument in the hands of the wealthy and privileged. They wanted to preserve the individual from the hazards, the waste and the injustice of a competitive economy *and* from the pressure of a gigantic, monstrous, many-tentacled State. They persuaded themselves that this monster owed its being to poverty, exploitation

---

[1] I say *for the most part* because in some ways they *are* impressive. Saint-Simon was perhaps the first to see the need for economic planning on a large scale in an industrial society, and this planning – which he called administration as distinguished from government – differed in kind as well as in scale from ordinary business management. Proudhon, moreover, was a shrewd critic of parliamentary democracy.

and inequality – that the same causes which had made force necessary had also allowed bureaucracy to flourish. It seems not to have occurred to them that in mediaeval Europe (not to speak of other parts of the world) where the governmental machine had been much smaller and simpler than in the Western Europe of their day, there had been as much inequality and perhaps more oppression. They favoured small communities in which there would be little or no officialdom, in which such administration as might be needed would be done in their spare time by men always under the eye of their fellows. They deluded themselves into believing that the most important decisions affecting men's lives could be taken within these communities, even in a region as technically advanced and as socially mobile as Western Europe in the first part of the nineteenth century. With this belief to sustain them, they felt themselves justified in sparing but little attention for the administrative structure which they did not deny would need to be superimposed on the communities they described more fully, and often in loving detail.

That the political theories of the early socialists who produced anything deserving the name of political theory were unrealistic, can hardly be denied. But we must – when we consider Marx's accusation against them that they were utopian – make a distinction which Marx did not make. What is it that is unrealistic about their theories? Is it their accounts of how the society of equals would be organized, or is it their beliefs about how it would come into being? These accounts we have already discussed and have conceded that they are unrealistic. But this is not what Marx had in mind when he called the early socialists utopian. He was not concerned so much with the shortcomings of this side of their theories as with the inadequacy of their views about how society could be changed. True, he refrained from the elaborate descriptions in which they delighted, but his conception of an egalitarian society – though he gave only the briefest and broadest indications – owed much to these descriptions. He followed the example they set in predicting the disappearance of the State, both as an organ of force and as a centralized administrative hierarchy. If, then, Marx and Engels were less utopian than the early socialists, it must be because they had more realistic ideas about how society could be transformed.[1] I shall come back to this question later in another connection.

---

[1] There is also a third sense in which wholesale reformers may be called utopian. We may not trouble to criticize them on the ground that their visions of the ideal society are unrealistic. We may think it wasted labour to object to these visions on specific grounds; we may object more generally that it is unreasonable to prepare

4. *Their 'Materialism'*

Rousseau condemned society for multiplying men's wants indefinitely. He was no ascetic and did not preach austerity; he did not think it good for men's souls that their desires should be frustrated or the flesh mortified. That society was best which produced in men no desires they could not satisfy. Society, as he knew it, was evil because it caused men to want so much that they could not get and so much that did not satisfy them when they got it. That was one reason why he preached the simple life.

Another reason connected with this one was that he disliked the social and political effects of an extensive division of labour. The more numerous men's wants, the greater the division of labour needed to produce what satisfies them; and the greater the division of labour, the larger the number of persons on whose labour each man depends. But Rousseau thought that a political community could not be truly independent unless it was economically self-supporting, or at least not dependent on foreigners except for what its citizens could easily do without. More important still, he believed that a large community could not be truly democratic. Therefore, where there is an extensive

---

schemes for the future because men, being limited by the ideas of their own time, cannot predict what the future will be like, since those who come after them will have ideas different from theirs. Marx and Engels, when they called the more speculative of the early socialists utopian, also had such an objection in mind. Now, it might be held that this is an objection which would come better from Burke than from them. If what is to come after cannot be foreseen, is not the revolutionary – the man who wants society completely transformed – merely destructive? He aims at putting an end to what exists without knowing what will take its place. What reason can he have for believing that the unknowable future will be better than the past?

But it is to do less than justice to Marx and Engels to turn the tables on them in this way. True, sometimes they speak as if – the moral values of each age being peculiar to it – there can be no sense in saying that one age is better than another; and sometimes, also, they speak as if it were impossible to predict what our successors will think desirable. And yet, in spite of this, they are believers in moral progress: believers in more than the extension of human knowledge and power. They believe that the course of history is a gradual progress to a type of society whose moral values will be in keeping with the ambitions and opportunities which men will have inside it. They also believe that we can already know what the basic values of that society will be – that we can know that it will be a society of equals. At the same time, by calling the early socialists utopian, they imply that we cannot know how that society will be organized. This position, so far, is not unreasonable. But, given that position, it is unreasonable to predict the withering away of the State, if this means the disappearance of bureaucracy. For, if we do not know how the society of equals will be organized, how can we know that it will dispense with bureaucracy? Can we know it, because bureaucracy is incompatible with equality? But how can we know that future generations will not know how to reconcile bureaucracy with equality?

division of labour, a community large enough to be self-supporting is too large to be democratic; it is too large to allow all its members to take an active part in the making of law. It cannot be a true society of equals because it is divided into two parts, of which the smaller makes the laws and the larger is required to obey them without having helped to make them. Moreover, production for and dependence on distant markets make producers and consumers dependent on middlemen who grow rich at their expense. Economic and political inequalities reinforce one another. This reason for disliking the multiplication of wants goes, in Rousseau's mind, with the belief that where there are great inequalities, men come to have insatiable ambitions and implacable resentments. They have wants which stand in the way of their getting happiness; they are moved by an obsessive need to preserve and to enhance the marks of their superiority. They do not want what really satisfies them, but what they imagine gives them worth in the eyes of others. Rousseau did not use the word *competitive*, which belongs to a later period when the influence of the classical economists affected all types of social theory; but he certainly hated what later came to be known as the competitive spirit. He was not an economist; he did not have in mind the competition of entrepreneurs for the market or of workers for jobs. The competition he deplored was the ceaseless striving to get ahead of others and to appear important to them; and, though he was no economist and had only the vaguest ideas about the functioning of the economy which Adam Smith was to describe, he did claim to see a close connection between its size and complexity and this striving.

The early socialists condemned both the sort of competition which offended Rousseau and the sort described by the economists. But they did not follow Rousseau in deploring the multiplication of wants. On the contrary – like Mandeville and Hume, like Bentham and the Utilitarians, like most of the Encyclopaedists – they welcomed it and took it for a mark of progress. The more men's wants multiply, the greater the need for peaceful collaboration between them and the greater the cohesion of society, provided, of course, that wants do not increase faster than the ability to satisfy them. What was wrong with industrial society was not that it multiplied men's wants, for it also multiplied the wherewithal to satisfy them. What was wrong was that it was so organized that it gave the largest rewards to idlers and the smallest to the industrious who could not afford to purchase the fruits of their industry. It was also wasteful, producing more than was needed to satisfy some wants and too little to satisfy others; its economy was blindly competitive and liable to sudden and disastrous crises. The remedy was to organize production more rationally and to distribute what was produced more justly.

Saint-Simon was perhaps the most whole-hearted exponent of these views. Of the major French socialists, he was the farthest removed in spirit from Rousseau. The same cause which multiplies men's wants not only increases their capacity to satisfy those wants but also enhances the social importance of a class enlightened enough to know how to organize production rationally and how to distribute its fruits justly. The cause is the progress of science and technology, and the class are the leaders of industry. It seemed obviously desirable to Saint-Simon that production should increase as rapidly as possible, so long as it increased smoothly and was aimed at satisfying the wants of all classes. In this he had much the same conception of happiness as Bentham. The more we want, provided we can get what we want, the happier we are. The workers, the most numerous and poorest class, have more unsatisfied wants than the other classes, and therefore it is the prime duty of society to satisfy their wants.

Proudhon did not have the same enthusiasm as Saint-Simon for increasing production; he was more concerned to ensure that the worker got the full product of his labour, and to decrease the authority of man over man. He cared more for equality and freedom than for productivity. Nevertheless, he welcomed the use of machinery and the wealth it brought. He was always the friend of the small man against the powerful and the rich, and shared more of Rousseau's likes and dislikes than any of the other socialists. But he did not preach the simple life or condemn the technical progress which made life complicated. Nor did most of the other socialists, English and French. When Owen (in the memoir known as *Mr. Owen's Report on the Poor*) explained that the widespread distress in England after the Napoleonic wars was due to a great increase in machine production – stimulated by the needs of a country at war and followed by an abrupt falling off of demand with the coming of peace – he took care to add that to destroy this machinery would be absurd. He wanted an England continually growing in wealth, and we may assume that Thompson, a good Utilitarian, also wanted it. Hodgskin's quarrel with the capitalist economy was not that it multiplied men's wants and complicated their lives beyond the point compatible with freedom and equality; it was merely that it deprived the worker of the product of his labour. Hodgskin believed in progress, and thought of it (after the fashion of his day, which was the fashion of almost everyone except Rousseau) as both material and moral. The natural increase of population, leading to an extended division of labour and to the accumulation of knowledge and technical improvements, makes for progress. It is true that some of the early socialists disliked factory production, but they disliked it because it made work monotonous and degrading, and not because a rapid increase in wealth multiplies wants and produces a type of society in which men are unable to be equal and free.

There is one important, though only partial, exception to this general statement. Fourier certainly shared some of the fears which moved Rousseau to extol the simple life. He believed that in industrial society there are three kinds of waste: there are idlers who in a properly constituted society would be producers; there is inefficiency; and there are things produced in abundance giving little or no pleasure. It was the first two kinds of waste, more than the third, that Fourier attacked. But he did also attack the third kind, saying that in industrial society the rich accumulate luxuries which add nothing to their happiness, while the poor envy them their lot. Thus we have society divided into two classes, neither of them truly satisfied, of which the poorer envy the richer largely because they have illusions about them. This is an argument very much in the style of Rousseau. So also is Fourier's attack on commerce. Widely felt emotions, he tells us, are rarely mistaken, and in most countries traders have been despised. He approves Christ's rebuke to the merchants driven from the temple: 'You have made of my house a den of thieves.' He concedes that the ancients went perhaps too far in their contempt for traders, but that is a better fault than to exalt them, as is done in industrial society. For there the merchant and the banker call the tune. They are the middlemen, the controllers of the market, the speculators who levy tribute on consumer and producer, and who create disorder by their manoeuvres to increase their profits. Fourier sees free competition in industrial society leading inevitably to a kind of mercantile feudalism – to the dependence of the producer (both the manual worker and the manager) on the merchant and the banker, the real masters of society. These are arguments quite in the spirit of Rousseau, though they are clearer and better worked out than anything on similar topics from Rousseau's pen. The phalanx is an economy organized to do without the middleman – the manipulator of the market and creator of insecurity, the man more interested in making profits than in seeing that needs are met. The phalanx excludes him but welcomes the honest owner of property, who, by joining it, thereby proves that he wants his property used to good effect. The phalanx also excludes the factory and includes only the workshop, because the factory makes the producer a mere tender of machines, taking all pride and pleasure out of his work, because it is unhealthy, and because the goods it produces are shoddy.

Yet Fourier did not follow Rousseau in praising the simple life. Nor did he attack the economy of his day because it extended the division of labour too far and made life too complicated to allow of genuine democracy. His reasons for keeping the phalanx small had nothing to do with the conviction that men can be equal and free only when they can all take a direct part in making the laws they are required to obey. Fourier was an ardent hedonist. He believed that in the phalanx all men's pleasures, physical and mental, would be more varied and more exquisite than the pleasures of the rich in contemporary France. He was not himself a voluptuary; he was too poor and also too much a man with a mission for that. But the men and women living in his phalansteries were to enjoy life abundantly, uninhibited by the scruples which now spoil the pleasures of civilized man.

In 1848, in a debate in the Constituent Assembly as to whether the *droit de travail* (the right of the worker against the State that it should provide work for him when he is unemployed) should be included in the constitution, Tocqueville asked, 'What then. . .is socialism?' and answered his own question in these words: 'It is a vigorous, sustained, immoderate appeal to the material passions. . . .As has been claimed, "It wants the rehabilitation of the flesh". . .and. . .unlimited consumption.'[1] Tocqueville was seldom grossly inaccurate, even in his attack upon what he detested. The socialists did not preach the virtues of poverty; they wanted the poor to live abundantly, as the rich lived. They wanted wealth to grow fast, believing that the faster it grew the happier men would be, provided only that wealth were justly distributed. What Tocqueville forgot is that the Encyclopaedists in France and the Utilitarians in England had appealed no less vigorously to the same passions, with only this difference – that their appeal, though addressed formally to all men, was directed in practice almost entirely to the educated classes, while the socialists directed their appeal either to the poor or to the consciences of the rich on behalf of the poor.

Durkheim makes this materialism – this assumption that the multiplication of wants is desirable so long as they can be satisfied – one of the two distinguishing marks of nineteenth-century socialism as compared with older egalitarian and communist doctrines; the other

---

[1] 'Discours prononcé à l'Assemblée Constituante dans la discussion du projet de Constitution (12 September 1848), sur la question du droit de travail', in the *Oeuvres complètes de Tocqueville* (Paris 1864–66), IX.539–40.

is the desire for some form of social control of production. Plato, he says, was not concerned to increase wealth or to rationalize production; he wanted the rulers to own all things in common because he believed that this was a condition of their being whole-heartedly devoted to the good of the State. Sir Thomas More was concerned with the individual rather than the State, and his Utopia is so organized as to make its citizens virtuous and contented. Though in Utopia everyone works and no one goes hungry, it is not thought desirable that wealth should increase indefinitely, and the Utopians do not ask themselves how production should be controlled in order to be more efficient. Durkheim sees the same indifference to the increase of wealth and the social control of production even in eighteenth-century writers who attacked the established system of property before 1789 – even in such writers as Mably and Morelly. If they wanted private property abolished, it was because they thought it corrupted morals; it was not in order to make easier the rational control of production, nor to satisfy material wants more abundantly.

Durkheim is substantially right, though he makes the contrast rather too sharply. More's Utopians do not aim at increasing wealth indefinitely; they aim rather at reducing the labour needed to produce the necessaries of life so as to leave as much time as possible for the cultivation of the mind. Nevertheless, the Utopians live commodiously, and the aged and the sick are provided for. There is social control of production; the phylarch or head bailiff, elected annually, by every group of thirty families, allots work and sees to it that it is done properly. Everyone who has not earned exemption from manual labour by proving himself worthy of promotion to the order of scholars must be trained for husbandry and must engage in it, and must also learn and follow a useful trade. In Utopia there is elaborate direction of labour and therefore also planned production. But all this is not done to make production more efficient, as Adam Smith or Saint-Simon or Owen would have understood efficiency; it is not done to ensure that available resources are used to produce the greatest possible quantity of goods and services; it is done to enable the Utopians to live healthy and virtuous lives. So, too, Morelly does not confine himself to proposing common ownership on the ground that private property is corrupting; he also proposes the direction of labour, public works to absorb unemployment, and the closing down of unprofitable industries. He wants to ensure that production as a whole satisfies all needs and that no one is overworked. The communist economy described in the *Code de la nature*, which is only one (and the most extreme) of several projects prepared by Morelly during the course of his life, involves just as much social control of production as the schemes of Saint-Simon, Fourier and Owen. But Morelly never says or even implies that the indefinite increase of wealth is desirable, and his conception of efficient production is not the same as that of the economists and nineteenth-century socialists. It matters to him that the idle should not exploit the industrious, that all who can should work, that no one should be unprovided for, that the vices born of inequality should disappear; but it does not matter to him that production should be so organized as to make men much wealthier than they are. Though he approves of lavish spending on public monuments and festivals, he expects the citizens to live modestly. The communists of the eighteenth century mostly favoured sober living; it was much more Voltaire, Mandeville and Montesquieu, and after them the Encyclopaedists and Utilitarians, who took the accumulation of wealth for a mark of progress and who approved of high living. It was not till the nineteenth century that the champions of the poor – the preachers of equality, the scourges of the idle rich – came to be materialists, in the sense meant by Tocqueville when he spoke of their attachment to 'unlimited consumption'.

5. Their Feminism

Several of the early socialists were ardent feminists. It was indeed to this part of their doctrine (and to an aspect of it likely to shock the bourgeois) that Tocqueville referred, in the speech from which I quoted, when he used the phrase *the rehabilitation of the flesh*. That phrase was invented by Enfantin, who after Saint-Simon's death proclaimed himself one of his disciples; it expressed Enfantin's belief in easy divorce and dislike of the chastity and continence preached by the Church. Fourier, though he thought easy divorce unsuited to the social system of the period in which he lived – the period he termed *civilization* – predicted it for the next period, and even foresaw the eventual disappearance of marriage. He said of the *civilized*[1] that they demand unlimited freedom of trade, where fraud and trickery cry out for restraint by law, but wish to deprive of all freedom the one passion, love, which must be free if men are to be happy and good.

---

[1] This word *civilized* has for Fourier an historical reference, since it refers to people living in the fifth period of social evolution, that of *civilization*. It also has, for him, a pejorative sense, because the social order of the fifth period is, he thinks, irrational and destined to pass away, and indeed in some respects is already passing away. The *civilized* are, in the eyes of Fourier, absurd and also apparently backward.

Attacks on the sanctity of marriage have in themselves nothing to do with feminism; they had been made in the eighteenth century by men whose object had not been to improve the position of women. It is only when existing forms of marriage and conventions of sexual morality are thought to lay a much heavier burden on women than on men that the attack on them deserves to be called feminism. But Fourier and the disciples of Saint-Simon did so regard them. They believed that men had made chattels and servants of women, and that nothing proved this better than the way that women were given in marriage and the wifely duties laid upon them by custom and by law. Some of the disciples of Saint-Simon, to mark their sense of women's equality with men, called God both the Father and the Mother of mankind, and sent a mission to the East to welcome the Woman Messiah, whose coming they expected, of all unlikely places, in Constantinople. Their feminism was as absurd as it was sincere.

Fourier thought it one of the great advantages of the communal living which he preached that it would free women from drudgery in the kitchen and the nursery. The small family living in the small house cannot but deprive the married woman of the opportunity to cultivate her mind, tying her to the home and to menial duties. He even put it forward as a general thesis that social progress can be measured by the extent to which women have moved towards liberty, and decadence by the extent to which they have been deprived of it. Such statements are probably not meant to be taken literally. Fourier no doubt believed that there are other forms of progress besides women's emancipation, and he certainly had no warrant for holding that progress is never made in any direction without also being made in this.[1] But the statement, though palpably false if taken literally, does show how strongly Fourier believed in the emancipation of women.

The disciples of Saint-Simon were not democrats, and were therefore not moved by their feminism to demand political rights for women. Fourier's hopes were confined to the community of the future, the phalanx, where the occupations open to men would also be open to women, who would presumably take part in choosing what officials might be needed; he was not concerned to extend the franchise in merely civilized communities. The most fervent advocate of political rights for women was Thompson, whose *Appeal of One Half the Human Race, Women, against the Pretensions of the other Half,*

[1] Fourier did not deny that the ancient Greeks made great progress in several directions between the Homeric and the classical periods. But women enjoyed greater freedom in the first of these periods than in the second, and there is no reason to believe that Fourier was unaware of this.

Men, to retain them in Political, and thence in Civil and Domestic, Slavery appeared in 1825. Thompson's book was directed against James Mill who, in his article on 'Government' in the supplement to the *Encyclopaedia Britannica* of 1820, had said that the interests of women were included in those of their menfolk, their husbands or fathers, and so, without actually denying the vote to women, had implied that it was not important that they should have it.[1] How, asks Thompson, can Mill, who admits that man is a selfish creature seeking to make others subservient to his will, assume that women's interests are included in those of men? Even children's interests are not included in those of their fathers, or else it would never have been necessary to pass such a law as the Factory Act. The reason for not giving the vote to children is not that their interests are included in their fathers'; it is that they do not know how to use the vote to protect their interests, that they do not know how to use the vote rationally. But Mill does not suppose (what Thompson takes to be obviously false) that women cannot use the vote rationally. Nobody's interest is included entire in anyone else's, and if we tie one person to dependence on another, we enable that other to exploit him or her, and so create a situation making for a greater divergence of interest. And, in any case, it would not be enough to have men, even though they were unselfish, look after women's interests, for women's abilities, like men's, are developed by their having to care for their own and the common interest.

Proudhon was conspicuously not a feminist. Not that he believed in the inferiority of women to men. But he wanted to preserve the family, and therefore resisted any claims made on behalf of women which seemed to him to weaken that institution. He, who wanted to loosen all other social ties, wanted to keep family ties as strong as ever. The child learns to be sociable and just inside the family, where he is under parental discipline, where he is controlled and punished by those who love him. Proudhon believed that the best type of family, the type best suited for the training of the young, exists only where monogamy is the rule and divorce is rare. Women are not inferior to but different from men, and they are happiest and most useful as wives and mothers; they are the creators and preservers of the family, of the most tightly knit and important of social groups, because it is inside it that the child becomes a social and moral being. But, admirable though the family is, larger social groups must not be families writ large; for the family is by nature hierarchic and under paternal authority, while all larger social groups ought to consist only

[1] See Mill's 'Government', in *Utilitarian Logic and Politics*, op. cit., p. 79.

of equals, of men who are not under authority but are bound only by agreements voluntarily made and by a moral law whose sanction is the individual's own conscience. The family is unique; it prepares man by love and coercive discipline for the larger society in which he is eventually to achieve justice without coercive discipline. The discipline of the family will always be needed to educate the child into a rational and sociable adult; it will still be needed when grown men shall have become capable of society without coercive discipline. And to Proudhon it seemed to go without saying, or rather without needing to be proved, that the head of the small monogamous family must be the husband and father, even though the wife and mother is the centre of it and exercises the deeper moral influence.

Marx called Proudhon a *petit-bourgeois* writer, and Marxists have ever since followed this example. There is nothing *petit-bourgeois* about Proudhon's anarchism or his dislike of nationalism, Jacobinism and Bonapartism; the *petit bourgeois* does not want to destroy State power, even though he resents bureaucratic interference with his small business. He does not want the State to tell him what to do with his own, but he does want it to protect him both from the propertyless and from the wealthy. In France, in Proudhon's day, the *petit bourgeois*, when he feared disorder, was inclined to Bonapartism, and when he feared the wealthy, to Jacobinism, both of which Proudhon despised. But Proudhon's defence of the small family, whose natural head he took to be the father, would certainly have been very much to the taste of the lesser bourgeoisie and also of the peasants, whom Marxists have often assimilated to that class.[1] It is, however, possible to insist upon the need to preserve this type of family without treating the father as any more its natural head than the mother.

It is not his wanting to preserve the small family which makes Proudhon manifestly not a feminist; it is rather his defence of paternal authority, and – even more important – his failure to take into account the possibility that, though woman's capacities may be different from man's, she needs to have the same civil and political rights as man if she is to make the best of them. Proudhon believed that men and women excel in different ways, that men have in larger measure the

---

[1] The *bourgeois*, great or small, is, as his name implies, a town–dweller. The point of calling the peasant a *petit bourgeois* is that he is supposed to share many of the political and social attitudes of the artisan and the shopkeeper, the *petit bourgeois* in the strict sense. The supposition is largely correct when made about French peasants in the last century, except that they were much more inclined to Bonapartism than to Jacobinism. It is much further from the truth when made about peasants in Russia and other Slav lands in this century.

qualities making for social superiority outside the family – such as physical strength, power of reasoning and consistency of purpose – while women are more intuitive, have more grace and delicacy of mind and a greater capacity for love. He admitted that the qualities in which they excel are as admirable and as useful to society as any, but he thought them qualities better suited to family life than to conspicuous achievement outside it.

He might have been right. Certainly, many men, and perhaps also many women, would agree with him that the two sexes differ greatly and even that they differ much as he said they do. There is nothing new about his views as to how men and women differ. But it is important to notice that a man or woman might share these views and yet be an ardent feminist. There are two kinds of feminism. We may hold, with Mary Wollstonecraft, that, while women can do all that men can, they have been unjustly deprived by men of the opportunity to do any but menial tasks; or we may hold that women, being by nature different from men, will not, except rarely, want to engage in most of the occupations traditionally reserved for men, but that this is no reason for not giving them the same civil and political rights as men. The socialists who were also feminists did not distinguish between these two kinds of feminism, and therefore did not consciously adhere to either in preference to the other. But I suspect that Enfantin and Fourier were both feminists of the second kind; they probably agreed with Proudhon that women differ greatly from men. They certainly did not want to make men out of women; but they thought that women could not make the best of their capacities unless they were given the same freedom as men, unless they were removed from the tutelage of the other sex. Enfantin and Fourier did not believe in strict monogamy and the close family circle; but it is possible to believe in them without denying that women should have the same rights as men. It is possible to put a high value on chastity and monogamy – to admit that the two sexes differ greatly, mentally and morally as well as physically – and yet to make a strong case for their both having the same civil and political rights. It is possible to insist strongly on natural difference and no less strongly on social equality.

Women feminists have been more inclined to the first kind of feminism than to the second. This is certainly true of Mary Wollstonecraft, whose *Vindication of the Rights of Woman* appeared in 1792; of the English suffragettes before 1914; and perhaps also of Flora Tristan, who was a socialist as well as a feminist. Mary Wollstonecraft and the suffragettes insisted that women are as good as men in all the ways in which men have claimed to be superior; they argued that if women have not in the past excelled in these ways it is because they have been kept down by men; they looked forward to women playing as great a part as men in every sphere hitherto reserved for men. They denied to men every superiority except greater physical strength. They have been accused of a lack of proper pride in their sex, of being envious of the male, of suffering from an acute sense of inferiority unconsciously revealed by the kind of argument they use to show that women are as good as men – arguments tending to prove, not that women's peculiar qualities are as valuable as men's, but that women, given the chance, could do all that men do equally well. This kind of feminism, so its critics say, may in the long run prove burdensome to women, making them competitors with men in spheres where masculine values prevail and where women are therefore likely to be at a disadvantage.

Such criticism, for what it is worth, cannot be justly made of the socialists who were also feminists, for they were mostly feminists of the second kind; they did not want to make women more like men but to give them as good a chance as men to make the best of whatever gifts Nature had endowed them with. This is especially true of the French socialists, perhaps because theirs is the country where women have been most appreciated for being what they are.

II. SAINT-SIMON'S ACCOUNT OF SOCIAL CHANGE. WERE THE EARLY SOCIALISTS UTOPIAN?

I have considered what is common to Rousseau and to the early socialists and also where they differ from him. This comparison serves to draw attention to the ways in which criticism of the established order changed as a result of the French and the industrial revolutions. The early socialists were all radicals of the post-revolutionary epoch, familiar with the hopes raised by the revolution and the disillusionments which followed it. They had lived through immense changes; they had witnessed what had been until then the boldest of all attempts to reconstruct a great society. They were used to change and expected more of it. For all that they deprecated violence, they were revolutionaries in a sense in which Rousseau never was; they aspired to a decisive influence on the course of change. Rousseau had predicted the revolution but had never sought to hasten its coming, or to advise men what they should do when it came. If he was a prophet, he was so rather in the style of the Old Testament; he saw evils all around him and foretold calamity. He saw no connection between the course of events which he deplored and the just society which he described but whose coming he never really hoped for.[1] And he lived before the age of factory production, of which the economists and early socialists took so large account.

Marx, though he claimed to be a scientific socialist in some sense in which the early socialists were not scientific, admitted his debt to them. He had, he believed, superseded them, but he had also taken up elements of their theories into his own. If not always a just, he was, on the whole, a generous, critic of the early socialists – that is to say, generous to most of them except to Proudhon, who was, in any case, more a contemporary than a precursor. What he learnt from the French socialists was, of course, different from what he learnt from the English, for their interests were by no means the same. Though the early socialists were believers in progress; though they were aware that a long process of change had been needed to make society as they knew it; though they held or hoped that it had at last become (or was soon to be) propitious to socialism, they for the most part produced no theories about the course of history. And those of them that did so were French, which is not surprising. For the French had had a great revolution, and it was only natural that they should speculate about it and its causes. Of these philosophies of history (or theories about the course of history) only one, Saint-Simon's, need detain us, not only because Marx owed more to it than to any other, but also because it is much the most interesting in itself. It is more perceptive and suggestive than Fourier's account of the first eight of the thirty-six periods which he allotted to human history, and more of a piece and clearer than Proudhon's far-ranging reflections on the great revolution and the destiny of man. Saint-Simon and Proudhon, because of their extensive interest in history, had more developed ideas than the others about social classes, their rise and decay, and their changing rôles. If they were not the most class-conscious of socialists, they were certainly the socialists who, except for Marx, produced the boldest and most ingenious theories about classes. But the most arresting

---

[1] Goethe is alleged to have remarked that with Voltaire one world ends and with Rousseau another begins. This is true in the sense that Rousseau gave birth to ideas only half understood in his own day, and destined to be more fully understood in a society very different from the one he knew, whereas Voltaire came closer than any other man to being the epitome of his age. Yet Voltaire, very much at home in the society which he dominated intellectually, had not the same forebodings about the future. He was, on the whole, a cheerful pessimist, while Rousseau, who was almost never cheerful, dared not hope in the future, even though he believed in the providence of God and quarrelled with Voltaire for denying it.

psychologist among the early socialists was certainly Fourier; he made
what he believed to be an exhaustive analysis of the human passions,
and sought to show how they are frustrated in the commercial and
industrial society of his day and can be given a free and harmless
outlet in the phalanx, the only fully rational society because the only
one fully adapted to human nature.

As philosophers of history, as speculators about social classes and
their historic rôles, as social psychologists, the French socialists have
more to offer than the English ones. But as economists, and more
particularly as critics of classical economics, it is the English socialists
who excel. The only one of the major French socialists to attempt a
sustained criticism of the classical economists was Proudhon, and he
was nowhere near as acute a critic as either Hodgskin or Thompson. If I
may hazard a generalization, I should say that the French socialists were
broader in their interests and more imaginative, while the English were
more lucid and more rigorous. Owen, no doubt, was both narrow and
vague, as businessmen are apt to be when they take to social theory in
middle age; he was much more popular than Thompson or Hodgskin,
and made a much greater impression on his contemporaries, but to the
student of theory he is perhaps the least interesting of the three.

1. Saint-Simon on the Course of Social Change

It is in the eighth and ninth letters of *L'Organisateur*[1] that Saint-
Simon describes in broad outline the course of social evolution which
transformed feudal society into the industrial society which he urges
the industrialists, supported by the scientists and artists, to take over.

What Saint-Simon calls the feudal and theological system of the
Middle Ages was born, he tells us, in and after the fourth century
of our era, with the triumph of Christianity and the irruption of the
barbarians into the Roman Empire. This system was fully mature
by the eleventh century, but as soon as it reached maturity the seed
of its destruction – the enfranchised commune – appeared inside it.
Before the advent of the commune, the craftsman had been the mere
servant or creature of the feudal lord, as much dependent on him as

[1] It has been said that *L'Organisateur* was written for Saint-Simon by Comte. But
it was published as coming from the pen of Saint-Simon, and the ideas in it are
probably his. Where, as in the third part of the *Catéchisme des Industriels* – the part
called *Système de politique positive* – Comte interprets the master's thoughts very
freely and neglects a part of it which seems important to the master, the work
appears under the name of Comte, who is styled a pupil of Henri Saint-Simon.
But these problems of attribution are not our concern.

the serf who was tied to the soil. With the commune's appearance, the craftsman became an independent producer. Hitherto the wealthy and the powerful had not been producers of wealth; they had not been engaged in industry; they had not been what Saint-Simon calls *industriels*; they had been feudal lords and churchmen. The emergence of the commune made it possible for the producer of wealth – the *industriel* – to grow wealthy and in the course of time to acquire social influence and power.

But until the feudal and theological system was in decay, the feudal lords and the men in Holy Orders were not parasites; they performed useful functions. The feudal lords maintained order and protected their dependants from attack; the Church maintained the cultural and moral unity which every society needs. Saint-Simon even says that the feudal system was natural to a society in which the principal means to national prosperity was war.[1]

At about the time that the communes emerged, science was introduced into Europe by the Arabs. According to Saint-Simon's account of the matter (which is not necessarily true), the feudal lords required passive obedience, while the spiritual power demanded complete submission to its teachings. But industrial power is of its nature less arbitrary than military power; the man who directs the labour of others in order to create wealth does not demand passive obedience of his subordinates. He is a man whose skill and experience are greater than theirs, and whose authority over them rests largely on a superiority as evident to them as to him. So, too, masters of science do not demand blind submission of their students; they offer them truths which they support with evidence. The authority of the scientists depends as much (and indeed more) on acknowledged ability as that of the leader of industry; it depends on his ability to offer explanations which satisfy the critical intelligence of those who hear him. Thus the spirit of the old society was quite contrary to the spirit of the new classes growing up inside it – the new society centred in the chartered towns and in the universities founded in them.

Conflict between the old and the new was inevitable but could

---

[1] This, surely, is an absurdity which serves to obscure what is valuable in Saint-Simon's thought. All wealth, as he knew it, is created by labour, whereas war destroys wealth. War may enable some nations to plunder others, but it impoverishes the plundered much more than it enriches the plunderer. It is nonsense to say that in a feudal society war is a means to national prosperity, whereas in an industrial society the means to it is work. The important point which Saint-Simon makes is that, in the first type of society, wealth and power belong to a military caste and a church, while in the second they belong to producers of wealth.

not break out openly while the emergent classes were still weak. The craftsmen in the towns who had obtained charters from kings and feudal lords did not look upon themselves as the enemies of those who had enfranchised them, nor did the universities look upon themselves as enemies of the Church. They did not, and could not, see themselves as the beginnings of a new social order destined to replace the old; they had no conception of themselves as involved in a necessary historical process. For generations they accepted the superiority of the established authorities, of the territorial magnates and the Church. But, inevitably, they acquired interests and attitudes incompatible with the old order.

It was not until the sixteenth century that the old society was openly challenged by the new society to which it had given birth. Luther and the other reformers successfully attacked the authority of the Pope and thereby irretrievably weakened the Church, which had until then dominated society intellectually – and weakened it so much that, even in the countries that remained Catholic, the Church, from being a rival of the monarch, became his subsidiary ally. The struggle against the Spiritual Power occupied the sixteenth and seventeenth centuries, and then came the struggle against the Temporal feudal Power. The commons[1] were too weak to challenge both the monarch and the nobles; and so in England they allied themselves with the nobles against the monarch, while in France they allied themselves with the monarch against the nobles. To contemporaries in these two countries (which Saint-Simon regarded as the most advanced), the main conflict seemed to be in each case between the monarch and the nobility, with the commons playing a minor part; but the historically important conflict in France as well as in England was between the commons and one part or other of the old Temporal Power.

At this point of his narrative, Saint-Simon assesses the importance of three great events: the discovery of America and of the route to India, the invention of printing, and the theories of Copernicus and Galileo. Unless there had been a large increase in trade and considerable scientific progress in the Middle Ages, the journeys of

---

[1] The word *commons* is used here in the same sense as Saint-Simon used the French word *communes*; it refers to the townsmen, the third estate of the *ancien régime*; it therefore excludes the gentry, whose representatives sat in the English House of Commons. The English gentry are equivalent to what the French would call *la petite noblesse*. It would be absurd in a summary of this kind to stop to criticize the many doubtful or misleading statements which Saint-Simon makes; our purpose is not to enquire into the truth of his account of social and political evolution in Western Europe but to consider what kind of account it is, what factors are treated as the most important in explaining social change.

the great navigators would have been impossible, but they in their turn encouraged trade and stimulated enquiry; the tight little world dominated by the feudal lords and the Church was suddenly and greatly enlarged. The invention of printing ensured that the discoveries of scientists and their speculations could reach many more minds than before; it multiplied the impact of mind on mind and so made intellectual activity much greater. The theories of Copernicus and Galileo, offering simpler and clearer explanations better supported by the facts, were fatal to the anthropomorphic theology of the Church; they could not be accommodated to that theology and therefore, as they were more widely accepted, inevitably undermined the authority of the old Spiritual Power.

By the eighteenth century the commons had become strong enough to challenge the entire old order, and science had developed so much, had acquired so great a prestige, that the Protestant attack on the spiritual authority of the Papacy could be expanded into a general attack on every attempt to impose beliefs by coercive methods. It was then that the claim was made for complete freedom of private judgement. 'Thus', we are told, 'the eighteenth century carried the attack on the two Powers (the Temporal and the Spiritual) to its ultimate limits, and completed the ruin of the old system in its parts and as a whole'.[1]

Unfortunately, in France, Louis XIV, having humbled the nobility, abandoned the alliance with the commons and sought the friendship of the defeated power. This mistake, which was continued by his successors, led in the end to the French Revolution. Saint-Simon, when he says this, is not suggesting that, if the three Louis had not made this mistake, the old monarchy could have lasted indefinitely. The old regime was bound to have come to an end, but if the French kings had continued their alliance with the commons – with the rising industrial class – it would have ended without violence. The French Revolution destroyed the monarchy, an institution still popular in France and well adapted to lead the country through the last stages of transition to the full industrial society. The destruction of the monarchy was therefore also a mistake, though the last three kings were to blame for creating the situation which caused the mistake to be made. The monarchy, still having an important function to perform, was re-established. It is interesting to notice that, in speaking of the French monarchy, Saint-Simon passes a judgement which brings to mind one of the fundamental doctrines of Marx. He says, 'The royal

[1] *L'Organisateur*, Huitième Lettre, *Oeuvres de Saint-Simon et Enfantin*, XX.104.

power was soon reconstituted, because it was in France at once the head and the heart of the old system, and could only disappear with it; and a system can only disappear to the extent that another already exists entirely formed and ready to take its place immediately'.[1]

It is only now, looking back on the past, that we can properly understand it; it is only now that historians have accumulated the facts which enable us to discern a necessary course of social evolution. The commons had no sense of the process in which they were involved; the kings who needed money and invited the commons to meetings of the estates to vote taxes did not know that they were strengthening the class destined to destroy the old system. The scientists who put forward the hypotheses incompatible with theology did not know that they were the agents of a vast cultural revolution. The commons, in promoting their interests and making the most of their opportunities, did not know that they were gradually transforming the social order.

The expansion of industry and the progress of science have changed the nature of authority. In industrial society everyone makes a contribution, everyone is a collaborator, and everyone understands that he is engaged in an elaborate enterprise with others. Hierarchy is grounded in differences of ability obvious to all, and social discipline need no longer be military in character, consisting of arbitrary command and unquestioning obedience. In the old society, those who produced no wealth received the greater part of it, and it was therefore necessarily a society of masters and servants. Already, in many industrial enterprises, order results from force of habit and a sense of the common interest, and so it will be eventually in society as a whole. Already, those who are not scientists have learnt to trust those who are; they believe, without being able to prove it, that the earth is round, that it revolves round the sun, and more besides. But they are not credulous, for the beliefs they accept are subject to verification by persons competent to verify them. Even the scientist outside the sphere of his own competence accepts things on trust, just as the layman does. Thus it is that science and industry bring into being a new kind of hierarchy, a new kind of authority,

---

[1] Ibid., pp. 105–6. The second half of this sentence illustrates something else which Saint-Simon shares with Marx: a difficulty in finding words to express his meaning exactly when what he means is at all complicated. His actual words suggest that the old system survives entire until the new system is entirely formed. But Saint-Simon has already shown the old system in process of disappearing as the new system emerges. What he really means is that the old form of government cannot disappear until the new system is completely formed, which suggests that what completes the forming of the new system is the emergence of a class willing and able to take over the direction of society; but that is not what he says.

not known before – a hierarchy and an authority based on proven ability and tested knowledge. Culturally and morally, the people have been weaned away from the old system of authority, temporal and spiritual, and so they 'no longer need to be governed, that is to say commanded. It is enough for the maintenance of order that matters of common interest should be administered'.[1] The people are already mature enough to do without government, and yet they are still governed. The parliamentary regime and full liberty of conscience are the furthest concessions that the old system can make to the new forces arising in its midst without its completely disappearing. The new system, industrially and intellectually, is fully developed; it pervades society but does not yet dominate it. By this Saint-Simon means that the industrial class have not yet taken over control of society; they still do not administer matters of common concern; they have not yet stepped fully into their inheritance. He conceives it to be his mission to persuade them to do it and to persuade the monarch to help them do it. That is why so many of his open letters are addressed 'to the King and to men of industry' or to '*MM les députés* who are men of industry (*industriels*)'.[2]

In the tenth letter of *L'Organisateur*, Saint-Simon considers the situation since 1814. He expects a smooth transition from the parliamentary regime to the sort of administration he has in mind. The leaders of industry already form a large part of the electorate; they have only to vote members of their own class into the chamber quite to alter its character. They have only to take the opportunities open to them, and this they are bound to do in the end. They will then set up an administration along the lines suggested by Saint-Simon in the sixth letter, whose contents we have already touched upon.

He protests that there is nothing utopian about the scheme proposed in the sixth letter; it may seem new, and indeed is new, but it is something for which history has prepared the way: 'It is not I who have formed the constitutional project whose basic principles I have expounded; it is the mass of the European population who have laboured to shape it during the eight centuries which have preceded this one.'[3] He invites his readers to enquire whether his account of the broad course of events since the eleventh century is accurate and whether his project fits in with it, for this is the only valid line of criticism.

[1] *L'Organisateur*, Neuvième Lettre, pp. 144–5.
[2] But not the letters which make up *L'Organisateur*; they are addressed by the author to his compatriots.
[3] *L'Organisateur*, Dixième Lettre, p. 180.

Saint-Simon was not as successful as he had hoped to be in persuading the leaders of industry to take over the direction of society. This lack of success moved him to sharper criticism of the French Revolution and of the ideas associated with it – ideas which were, he thought, turning men's minds away from essentials. During the period of transition from a feudal to an industrial social order, two groups had appeared – the lawyers and the metaphysicians – who now stood in the way of progress. Originally their functions had been useful; the lawyers had served the royal power against the feudal nobles by undermining their privileges, and the metaphysicians had loosened the hold of theology on men's minds. The metaphysicians had, in a sense, been the intermediaries between the theologians and the scientists. They erected their theories on a theological foundation and yet claimed the free exercise of reason. The lawyers, in turn, having once been the agents of the feudal lords, produced a monarchically inspired jurisprudence hostile to feudal pretensions. Unfortunately, when the French Revolution destroyed what remained of clerical and feudal power, the scientists and industrialists – the natural leaders of the new society which had emerged over the last six centuries as a result of their activities – instead of ruling it, left its government to the lawyers and professional politicians. There cannot be an abrupt transition from one system, be it social or intellectual, to another; there is necessarily a long course of change leading from the one to the other, and in this intervening period there emerge institutions, attitudes of mind and social groups which will disappear as soon as the new system is fully established. Liberalism is such an attitude; it is the philosophy of the lawyers and metaphysicians who played so prominent a part in demolishing the old system and in making the French Revolution. This philosophy has acquired an immense prestige, but it is at bottom negative. As the creed of the politicians, the fashionable doctrine of the rights of man was the absurd offspring of pseudo-science – the product, Saint-Simon supposed, of high metaphysics applied to high jurisprudence.[1] The ideas of liberty and equality, as proclaimed by the liberals, effectively challenged the privileges enjoyed by classes which, as the old system decayed, ceased to be useful to society; that was their true and important historical function. But as ideals to be realized in the new society, they are useless and even harmful.

It is absurd to consider every citizen competent in political matters, which are more difficult to understand than, say, chemistry, where

---

[1] See *L'Industrie*, Deuxième and Septième Lettres, and the *Système industriel*, preface, *Oeuvres de Saint-Simon et Enfantin*, XVIII.158 and 175–81, and XXI.8–19.

the authority of experts is undisputed. It is only because politics is not a science that this assumption of universal competence can pass muster; its absurdity will be fully apparent when the study of society and administration has become scientific. Saint-Simon even accuses the lawyers and metaphysicians, whom he calls a bastard class born of the decay of the feudal system, of wanting to become a privileged order. They made the revolution in the name of all Frenchmen but now want to dominate the France which has emerged from the revolution. These negative conceptions of equality and liberty now stand in the way of the positive principle suited to the new industrial society: *from* everyone according to his capacity, and *to* everyone according to his contribution. This is the true principle of equality, which gives to every man rewards and authority in proportion to his ability and willingness to serve the community.[1] And so Saint-Simon, during the last years of his life, thought it his mission to combat the false ideals of the liberals and democrats as well as to persuade the leaders of industry to take charge of society; or, rather, he saw these two things as parts of the same mission.

I shall argue, in discussing Hegel's philosophy of history,[2] that, though it treats history as a necessary course of change, it does not explain how any one stage in that course leads to the one after it; it gives us an account of a variety of stages and seeks to explain how in the later stages the essential nature of Spirit is more adequately realized than in the earlier, but it does not show how the earlier stages change into the later ones. This criticism cannot be made of Saint-Simon; he does offer an account of how feudal society evolves into industrial society. No doubt, his account is far from satisfactory, but it is an attempt to do something which Hegel never attempted. If we were to describe a child's condition, physical and mental, at various stages of its growth, explaining how at each stage it was closer to maturity than at the stage before it, we should be using Hegel's method; but if we tried to explain how it had passed from each stage to the next, we should be using the method of Saint-Simon and of Marx.

Saint-Simon's account is open to two kinds of criticism: we can object to his interpretation of the facts, or we can object to the

[1] See *L'Industrie*, Sixième Lettre; the *Système industriel*, tome II; and the *Catéchisme des Industriels*, premier cahier, ibid., XVIII.163–4, XXII.17 and XXXVII.35, 42 and 61. In the *Système industriel*, Saint-Simon calls the negative and arbitrary conception of equality 'le dogme de l'égalité turque', the exact opposite of the positive principle of 'l'égalité parfaite', upon which, as he claims in the *Catéchisme des Industriels*, the system of industrial society is established.

[2] See *Man and Society*, vol. III, pp. 54–60.

concepts he uses and the assumptions he makes. It is, of course, the second kind of criticism, rather than the first, which interests the social and political theorist, and I shall confine myself to it.

There is no harm in speaking of periods of transition. If, like Saint-Simon, we consider the social and political order in Western Europe as it was in the eleventh century and as it is in our own, we can treat the intervening centuries as a period of transition. Our aim is then to explain how one social and political order was transformed into another, and since that is our aim, whatever falls in time between the two belongs properly to the period of transition; but if our purpose had been to explain how the social and political order of the ninth century was transformed into that of the sixteenth, then the eleventh century would have been transitional. True, the social and political order is always changing; it changed not only during the eleventh century but in every year of that century. Nevertheless, since social change is always gradual (though sometimes much more rapid than at other times), we can, if we take a relatively short period, speak of the social order during that period as if it were unchanging. Indeed, we not only can but must; it is a condition of our explaining a course of constant change that we should select points along it and show what happened between them. But the points are not really points; they are periods of time and there was change while they lasted. We ignore this change and attend only to what remained the same during each period, since our purpose is to explain the great changes which occurred between the periods and not the small changes within them. It would be absurd to criticize Saint-Simon for treating the eight hundred years separating the eleventh from the nineteenth century as a period of transition, if he had had no other purpose than to explain how the social order at the beginning of that period was transformed into the social order at the end of it.

But he did have another purpose; he wanted to show that, since the eleventh century, there had been social disintegration as well as social change. He spoke of the social order of the eleventh century – as he spoke of the future fully industrial society – as if it were a social order in some sense in which there was no social order in, say, the sixteenth or the seventeenth century. In the sixteenth century there were philosophy and religion and government and production just as there had been in the eleventh; there were many kinds of institutions, theories and attitudes of mind. In both centuries men engaged in different kinds of activity, which reacted upon one another. These kinds were just as characteristic of the age in the sixteenth century as they had been in the eleventh. But the institutions and beliefs of the eleventh century constituted – so thought Saint-Simon – a social and moral order in some sense in which those of the sixteenth century did not.

What could this sense be? Did the socially important beliefs – the beliefs about man's place in the world, about right behaviour, about what was worth having and doing – which people held in the eleventh century, form a coherent whole? Were they consistent with one another? Were these beliefs in keeping with existing institutions? Saint-Simon evidently thought that they were. And he believed that, in the sixteenth century, socially important beliefs were much less consistent with one another and much less in keeping with established institutions. No doubt, they could not have been completely inconsistent with one another or completely out of keeping with institutions, or else there would have been no stability and no peace, no society. But the degree of consistency and compatibility was much smaller in the sixteenth than in the eleventh century. Saint-Simon's disciple, Bazard, in lectures which were later published under the title, the *Doctrine of Saint-Simon*, used the terms *organic* and *critical* to mark this distinction between periods when the degree of such consistency and compatibility is high and periods when it is low. Ancient Greece, before the time of Socrates, had passed through an *organic* period and so had Western Europe in the Middle Ages. Europe was now at the end of a *critical* period, the period inaugurated by Luther and the reformers, and on the threshold of an *organic* one, when industrial society would be fully mature. So Bazard told his listeners in the lecture-room in the rue Taranne.

But, we may ask, why did Saint-Simon and Bazard believe that the Middle Ages were an *organic* period, in this peculiar sense? What was the evidence which satisfied them? I am not asking whether what they took for facts really were facts; I am asking only what kind of facts they thought would establish their conclusion. In the Middle Ages there existed a single Church to which everyone in the West belonged, a Church whose doctrines no one questioned. At least Saint-Simon and Bazard believed that it was so, and we can, for our purpose, suppose that they were right. But can we conclude, as they do, that where there is a Church teaching unquestioned doctrine, socially important beliefs are mutually consistent and in keeping with established institutions? Can we come to this conclusion even if we suppose that Church to be the most powerful of social organizations, dominating all the others?

It seems to me that we cannot; it seems to me that a society dominated by such a Church is no more likely than any other to be *organic*. What reason have we for thinking that the beliefs which constitute orthodoxy – the beliefs placed by the powerful Church out of reach of open criticism – are consistent with one another? No doubt, they are held to be mutually consistent by the body which propagates them. But an orthodox set of beliefs is not put together by impeccable logicians who know all the relevant facts; nor is there a process of natural attraction among beliefs ensuring that they never come together to form an orthodox corpus of doctrine unless they are consistent with one another. An orthodox system of doctrines building up over a long period of time in a large and variegated society is most unlikely to contain only mutually consistent beliefs and beliefs in keeping with established institutions. True, beliefs which have important practical consequences are continually being adapted to one another and to existing institutions; but this happens in all societies, and as much in those where there is no orthodoxy as in those where there is. In all societies, there are factors making for greater consistency and compatibility and factors making for less, but there is no reason to believe that the first kind are stronger where society is dominated by a powerful Church or party propagating an orthodox body of doctrines than where it is not. Therefore, the mere fact that there was a Church in the West whose authority was virtually undisputed in the eleventh century, while in the sixteenth there was not, is not good evidence that the earlier period was any nearer being *organic* than the later. It may have been, or it may not. Neither Saint-Simon nor Bazard produced evidence which would help to settle the question.

The distinction between *organic* and *critical* periods, or organic and critical societies (for these terms can be applied as readily to societies as to periods), is not so much improper as useless for Saint-Simon's purpose, which is to explain the course of social evolution. Admittedly, socially important beliefs can be mutually consistent or inconsistent, and beliefs can be compatible or incompatible with institutions; they can serve to maintain them or to destroy them. How beliefs and institutions affect one another must always be of absorbing interest to the student of society. And these inconsistencies and incompatibilities are, no doubt, much greater at some times and places than at others. But, unless there is a discernible alternation – a flux and reflux as of the tides, a period when consistency and compatibility decrease following regularly on a period when they increase – the distinction between the organic and the critical, as Saint-Simon and Bazard make it, does not provide us with a pattern of social change. And even this is not enough. Each organic period must differ from the one before it, the beliefs reaching a high point of consistency with one another and of compatibility with institutions being no longer what they were when harmony was last attained. Otherwise, there is no point in speaking of a social order which gradually disintegrates and gives way to another building up inside it; there is no point in treating history as Saint-Simon treated it and Marx was to treat it after him. Saint-Simon believed that there is a discernible alternation or rhythm, and also that he had produced evidence to support his claim. Unfortunately, he was mistaken. He predicted that, in the mature industrial society, there would be mutually consistent beliefs compatible with established institutions; he predicted that industrial society would be what Bazard was to call *organic*. But industrial society, as he described it, would not be dominated intellectually by a dogmatic Church; authority inside it, administrative and intellectual, would be different in kind from the authority known to mediaeval Europe. The universal acceptance of that authority, if ever it occurred, might be evidence that society was organic – that it was a social and moral order in a special sense in which not every society is one. But the unquestioned authority of the Church in the Middle Ages is no more evidence that mediaeval society was organic than the unquestioned authority of the Communist Party is evidence that Soviet society came to be so in our day.

Saint-Simon offers us another criterion besides the two I have discussed (which are the mutual consistency of socially important beliefs and the compatibility of these beliefs with established institutions) for distinguishing the two types of society which Bazard calls *organic* and *critical*. Industrial society, to be fully mature, must have *a positive purpose*; it must aim at increasing production, especially for the benefit of the poor. This requirement, that the new industrial society should have a positive purpose, was insisted upon even more strongly by Saint-Simon's disciples than by the master himself. In the third notebook of the *Catéchisme des Industriels*, written by Comte while he was still attached to Saint-Simon, we are told that 'any social system. . .aims at directing all particular forces towards some general goal. For there is no *society* except where there operates a combined general action'.[1] The whole tenor of Comte's argument makes it clear that he considers that a society is not properly a social and moral order unless 'all particular forces' are directed to a 'general goal', unless its leaders have a common purpose which is generally accepted and to which all private purposes are subordinate. A society lacking such

---

[1] *Catéchisme des Industriels*, troisième cahier, *Oeuvres de Saint-Simon et Enfantin*, XXXVIII.45.

a purpose is in a state of moral disorder. Saint-Simon and Comte preached the need for such a common purpose to men living in a society which (in their opinion) was in a state of moral disorder; and they found mediaeval society superior to their own in at least one respect, in having a common purpose.

Clearly, by a common purpose Saint-Simon means something more than common notions of justice maintained by a government enjoying the confidence of its subjects. In one of the letters which make up the *Système industriel*, he says that 'society does not live on *negative* ideas, but on *positive* ideas. It is today in extreme moral disorder; selfishness is spreading at an astonishing rate; and everything is tending to isolate man from man (*tout tend à l'isolement)'.*[1] The *negative* ideas which Saint-Simon had in mind were the ideas of the French Revolution; and he called them negative partly because he thought that they had been used to attack the privileges of the nobles and the Church, and partly because, in his opinion, they did nothing to strengthen men's devotion to the community and their sense of belonging to it. They served only to remove obstacles in the way of each man's pursuing his own ends. The French Revolution, he claimed, had left no monuments to its achievements, no political institutions and no philosophy suited to a mature industrial society. If (what was in fact far from being the case) all Frenchmen had accepted wholeheartedly the doctrine of the rights of man and had supported a government willing and able to maintain them, France would still have lacked a common purpose, as Saint-Simon understood it. To have a common purpose, men must do more than share certain notions of justice; they must be engaged in some common enterprise. In other words, in order to have a common purpose in Saint-Simon's sense, they must be agreed about something more than the rules which have to be enforced if each man is to pursue his private ends with as little interference as possible from others.

There is no need for us to quarrel with Saint-Simon and Comte for giving this meaning to the expression *a common purpose*. But we can object to their saying that, where there is no common purpose in this sense, there is *moral disorder*. Of course, if the expressions *having a common purpose* and *belonging to a moral order*, as they use them, were equivalent, we could not object. But they are not equivalent. Moral disorder is something which, in their opinion, results from lack of a common purpose. Now, we can reasonably doubt whether this assertion is true; we have the right to expect those who make it to produce arguments to support it. What is moral disorder, if it

[1] *Du Système industriel*, tome II, ibid., XXII.51.

is not lack of a purpose common to the whole community and taking precedence over other purposes? Presumably, it is either serious disagreement about what is right or desirable, or it is adherence to values which are seriously incompatible. What reason is there for believing that there will be moral disorder in this sense where there is not a common purpose in the sense understood by Saint-Simon?

No doubt, in all societies there are many common purposes; there are purposes shared by smaller or larger numbers of persons. No doubt, too, it is as much by working together for the attainment of common purposes as by learning not to interfere with one another in the pursuit of private ends that men acquire a common and internally consistent code of morals – to the extent that they do acquire one. But these are not the common purposes which Saint-Simon has in mind; for such purposes are limited, though there are many of them and everyone shares in some. There can be an immense number of purposes of this kind, varying in extent and importance, even in a society where there is no common purpose in the sense of Saint-Simon – even where there is no purpose, shared by the whole community, taking precedence over all other purposes.

Why, if there is to be moral order – if there are to be no serious disagreements about the right and the desirable, no adherence to values which are seriously incompatible – need there be a pre-eminent purpose shared by everyone? Where has there ever been such a purpose, except in time of war? Certainly, we cannot assume that, where there are rulers able to mobilize the resources and the labour of a community for some vast enterprise to which they attribute supreme importance, the people generally share their purpose. We cannot assume that they willingly participate in it or that they sympathize with it. They may have many motives for doing what is required of them by their rulers. Even where there is widespread sympathy for the supreme purpose, moreover, as there often is in time of war, there may still subsist other purposes, private or shared by smaller groups, which conflict with the supreme purpose and yet are no less important to those who have them. A vast enterprise may affect the persons involved in it (even when they are involved willingly, as the majority of Englishmen were in the endeavour to defeat Hitler's Germany) in ways unforeseen and unnoticed by either the directors of the enterprise or those they direct; it may, even where there is genuine and widespread enthusiasm for the enterprise, increase moral disorder, if by moral disorder is meant serious disagreement about moral values or adherence to values which are seriously incompatible. When do nations come closer to having a common and supreme purpose than in time of war? And when are they more liable to moral disorder?

No doubt, the mature industrial society, if it were as Saint-Simon conceived it, would have a purpose common to all its members, and a purpose important to them; and it would also be a true moral order, with no serious disagreements or inconsistent moral values. It would be *organic* in both the senses we have discussed; it would be what Saint-Simon meant by a moral order and would have what he understood by a common purpose. In such a society there would be no need for coercion, and the predominance of all who exercise authority would be the fruit of a competence universally recognized. But, if there were such a society, it would be the first society to be organic in both of these senses in time of peace. It may be that there have been primitive societies which were organic in the first sense, in which there were neither serious disagreements nor seriously inconsistent moral values, but primitive societies do not have common purposes except in time of war. And there is no more evidence that mediaeval society was organic in the second sense than there is that it was so in the first.

No doubt, there were small communities in the Middle Ages which were organic in both senses for perhaps years at a time: religious houses whose members were devoted to a common faith and a common way of life. And it may be that there were more such communities in the twelfth century than when Saint-Simon was alive. But that is nothing to Saint-Simon's purpose. He had in mind, not religious houses or other closed communities, but mediaeval Western society taken generally. In what way were Western Europeans in the twelfth century nearer to having a common purpose than their descendants in the eighteenth or early nineteenth? Even if we suppose (what is probably untrue) that they were Christians who understood the teachings of their Church, who shared the same conception of God, who aspired to the same Heaven, this is not enough to give them a common purpose in Saint-Simon's sense. The Church, merely by endeavouring to assist every Christian to deserve Heaven, no more serves a common purpose than does the State by affording to every citizen secure possession of what he owns. In the society condemned by Saint-Simon for being in moral disorder, men were perhaps as much attached to their property as their ancestors had been to God and to hopes of an after-life. The State, by maintaining the law, assists all men to preserve their property, which they all desire to do, but that is not enough to ensure that it serves a common purpose. To have a common purpose, men must do more than pursue similar private ends and be assisted by Church or State in doing so. This is how we have to interpret the sense in which Saint-Simon speaks of a common purpose, if his attack on the individualism of the French revolutionaries and of the liberals who came after them is not to be pointless. That being so, we have also to conclude that mediaeval Europe lacked a common purpose as much as the Europe familiar to Saint-Simon, who (though he believes otherwise) gives only one example of an organic society: namely, the mature industrial society whose coming he foretells, and to which, because it does not exist, he can, within limits, attribute what qualities he pleases.

Saint-Simon believed that there ordinarily is, and that there ought always to be, a close connection between the social order and the form of government. He also believed that a form of government can survive the social order out of which it arises and to which it is adapted. He sometimes spoke as if the form of government were the last thing to disappear, as one social order gives way to another. These are beliefs which we can also find in the writings of Marx. Saint-Simon tells us that the industrial class has been growing in wealth and social influence for centuries, and that it ought now to 'direct' society or, as he also puts it, to 'administer' its affairs. There was a time when the feudal nobles were the wealthiest class and the common people lived mostly on their estates and in their protection, so that it was therefore inevitable and natural that the nobles should govern.[1] But they have since lost their social importance, and it is now natural and inevitable that the socially predominant class, the leaders of industry, should become the 'directing' class. As Comte puts it, 'The political order is, and can only be, the expression of the civil order, which means, in other words, that the socially preponderant forces necessarily end by becoming the directing forces'.[2] Presumably, it is *natural* that the leaders of industry should 'direct' society because, human nature being what it is, those who have some forms of power (e.g. wealth or

[1] Neither Saint-Simon nor his disciples (who follow him on this point) had any notion of how his argument in fact applied to the feudal lords. Their social superiority resulted from their political functions, from the protection they afforded to their dependants, from the justice dispensed by them or in their name. They did not govern or 'direct' society because they were wealthy or had a high social position; they were wealthy and had that position because they governed. It is odd to say of them that they ought to have governed, or that it was *natural* they should do so, because they were wealthy and socially predominant. Their case differed completely from that of the leaders of industry, who had acquired great wealth and influence in a society in which they exercised no political functions.

[2] *Catéchisme des Industriels*, troisième cahier, *Oeuvres de Saint-Simon et Enfantin*, XXXVIII.98.

managerial skill) ordinarily aspire to, and are well placed to obtain, forms which they do not yet have (e.g. political power); and they ought to 'direct' society because, society being what it is, they are the most likely to 'direct' it for the common good.

There is no need, at this stage, to contest the claims made by Saint-Simon on behalf of the leaders of industry, who were so much immersed in their own affairs that they never aspired to the rôle which he reserved for them. Nor need we enquire what warrant there is for assuming (as Saint-Simon does) that it is the social order which determines what class shall control society and by what methods. There is good reason to doubt whether it is proper to make so sharp a distinction between social predominance and political power. But these are matters best left to a later stage, when we come to discuss the political theories of Marx and Engels.[1] For the moment, it is enough to point to the absurdity of Saint-Simon speaking of the form of government in France after 1815 as if it were the last important survival from a social order which had been in its prime some six centuries earlier. He called it a relic of the feudal system, though the form of government in France had changed since the high Middle Ages just as drastically as the relative importance of the social classes or the system of production. Indeed, Saint-Simon knew this, for it was too obvious to be ignored even by an intellectual enamoured of his own theories; he knew it and often admitted it, at least implicitly. The feudal nobles had been exalted and powerful in their prime by virtue of the services they had done, and these services, if they are examined, are seen to be political; the nobles in the Middle Ages governed. Since that time, they had ceased to perform those services; they had ceased to govern. The kings of France had gradually taken over the functions of the nobles, and France had acquired a centralized monarchy. Saint-Simon, far from denying this, tried to explain how it had happened. It was therefore absurd of him to speak of France's government in the 1820s as if it were a survival from the Middle Ages, a remnant of feudalism.

Though he distinguishes between the social and political order, and speaks of the second as if it were determined by the first, Saint-Simon never says anything to suggest that he is, in the same sense as Marx, an economic determinist. The event which he sees as the conception of the new industrial order in the womb of the old feudal society is not a technical invention or a change in a method or pattern of production, a shift of labour and resources from one to another line

[1] See *Man and Society*, vol. III, ch.4, pp. 238–62.

of production; it is the enfranchisement of the communes, or the grant of rights by the nobles to the craftsmen. He also attaches importance to the introduction into mediaeval Europe of sciences cultivated by the Arabs. As science flourishes, theology decays; but science is not, in his eyes, the handmaid of industry. The technical invention which he singles out as being the most important of all is the printing press, which makes knowledge spread much more quickly and therefore arouses curiosity in many more minds. Science makes possible all kinds of technical improvements, and Saint-Simon is well aware that it does so; but that is not what strikes him most forcibly. He is more impressed by how science affects men's conceptions of the world and of their place in it. Durkheim[1] says that he treats the accumulation of knowledge as the prime cause of social change, and although Saint-Simon is not unambiguous, the weight of evidence favours Durkheim's hypothesis. Comte, in his section of the *Catéchisme des Industriels*, which he wrote while still an avowed pupil of Saint-Simon, distinguishes between the theological, metaphysical and positive stages in the evolution of mankind; these are distinctions turning entirely upon the character of what men take for knowledge, upon how they look upon the world and themselves.

2. Their Illusions

Among the early socialists, only Saint-Simon (assisted by Comte) and Bazard[2] have philosophies of history sufficiently developed and *plausible*[3] to be worth comparing with Marxism. Just as Marx's view of his own age is intimately bound up with his conception of the past and his hopes for the future, so too is Saint-Simon's. Just as Marx's advice to the proletariat is the fruit of a wisdom derived from much thinking about the past, so too is Saint-Simon's advice to the leaders of industry. Just as Marx treats political history as essentially the record of a struggle for influence and power between classes, some of

---

[1] See Durkheim, *Socialism* (New York 1962 edition), ch. 6, p. 128.

[2] Bazard's account of the course of social evolution is substantially like Saint-Simon's. Bazard put himself forward as an interpreter of Saint-Simon, and not as an original thinker, though he was, in fact, a very free interpreter. But the differences between their two accounts, interesting though they are in themselves, do not raise important issues for us, since we are more concerned to examine the concepts they use to explain the course of events than their actual explanations.

[3] I intend no disparagement by this word. Saint-Simon and Bazard were excited by the past and perceptive about it. The historian, while rejecting their theories, might be impressed by them, as he would not be, I suspect, by Fourier's tidy division of the past and future into periods and phases.

which are growing stronger and others weaker through the operation of causes of which they are unconscious, so too does Saint-Simon. Just as Marx assumes that the proletariat (unlike other classes whose action has transformed society in the past) must be enlightened about its historic rôle in order to perform it, so Saint-Simon makes the same assumption about the leaders of industry. They both believe in progress and the need for a controlled economy; they both condemn militarism, liberalism and the organized churches; and they both predict the advent of a perfected society without government, which will enable men to be not only more equal but freer than they have ever been, because not subject to force. In all these ways Marx stands closer to Saint-Simon than to any other of the early socialists.

While Proudhon had no philosophy of history, no conception as definite and elaborate as Saint-Simon's or Marx's of a course of social evolution lasting many centuries, he did philosophize about the past and the present; he took as passionate and as enduring an interest in history, and was as much steeped in it, as either of them. And it deserves notice that he too ascribed historic rôles to social classes and fashioned his advice to them accordingly. Saint-Simon directed his message to the leaders of industry, looking upon them as spokesmen for all who earned a living by producing wealth; Marx directed his to the urban proletariat; and Proudhon his to all who made a living in a small way, whether they worked for others or were their own masters. With all three of them, there is a close connection between their views about history and the direction of their political efforts; there is also an extensive interest in social classes, their rivalries, their opportunities and their destinies.

Several of the other socialists took as active a part in politics as they did. Both Owen and Thompson did so, and were by no means lacking in realism. They understood the importance of the trade unions and tried, with considerable success, to win them over to their views. They collaborated with the workers and came closer to gaining their confidence than Marx ever did. They were not without shrewdness. Nor were the schemes they produced fantasies unrelated to existing conditions. Both the reports prepared by Owen – the first at the request of a committee chaired by the Archbishop of Canterbury in 1816, which came to be known as *Mr. Owen's Report on the Poor*, and the later *Report to the County of Lanark* of 1821 – are quite sensible schemes. They were sympathetically received by the bodies, consisting of practical men, to whom they were addressed. These reports proposed the setting up of communities which (though more modest) were just as truly socialist as the ones that Owen set up years later at New Harmony and Queenwood, when he had become more obstinate and reckless. Owen's schemes for co-operation were by no means as impractical as his theories about human nature were simple-minded. If he is open to the charge of lack of realism, it is less his schemes than his theories which make him so. The schemes were not in themselves unworkable, and it was not unreasonable to hope that they might be adopted. Thompson, less simple-minded than Owen as a theorist, was not more impractical. As much can be said, moreover, of Louis Blanc; his proposals were moderate enough, and he was not unreasonable in hoping that some of them might be adopted, though, as a matter of fact, they were not. The national workshops established soon after the February Revolution of 1848 differed in important respects from the ones he had proposed before the revolution, and there were, furthermore, prominent persons who did what they could to bring them into disrepute. Of all the proposals made by the early socialists in England and France, we can either say that they were not adopted or that, if they were, they did not work; but, as I hope to show in a moment, that does not in itself bear out the Marxist charge that the early socialists were utopians.

If we compare Saint-Simon and Proudhon with Owen and Louis Blanc, we see that the first two, whose interest in philosophy and history was much the greater, had a deeper understanding of society and their own age, while the last two made the more timely and the more practical proposals. The leaders of industry, so assiduously courted by Saint-Simon, took no notice of him; and the workers, though they warmed to Proudhon when he defended them after the June Days or when he attacked the bureaucratic state, were not much interested in his proposal for a *Banque du peuple*. Proudhon's very considerable influence was almost entirely negative; the workers shared little more than his dislikes and suspicions. He was, at times, very much their spokesman, closer to them perhaps than any other socialist. He spoke for them as Cobbett spoke for the village labourers in England. But he gave them no practical advice which they were inclined to take. He was, at times, as popular with the French workers as Owen with the English ones, but he never had the same power to move them to attempt what he advocated. And he never had the ear of ruling circles to the extent that Owen still had it when he produced his *Report on the Poor*. Nor did Proudhon make practical proposals which aroused even the same degree of interest as those of Louis Blanc, either among the workers or among the more radical sections of the middle-class parties. Clearly, Owen and Louis Blanc put proposals which attracted wide attention among men active in politics; and, just as clearly, Saint-Simon and Proudhon – whose judgements about the past and whose criticisms of the present cut so much deeper, and whose views about society and government were so much fresher and more perceptive – did not.

What, then, was it about the early socialists that was utopian or unrealistic? Was it their theories about how the society of equals would be organized? Or was it their beliefs about how it would come into being? I have conceded that their theories were to a large extent unrealistic; but this, I suggest, was not the real point of Marx's criticism when he called them utopian. Having only the vaguest ideas himself about the society of equals, he was not much interested in the shortcomings of this part of their theories; he was not concerned to show that a large economy could not be managed as Saint-Simon proposed that it should be or that a community organized in the manner of Fourier's phalanx would soon break down. His own ideas about the future, vague though they were, owed more than a little to the speculations of the early socialists. His real objection to them was that their beliefs about how society could be transformed were based on illusions. I do not want to reject this verdict so much as to qualify it, and I also want to examine one of the assumptions on which it rests. For it often happens that a conclusion which is right or partly right rests on arguments and assumptions which are mistaken.

We have seen that Saint-Simon based his political tactics on a theory of social evolution which he believed gave him a more profound insight than that of other thinkers into the realities of the situation. He was aware that his ideas might seem bizarre to others, but that, he thought, was only because they had not seen, as he had, how the present had emerged from the past. He was as firmly convinced as ever Marx was that he saw deeply into the forces moulding his own age, and that he was therefore well equipped to enlighten the class to whom he addressed his message about their true interests. No more than Marx, did he appeal to 'eternal' principles of justice or to unchanging human nature. And the claims which he made for himself, openly or tacitly, were not altogether unjustified. He did have a deeper insight, in many ways, than his contemporaries, and he did owe it in large part to his excursions into history. And yet he was also what Marx accused him of being when he called him utopian; he was unrealistic. Many things which other people did not see were clear to him, but others more obvious escaped his notice. Even in his day, a man had to shut his eyes to much that took place around him to be as convinced as he was that the 'leaders of industry' were trusted by the workers or cared much for their good. Why should he have supposed that he could interest them in running the nation's economy principally for the benefit of 'the poorest and the most numerous class', whose welfare he had so much at heart? He failed to notice a divergence of class interests which was already obvious to several of the classical economists (and more especially to Adam Smith and Ricardo) as well as to Sismondi. It was a much grosser error of judgement on his part to suppose that he could induce the leaders of industry to manage the nation's economy for the common good than it was on Owen's part that he could find men of goodwill to put up the money to finance his schemes. If Saint-Simon had not been blinded by his hopes, it might have occurred to him that businessmen in the highly competitive economy of his day were too much engrossed in making profits and avoiding ruin to lend an ear to such proposals as his – that they were even less disposed by the nature of their occupations to accept responsibility for the welfare of the poor than the servants of the Crown had been under the old monarchy. It is easy to see how blind to many realities Saint-Simon was, even if we compare him with some of his contemporaries.[1] To a man like Marx, in whose eyes the divergence of interest between capitalists and wage-earners was the essential feature of the age, he must have seemed in some ways very foolish.

It would not be difficult to make a case against each of the early socialists, showing that, in one way or another, his hopes were unreasonable; that the methods he used or advocated to induce governments and private citizens to try out his schemes were unlikely to succeed. This is not surprising. The understanding of the early socialists, both of government and of production, was limited; they lived at a time when the social studies were scantier and less cautious (though not perhaps more confused) than they are now. They were often and widely mistaken, both in their explanations and their forecasts. And it may be that Marx and Engels, though they too made serious mistakes, had a deeper understanding of society and

[1] Perhaps Saint-Simon, born a nobleman, remained all his life influenced, though unconsciously, by attitudes typical of his class. To the eighteenth-century nobleman, the most striking social cleavage was the one separating his own class from the rest of society. The *industriels* all belonged to the unprivileged orders, and in the eyes of Saint-Simon were workers on whom the drones, his own class, were parasites. According to André Lichtenberger (see his *Socialisme et la Révolution française* [Paris 1899], ch. 10, p. 295), it was in about 1793 that the old social division of France into the privileged and the unprivileged became politically less important than the division into rich and poor. Saint-Simon was then already thirty-three years old.

fewer illusions than their precursors. This claim is still made on their behalf, even by some of their more severe critics, and I shall not contest it, partly because I suspect it may be true and partly because it does not affect my argument.

Marx and Engels did not confine themselves to pointing out the various mistakes made by the socialists whom they called *utopian*; they did not merely say that it was simple-minded of Saint-Simon to believe that he could persuade the leaders of industry to take his advice, that it was unlikely that communities of the types advocated by Owen or Fourier could operate successfully in the existing social environment. If that were all they had said, we should have to agree with them in principle, even though we might insist that some of the early schemes and proposals were much nearer being realistic than others. But Marx and Engels were not really concerned to make a separate case against each of the utopian socialists, showing just why his proposals, made at the time they were made, were unrealistic; they set much greater store by a general argument directed against them all, a blanket condemnation. It is this general argument which seems to me mistaken.

The error of the utopian socialists generally, according to Marx and Engels, was that they supposed that it was possible to transform society by appealing to the privileged classes. But the privileged classes owe their privileges to society's being what it is; it is therefore their interest that it should not change in any way which destroys or greatly reduces their privileges. Classes cannot be persuaded to do what is against their class interests, and they will not allow it to be done by others unless they are too weak to prevent it. Therefore, since the transformations desired by the socialists involved the destruction of privileges, they should have aimed at persuading, not the privileged, but the unprivileged. There is only one really effective method for putting an end to exploitation, and that is to enlighten the exploited and to encourage them to organize themselves until they are strong enough to put an end to the system against the will of the exploiters. Marx could perceive, as Saint-Simon did not, the need for organizing mass movements. He had a better sense of the actual, even when he was discussing the past. Perhaps he understood the deeper causes of the French Revolution no better than Saint-Simon, but he was much more interested in the revolutionaries, their predicaments and their motives for action. He understood why the political allies of 1789 parted company in later years; why Mirabeau, Lafayette and the Girondins all failed; and how the Jacobins eventually became masters of France. What men like Robespierre felt in their bones – what they knew by a kind of instinct – Marx could explain. He understood how revolutionaries behave, what kinds of decisions they have to make, better than any of the other great socialist writers. That is a major reason why, though he never succeeded himself in bringing about a revolution, his writings have proved so attractive to revolutionaries. Saint-Simon had no such understanding; he was a social theorist and nothing more. The early socialists were *utopian*, in the eyes of Marx and Engels, not so much because of the many mistakes they made in sizing up the situation in which they acted, but because they believed that it was possible to reconcile the interests of the propertied and working classes by appealing to a sense of justice common to all classes.

In the next volume, where I deal with Marxism at considerable length, I examine more closely the Marxian conception of a class interest and also enquire what could be meant by saying that the interests of two classes are *irreconcilable*. I shall not anticipate here what I say there, for these are difficult matters and cannot be discussed briefly. Suffice it to say, for the moment, that the mistakes made by the early socialists are not in themselves good evidence that Marx and Engels are right when they say that it is wasted labour appealing to privileged classes to transform society. Yet many people have supposed otherwise; they have been inclined to accept the charge brought by Marx against the early socialists because they have been impressed by their lack of realism. The early socialists had many illusions; they tried to persuade the unpersuadable. This is a widely accepted verdict on them. The first part of it, that they had many illusions, is true – as it nearly always is true of those who have great hopes and are active in their service. It is a judgement which applies as truly to Lenin as to Owen. The second part of the verdict, properly qualified, is also true. The 'leaders of industry' cared nothing for Saint-Simon's arguments, and even the prominent men who listened to Owen or Louis Blanc were disposed to go only a little way in taking their advice. The appeals of the early socialists, to the extent that they were addressed to the powerful and the rich, did mostly fall on deaf ears. But from this judgement on their doctrines (which in any case needs to be qualified) to the general conclusions reached by Marx, there is a long leap and one made in the dark.

The early socialists appealed to the workers as much as to the propertied class, and had as many illusions about them. Owen appealed to both classes and got a considerable response from both. If he failed to achieve what he hoped to achieve with their help, it was not really because the class interests of the privileged stood in his way. The experiments at New Harmony and Queenwood did not fail because governments took steps against them or because of the hostility they aroused; they failed because they were badly run, and so too did the Orbiston community founded on his principles. The National Equitable Labour Exchange, which he set up in Gray's Inn Road in 1832 for selling goods at prices varying with the time needed to produce them, failed because the goods were priced either too high or too low as compared with ordinary market prices. Of all Owen's schemes, only the Grand National Consolidated Trade Union frightened the propertied and the government – and perhaps inspired the action taken against the Tolpuddle martyrs – but its collapse was due more to internal weakness than to pressure from outside. If we read accounts of the experiments promoted by the early socialists and their disciples, we nearly always find that their failure was due primarily to bad organization or lack of discipline and not to the hostility they provoked.

Now this, it may be objected, does not really meet the Marxian argument, which holds that the experiments of the early socialists failed not so much because they provoked the government and the propertied classes into taking action against them as because they were made in an unpropitious environment. Take, for example, Owen's National Equitable Labour Exchange; it did not fail because of hostile action taken against it but because it was an experiment made in a market economy. The surrounding system doomed it to failure without anyone's needing to take action to ensure that it failed, and even without anyone's noticing that, if it did succeed, it might eventually destroy the system. The social system prevents, as it were automatically, the success of experiments which threaten it, even though the classes whose interest it is to preserve the system do not feel themselves threatened by the experiments and take no action hostile to them.

This explanation is ingenious, but what reason is there for believing that it is true? As anyone who looks at the experiments tried or inspired by the early socialists can see, there were many reasons other than this to explain their failure. Are we then entitled to say that, if they had not failed for these other and more obvious reasons, they would have failed for this one? What is the evidence to support that conclusion? Much the more numerous and more weighty reasons – the ones which thrust themselves upon us as we read the accounts (most of them written by persons with strongly socialist sympathies and often deeply influenced by Marxism) – have no logical connection with this reason, which is usually brought in to the rear of them, as if to set the seal of Wisdom upon them. But the evidence to support it is weak indeed. Did the National Equitable Labour Exchange fail because it was tried in the midst of a market economy? Very probably it did. But what does that prove? That the market economy dooms to failure every experiment whose success would destroy the system on which the privileges of the propertied classes rest? This is a extraordinary conclusion to draw from that piece of evidence and a few others like it.

It is also a conclusion which contradicts other parts of the Marxian theory. For Marx holds, as Saint-Simon does, that in every social system (except the last) there emerge the forces destined to destroy it. What, then, are these forces? They are practices and institutions which prove to be in the long run, incompatible with the system in which they first appear and are tolerated. These practices and institutions arise, presumably, because some sections of the community believe them to be in their interest. The feudal lords who enfranchised the commons did so, either because they thought they had thereby something to gain or because demands were made on them which they saw no good reason for refusing. The trade unions threatened the interests of the propertied classes rather more obviously than did the National Equitable Labour Exchange, and were also, though in a different way, out of keeping with a free market economy. Parliament, dominated by the propertied classes, first made *combinations* illegal and then allowed them. Were the workers already too formidable for Parliament to dare to deny them the right to combine? This is not the verdict of the historians. But the workers became, as Marx saw, a much more formidable class for being allowed to combine. Those who pressed for the repeal of the Combination Laws appealed to ideas of justice very widely held in England. We need not call them 'eternal' ideas; they have been denied or neglected or unheard of in some countries. In the early nineteenth century they formed part of a culture favourable to the predominance of a small section of the community, and yet it was possible to appeal to these ideas to persuade that section to allow practices which eventually helped to transform the social order.

Law and morality, even in a society of unequals – even when they serve to support the claims of the privileged – also often allow practices which, sometimes quickly, sometimes slowly, subvert the society which tolerates them. A conception of justice or liberty or property which, far from being eternal, was perhaps unknown several centuries ago and which in the past has made easier the enrichment of some at the expense of others, may come to be used to justify innovations fatal to a supremacy which rests on wealth. Very probably, the innovations will modify the conceptions originally used to justify them, and the old social order may thus be subverted all the more quickly. When a social class rises in importance and challenges the supremacy of another, the legal and moral conceptions favourable to the established order do usually change; but that does not touch my present argument, which is that the old conceptions could be used to justify practices subversive of the old order. We can say this without assuming that there is, in any sense in which Marx would deny it, an 'eternal' justice, and without denying that, where there is social inequality, current ideas of what is just usually support the pretensions of the rich and the powerful. There is evidence in plenty that the privileged are apt to resist proposals which they believe are against their interests, but there is also evidence that they sometimes take the initiative in making reforms raising the status and improving the lot of the unprivileged. The privileged accept for generations conditions of which in the end they come to be ashamed, though they do not suffer from them. Is it always fear of revolution which causes them to change their minds?

Certainly, the better organized and the more enlightened the poor, the more liable to persuasion are the rich. It is a fair criticism of several of the early socialists, though by no means of all of them, that they devoted too many of their efforts to persuading the rich and the powerful and too few to persuading the poor. It applies to Saint-Simon and to Fourier. But if a general charge is to be brought against the early socialists, it is not that they tried to persuade the unpersuadable, seeking to transform society without the massive and organized support of the workers; it is rather that they believed that society could be transformed according to a recipe prepared beforehand. To say this is not to repeat against them what Burke said against the French revolutionaries, for he condemned every attempt to make large reforms. Nor is it to condemn the making of plans in advance, nor the description in detail of ideal societies. It is sometimes desirable to make large changes quickly, and it is certainly wise to prepare a plan beforehand, provided we do not adhere to it rigidly as we try to execute it. For all plans are (or ought to be) provisional; they are based on limited knowledge, and ought to change as knowledge increases. The changes in group attitudes and interests which create a need for large reforms, moreover, are not effects of any one man's criticism of the established order or vision of a just society; they arise, in so far as their causes are intellectual, from the impact of many theories on many minds. Western Europe has changed enormously in the last six or seven generations, and one of the important causes of this change is the preaching of socialist doctrines; but none of the doctrines foretold the course of change. The socialists helped to formulate the ideals which have guided the reformers and the concepts they have used to state their problems and to find solutions of them; they have transformed both the language of politics and the aspirations of mankind; but they have not produced plans which men could follow, even in broad outline, in the attempt to realize these aspirations.[1]

I would not say that it is virtually impossible to transform a large society more or less according to a plan scarcely changed in the course of execution. Certainly, it has not been done in the West or in the Soviet Union, no doubt because they are parts of the world where there has been *unprecedented* change. The reformers in the West and the revolutionaries in Russia were *pioneers*; they were moving in directions in which no one had moved before them. Russia as she now is was no more foretold and desired by the Bolsheviks in 1917 than the West, as it now is, was foretold and desired by the radicals and socialists of the nineteenth century. Yet it may be that reformers active in countries which – judged by standards they themselves accept – are backward when compared with certain other countries, can produce beforehand a vast and intricate scheme of transformation and adhere to it, at least in broad outline. But they are not taking for their model an ideal society unlike any that exists; they are following along a road already trodden before them; they are aiming at something similar to what has already been established outside their own country. They will want to avoid, no doubt, the 'mistakes' of their precursors, but they will have a fairly clear and detailed idea of their goal and of how it can be achieved. They are not engaged in exploration but only in catching up others who, in their opinion, are in advance of them.

Marx and Engels have themselves been called utopian. But this sort of *tu quoque*, though tempting, is not really justified. They produced no plan of an ideal community, as Saint-Simon, Owen and Fourier did, believing that the time had come already to put it into practice.[2] Those who call Marx and Engels utopian mean to suggest that they

---

[1] The greatest and most rapid deliberate transformations of society have been made by disciples of Marx, who refrained from producing an ideal model of post-revolutionary society. But, in spite of Marx's reticence in this respect, he did say enough about socialism and the dictatorship of the proletariat to warrant our saying that none of the societies created by his disciples is *socialist* or *proletarian*, as Marx understood those terms, or shows any sign of becoming so.

[2] I take it that no man is utopian, in Marx's sense, unless he produces an ideal model and mistakenly believes that it can be realized immediately or in the near future. The author of *Utopia* was therefore not utopian in this sense, and neither was Plato or Rousseau.

were so in the same sense as they accused the early socialists of being so, and the suggestion is false. Yet they may have been, though in a different way, as unrealistic as the men whose lack of realism was so obvious to them. For, though they produced no model of an ideal community, they did express some general, mostly negative, opinions about what society would be like after the proletarian revolution – opinions largely inspired by the early socialists; and they also held strongly to certain beliefs about how bourgeois society would come to an end. And, surely, a man is lacking in realism if he holds those opinions together with these beliefs. If the proletarians are to organize politically in order to capture the State from the bourgeois, why should the State wither away? Within a very numerous class, politically organized, there is necessarily a structure of authority; there are leaders accustomed to power and eager to keep and enlarge it. Those who gain control of a great community, no matter what their class origins or class support, have an interest in maintaining that control. If, moreover, already before the collapse of bourgeois society, the average size of the unit of production has grown rapidly, and every part of a vast economy has become more closely dependent on the other parts, then the workers, when they take control, must either maintain a numerous and centralized bureaucracy or else must revert (at enormous material sacrifice) to a much simpler system in which units of production are smaller and there is less need for the economy as a whole to be controlled from the centre. Is a man more lacking in realism if he holds, with Proudhon, that the workers must boycott the State and must abandon their capitalist employers to start ventures of their own; or if, with Marx, he holds that, when the workers have captured the State and have taken control of a vast and closely knit economy, bureaucracy (that is to say, a centralized administration remote from the ordinary citizen and taking important decisions which closely affect him) will quickly disappear? Is not a man in the second case as much inspired by fantasy as in the first, as much the victim of illusion? The revolutions of the past, which both Marx and Proudhon called *bourgeois*, had strengthened the State, as they both noticed. Why then should the proletarian revolution destroy it or set in motion a process which would cause it to disappear?

3. Their Dislike of Violence

We have seen that most of the early socialists believed that, in the ideal communities they described, there would be no need for organized force. We have seen why they held this belief, and why Rousseau did not hold it of his ideal community. In this matter, Marx and Engels agreed with them and not with Rousseau, for the 'withering away' of the State implies the disappearance of organized force. And yet, in spite of this agreement, Marx and Engels did not dislike and distrust force as the early socialists did; they were not pacific by temperament. Their doctrine is altogether more combative and angry.

The early socialists were not revolutionaries; they deprecated the use of force against established authority, even when they strongly disapproved of that authority. Saint-Simon and his disciples, Fourier, Considérant, Owen, Thompson, Bray, Cabet, Leroux, Louis Blanc and Proudhon: they all hoped to achieve their objects by peaceful means. They disliked violence, and though they could not deny it in the past, they envisaged a future free from it, and, by and large, attained without it. Of the English and French socialists who were important before the rise of Marxism, only the Blanquists believed that the established system must be destroyed by violence and were willing to resort to violence to destroy it.[1]

It might be said that this objection to violence was an effect of misplaced optimism – that it was connected with those aspects of their teaching which moved Marx to call the early socialists utopian. But that judgement would not apply to them all, for by no means were they all optimists. Saint-Simon and Fourier preached mostly to the propertied and educated classes, expecting to convince them by argument, and took little notice of how widely the interests of the propertied and the propertyless diverged. Owen, at one time highly respected in governing circles, never lost faith in his own powers of universal persuasion. These three pioneers were incorrigible optimists. But others, like Leroux and Louis Blanc, though they said (and no doubt believed) that it was in the *true* or long-term interest of both capitalists and workers that society should be greatly changed, were well aware of how deeply the rich feared the poor and the poor hated the rich. They wanted to make great reforms precisely in order to avoid revolution. Cabet, whose influence on the French workers was at one time very great indeed, said that, if he held a revolution in his fist, he would keep that fist shut, even if it meant his having to die in exile. He knew that there was danger of revolution in France; he knew

---

[1] The Blanquists were, I suppose, *socialists,* though they were in practice concerned only to destroy what they believed to be evil without troubling themselves about what would take its place. Still, they were opposed to forms of property which they believed allowed the idle to exploit the industrious, and they did look forward to a type of society in which the workers would organize production and exploitation would cease.

how angry and how ready for violence were the workers in Paris and in other towns. But he also believed that the communist society he advocated could not be established by force, and therefore thought it his duty to dissuade the workers from violence. Thompson did not expect to persuade the rich to reform society for the benefit of the poor; he hoped rather to help the poor to help themselves, which he thought they could do without resorting to force. In general, we may say that, as one decade succeeded another and society became more industrial, the socialists grew more sharply aware of the hatreds and suspicions dividing the rich from the poor; the facile optimism of the earliest socialists gave way to more sober expectations and to more urgent fears. This was especially true after the July Revolution of 1830 in France and the passage in 1832 of the first Reform Bill in England – two events which aroused great hopes among the poor and led to great disappointments. Class antagonisms had never seemed deeper, and there was widespread fear of revolution. Yet the socialists, with rare exceptions, remained social pacifists. They mostly refused to believe that the violence which threatened society, and whose causes were perhaps as well understood by them as by any of their contemporaries, could bring their countries nearer to the social order which would remove these causes. They did not share the faith of Marx that the violence produced by the ills of society could purge society of those ills.

Proudhon did occasionally come close to arguing that class war and violence were inevitable, but he never advocated violence. At times, the situation in France seemed to him so tense that he could not see how violence was to be avoided. Yet his attitude to it was not so very different from, say, Tocqueville's; he sometimes saw the hatred between classes leading France into an *impasse* out of which there might be no issue except by violence. His sympathies were with the workers, as Tocqueville's were not; he felt a need to defend them when they were most reviled, which was apt to be when they had resorted to violence, as after the June Days of 1848. It was not the workers on the barricades who were to blame, he said, so much as the authorities whose indifference to their sufferings had driven them to such lengths. But, though he sometimes condoned violence, he never preached it and never foretold it with relish. He never looked forward to the workers *smashing* anything or anybody. The cult of violence of the Blanquists and some of the extremer radicals seemed to him sometimes disgusting and sometimes ridiculous. He abominated the Jacobins of '93 and despised their nineteenth-century imitators.

What explains this early socialist dislike of violence? We might expect it in England, but it was not less marked in France.[1] We cannot, as we have seen, explain it by postulating a simple-minded belief in the efficacy of persuasion by argument. Perhaps the French socialists, reflecting first on the great revolution and afterwards on the revolution of 1830, had noticed that those who did the fighting, who took the risks, did not get the rewards. Perhaps, to men of ideas, violence rarely seems attractive when it is seen close at hand, when there is more than book-knowledge of it. Perhaps many of the early socialists, precisely because they had fairly well-defined ideas about what they thought needed doing, were afraid that violence would make it less likely than ever that they would be listened to. Perhaps Proudhon and Cabet, born of working-class parents, were afraid that the grievances of their class would be used by revolutionaries of bourgeois origin for their own purposes. Perhaps the cult of violence in intellectual circles varies inversely with experience of freedom or with civic courage, and is therefore less to be expected among the English and the French than among the Germans and the Slavs.

---

[1] Indeed, it was *more* marked in France than in England; for the English socialists did not feel the same need to condemn violence, since they lived in a country at that time less given to it.

CHAPTER 7

The Early Socialists, French and English II

I. HODGSKIN AND THOMPSON AS CRITICS OF CLASSICAL ECONOMICS, AND FOURIER'S IDEAL SOCIETY

The early socialists contemplated the same economy as Adam Smith or Ricardo. But, whereas the classical economists saw it as a system ensuring that, on the whole, available resources were put to the most productive use, the socialists condemned it as wasteful. These two almost contradictory judgements passed on the same system are not to be explained by a difference of opinion about what constitutes productive use. It is not that the economists wanted the total product, measured in money or in some other external way, to be as large as possible, while the socialists had in mind the optimum satisfaction of wants. The economists, just as much as the socialists, thought it desirable that men should so use their energies as to produce with the least effort what was needed to satisfy their wants. They both assumed, as Bentham did, that no man's satisfaction is more valuable than another's unless it is greater. True, the socialists aimed at kinds of equality to which the economists were indifferent, but there was one conception of equality common to them – the conception implicit in Bentham's greatest happiness principle. The economists, moreover, were as convinced as the socialists that, beyond a certain point, every successive addition to a man's income procures him a less than proportionate satisfaction. They both knew that competition brings ruin to the unlucky and the weak, that in a free market economy the adjustment of supply to demand is always imperfect and involves losses. The economists were not really blind to the waste and the suffering caused by the system they described, but they thought it a price worth paying, because the advantages of the system outweighed its disadvantages. The socialists believed the contrary, and naturally, believing what they did, they paid greater attention than did the economists to the disadvantages and less attention to the advantages. They did not argue with the economists or challenge their assumptions so much as lay heavy emphasis on what the economists tended to neglect. But there were two early socialists to whom this judgement does not apply: Thomas Hodgskin and William Thompson.

The early socialists were not moved primarily by the belief that inequality diminishes happiness by preventing available resources being used to produce what satisfies the most wants; nor yet by a pure love of equality, a feeling that every man ought to get a return in proportion to the contribution he makes. They were moved, above all, by the belief that poverty, insecurity and ruthless competition are degrading. Men who become socialists, even though they have a taste for abstract argument, are not moved in the first place by the pure desire that certain abstract principles of justice should be put into practice; they are moved by sympathy with the poor and are perhaps also offended by the indifference and smugness of the fortunate. Even Hodgskin, who attacked some of the assumptions made by the economists, was not arguing with them for the sheer love of argument; he was not merely enjoying an intellectual exercise; he attacked their assumptions because they were used to justify a system which he condemned for the suffering and degradation involved in it. But he did not expatiate on the suffering or seek to describe the degradation; nor was he concerned to show how the system frustrated the individual and prevented his attaining happiness. Others were less reticent; they were copious and explicit when they spoke of the sufferings of the poor and the heartlessness of the rich. But only one of them, Fourier, produced an elaborate theory about the human passions, their frustration in existing society, and the type of community in which they could have free and harmless expression.

1. Hodgskin and Thompson

In *Labour Defended against the Claims of Capital* of 1825, Hodgskin is concerned to do only one thing: to refute the argument of the classical economists that the capitalist performs a useful function and is therefore entitled to his reward.[1] He quotes these words from

---

[1] Though the classical economists took it for granted that the capitalist is *entitled* to his reward, they were in practice more concerned to explain how wealth was produced and distributed than to justify its being so distributed. Explanation

James Mill's *Elements of Political Economy*: 'The labourer has neither raw materials nor tools. These are provided for him by the capitalist. For making this provision the capitalist of course expects a reward.'[1] Mill gives us to understand that the capitalist not only expects but expects justly; and that is what Hodgskin sets out to disprove.

The economists say that the labourer, in order to work, must live, and cannot live on the product of his own labour before that product is completed and sold. The capitalist provides him with the wherewithal to live while he is producing, and for this indispensable service gets his reward. But, says Hodgskin, the capitalist does not in fact possess ready prepared the commodities needed by the labourer. He possesses only money which he uses to pay the labourer for his labour before the product of that labour is sold. The labourer spends his money on what other workers have produced. Hodgskin is at great pains to show that capitalists do not in fact have a large quantity of food, clothing and so on in store to supply their workers while they are at work, and that, in any case, only a small part of what workers need is produced much in advance of their needing it. By so doing he rather obscures the essential point of his argument, which is this: What the worker needs to keep him alive while he is working is itself the product of labour; and the only reason why he cannot buy it and also get the whole price fetched by what he produces when it is sold is that he has no money unless he sells his labour to the capitalist. If he had the money he could buy what he needed while he worked and then get the full market value of his product; but, having no money, he is obliged to sell his labour and to allow the purchaser of it to sell what that labour produces.

In the language of the classical economists, the commodities needed to supply the worker while he worked (or the money to buy them) were known as *circulating capital*, while the machinery and tools he used and the buildings in which he worked (or the money invested in them) were known as *fixed capital*. Hodgskin argues that the capitalist is no more entitled to a reward as a provider of *fixed* than as a provider of *circulating* capital. Fixed capital is itself a product of labour, and is useful only while labour is applied to it (that is to say, as a tool). The capitalist neither produces it nor does the work which makes

---

passes over into justification more perhaps with McCulloch and James Mill than with Smith, Ricardo and Malthus: and it is McCulloch and Mill that Hodgskin quotes.

[1] *Labour Defended against the Claims of Capital*, ed. G. D. H. Cole (London 1964 edition), p. 34. The passage is drawn from the introduction to ch. II, sect. 2 of Mill's *Elements of Political Economy*, first published in 1821.

it useful. For a nation to have fixed capital (and it must have it if it is to put labour to the most productive use), only three things are necessary: knowledge and ingenuity for the inventing of machines, ability to arrange for their construction and profitable use, and the skill and labour to use them. These abilities and skills are manifest in labour – in useful work – and are at bottom so many forms of labour. The capitalist does not really provide them; they are provided by the men who actually do these kinds of work, and the capitalist merely purchases their labour. Since men labour in order to produce what satisfies their wants, there is no need for capitalists to purchase labour to ensure that useful work is done: by purchasing labour they merely enrich themselves at the expense of those who labour. And we have seen that Hodgskin does not mean by labour only manual labour; he means also the work involved in ensuring that manual labour is put to the most productive use, the work of the inventor and of the manager. 'No subject of complaint is', he thinks, 'more general or more just than that the inventor of any machine does not reap the benefit of it. . . .Thousands of capitalists have been enriched by inventions and discoveries of which they were not the authors'.[1] And later he says, 'The labour and skill of the contriver, or of the man who arranges and adapts a whole, are as necessary as the labour and skill of him who executes only a part. . . .But because those who have been masters, planners, contrivers, etc., have in general also been capitalists, and have also had a command over the labour of those who have worked with their hands, their labour has been paid as much too high as common labour has been under paid'.[2] In other words, to direct the labour of others to make it more productive is useful work entitled to a reward, but a man need not be a capitalist in order to do it. The capitalist does not owe his high income to his doing this work; he owes it to his ability to purchase labour and to sell what it produces. Because wealth is distributed as it is, those who do the planning and contriving are mostly capitalists; they therefore do some useful work, but their incomes are far greater than what their work entitles them to.

In the last pages of his short book, Hodgskin foretells that the workers, as they gain in knowledge, will examine closely 'the foundations of the social edifice', and will dig them up and not restore them 'unless justice demands their preservation'.[3] He is certain that

[1] *Labour Defended*, pp. 63–4.
[2] Ibid., pp. 88–9.
[3] Ibid., p. 102.

'till the triumph of labour be complete. . .till *man* shall be held more in honour than the clod he treads on, or the machine he guides – there cannot, and there ought not to be, either peace on earth or goodwill amongst men'.[1]

We have here as vigorous an account (and a more concise one) of exploitation as we can find in the writings of Marx; we have the argument that where the capitalist flourishes, capital (the clod and the machine) is more valued than the man who produces or works it; and we have the prophecy that, until labour gets its full reward, there cannot be true social peace. We have here by no means all, but at least some, of the bare bones of Marxism.

Thompson's purpose, in his *Inquiry concerning the Distribution of Wealth*, is also to contest the claims made, openly or by implication, by the economists in favour of the capitalists. But, as a disciple of Bentham who accepts the greatest happiness principle, he is disturbed by the master's argument that, where security and equality conflict, the second must be sacrificed to the first. Bentham had allowed that, once a man has enough to live on, each successive increment of wealth brings him a diminishing return in happiness, and had therefore admitted that, *ceteris paribus*, the more equal the distribution of wealth the greater men's happiness. But he had then gone on to argue that there was another principle involved, even more important than this one: men suffer more for being deprived of what they reckon on having than they are pleased by getting what they do not expect. If men are to be happy they must have security: they must be able to reckon on getting what law and convention have led them to expect and to believe they are entitled to. Equality is good but security is better (i.e. more conducive to happiness), and therefore, when the two conflict (as they often do), it is security which is to be preferred.

Thompson might well have called in question the relative importance attributed by Bentham to these two principles. Did Bentham really mean to be taken literally? Did he really mean that, *whenever* security and equality are in conflict, there is more to be gained than lost by sacrificing the second principle to the first? Presumably not, for we cannot suppose him to have been so unrealistic as to have held that no increase in equality, however great, if it deprives anyone of what he expects and believes he is entitled to, can add to happiness more than the deprivation takes away from it. Did he mean, then, that an increase in equality, if it diminishes security, *usually* affords less happiness to those who benefit by it than unhappiness to those

[1] Ibid., pp. 104–5.

who lose by it? Though this is not absurd on the face of it, it is also not obvious. To make the assertion without producing arguments in support of it is not enough. No doubt, when two men are more or less equal in wealth, the chances are that, if we deprive one of them of £100 which we give to the other, we cause more pain than pleasure. But, if equality is a valid principle at all (and Bentham admitted that it is), it follows that, the greater the inequality of wealth between two persons, the smaller the chance that, if we take something from the richer of the two to give it to the poorer, we are causing more pain than pleasure, and the greater the chance that we are doing the opposite. Did Bentham believe that in the England or the Europe of his day (for these were the only parts of the world with which he was at all familiar) inequalities of wealth were not yet great enough to make it likely that, if the rich were taxed heavily for the benefit of the poor, the poor would gain in happiness more than the rich lost? If he did believe it, it was presumably a matter of faith, for he certainly produced no reasons to support his belief. Bentham, the great champion of calculation and measurement to decide social issues, was sometimes extraordinarily self-confident in his judgements, speaking as if a vast experience enabled him to take the measure of things without putting himself to the trouble of actually measuring them, like a shrewd old farmer who can tell at a glance which of two almost identical bullocks is the heavier with no need to use the scales.

But Thompson did not attack Bentham on these lines. He did not say that it is absurd to put it forward as a general rule that to preserve security is more important than to increase equality (or the other way about), since the relative importance of the two varies with the degree of inequality. Nor did he say that equality is more important than security. He tried, rather, to argue that the worker does not have security unless he gets the whole product of his labour. The worker feels that he is entitled to this whole product or to its equivalent, and feels deprived of what is justly his when he does not get it. The closer he is to getting it, moreover, the stronger his incentive to work.

The problem, then, is to reconcile the labourer's right to the whole product of his labour (which Thompson calls his *security*, using that word in a sense which is similar to and yet not quite the same as the sense in which Bentham used it) with the principle of equality – the principle that the more equal the distribution of wealth the greater the total happiness. His solution is to put forward two rules: the first, that what is not a product of human labour ought to be distributed equally; and the second, that every departure from the rule – *secure to the labourer the value of his whole product* – ought to be in favour of equality. Thus Thompson surmounts the difficulty created for him by Bentham's assertion that security is to be preferred to equality when the two conflict, not by denying it, but by defining *security* in a way which greatly reduces the divergence between the two principles.

The objection to this sort of argument is that it involves an unusual, and perhaps improper, use of words. Unless the worker expects and feels entitled to the whole product of his labour, it is a misuse of language to say that he is *secure* only if he gets it. As the word is ordinarily used by social and political theorists, a man is *secure* when he can enjoy his established rights, legal and conventional. By saying that the worker is secure only if he gets the whole product of his labour, Thompson implies that he expects to get it or at least feels entitled to it. But this is unlikely in a community in which for generations workers have received less than the whole product of their labour and are brought up to respect established rights of property. True, if the matter were put to them, they might agree that – in a community very different from their own and ideally superior to it – they would receive the whole product of their labour; they might be persuaded that, if there were greater justice in the world, they would work less and get more. It is perhaps not difficult to convince the poor that, in strict justice, they are entitled to more than actually comes their way. But then they ordinarily do not expect strict justice; they only dream of it. Such dreams, delicious though they may be, do not produce expectations whose disappointment causes a deep sense of grievance. The poor are not insecure because they get less than they would get if a kind of justice other than they are used to were done to them, attractive though they may find that justice when it is brought to their notice; they are insecure only when they cannot rely on getting what they expect to get because it is what they are entitled to, according to notions of justice which are widely accepted in practice or which seem to them practicable in the world as it is.

Against the claim made on behalf of the capitalist that he performs a service which entitles him to the reward he gets, Thompson argues that this is only one, and the less reasonable, of two alternative claims. It has been held that the capitalist should get the whole difference between what is produced by workers using the capital he provides and what they would be able to produce without it; but it can also be held that he should get only an allowance for the depreciation of his capital and as much more as would enable him to live as comfortably as the workers. The first alternative leads to great inequality, while the second leads, if not to equality, to something not far removed from it, and is therefore the better of the two.

The economists, who prefer the first alternative, mistakenly believe that profits and interest depend on the amount of capital accumulated by the community. If capital remained in the hands which produced it, the price that a man could get for putting his capital at another man's disposal would be small; it is only because those who own capital are few, while those who need it are many, that its owners can get so high a price for the use of it. The concentration of capital in a few hands ensures that workers get much less than the whole product of their labour; it reduces their incentive to work and so prevents the community from becoming as wealthy as it would otherwise be. It also ensures that the wealth which is produced gives less happiness than it might, for that is the usual effect of inequality.

In 1827 Thompson published a reply to Hodgskin's *Labour Defended*, calling it *Labour Rewarded*.[1] He attacked Hodgskin for wanting to make the economy even more competitive by merely getting rid of the exactions of landlords and capitalists.[2] Competition leads to periodic crises, and in any case can never be really free unless no one at the outset of his career has greater wealth or knowledge, greater freedom of action, or greater access to means of production than anyone else. It is possible to go a considerable way towards ensuring that competitors start with equal advantages, but it is never possible to go the whole way. Moreover, competition leads to over-exertion, which endangers health and prevents mental improvement. If men are to continue using machinery on a large scale (and they ought to do it since it vastly increases production and therefore the power to satisfy wants), it is impossible to assess exactly each man's contribution to the common product and the reward to which he is entitled.

Therefore, says Thompson, instead of competition there should be co-operation, and all who contribute should receive the same reward. Otherwise – since all who work willingly expect equal treatment – by giving larger rewards to the meritorious, we undermine security. In a

---

[1] Or, to give it its full title, *Labour Rewarded. The Claims of Labour and Capital Conciliated; or, How to Secure to Labour the Whole Products of its Exertions.*

[2] It is sometimes said that Hodgskin was not a socialist because he did not advocate co-operative production or any sort of public or communal control of production. Certainly, by Durkheim's criterion (see his *Socialism*, ch. 1, pp. 54–63), Hodgskin was not a socialist. But, then, it has also been said that Saint-Simon was not a socialist because he did not condemn unearned incomes. The word *socialist* has been used in several different ways. If we are not to use it in a way which obliges us to deny that a Hodgskin or a Saint-Simon (or, for that matter, a Proudhon or a Fourier) is a socialist, we ought to allow that any man is a socialist who advocates *either* public or communal control of production for the benefit of the poor, *or* the abolition of types of property which enable some men to live from the labour of others.

co-operative community the workers provide a ready market for one another; they produce only what they need. There is no waste from the failure of supply to meet demand. Thompson advocated the setting up of small communities, which should increase in size gradually until they consist of two thousand persons. A community of more than two thousand is too large to manage its affairs democratically and efficiently, whereas, if it is appreciably smaller, it cannot be self-sufficient and prosperous, providing its members with an ample living. Thompson expected the workers to finance these communities out of their own savings and looked for support to the trade unions. Like Hodgskin, he had little faith in the propertied classes and believed that the labouring poor could improve their wretched condition only by their own exertions.

2. Fourier

'My theory', Fourier tells us, 'aims at using the censured passions (*les passions réprouvées*) as nature gives them and without changing them in any way. That is all there is to it, the whole secret of passionate attraction. There is no questioning whether God was right in giving such and such passions to human beings; the associative order (*l'ordre sociétaire*, or the social order in which men are true partners – the name that Fourier gives to the type of community he favours) uses them without changing them at all and as God has given them'.[1] Fourier delights in attacking the 'moralists', meaning presumably not everyone who offers advice to men about how they should live (for he does that himself) but those who teach the sort of morality which makes a virtue of restraining the passions. The morality of the moralists whom he condemns impels man to be at war with himself; it rests on the assumption that God does not know how to fashion men's souls wisely but needs a Plato or a Seneca to improve the work of His hands. The 'moralists' have taught man that he must get the better of his nature, as God made it – that he must tame it. But this, Fourier tells us, is quite to mistake the matter. Man must not repress his nature but must create the sort of community where it can have free play. The natural passions, which have harmful effects in society as it is today, will find full and harmless scope in communities of about 1600 persons, properly organized. Fourier claims to have discovered the key to that proper organization, and offers it to mankind.

---

[1] *Théorie de l'unité universelle*, 2nd ed., vol. IV, Livre Deuxième, sect. IV, ch. 3, in the *Oeuvres complètes de Fourier* (Paris 1841–58), V.157. I am responsible for the translation from the French.

Fourier the psychologist – the interpreter of the passions – in some ways recalls Hobbes; there is the same love of definition, enumeration and order, and the same unspoken conviction that he has taken the full measure of mankind. Man, we are told, has five sensitive passions; they are the five senses, and they tend to luxury. Perhaps it would be better to say that the object of many desires is to gratify the senses, and that these desires can be roughly classified according to the sense or senses they aim at gratifying. Fourier insists against the 'moralists' that these five passions (or, as we might prefer to say, these sensuous desires) ought to be satisfied as much as possible; he approves of luxury provided it does not lead to boredom or disgust. Man also has four affective passions which make him sociable: friendliness, love, ambition and parental feeling.[1] And, furthermore, he has three distributive passions, the *cabalistic*, or passion for intrigue; the *composite*, or desire for satisfactions which are of more than one type (for instance, a desire for an experience which satisfies both the senses and the intellect, like a good dinner in good company); and the *butterfly*, or passion for variety. It is above all the distributive passions which have been misunderstood and called vices; they are the pre-eminently worldly passions; and the 'moralists' have castigated them as impediments to virtue. They are passions denounced under such names as vanity, deviousness, hypocrisy, triviality and inconstancy. They are also the passions which have produced most of the refinements of art and social life. Besides these twelve passions, there is another, a thirteenth, which is unlucky in at least one respect, for Fourier could find only ugly names for it; he called it *harmonisme* or *unitéisme*, and described it as the natural inclination which a man has to reconcile his own happiness with other people's. Presumably, man does not seek this reconciliation deliberately; it is rather that he is inclined to get happiness from what gives happiness to others, that he tends to put a higher value on shared than on solitary pleasures. Fourier's problem is to find a form of association in which these passions are not repressed but are given a free course and yet serve to hold the association together.

Society, as at present constituted, is both repressive and wasteful. Parents, in order to prepare their children for life in it, feel bound to restrain their passions, and the children secretly rebel against parental

[1] Fourier uses the word *paternité* to denote the fourth affective passion. Clearly, he does not have in mind fatherhood, the condition of being a father, nor the sexual desire which causes a man to become a father; he means presumably some passion which is satisfied in paternity. And, since he uses the word *man* in the sense of *human being*, he means a passion which is also satisfied by maternity.

authority. Thus neither parents nor children feel for one another as they should feel; their love is spoilt by resentment and fear, and they get as much pain as pleasure from each other's society. Production cannot but be disorderly because it must respond, in large measure, to the speculations of middlemen who levy tribute on producer and consumer alike and who by their manoeuvres create monopolies and cause bankruptcies. Sismondi has admitted that consumption is 'upside down' because effective demand is determined by the whims of the unproductive and not the needs of producers. There are other absurdities: As man's power to create wealth increases, the rich grow richer while the poor remain in their poverty and are less secure than they used to be; the rich accumulate possessions which add nothing to their happiness while the poor are consumed with envy. Waste is enormous because there are idlers, because there is inefficiency, and because much is produced which is not wanted or does not satisfy.[1]

The remedy for these ills is the *phalanx*, a community of from 1000 to 1600 members differing in age, fortune, experience and character. In this community all work is voluntary, and workers are put into groups according to the work they do, a group being formed for every different kind of task. Groups doing similar work are arranged in series, each group taking its place in the series between the two groups whose work is most like its own. Fourier supposes that workers will join a group because they are attracted by the kind of work it does, and supposes also that there will be considerable rivalries between contiguous groups in a series. Every worker will want to join several groups and to work in each for only a short time. In this way the community will benefit from a wide division of labour and from the incentive to work which springs from emulation, while the worker will find an outlet for several talents and will do work which gives him pleasure. Fourier expects that there will be at least fifty to sixty series in a phalanx, and probably many more. It may well be that there will be more groups than workers, so that every worker will

[1] Fourier reckons up the waste thus: three-quarters of the housework done by women in the towns and half done in the country would not need doing in a rationally organized community; nor would three-quarters of the work done by domestic servants, all the work done by the armed forces, by customs officers, and by 'sophists' (i.e., lawyers), nine-tenths of the work done by merchants, two-thirds of that done by transport workers, and half of that done by manufacturers, taking into account the shoddiness of what they make. There is also the waste involved in unemployment, in the idleness of the rich, and of prisoners and of the preventably sick, in crime, begging and prostitution, and in the uselessness of the studies and games of children. In the eyes of the reckoner it is a formidable tally, because he sets it up against the phalanx, the hive of industry, full of healthy, happy and busy workers.

belong to many groups and each series will therefore work for only short periods. The system aims at making the best use of the three distributive passions: the butterfly passion for variety, the composite passion for blended or multiple satisfactions, and the cabalistic passion for intrigue. These are reprobate passions in actual society, repressed and harmful, but in the phalanx they are respectable and useful. How the passion for variety is given a wide field needs no explaining; and it is almost as easy to see how the other two are provided for. The worker in the group gets the satisfactions that come from competition as well as those that come from co-operation, for his group is striving to do better than those closest to it in the series. He helps to decide how the group will work and also takes part in the work; he is both manager and worker. Every different kind of work which he chooses to do offers him a different blend of pleasures. Since every group is the rival of other groups, there is constant scheming to do better; there is room for the arts of persuasion and manoeuvre, and the passion for intrigue is satisfied.

The distributive passions are not satisfied only in the work done by the groups arranged in series; they are satisfied also in other ways, in the loosening of the ties which bind men and women to one another and to their children, in the very different and less restrictive ties resulting from a widening of the circle of intimacy. So, too, the sensitive and affective passions are satisfied in the working groups as well as outside them. Yet it is mostly to social activities outside the groups that Fourier looks to give a head to the sensitive and affective passions, whereas it is to these activities and to the groups equally that he looks to set free the distributive passions. The passion for variety is satisfied by the absence of restrictive family ties as much as by the freedom to do many different kinds of work, and the passion for multiple satisfactions as much by common meals and other forms of social intercourse as by work which is both co-operative and competitive. Only the passion for intrigue is perhaps better satisfied in the working groups than outside them.

The members of the phalanx are to live in one large building, the *phalanstery*, where they take their meals and leisure together, though they also have separate apartments to which they can retire when they feel the need for privacy. Fourier derived great pleasure from describing the life of the phalanstery, the excellence and delicacy of the food, the comforts of the building, the variety of the entertainment, the warmth and politeness of social intercourse, and the doing away with many unpleasant forms of housework. It is the vision of a bachelor with a taste for good living, a tenderness for women and charity towards children, and with a strong dislike for the intimacies and stuffiness of family life. The small family, he thinks, stifles its members; there may be affection between them but they are also held together by bonds which they find irksome and cannot undo. The family is not what Fourier understands by *an harmonious group*; for a group is *harmonious* when the passion which in fact holds it together is also the tonic passion or the passion of display (*passion d'étalage*), the one it exhibits to the world. The family, as we know it, is supposed to be held together by love; much of its behaviour (especially the front it puts to the world) is inspired by the need to give evidence of love; and yet it is in reality held together more by material needs and social conventions. The family is, as Fourier puts it, *a subversive group*, a group in which the real and the tonic passions are different. In the phalanx all groups are harmonious; the passions that hold them together are the passions manifest in the outward behaviour of their members.

The phalanx must be recruited from all classes, and no one must be called upon to make a great sacrifice on entering it. If the rich do not enter it, its resources will be meagre and it will have less to offer its members. The rich must enter voluntarily, hoping to live the better for doing so, and they must not be deprived of their wealth, which must be treated as an investment they have made in it. They will, says Fourier, get a better return on their money in the phalanx than they could get outside it. Of the annual wealth produced by the phalanx and distributed to its members, capital should get four-twelfths, talent three-twelfths, and labour five-twelfths, or less than half. But Fourier's concern for the rich is not quite as great as might appear. The return on capital is to diminish with each successive thousand francs invested, and the workers who come into the phalanx without capital are encouraged to save, so that soon all the workers are likely to be capitalists as well, getting a proportionately much larger return on their investments than the rich.[1] And, of course, capital is

---

[1] It may seem that, if the return on each successive amount invested is to diminish, the rich man with a large sum to invest can hardly get a better return in the phalanx than outside it. True, Fourier believed that productivity in the phalanx would be immensely greater, so that, if holders of capital received one-third of the distributed product, the return that any man would get on the first amounts invested would be several times greater than he could expect to get outside. Even so, the really wealthy man could hardly expect to get a better return on his capital in the phalanx, and must probably get a much worse one, especially as Fourier supposed that the return would diminish steeply with every thousand francs invested and never envisaged a rate of interest of more than 50 or 60 per cent, even on the first shares. Perhaps the 'rich' men he had in mind were merely solid well-to-do bourgeois and not men with great fortunes of francs to invest.

to be managed, not by the individual investor, but by the community through its appointed agents.

Once the phalanx is a going concern and its members are used to the work and leisure it provides, the rich will not want to spend their money on themselves; they will spend it rather on the community as a whole or on some part of it with which they are closely connected. The life of the phalanx will be such that differences of income will not there have the significance which they now have. The rich will work as much as the poor, and the poor will be able to save and invest. Who will resent the wealth of a man whose capital is ten times greater but who lives more or less as other men do and is a close collaborator with them? Fourier's purpose is neither to preserve the wealthy in their riches nor to dispossess them; it is rather to draw them into a community where their wealth will be useful but will cease to divide them from the poor, where there will still be inequality (though much less than before) but where inequality will have no harmful effects. In the phalanx everyone will have adequate food, clothes and lodging, even though he does not work; but the spirit of the community will be such – and the work it offers so attractive – that no one will be idle unless he is incapable of work. Where most work is unpleasant or unsatisfying, where most men work only because they need money, to offer them even a bare living regardless of the work they do is to encourage idleness; it is to make the lazy parasites on the industrious. But in the phalanx, work, even though it is not always easy, is always attractive. In the phalanx the rich will reject the notion, now so widely accepted, that many must be poor if some are to be rich. This notion (which Fourier calls, rather oddly, the 'political principle' of the civilization he abominates – meaning presumably that it is there taken for granted and not that it serves as a guide to policy) will give way to another: that the poor must enjoy a degree of affluence if the rich are to be happy. Even donkeys will be better lodged and cared for in Harmony (which is one of the names that Fourier gives to the social order he approves of) than the peasants now are in France.[1]

Man is by nature good, but society has corrupted him. What proves better the vagueness of this maxim than that it serves to express Fourier's doctrine as much as Rousseau's? For the two doctrines are very

---

[1] Fourier was fond of animals. We are told that it is a rule in Harmony that whoever ill-treats an animal is himself more of an animal than the creature he ill-treats. As we are not told what are the practical effects of this rule, we must suppose that it is not so much a rule as a sentiment. It is an odd sentiment in a community of animal lovers. Is it also the rule in Harmony, where there is so much tenderness for all man's present victims, that whoever ill-treats a woman is more of a woman than she is?

different. If we look at Rousseau's description of the education of Emile, we see that the boy is faced one after another by problems which need energy, and often also courage, as well as intelligence, to solve; he learns, not without difficulty, that he cannot have all that he wants, that he must control his desires, that he must become his own master. Though Rousseau sometimes speaks as if Emile were never thwarted by human beings, but only by his physical environment, this is not at all borne out by the facts as they are described. The boy has to learn to live with others, to moderate his demands on them, to forgo what he could not get except by making them subservient to his wishes, which he is too weak to do. He must learn self-discipline, not only that others may have peace, but that he should be capable of freedom. The tutor does not remove all obstacles, apart from those which Nature imposes, out of the boy's way; he does not create a condition in which the boy can give play to all his passions without harm to himself or to others. He does not insulate him from society; he merely sees to it that society does not present him with problems which he is too weak and immature to solve. Society both stimulates and represses. The function of education, as Rousseau describes it, is to ensure that the child, by his own efforts, is able to come to terms with society in such a way that his need for autonomy and self-respect is satisfied. Though this need is itself a product of social intercourse, the pressures of society on the individual – especially while he is still a child and immature – may make him incapable of satisfying it. The aim of the tutor is to preserve the child from these harmful pressures until he is strong enough to resist them. But he does not acquire this strength in isolation from society; he acquires it by solving social problems which are within his powers, by exerting himself, by becoming his own censor. The tutor tries, as far as possible, to ensure that the child learns from experience; he does not demand unquestioning obedience; he seeks to avoid situations in which the child yields to adults merely because he fears their power. But he does not preserve the child from having to take account of the wishes of others. Repression is inevitable in any society, even the most perfect; and the best that we can do is so to educate the young that they can find freedom and happiness under self-discipline compatible with social harmony. This, I believe, is the essential doctrine of Rousseau in *Emile*.

But it is not the doctrine of Fourier, who usually speaks as if in the phalanx there were no need at all for self-discipline – as if nobody, whether child or adult, would ever want to do anything incompatible with social harmony. True, he does not always speak in this way; he does, when he describes the process whereby children educate one another, acknowledge that a child learns to behave partly by being rejected by other children and altering its ways in order to be accepted by them. He does sometimes admit, indirectly, that in every society education involves repression. Yet the whole bias of his doctrine is to suggest the opposite. He does not say, as Rousseau does, that, though the passions we are born with are neither good nor bad, we must ensure that society – which in any case will profoundly modify them – does not pervert them; and that we can do this only by creating a social environment which enables the child to become, largely by its own efforts, a reasonable adult. He is not even much interested in the process whereby a child becomes a grown man or woman, and seems almost to take it for granted that human passions are little affected by the social environment, so that all that matters is that they should have free play. He speaks almost as if the passions were like water, whose flow can be stopped but whose nature is not changed by the stopping. Man is cramped in society as it is now constructed, and therefore must have room to stretch himself. This is not at all the doctrine of Rousseau and takes far less notice of the facts.

Several of the other socialists favoured easy divorce, but none of them attacked the close family of the Western type with the ardour of Fourier. He did not want it broken up immediately, and even criticized Owen for being in too great a hurry to make divorce easy. The close family is part of the established system, and it is a mistake to undermine it while that system lasts. *Phanerogamic morals* (or, in plain English, free love) are suited only to Harmony – to the phalanx after its members have worked and played themselves free of the restrictive conventions of civilized society. Fourier, who found Owen impatient and superficial, prided himself on his prudence and judiciousness; he disliked rival theorists but had no wish to shock the well-to-do and the respectable.

The close family cannot be defended against some of Fourier's strictures upon it. There is often a pretence of love where no real love is felt, especially between persons bound to each other by ties which, for one reason or another, they cannot bring themselves to break; and the tyrannies of the possessive are the most unbearable of all. The worst cruelties, the deepest betrayals, the most elaborate and degrading insincerities are reserved for the family circle. There is nothing nastier, when it is nasty, than family life. We can admit this, and yet defend what Fourier attacks. Every close tie is apt to make demands on us which are excessive, and yet we feel the need for such ties. The passions for whose sake Fourier (a bachelor) would destroy the family are perhaps products of family life. The sort of love upon which he set so high a value might not exist in a society where there were no enduring bonds between men and women. Even the capacity for the friendships which for some men (especially bachelors) take the place of love – a capacity acquired in childhood – may develop in the intimate family circle. Fourier supposed that in the phalanx men's passions would be deeper as well as more varied – that men would live more intensely. It never occurred to him that the capacity to feel strongly is acquired in the closest and most demanding of human communities, in the hothouse which is the family; nor yet that the looser ties, which to him were the most precious, might lose their savour if the closer ties, which he feared, were abolished.

II. THEIR ATTITUDE TO RELIGION, NATIONALISM AND WAR

The *philosophes* in France and the Utilitarians in England were, for the most part, hostile or indifferent to Christianity; some of them were atheists and others deists, and the few whose devotion to Christ it would be uncharitable to question (since they were in Holy Orders) gave little outward evidence of faith. But the early socialists, with two important exceptions, were not hostile to organized religion, and several of them were friendly to Christianity. They were not orthodox Christians; they did not accept whole-heartedly any of the established creeds. Indeed, we may question whether, strictly speaking, they were Christians, for they may not have believed in the divinity of Christ or even in a personal God. But they spoke sympathetically of religion in general and of Christianity in particular, dissociating themselves from the *philosophes* who had attacked them. They also sometimes put themselves forward as spokesmen of God. 'Listen,' says the Innovator (whose opinions are those of Saint-Simon) to the Conservative, 'listen to the voice of God speaking to you through my mouth. Become good Christians once again'.[1] When Fourier speaks of the social order he has invented and delights in, he remarks, 'At the sight of this societal fairyland. . .we shall witness a frenzy of enthusiasm for God, the author of so beneficial an order';[2] and in several places he introduces

---

[1] *Nouveau Christianisme, Oeuvres de Saint-Simon et Enfantin*, XXIII.192.
[2] *Le Nouveau Monde industriel et sociétaire*, sect. IV, notice VIII, ch. 31, *Oeuvres complètes de Fourier*, VI.287.

what he recommends with the words, 'God has willed'. But we are not so much concerned with the personal faiths of the early socialists or how close they stood (in their own eyes) to God, as with their attitude to religion. They did not think of it as the 'opium of the people', and wanted rather to reform than to abolish it.

Nearly all the early socialists were indifferent to one of the strongest sentiments of their age, nationalism. This indifference is not peculiar to them among the social and political theorists of their time; it is as marked in the Utilitarians. But Saint-Simon and Proudhon were more than indifferent; they were strongly hostile to it, and their arguments are worth noticing. Saint-Simon, educated before the French Revolution, was used to thinking of Europe as a cultural whole and looked upon nationalism as a relic of the past. It was unsuited to the times, he thought, and he even persuaded himself that it was already giving way to more generous and more appropriate sentiments. Proudhon, born almost fifty years later, believed as strongly that nationalism was out of place, but saw it as a growing menace.

1. *The Abuse and Use of Religion*

The two socialists conspicuously hostile to religion were Owen and Proudhon. About Owen's attitude to it, little need be said. It was very much like an attitude common in educated circles in the eighteenth century in both England and France, though more aggressive in France than in England because the Catholic Church had long been more intolerant and formidable than the Church of England. Even in the decades before the French Revolution, it had still been more dangerous (and also more exciting) to attack the Established Church in France than in England. Men like to think themselves braver than they are, and find it exhilarating to take small risks boldly, especially when they can take them in good company.

Owen believed what the eighteenth-century rationalists had taught: that men, while they were still too ignorant to explain the world rationally, had taken to religion, but were now growing out of it – a process which persons of goodwill and good understanding must want to hasten. That belief alone might not have sufficed to move him to attack religion. He had another and more pressing motive for doing so. The churches taught that man is responsible for his own actions, and can justly be blamed and punished for the harm he does. It was this doctrine that Owen believed to be the most pernicious of errors. It had caused men to devote their energies to detecting and punishing crime and to neglect what really matters, which is to remove its causes. Not until they are persuaded that character is a product of environment will they cease punishing the individual and set about reforming society – will they then take the course which is the only sure road to happiness. But, once they are persuaded, they will act upon this truth, for such is their nature. And so to Owen it seemed that the churches were teaching a doctrine which prevented men taking his salutary advice.[1]

It is often difficult to make out just what it is that Proudhon disliked about what he attacked. Did he object to religion because its teachings are false? He seems to have shared Condorcet's belief that religion thrived while men were ignorant but that there is now no place for it. Yet he did not agree with Condorcet that religion, though inevitable in the past, had been harmful even then; he said that religion had been useful in the past, but he did not make it clear just how it had helped to induce men to behave well while they were still too little enlightened to see that good behaviour was in their own enduring interest. Perhaps he believed that, while organized force was still necessary to maintain social discipline, religion provided supplementary sanctions. Perhaps he believed that, at a time when men were still too ignorant to know how to remove the social causes of their wretchedness, it was good that they should have religion to comfort them.

Whatever his views about the past, he saw no need for religion

[1] Owen was a poor tactician. It should have occurred to him that nobody denies that character is deeply affected by environment. Since his object was to persuade his contemporaries to change the environment which, in his opinion, produced crime and misery, he was ill-advised to raise the issue he did raise. He had no need to attack the churches for teaching that men are responsible for their actions and ought to be punished for the evil they do; he would have done better to enlist their support in his endeavours to change the social environment in order to reduce the temptations which move men to do evil. The churches were not committed by their creeds to leaving the environment unchanged. Those who hold to the doctrine of responsibility which Owen rejected are not logically committed to resisting social reform, and it is not at all obvious that they are psychologically disposed to resist it. By offending the churches, Owen did more harm than good to his own cause. The truth is that he was so much excited by his doctrine that men are not responsible for what they do (of which he sometimes spoke as if he were its discoverer) that he could not help attacking whoever denied it. He attacked first, and then justified his attack by putting forward mistaken opinions about the practical consequences of denying his doctrine. His arguments in support of this doctrine, moreover, are so weak and ambiguous as to create the impression that he has raised an issue beyond his intellectual powers. Men who have been successful in business – and in this they resemble politicians – when they engage in controversy of that kind sometimes give the impression of great arrogance, because they have strong convictions and yet are blind to the weaknesses of the position they take up. Though their arrogance, being simple-minded, rarely gives offence, its absurdity causes them to be dismissed as cranks.

in the present. Religion is now worse than useless; it is harmful. It is an obstacle to progress because it turns men's minds away from reforming society, now that it is at last in their power to do so. It attributes all the virtues proper to man to a God without whom man is nothing. It thus weakens man's self-confidence, his sense of his own dignity; it puts him in perpetual tutelage. Perhaps in the past, while his understanding and powers were small, it was good that he should create for himself an image of benevolent omnipotence and take shelter under it. But now he must dare to see himself without a master anywhere; he must trust in his own powers; he must strive to realize justice here and now, and not look for it in an imaginary world beyond death. Man cannot reach maturity in the shadow of a God fashioned by his own hopes and fears. Proudhon is not concerned to prove that religion is false; he is content to hint at its origins and to condemn it for the harm it now does. He condemns it for a reason almost opposite to Owen's; he accuses man of taking refuge in God to escape his worldly responsibilities, which are the only true ones.

Much the most interesting of the early socialists, when he speaks of religion, is Saint-Simon. He tells us that every society needs a system of beliefs which not only explain the world but also determine the goals of human endeavour. Otherwise men will have no firm principles to guide them; they will be morally at sea and therefore disturbed and unhappy. In the Middle Ages there was such a system: theology purported to explain the world – all other studies being subordinate to it – and it also provided a morality acceptable to men at that stage of social evolution. The theology and the morality were intimately related to one another, so that whoever accepted the first found it reasonable to accept the second. If the world were as the theologians described it, it was the task of wisdom to do what the moralists prescribed. Saint-Simon agreed with such Catholic writers as Maistre and Bonald, who condemned the moral anarchy of their age, contrasting it unfavourably with the Middle Ages. Indeed, he generally rather preferred the conservative and even frankly reactionary political theorists to the liberals. He could understand what it was in the old order – a society united in faith and capable of greatness – that attracted such writers.

But he thought it impossible and undesirable to restore the hold upon men exercised by religion as the Middle Ages had known it. The progress of science has destroyed many of the beliefs on which that religion rested; it is therefore beyond anyone's power to revive it, and men must not be deceived by attractive memories or romantic phrases. If it could be revived, it would have to be to the detriment of the positive sciences to which men owe opportunities of happiness unknown to any previous age – though they are opportunities still largely untaken. The great merit of the philosophers of the eighteenth century, especially the Encyclopaedists, was that they had shown that the new sciences were incompatible with old religion. They had sapped the faith on which the *ancien régime* rested. Though religion still survived, after a fashion, it was no longer what it had been, the acknowledged mistress of the house; it was a decayed and almost useless servant, kept on for old time's sake. The work of the Encyclopaedists had been needed; it was foolish to regret what they had destroyed. What is required now, therefore, is not a return to a system of beliefs suited to a different type of society, but an advance to a new system suited to a new society. The positive sciences – the sciences that study the facts and produce theories to explain them which are subject to verification – have made progress enough to debilitate the old religion beyond hope of revival; but they have not yet advanced to the point where they can do for society all that religion once did. There is still one large gap in men's knowledge; they know much more about the world external to them than about themselves and the communities they form. Before science can take the place of religion, this gap must be filled; there must emerge a science of man in society, a science which one of Saint-Simon's disciples, Bailly, called *social physiology* and to which another, Comte, later gave the name of *sociology*. Saint-Simon believed that he had himself laid the foundations of this new science. Until it was developed, philosophy must remain lame and inadequate, he thought, while the so-called science of politics laboured under an even heavier disability. Politics could not become a genuine science, except as a branch of another science not yet born. But mankind have been discussing politics for over two thousand years. These discussions, which go under the name of *political theory* or *political philosophy*, are a form of metaphysics, a kind of sophisticated nonsense disguised as sense. Political theory can nevertheless be dangerous, because it creates in men the illusion that they understand society when in fact they do not. The method of the new science of social physiology must be historical. But history, in Saint-Simon's time, was regarded as little more than a branch of literature. The exact and well-documented study of the evolution of human societies was still unknown in the first decades of the nineteenth century. Saint-Simon's own attempts at reconstructing the past were clumsy and precarious. He guessed at more than he knew and was too apt to think well of his guesses.

When the circle of sciences is completed, when man has learnt to use the same methods in studying himself as he already uses in studying the world external to himself, there will arise a philosophy entirely in harmony with science.[1] This philosophy will not purport to give men knowledge of a reality lying behind the phenomena studied by the scientist; it will merely explain how the aspects of reality studied separately by the special sciences form a single universe. It will be the science of sciences, not as directing the others what they should do, but as putting together into a whole what they produce, which must, as they produce it, be fragmentary. Philosophy will therefore be a kind of compendium of the sciences, though it will call for intellectual gifts as rare as any possessed by the special scientists. It is to philosophy thus conceived that Saint-Simon looks to do for industrial society what theology did for feudal society: to provide it with a cosmology intimately connected with a morality suitable to the age. He even proposed that the *Institut de France* should prepare a catechism to be taught in all elementary schools. That body was, he thought, a congregation of the finest intellects, many of them learned in the sciences, and therefore the most competent to devise a moral code suited to a society dominated by industry and science.

Later, in the last years of his life, he seems to have changed his mind considerably, though perhaps without himself noticing the extent to which he had done so. Durkheim[2] suggests that Saint-Simon began by believing that men, though predominantly self-regarding, can become enlightened enough to follow their own advantage without harming one another. In other words, he believed in a natural harmony of interests: it is the long-term interest of every man that he should accept rules which, while they prevent his doing harm to others, also prevent their doing harm to him. Men are unhappy, not because they are egoists, but because they are unenlightened egoists. It is possible to discover rules which are in the long-term interest of them all, and to persuade them to accept these rules. But the rules must be suited to the type of society in which men live, and must be inculcated by

---

[1] Saint-Simon did not suppose that mankind were on the verge of producing, in every sphere, scientific theories which could not be improved upon. He looked forward to indefinite scientific progress. The circle of the sciences would be *completed* when men used scientific methods in every field of enquiry; its completion would not therefore mean that there would be no further progress. Yet Saint-Simon did not foresee the sort of revolution in science we have lived through in our century; he supposed that the principles discovered by Newton would be accepted always, and that progress would take the form of building upon principles such as these and not of discarding them for others. His conception of scientific progress was in important ways different from ours.

[2] See his *Socialism*, ch. 9, pp. 226–8.

methods likely to be effective. Saint-Simon therefore long believed that some such body as the *Institut de France* could decide both upon the rules and upon the methods. It was a task for which intellectuals, learned and dispassionate, were eminently fitted. But later he changed his mind, experience having taught him that the obstacle to progress is as much egoism as ignorance. It is not enough to enlighten the selfish; it is also necessary to combat their selfishness.

To combat selfishness, we must do more than educate men about themselves and teach them how best to reconcile their interests with other people's; we must strengthen sentiments in them which are not made strong merely by extending their knowledge. The Encyclopaedists had not understood the value, in its great days, of what they had destroyed. What religion had once done and could no longer do, must not be left undone. Man cannot live without faith, or, rather, though individuals can sometimes do so, whole communities cannot, for what holds a community together is always a common faith, a system of shared beliefs directing their ultimate loyalties. We must teach men to love one another. But we cannot teach them to love one another by showing that otherwise they will be unhappy, for it is of the nature of love that, though it brings happiness, men cannot be brought to feel it by being persuaded that without it they will not be happy. And so – all this according to Durkheim – Saint-Simon, though without admitting it to himself, lost faith in the ability of a philosophy derived from science to provide a morality suited to industrial society; he lost faith in the wisdom of intellectuals and scientists and turned back to the morality of the gospels. He did not, however, turn back to Christian theology; he did not believe in the divinity of Christ, nor even perhaps in the existence of a personal God. He cared only for Christian morals, and saw no logical connection between them and Christian theology. He remained what he had perhaps always been, a pantheist with vague beliefs about a divinity immanent in all things.

Now this, though Saint-Simon might not know it, was to abandon the doctrine that every moral code goes along with a philosophy, or general theory about the universe, appropriate to it. The Christian moral code appeared in the world centuries before even the first beginnings of the industrial society in which alone (according to Saint-Simon) it could be applied fully. When Jesus taught His followers, civilization was still in its infancy and society was divided into masters and slaves; it was not yet possible for men to organize society in the spirit of the doctrine of love which He preached to them.[1] He sowed

---

[1] So Saint-Simon tells us in his *Nouveau Christianisme*, op. cit., pp. 165–8.

a seed which, for nearly two thousand years, still could not ripen into a full harvest. Both Catholics and Protestants have neglected the core of His teaching. Men have made progress in every science except the most important of all, which is the science of morals. And Saint-Simon makes it clear that progress in this science does not consist in finding better principles than those taught by Jesus; it consists only in discovering how to apply His principles. Nor does Saint-Simon say that, in all the generations since Christ taught, no one has understood His moral teachings and tried to live up to them; he does not say that men have possessed the letter of those teachings for centuries without ever having understood their spirit. He says only that the social order was an obstacle in the way of men's receiving them and acting upon them. While that order lasted it was difficult but not impossible for them to understand Christian doctrine fully, and difficult also to act upon it when they understood it. But, presumably, these difficulties did not arise because men lacked the knowledge which science provides; they arose for two quite different reasons. Men were still deeply influenced by the moral values of a society divided into masters and slaves, so that, even when they were sincere Christians, they often did not aim at what sincere Christians should aim at. They made mistaken decisions about what they ought to strive for. And, even when they did not make mistakes of this kind, but, rather, wanted what they ought to have wanted, it was difficult for them to achieve it.

If that is so, then the connection between science and the morality of which Saint-Simon approved is not what he, in his earlier writings, supposed it to be. The knowledge which comes with science adds nothing to man's understanding of this morality, which is, indeed, an *understanding* different in kind from scientific knowledge or opinion; a man could *understand* – could acknowledge and inwardly digest this morality, could possess it in the spirit as well as in the letter – and yet have little or no science. He could be as scientifically ignorant as the most ignorant of the Apostles. The connection between science and this morality is merely that the progress of science is one of the causes of the disintegration of the old social order whose values and behaviour stood in the way of men's receiving Christ's teaching in the spirit of the teacher and acting upon it. This is the revised doctrine of the *Nouveau Christianisme*; or perhaps we should say (to avoid attributing to Saint-Simon opinions which he never put into words), it is the doctrine about the connection between science and morality implicit in the *Nouveau Christianisme*. But we have to admit that Saint-Simon probably never saw the implication; there is no evidence that he was aware how far he had broken away in the *Nouveau Christianisme* from his earlier teachings.

Saint-Simon was right in believing that mediaeval theology and cosmology were closely bound up with the moral values of mediaeval society. He was mistaken in supposing that the cosmology and ethics of the Middle Ages formed a system of mutually consistent beliefs, but he was right in holding that they deeply influenced each other. But then, as he himself insisted, the mediaeval explanation of the world was not *positive*; it was not scientific. It pretended to a knowledge not got from experience; it put forward hypotheses incapable of verification. The function of mediaeval cosmology was partly to strengthen the hold upon men of the values asserted by mediaeval ethics. The contrary was also true: mediaeval moral values were made to square with the mediaeval conception of a universe created and controlled by a God more wrapped up in man than in any other of His creatures.

But a philosophy which is merely a compendium or summary of the special sciences[1] cannot stand to any system of values as mediaeval cosmology stood to mediaeval ethics. Such a philosophy is morally neutral. No doubt, someone who accepts it will be inclined to reject (in large part, if not completely) a cosmology of the mediaeval type; and his rejection of it will also incline him to reject many of the values of mediaeval society. The man who will take for true only what the sciences vouch for is likely to have moral values different from those of the man who believes in a divinely ruled universe and a life after death. But the effect of science on morals is entirely negative; it merely destroys or weakens beliefs which incline men to accept certain values. It does not itself incline them to accept other values. This is because it consists of beliefs different in kind from those contained in the cosmologies it undermines. No doubt, there are some values common to all societies and without which no society could endure. If an unscientific cosmology which serves to support them along with other values is destroyed, they will survive its destruction, even though they are temporarily shaken by it. These are values indestructible by

---

[1] This is a different conception of philosophy from that of some (perhaps many) contemporary philosophers who disparage or neglect theology and metaphysics. They do not look upon philosophy as the summary of the special sciences but as the explanation of what is involved in experiencing, knowing, reasoning, making moral judgements, etc. The philosopher in this sense is concerned with scientific method but not with explaining what the sciences, between them, make of the universe.

science or by philosophy as understood either by Saint-Simon or by some present-day philosophers. But they are not values supported by science or by philosophy in the sense that mediaeval morals (including such values) were supported by mediaeval cosmology. The experience which, apart from unscientific cosmology, inclines men to accept these universal and indispensable values is not science or philosophy as Saint-Simon and some philosophers of our time conceived them; it is an experience common to the illiterate peasant and the most gifted scientist or philosopher. Though the social scientist may enlighten us about that experience, the knowledge he provides will still not stand to those values as theology did to morals in the Middle Ages.

Saint-Simon wanted too much: he wanted to reject religion on intellectual grounds and to get from science the assurance and comfort which religion gives to those who accept it. And when he found he could not get it – when he was moved to write the *Nouveau Christianisme* – he refused to admit his disappointment; he continued to speak of the old theology as unacceptable because it conflicted with science and to speak of science as the cause of progress. But he no longer looked to science or to a philosophy, either derived from science or explanatory of it, to support morals. Nor did he confine himself to repeating the moral teachings of Jesus and to showing how they could be followed in industrial society; he resorted, as his disciples did after him, to a verbose and cloudy pantheism, as if he wanted to tap all the emotions connected with the old religions without committing himself to any of their explicit doctrines.

2. Fraternity

Seeing that hostility to the Church and to Christianity was so much more conspicuous in the eighteenth century in France than in England, it is surprising to find the early French socialists so friendly to religion, if not to the Catholic Church.[1] There was more religiosity among them than among the early English socialists. The German radicals who came to Paris preferred Proudhon to the other French socialists because he stood out among them as an enemy of religion. These radicals came from a country where most of their kind were against

---

[1] The disciples of Saint-Simon, though they rejected Catholic dogma and criticized the Church for making a virtue of asceticism, were in one respect closer than any of the other socialists to Catholicism. They wanted to organize a Spiritual Power, an intellectual élite, whose pronouncements on matters of theory and morals should be final. They criticized liberty of conscience as leading to intellectual and moral anarchy.

religion, and the attachment to religion of the French socialists seemed to them old-fashioned and out of keeping with 'advanced' views about the organization of society. Many of the French socialists, despite their hostility to the established hierarchy, temporal and ecclesiastical, clung to the Christianity of the gospels, as the Anabaptists had done in Germany in Luther's time; they clung to it for all the world as if Voltaire and the Encyclopaedists had never been heard of. And to some of the young German radicals in Paris this seemed, after the great flood of the French Revolution, positively antediluvian.

There is, of course, no logical incompatibility between socialism and Christianity. Christianity, in itself, is neither radical nor conservative. To the extent that it turns men's thoughts to another world, or inclines them to believe that their relation to God is more important than their relation to other men, it may weaken their motives for wanting to change this world. St Paul preached obedience to the established powers, and the churches have often taught men that they ought to be content with their earthly lot, because, no matter what it is, they can obey God's law and receive His reward. Yet Christian morals can be understood as much in a radical as in a conservative sense. Many Christians have held that it is possible to follow the teachings of Christ without attempting in any way to change the established order, while others have believed that that order must be changed if men are to live as Christ taught them to do. The second position is logically just as sound as the first. Certainly, it is not less sound than the first merely because it has been less often adopted, or, rather, less often until quite recent times. Nor is Christian theology in any way incompatible with socialism. The religiosity of the French socialists, if it seemed out of keeping with their socialism, must have seemed so only because, for historical reasons, radicalism was associated in the eyes of many with hostility to the Christian faith.

I suspect that the French socialists were attracted to Christianity mainly from two motives, both of them connected with the great revolution. For they were disappointed in that revolution. It had proclaimed three principles, liberty, equality and fraternity, but had taken little notice of the third. It had removed many barriers and privileges; it had established a kind of equality of opportunity. It had created a society in which it was easier than it had been for the able and the energetic to make successful careers. It could, of course, be criticized for not having gone far enough in that direction – for not having ensured that the child of poor parents has as much chance to make good as the child of rich ones, for not taking the principle of equality of opportunity to its logical conclusion. And it was criticized for this reason by the socialists. They argued that, to the extent that competition is inevitable or is good for society, justice requires that all who have to compete should have the same advantages. Since some are born abler and stronger than others, they cannot have the same natural advantages, but society ought to aim at eliminating all other inequalities. If competition there must be, let it be fair.

Yet the faith of the early socialists in competition, no matter how fair, was limited. They believed in more than equality of opportunity, and were concerned to do more than insist that the avowed supporters of that principle, proclaimed by the French Revolution, should be true to it. They believed also in another kind of equality. A competitive society, even though it does everything that can be done to ensure that competition is fair, inevitably raises some persons above others; and every society is to some extent competitive. But it must not exalt the competitive spirit, which is essentially selfish even when it makes for the common good; or otherwise the successful will despise those who fail, who will in turn envy them. The other kind of equality, the kind which takes no account of success or failure, is fraternity. It is equality between members of the same family or community, of whom each feels that the others belong to it as fully as he does himself; it is like the equality of Christians in the sight of God. It is the equality which justifies inequality, making it tolerable, enabling one man to say of another, *Let him be raised above me because he has more to give to the community to which we both belong*. The revolution, so it seemed to many of the French socialists, far from strengthening this kind of equality, had weakened it.

The French socialists also disliked the great revolution for its violence and the passions which it aroused – passions at least as strong as those which gave rise to it. They believed that these passions had prevented the revolution from achieving as much as it otherwise might have done. They were therefore attracted to a religion which both condemned violence and preached doctrines that seemed to them to justify the great changes they wished to make. What was later to be called the 'opium of the people' appeared to them a fence against passions which, if not controlled, might make it easier for the ambitious to use popular grievances to help them get power. The French socialists had seen this happen in their own country.

3. Their Dislike of Nationalism

One of the many ways in which Saint-Simon differed from the rationalist philosophers of the eighteenth century was in preferring the Middle Ages to antiquity. Condorcet, though he believed that progress was now inevitable because the forces making for it were stronger than all the obstacles in their way, did not hold that every age had been superior to the age before it; the course of events from the fourth to the eleventh century – from the decline of Rome to the domination of the West by the Church – did not look to him like progress. He saw no great advantage to mankind from the triumph of Christianity. But Saint-Simon claimed to see one: Christianity had taught men to transcend the narrow loyalties of the Greeks and Romans. It had superimposed humanity or philanthropy on the many patriotisms of the ancient world.[1] Christendom in the eleventh and twelfth centuries was a single community in a way in which the Roman Empire had not been; its unity did not consist in its all being subject to one prince or even in its having traditions and practices marking it off from the rest of the world. It consisted in the feelings that Christians had for one another as sharers of one faith. The old patriotism of the Greek or Roman had been inferior, not as being a sentimental attachment to the country of one's birth, but as excluding wider loyalties. What Saint-Simon objected to in the Roman was that he made service to his country the supreme duty of man.[2]

The spread of industry was making nations more than ever dependent on one another, Saint-Simon believed. Classes were coming to have more in common than nations. The industrial class in France had less to divide it from the same class in England than from the feudal nobility in its own country. Indeed, the industrial class had interests transcending national barriers as no class before it had had. The barons of mediaeval England might share many of the attitudes and prejudices of the barons of mediaeval France. To the outsider contemplating them both, they might have seemed very much alike.

---

[1] Saint-Simon did not consider the claim that the Stoics had done this several centuries before the Christians; he did not know how much both Christian theology and Christian ethics owe to the Greeks.

[2] It might be objected that Christians have in practice been as exclusive and as uncharitable to outsiders as ever Roman patriots were. Christians have sometimes taught that whoever does not share their faith will suffer everlasting punishment. Perhaps it was in part because Christians taught this while Stoics did not that Diderot, Condorcet and others preferred antiquity to the Middle Ages. Yet Saint-Simon was not as simple-minded as that comment might make him appear. He made much of what seemed to him good about Christianity because Condorcet and Diderot had passed it over, and also because he believed that it would survive what was bad. The appeal of Christianity was not confined to the sophisticated; it was altogether more exciting and wider than the appeal of Stoicism. Saint-Simon was attracted by all that is warm and generous in a religion which requires the giver of charity to respect its recipient, and condemns compassion when it is mixed with contempt.

But this similarity did not prevent their often making wars upon one another. Members of the new dominant class were not merely like one another from country to country; they had interests which drew them together. They formed the class destined, according to Saint-Simon, to create an international order which would bring peace to the world. As we have seen already, Saint-Simon's 'industrial class' included all productive workers, manual and administrative; it included men of business and captains of industry as 'the natural leaders' of that class. Saint-Simon made for both capitalists and proletarians the claim which Marx was to make for the proletarians alone: that their class interests, to the extent that they are aware of them, move them to oppose war.

This claim is not so much false as misleading. But I shall not contest it, for I could not do so without looking carefully into the concept of 'a class interest' – a task better left until I come to examine the Marxian theory, which makes much greater use of it. It is perhaps enough for the moment to say that capitalists probably stand to lose as much by war as proletarians do, if we estimate their gains and losses in terms of the preferences usually attributed to them. They are supposed to want to increase their wealth without their right to make use of it as they please being diminished, just as proletarians are supposed to want a better standard of living, greater security and perhaps also a larger say in the running of the businesses which employ them. There is no evidence that war is a greater obstacle to proletarians getting what they want than to capitalists doing so. But the feudal nobles, having quite different preferences, wanted what could not be obtained without war: they wanted danger and glory; they wanted to assert themselves in a society where they could best do it by making war. It would be wide of the mark to say that they sought to enrich their country, or even themselves, by making war, but it is true that they could not get what, as a class, they most wanted unless they made war. They were so placed socially that their ambition found its largest scope in war.

Saint-Simon disliked the scheme proposed by the abbé de Saint-Pierre in 1713 in his treatise on *Perpetual Peace*. Saint-Pierre advised the sovereign princes of Europe to set up a permanent congress of plenipotentiaries, pledging themselves to accept the decisions of this body. The scheme seemed as unrealistic to Saint-Simon as it had done to Rousseau, and for much the same reasons. The governments of Europe had been each other's rivals for centuries; they were deeply suspicious of one another, and their policies sprang from these suspicions as well as from ambitions which they were unlikely to abandon. Only when the nations had acquired governments of a different type – governments pursuing different ends from those they now pursued – would it be possible to set up a real international authority, a body able to make important decisions and to carry them out. Saint-Simon believed that governments, constituted as they were in his day, were moved by ambitions surviving from an earlier type of society. These ambitions were both dangerous and absurd in an industrial age, and would disappear as soon as industrial society acquired the kind of government (or, rather, administration) appropriate to it. He was therefore hopeful. True, nothing good could be expected from governments of the sort that Europe still had, but these governments had survived beyond their time, and something much better would soon take their place. When the last traces of the feudal order disappeared, there would be no more war, for the industrial class is by nature pacific just as the feudal class is by nature warlike.[1]

Proudhon was both less hopeful of the future and less scornful of the past than Saint-Simon. He did not look upon war as the profession of a class surviving from a decrepit social order about to disappear completely; he did not believe that the manual workers (who were included by Saint-Simon in the industrial class) were any more devoted to peace than other classes. The people, he said, admire the strong and the ruthless; and Proudhon, though himself a pacifist, came at times close to sharing this admiration. The popular attitude to war seemed to him neither absurd nor evil. The military virtues – courage, discipline, devotion to duty, self-sacrifice (virtues which are military not because soldiers always possess them but because they make a nation formidable in war) – rightly inspire respect. Success in war has in the past often been an effect of moral superiority. Proudhon, who admired courage in all its forms and who was also a man of the people, did not disparage it in the form best understood by the class he sprang from. Just as individuals who are self-confident and high-spirited are often combative, so too are communities, and self-confidence is good in both individuals and communities.

---

[1] Saint-Simon was not quite as consistent as I have made him appear. He said that 'the feudal class', dominant in the Middle Ages, was warlike, but he also spoke admiringly of the 'cosmo-political' character of mediaeval society, and even suggested that wars in the Middle Ages had been fewer and less 'important'. But why had wars been less 'important'? Presumably, because resources were smaller and authority less centralized, so that it was impossible to put large armies into the field. If resources were larger in later centuries, this was surely because of the expansion of industry, and if these resources could be more readily mobilized for war, it was because the State had grown strong at the expense of the feudal class. Saint-Simon's thesis – that industrial society is essentially pacific – clearly needs to be stated much more carefully than he stated it, if it is to be even plausible.

If, then, Proudhon condemned war, it was not because he believed it to be inherently evil or irrational. He condemned it because he believed that, in modern conditions, it is not only more destructive than ever before but also more brutal and more degrading. It has always been both good and bad: it has encouraged some virtues and set loose some vices. As communities grow larger and instruments of war more formidable, war gives less scope to the virtues and more to the vices. The combativeness natural to vigorous persons and communities persists and must be given an outlet other than war. But so long as the State, as we know it, endures, there will be danger of war. There will be lasting peace between nations only when the enormous concentration of power, which is the modern State, has been dissolved. In this connection, as in every other, Proudhon was suspicious of the vast organization which enables a few ambitious men to manipulate the masses. The danger of war, now that war has become terrible and degrading, does not spring from the combativeness natural to man; it springs from the political order which allows this combativeness to be exploited by a narrow ruling group. There is no social class conspicuously less warlike than the others. Peace will not come when some other class dominates society in the place of the now dominant class; it will come only when the apparatus of power which makes modern war possible shall have ceased to exist.

Proudhon was closer to the truth than Saint-Simon when he spoke of the causes of war, but his suggested remedy is too improbable to leave room for hope. The apparatus of power which he condemned is unlikely to disappear. Undoubtedly, it is a condition of war as we know it; if it did not exist, the kind of war which he feared (and which we have so much greater cause to fear than he had) would be impossible. But there is no comfort in this truth, for not only is it unlikely that the State will disappear; it is also, given what most people nowadays aspire to, undesirable. The State is a condition of the material prosperity that must exist if everyone is to have the opportunities which not only socialists but men of other persuasions now agree that he should have. We speak of the right of every man and woman 'to realize his or her potentialities'. We may be hard put to it to give a precise meaning to these words, but, whatever we understand by them, we mostly agree that they refer to opportunities still out of reach of most people, on account of their poverty or ignorance. Prosperity greater than the world has known in the past, though not a sufficient, is a necessary, condition of everyone's having these opportunities. This, at least, is a belief widely shared, and to which Proudhon subscribed. He wanted the prosperity which everyone sharing this belief thinks desirable; he wanted the prosperity but not the concentration of very great power in a very few hands, without which it is impossible. 'Be rid of the State and you will be rid of many evils, including war', is apt to appear useless advice to persons convinced that they have much to hope for from the State and who yet passionately desire peace.[1]

Proudhon did not share in French sympathy for Polish and Italian nationalism, for it seemed to him that those most eager to create large nation-states cared too little for the autonomy of smaller groups and the freedom of individuals. He saw how illiberal nationalism was or might soon become. He was a man of many loyalties. Far from disparaging patriotism, he thought well of it. But he was suspicious of the strident nationalism which swallows up all narrower loyalties, and which strengthens the State at the expense of associations closer to the individual or more sensitive to his needs.

He was alive to the dangers of what he disliked, but not to its causes or advantages. Why was it that wider loyalties were gaining strength at the expense of narrower ones? Could the Poles or the Italians, as individuals, get the freedom which Proudhon thought desirable, while as nations they remained under foreign rule? Could they shake off that rule unless they were united by devotion to a larger community? Nationalism is dangerous to freedom, and yet national independence is often a condition of it. To Proudhon, belonging to a nation long united and too formidable to be ruled by foreigners, nationalism was distasteful. What he valued most seemed to him threatened by it. He was perhaps too insular to imagine how what was distasteful to him could be attractive to a Pole or an Italian no less devoted to individual freedom than he was. He was a shrewd but a one-sided critic.

★ ★ ★

The early socialists are not to be reckoned among the most profound or subtle or broad-minded or lucid of social theorists. With two conspicuous exceptions – Saint-Simon and Proudhon – they had narrow views, and

---

[1] Proudhon also believed that war is an effect of the unequal distribution of wealth, whether between nations or inside them. Poor nations make war to get wealth, if their poverty does not weaken them to such an extent that they have no hope of success; and the wealthy classes in a nation sometimes provoke wars, either from cupidity and ambition or to distract the poor from their wretchedness. There is nothing new about these arguments, which are perhaps not worth refuting. Even if it were true that war has often been an effect of these kinds of inequality, it would not follow that with greater equality there would be less danger of war, for other causes of war might then operate more strongly.

Saint-Simon was careless and diffuse while Proudhon was obscure and elusive. It cannot be said of them – as it can of Rousseau, Hegel and Marx – that their writings, for all their defects, are worth close and repeated study, because there is so much in them. They also lack the rigour and clarity of the English Utilitarians. Judged by the standards we should apply to Rousseau, Hegel or Marx, they are men of small talents. Not that their theories are more open to criticism than those of these so much more gifted men; they are merely less comprehensive and less profound.

Nevertheless, taken collectively, the early socialists are intellectually rich. They are also important. In the field of social theory, it is they who, with Rousseau and Hegel, take us from the eighteenth to the nineteenth century. Like Rousseau, they put forward an ideal of equality which could not be realized unless society were transformed; like Rousseau and Hegel, they see the individual, a purposeful and moral being, as the product of his social environment; and like Hegel, they see him involved in a social process leading eventually to his emancipation. Most of the ideas that go to make up the social theory of Marx and Engels are already present, somewhere or other, in their works. The extent to which they anticipate Marx is obscured by the Marxian vocabulary, which owes more to Hegel than to them. There are, for example, remarkable similarities between Saint-Simon's account of social evolution in the West since the Middle Ages and Marx's account. There are also remarkable differences: Saint-Simon attributes less importance than does Marx to changes in methods of production and more to the progress of science, and he sees no deep cleavage of interest between capitalists and proletarians. But where Marx differs from Saint-Simon, he often agrees with another of the early socialists. He is the heir of them all, and also, of course, more than the heir. He elaborated upon the ideas he took over from them; he saw connections which escaped their notice; he took more than they did into account. It has been claimed for him, and not untruly, that he saw deeper than they did, which means, not so much that he went further than they went in the directions they took, as that he saw what they saw as they did not see it; for each of them saw only a part of the world which was the focus of their attention, while he came closer to seeing the whole. He was more versatile, more intense, more imaginative than they were. Repeatedly, he reminds us of them, and yet, when we stop to take his measure, he stands out clearly above them all, as Shakespeare does above the other Elizabethan dramatists. He absorbs and transcends them.

The early socialists, judged by the highest standards, were men of small talents but generous impulses. They have been, above all other social theorists, the interpreters of the aspirations and fears of mankind in the industrial age. It would perhaps be unjust to say that they have contributed less to enlarging our understanding of society than to formulating our social aspirations, for, as I have said already, taken collectively, they were prolific of good ideas. But certainly, if we take them individually and compare them with Marx, they have contributed less to our understanding and more to our hopes and fears. Marx called some of them *bourgeois* or even *petits bourgeois*. And yet they were not – in their habits, moral standards and personal ambitions – noticeably more bourgeois, *petits* or otherwise, than he was. They were not, any more than he was, preaching doctrines likely to attract the lesser *bourgeoisie*. Nevertheless, Marx's judgement upon them is not entirely untrue; they probably did sympathize more than he did with some aspirations of the 'little man', the craftsman, the shopkeeper and the peasant. They sympathized with his desire to raise his standard of living, his craving for equality, his love of independence, his mistrust of the middleman, his fear of organized power. But these feelings seemed to them as strong in the proletarian as in the man of little means. They were the spokesmen for all in society who were weak and hard put to it to defend their interests against the strong, who owed their strength either to wealth and privilege or to their position in some powerful organization. Certainly, their sympathy for the proletarian, for the man with nothing to sell but his labour, was not less than Marx's. Indeed, it may well have been greater. When they contemplated the situations of both the proletarian and the small man struggling to maintain a precarious independence, they saw much that was common to them. They looked steadily at what Marx was inclined to neglect, because they had no wish to draw the proletariat away from other classes.

They were, as Marx never was, advocates for the little man.[1] Hence their deep suspicion of the State, their dislike of bureaucracy, their preference for small communities where there is scant difference of status or none at all. No doubt, Marx too predicted the eventual disappearance of the State; and yet he gave little thought to it. It was something that was to happen after the revolution, and the best of his mind was given to explaining how the revolution would come and to hastening its coming. He merely foretold that men would be equal and free in the future, and did not stop to consider what their condition would be like when they were so.

[1] This, of course, is not equally true of all of them, and is least true of Saint-Simon.

The early socialists attended carefully to what he neglected; they never lost sight of the goal which made the journey worth taking; it was never beyond their horizon. The world, since their time, has become even more complicated, with even greater concentrations of power than they knew, and so their fears are more than ever our fears. And we still, in the West, share their aspirations. We want the poor to live more abundantly; we want equality of opportunity; we want security and independence. Though we have abandoned all hope that the State will grow weaker or disappear, we seek to make it our servant rather than our master. The merely rich or 'well-born' or highly educated are much less important than they were; we are all little men today, unless we are big men by virtue of some office we hold in the State or in some large organization in close contact with the State. We are all, in some respects, *petits bourgeois*; we share some of the fears and some of the aspirations of the early socialists. Their solutions may not tempt us or may seem to us impossible to attain, but the motives and sympathies which inspired them are still ours. In some ways they are closer to us than is Marx, in spite of the vast influence he has had and still has.

By temperament the early socialists were more sanguine, more charitable and less resentful than Marx. This is true even of Saint-Simon, the least *petit-bourgeois* among them. They were much more reluctant than Marx was to use force and much more afraid of the consequences of using it. They hardly spoke of the *masses* who figure so largely in Marx's thought, and their political vocabulary, compared with his, is conspicuously unmilitary.

They failed to reconcile their aspirations with one another. They wanted life made easier and more comfortable for the poor, and therefore (though with some exceptions) welcomed industrialism. Yet they often closed their eyes to the obvious, and would not see that the growth of industry, by making society more intricate and its parts more tightly knit, made centralized bureaucracy inevitable. They wanted the benefits of industrialism without accepting the hierarchy and bureaucracy inseparable from it. They therefore neglected matters of capital importance to persons who care, as they did, for equality and freedom as well as for material well-being. They did not ask themselves just what kinds of equality and freedom are desirable, and how far they can be achieved in an industrial society where there must be large-scale administration if there is to be the efficient and smooth production on which prosperity and security depend.

Industrialism and bureaucracy are necessary, if not sufficient, conditions of some kinds of equality and freedom, and are incompatible with others. What we need to discover is what these kinds and the others are. Unfortunately, when we raise this question, we get no help from the early socialists. Not even from Saint-Simon, though he roundly condemned the doctrine of the rights of man and the political democracy it was used to justify. He wanted administration by experts, who could not (so he thought) exercise their authority for the common good if they were responsible to the people, and he also wanted equality of opportunity. He never asked himself what equality of opportunity could amount to in communities in which every man's capacities and needs were determined by a self-recruiting élite.

The inadequacy of the political thinking of the early socialists is striking. It leaps to the eye as the poverty of Marx's political thought does not. Marx attacked bureaucracy and the State as fiercely as they did, but, since he never seriously attempted to describe the kind of society in which bureaucracy and the State would disappear, his writings do not bring home to us the full absurdity of the dream of an industrial society without bureaucracy and without the inequalities of power inseparable from it. Our attention is not drawn to the weakest part of his political thought, his theory of the State; it is drawn rather to the stronger part, to his beliefs about how classes struggle for power and what the working class should do to obtain it. Marx understood politics as none of the early socialists did. Not that he made – or would have made, had he had the chance – a conspicuously successful politician; but he was a profound observer of political events. He was, like Machiavelli, a frustrated politician, and frustrated as much by temperament as by lack of opportunity. Such men are sometimes born politicians – not born to get power, not born to success, but born to a deeper knowledge of how power and success are to be won.

Further Readings

A list prepared by Robert Wokler

CHAPTER 1 MONTESQUIEU

F. T. H. Fletcher, *Montesquieu and English Politics (1750–1800)* (London 1939). A scholarly study of the British perspectives of Montesquieu's political thought, addressing both the English focus of its doctrine of the mixed constitution and other themes, and its reception in England and Scotland.

Mark Hulliung, *Montesquieu and the Old Regime* (Berkeley and London 1976). An unorthodox interpretation of Montesquieu's critiques of political absolutism, divine right and *raison d'état*, deemed to derive not from a conservative standpoint but out of a longing for a constitutional republic along lines which anticipate Weber.

Henry J. Merry, *Montesquieu's System of Natural Government* (West Lafayette, Indiana 1970). An expansive study of the complex interrelations of government and society in Montesquieu's political thought, around his concern that rulers should respect differences between classes, so as to encourage toleration and socially relevant distributions of authority.

Thomas L. Pangle, *Montesquieu's Philosophy of Liberalism: A Commentary on 'The Spirit of the Laws'* (Chicago 1973). A study of Montesquieu's conceptions of human nature, freedom, commerce, religion and participatory republicanism, showing how, in contending with principles which challenged his own, he proved the most humane of liberal thinkers.

Melvin Richter, *The Political Theory of Montesquieu* (Cambridge 1977). Translated selections from Montesquieu's three major contributions to political and social thought, with a substantial and illuminating introduction devoted to their central themes and to the meaning of terms.

Robert Shackleton, *Montesquieu: A Critical Biography* (first published 1961, Oxford 1970). A meticulously detailed biography which locates Montesquieu's political and other writings in the specific contexts, and with much reference to the sources, that inspired them.

Judith N. Shklar, *Montesquieu* (Oxford 1987). An engaging intellectual biography which places emphasis upon the independence of courts of law both as the most central feature of moderate as distinct from despotic government and as Montesquieu's pre-eminent contribution to liberal thought.

Henry Vyverberg, *Historical Pessimism in the French Enlightenment* (Cambridge, Mass. 1958). An investigation of the genesis and different formulations, including those of Montesquieu and Diderot, of eighteenth-century French ideas of decadence and flux.

Mark H. Waddicor, *Montesquieu and the Philosophy of Natural Law* (The Hague 1970). An attempt to locate Montesquieu's scientific study of the diverse manifestations of positive law against the background of natural law philosophy.

CHAPTER 2 HUME

H. T. Dickinson, *Liberty and Property: Political Ideology in Eighteenth-Century Britain* (London 1977). A study of British political ideas and institutions from the 1680s to the 1790s, in the light of the principles and assumptions of persons engaged in campaigns to reform or (like Hume) to defend the social order.

Duncan Forbes, *Hume's Philosophical Politics* (Cambridge 1975). A spirited account of Hume's political thought, around his attempt to establish an experimental method with regard to morals, leading to a science of politics embraced by empirical natural laws.

Jonathan Harrison, *Hume's Theory of Justice* (Oxford 1981). A subtle, closely reasoned and sometimes critical assessment of Hume's conceptions of justice as an artificial virtue and of property defined in terms of rules, embracing interpretations of his account of the obligation of promises and the origins of government.

Albert O. Hirschman, *The Passions and the Interests: Political Arguments for Capitalism before Its Triumph* (Princeton 1977). A broadly conceived, compactly executed essay on the transformation of a seventeenth-century opposition between interests and passions into an eighteenth-century opposition between benign and malignant passions, developed in critical reaction to Hobbes's doctrine, by the so-called sentimental school of English and Scottish moral philosophers, from Shaftesbury to Hutcheson to Hume.

Shirley Letwin, *The Pursuit of Certainty* (Cambridge 1965). Contends that Hume's science of politics excludes the imposition of an ideal form of government, focusing instead on the need to safeguard existing institutions against the unchecked concentration of power.

David Miller, *Philosophy and Ideology in Hume's Political Thought* (Oxford 1981). A lucid interpretation of Hume's science of politics, including British politics as portrayed in his *History of England*, showing how its apparent inconsistencies stem from a sceptical conservative philosophical position.

G. P. Morice, (ed.), *David Hume: Bicentenary Papers* (Edinburgh 1977). Contains notable essays on Hume's ethics and politics by leading contemporary scholars.

Ernest Campbell Mossner, *The Life of David Hume* (first published 1954, repr. London 1970). An ambitious, erudite and always engaging intellectual biography of the highest calibre.

Nicholas Phillipson, *Hume* (London 1989). Draws attention to Hume, *the historian*, as he was at first best known and is still sometimes described, pointing to the ways in which his curiosity about human behaviour turned from general maxims to particular illustrations, with reference to British culture and politics.

John B. Stewart, *The Moral and Political Philosophy of David Hume* (New York 1963). An expansive treatment of Hume's conception of men's moral virtues, their principles of justice and forms of government, and the place of popular religions in politics.

Frederick G. Whelan, *Order and Artifice in Hume's Political Philosophy* (Princeton 1985). A detailed discussion of Hume's ethics and politics as elements of his science of human nature, with special reference to his account of the social formation of beliefs and character.

CHAPTER 3   BURKE

James T. Boulton, *The Language of Politics in the Age of Wilkes and Burke* (London and Toronto 1963). A literary analysis of British political controversies of 1769–71 and 1790–3, dealing mainly with Junius, Johnson and Burke, their style and rhetoric, and the audiences they addressed.

John Brewer, *Party ideology and popular politics at the accession of George III* (Cambridge 1976). An authoritative study of Hanoverian politics, ideology, propaganda and political ritual, particularly notable for its treatment of Wilkite radicalism.

Gerald W. Chapman, *Edmund Burke: The Practical Imagination* (Harvard 1967). A compelling account of Burke's political doctrines, seen as diverse campaigns of a statesman attempting, through his opposition of reform to revolution, to extend the same principles and restraints to all the subjects of the British Empire.

Carl B. Cone, *Burke and the Nature of Politics*, 2 vols. (Lexington 1957 and 1964). A comprehensive, well-executed biography and study of Burke's political career, the first to draw predominantly upon archival sources.

Isaac Kramnick, *The Rage of Edmund Burke: Portrait of an Ambivalent Conservative* (New York 1977). A study, in part psychosexual, of Burke's conservative and repressive social thought in its relation to his private life and personality, drawing much material from his correspondence and notebooks, and interpreting his vendettas against Warren Hastings and Jacobinism as obsessions against upstart licentiousness.

F. P. Lock, *Burke's Reflections on the Revolution in France* (London 1985). A contextual reading of Burke's main contribution to political thought, pointing to the circumstances surrounding its composition and to his use of rhetoric in defence of aristocratic Whiggism against both the French insurgents and their British radical admirers, and to the success of its impact on its readers.

Harvey C. Mansfield, Jr., *Statesmanship and Party Government: A Study of Burke and Bolingbroke* (Chicago and London 1965). An expansive study of the rôle of parties in England after the Glorious Revolution, embracing detailed treatments of Burke's defence of party government, when informed by both principle and popular prejudice, in response and opposition to the spirit of patriotism which Bolingbroke had counselled against the corrupt tendencies of court and country cabals.

Frank O'Gorman, *Edmund Burke: His Political Philosophy* (London 1973). A contextual reading of Burke's Whiggish conservatism, in the context of a career devoted to affairs of state and of the empire in Britain, Ireland and India, and with regard to the innovative revolution in France – a career collectively informed by the belief that only restorative political change should be encouraged.

Peter J. Stanlis, *Edmund Burke and the Natural Law* (first published 1952, Ann Arbor 1965). An interpretation of Burke's political thought as a set of diverse appeals to a principle of natural law in opposition to tyranny, chaos and injustice and as a moral and legal weapon against both radical innovation and existing abuses in government.

CHAPTER 4   ROUSSEAU

Bronisław Baczko, *Rousseau: Solitude et communauté*, trans. (from Polish) Clarie Brendhel–Lamhout (Paris 1974). A richly illuminating treatment of Rousseau's social philosophy through the antinomies of his own character and the tensions between his natural and civic identities.

John Charvet, *The Social Problem in the Philosophy of Rousseau* (Cambridge 1974). A critical reconstruction of Rousseau's political thought in three of his major works, showing the incoherence of his proposed resolution of the problem of social dependence in his vision of a new man, naturally conscious of the common good.

Maurice Cranston, *Jean-Jacques: The Early Life and Work of Rousseau, 1712–1754* (London 1983), and *The Noble Savage: Rousseau, 1754–1762* (London 1991). The first two volumes of the finest biography available, formed around Rousseau's *Confessions* and the definitive edition of his correspondence.

N. J. H. Dent, *Rousseau: An Introduction to his Psychological, Social and Political Theory* (Oxford 1988). A sympathetic reading of Rousseau's social philosophy, constructed round his notion of each person's self, both in its estrangement from others and in rightly ordered association with them.

Robert Derathé, *Jean-Jacques Rousseau et la science politique de son temps*, 2nd ed. (first published 1950, Paris 1970). A meticulous reconstruction of central themes in Rousseau's political philosophy, in the context of seventeenth- and eighteenth-century doctrines of natural law.

Peter Gay, *The Party of Humanity: Studies in the French Enlightenment* (first published 1959, London 1964). An urbane and refreshing collection of essays devoted to Voltaire and cosmopolitanism in the Enlightenment, including a useful bibliographical discussion of some modern interpretations of Rousseau.

Charles W. Hendel, *Jean-Jacques Rousseau: Moralist*, 2nd ed. (first published 1934, Indianapolis 1962). A detailed and perceptive interpretation of Rousseau's views on the social corruption of human nature and the alternative dimensions of uplifting morality, stressing the importance of a biographical understanding of the development of his thought.

Roger D. Masters, *The Political Philosophy of Rousseau* (Princeton 1968). A close reading of Rousseau's major writings on politics, education and the philosophy of history, pointing to their place as parts of a coherent and systematic doctrine.

James Miller, *Rousseau: Dreamer of Democracy* (New Haven 1984). An incisive and lyrical account of the Alpine images of Rousseau's view of democracy, and further material on Rousseauism in the French Revolution.

Patrick Riley, *Will and Political Legitimacy: A Critical Exposition of Social Contract Theory in Hobbes, Locke, Rousseau, Kant, and Hegel* (Cambridge, Mass. 1982). A broad interpretation of the philosophical foundations of social contract theory conceived as a tradition of discourse around notions of political voluntarism, and of Hegel's challenge to that tradition, with a salient discussion of Rousseau's idea of the general will.

Judith N. Shklar, *Men and Citizens: A Study of Rousseau's Social Theory* (Cambridge 1969). A notably vigorous treatment of central themes, framed round images of two lost utopias, one domestic, the other civic.

Jean Starobinski, *Jean-Jacques Rousseau: Transparency and Obstruction,* trans. Arthur Goldhammer, ed. Robert J. Morrissey (first published in French in 1957, Chicago 1988). A modern classic, probing the textual meanings of Rousseau's philosophy in all its manifestations and themes in the light of his inner experience and the contrasting metaphors of immediate sensation and opaque reflection.

Maurizio Virolli, *Jean-Jacques Rousseau and the 'well-ordered society'* (Cambridge 1988). A comprehensive reading of Rousseau's political thought, most illuminating on his republicanism.

CHAPTER 5   FROM BENTHAM TO JOHN STUART MILL

David Baumgardt, *Bentham and the Ethics of Today, with Bentham Manuscripts Hitherto Unpublished* (Princeton 1952). A learned commentary on Bentham's principal writings in moral and political philosophy, interspersed with critical reflections on modern interpretations and on the place of Benthamite ethics in relatively contemporary moral philosophy.

Stefan Collini, Donald Winch and **John Burrow,** *That noble science of politics: A study in nineteenth-century intellectual history* (Cambridge 1983). A profoundly illuminating study, in the form of a collection of essays, of the various British aspirations to develop a science of politics, and the historical, comparative, philosophical or economic methods appropriate to it, from its Scottish Enlightenment origins to its dissolution in the 1930s in Cambridge.

Maurice Cowling, *Mill and Liberalism*, 2nd ed. (first published 1963, Cambridge 1990). An iconoclastic account of Mill's crusading liberalism, perceived as aiming to elevate character and achieve social cohesion, in the context of a political philosophy and sociology designed not just to explain human conduct but to prescribe it.

John Dinwiddy, *Bentham* (Oxford 1989). A crisp intellectual biography of the foremost grand theorist of cost-benefit analysis, whose seldom noticed recognition of the aesthetic dimension of life led him to conclude that in poetry, as distinct from prose, some lines do not go as far as the margin.

John Gray, *Mill on liberty: a defence* (London 1983). A philosophically astute endorsement of Mill's own defence, in utilitarian terms, of a system of moral rights within which priority is accorded to the right to liberty, around a conception of autonomous choice central to the argument of *On Liberty* and Mill's other political writings.

Elie Halévy, *The Growth of Philosophic Radicalism*, trans. Mary Morris (first published in French in 1901–4, London 1972). Subject to frequent correction and revision but still a magisterial treatment both of Bentham's political programme and of the Benthamite School, an enduring classic contribution to British intellectual history.

Ross Harrison, *Bentham* (London 1983). A first-rate philosophical commentary on Bentham's theories of ethics, law, government and education, including particularly illuminating treatments of his critique of legal fictions, his conceptions of duty and interest, and his greatest happiness principle.

John Plamenatz, *The English Utilitarians*, 2nd ed. (first published 1949, Oxford 1966). A predominantly critical study of England's greatest contribution to moral and political philosophy, found wanting on account of the Utilitarians' shared supposition that society, government and morality were means to individual ends.

John C. Rees, *John Stuart Mill's 'On Liberty'* (Oxford 1985). A perceptive collection of essays posthumously assembled (by G. L. Williams) on the meaning, sources, intellectual context and modern interpretations of Mill's most famous work, with a particularly notable discussion of the principle of self-protection.

John M. Robson, *The Improvement of Mankind: The Social and Political Thought of John Stuart Mill* (Toronto 1968). A study of Mill's intellectual career, sources and meaning, which addresses his views on the conflicts between society and the individual that arise from the growth of civilization, and contends that he reached consistent conclusions by way of a unified methodology which subordinated sociology to ethics.

Frederick Rosen, *Jeremy Bentham and Representative Democracy: A Study of the 'Constitutional Code'* (Oxford 1983). An expert commentary on Bentham's constitutional thought, devoted to expositions of his doctrines of sovereignty and democracy, his treatment of the accountability of government, and his differences, with respect to representative government, from both James and John Stuart Mill.

Alan Ryan, *J. S. Mill* (London 1974). A particularly fine and illuminating commentary on the arguments and themes of all of Mill's principal writings.

Leslie Stephen, *The English Utilitarians,* 3 vols. (first published 1900, New York 1968). A loftily commanding disquisition, at once historical, philosophical and evaluative, of the politics and ethics of Bentham and the two Mills.

C. L. Ten, *Mill on Liberty* (Oxford 1980). An analysis of Mill's ideal of individuality and his principle of liberty, emphasizing the significant non-Utilitarian features of his arguments and paying considerable and often critical attention to his historical interpreters and philosophical disciples.

William Thomas, *The Philosophic Radicals: Nine Studies in Theory and Practice, 1817–1841* (Oxford 1979). A richly textured, subtly woven reading of both leading and lesser luminaries among the Philosophic Radicals, based substantially upon manuscript sources, with particularly notable essays on James Mill's science of politics and the Earl of Durham's expedition to Canada.

CHAPTERS 6–7 THE EARLY SOCIALISTS, FRENCH AND ENGLISH

Jonathan Beecher, *Charles Fourier: The Visionary and His World* (Berkeley 1986). The fullest and best biography of the most utterly utopian of the figures generally portrayed as utopian socialists,

Man and Society · Volume Two

including detailed treatments of his vision of the good society, his theories of human motivation and the immortality of the soul, and his accounts of the creation of the universe and the sexual significance of the artichoke.

Gregory Claeys, *Citizens and Saints: Politics and anti-politics in early British socialism* (Cambridge 1989). A penetrating study of Owenite democratic radicalism and its wider place in the history of political thought, embracing a discussion of the theory and practice of communitarian government and a treatment of the connection between Owenism and other British radical movements of the early nineteenth century, including Chartism.

Gregory Claeys, *Machinery, Money and the Millenium: From Moral Economy to Socialism, 1815–60* (Oxford 1987). A study of the economic ideas of early British socialists, concentrated upon Robert Owen, George Mudie, William Thompson and John Gray, who were united by a vision of public utility in a new age of material plenty, and by a theory of progress according to which labour was to be justly rewarded.

G. D. H. Cole, *A History of Socialist Thought,* vol. I: *Socialist Thought: The Forerunners 1789–1850* (London 1953). A spirited survey, in twenty-six short chapters, of early nineteenth-century doctrines of the co-operative and collective regulation of human affairs, including commentaries on Saint-Simon, Fourier, Owen and their schools.

Emile Durkheim, *Socialism,* trans. Charlotte Sattler, ed. Alvin W. Gouldner (first published in French in 1928, New York 1967). A contribution to sociology by way of a close, largely sympathetic, commentary on the doctrines of Saint-Simon and his followers, trading on the distinction between modern socialism, in its concern with the organization of production in industrial society, and ancient communism, as pertaining to shared consumption and the abolition of property.

J. F. C. Harrison, *Quest for the New World: Robert Owen and the Owenites in Britain and America* (New York 1969). A compelling history of the communitarianism of Owen and his followers, embracing his perception of the loss of social harmony in Britain in the early nineteenth century, his Enlightenment inspired search for a science of society, the establishment of communities along his principles in

Scotland, England and America, and the millenarian spiritualism to which the Owenite movement sometimes gave rise.

Robert C. Hoffman, *Revolutionary Justice: The Social and Political Theory of P.-J. Proudhon* (Urbana and London 1972). An excellent intellectual biography of a radical humanist of passionate convictions, a socialist who remained hostile to schemes for the reorganization of society, at once an anarchist and a libertarian.

Edward Hyams, *Pierre-Joseph Proudhon: His Revolutionary Life, Mind and Works* (London 1979). A biographical study of the intellectual, literary and political career of a fierce scourge of property and inequality, whose federalism and attachment to a people's bank are examined principally against the background of the 1848 French Revolution.

Georg G. Iggers, *The Cult of Authority: The Political Philosophy of the Saint-Simonians. A Chapter in the Intellectual History of Totalitarianism* (The Hague 1958). A study of the Saint-Simonian movement around Bazard and Enfantin, whose centralizing conceptions of planning and organization linking every phase of individual life to the power of the State were only partly inspired by Saint-Simon himself, and can be seen to have close affinity to modern totalitarian authoritarianism.

Christopher H. Johnson, *Utopian Communism in France: Cabet and the Icarians, 1839–1851* (Ithaca and London 1974). A study of the influence and appeal of the most successful propagandist, if not the greatest thinker, among the experimental communitarians of the early nineteenth century.

Frank E. Manuel, *The New World of Henri Saint-Simon* (first published 1956, Notre Dame 1963). A substantial, profoundly authoritative and stimulating intellectual biography, devoted both to Saint-Simon's career and to an interpretation of the texts which comprise his scientific, historical, industrial and religious doctrines.

Keith Taylor, *The Political Ideas of the Utopian Socialists* (London 1982). A solid introduction to the at once idealist and pragmatic doctrines of Saint-Simon, Owen, Fourier, the Saint-Simonians, Cabet and Weitling.

Sheldon S. Wolin, *Politics and Vision: Continuity and Innovation in Western Political Thought* (first published 1960, Boston 1975). A subtly conceived interpretation of some central traditions in the history of political thought, around the theme of the maintenance of order in spatial, temporal, economic and legal terms, embracing an account of the sublimation of politics in the modern age of organization, heralded above all by Saint-Simon.

Index

'Luxe, le commerce et les arts, Le',
190n
and men's wants, 291–3
and John Stuart Mill, 204, 270
and Montaigne, 152–3
and Montesquieu, 2, 14, 49, 206
and morality, 125–6, 131–2, 133–40,
143–50, 156
on natural goodness, 133–53, 166
and Plato, 150–2
on natural law, 124–5, 131–3
La Nouvelle Héloïse, 123
on obedience, 173–5, 200
on passions, 129, 131, 135–43, 171,
179
on patriotism, 192–8, 203
on pity, 135, 137
and Plato, 147, 150–3, 175
'Political Economy', 190, 192, 201n
on power, 189–90
on pride, 185–7
'Profession of Faith of the Savoyard
Vicar', 123–4, 144
on progress, 164, 271–4, 291–5,
302–3
Project of a Constitution for Corsica,
124, 149, 153, 184
and equality, 189–92
on property, 129, 183, 190–2
on rationality, 132–4, 143–6, 151–2,
179, 207–8
on religion, 123, 202, 205
on self-consciousness, 126, 133, 136,
142, 184, 207
on self-love, 135–42
Social Contract, 124, 131, 146, 148,
151
and equality, 183, 189–90
and freedom, 163n, 172, 202–3,
283
the general will in, 153–5, 167,
169, 172, 176
and law, 165, 178, 180
and sovereignty, 158, 160, 199n,
201
on society, 124–8, 132–3, 139–40,
146–7, 156–7, 171, 207–8, 261,
281–3
on sovereignty, 155–8, 166–8, 200–1
on the State, 163, 180, 195–6
and organized force, 281–2, 332–3
and totalitarianism, 200–1
on state of nature, 124–33
State of War, The, 129–30
on vanity, 128, 137–8, 141–2, 184–7,
204

on virtue, 137–9, 192, 204
on war and peace, 129–30
Russia, 41–2, 165
and revolution, 111, 331

Saint-Pierre, Charles Irénée Castel,
Abbé de,
Perpetual Peace, 365
Polysynodie, 160
Saint-Simon, Claude Henri de, xii, 275,
281, 371
on authority, 308–9
Catéchisme des Industriels, 304n, 311n,
315, 319n, 321
on Christianity, 358–61
on common purpose for society,
315–18
on egoism, 357–8
and feminism, 297–8
on feudal and theological society,
304–5, 310–11, 319n, 320, 364–6
on French Revolution, 307–8, 310–11
on government, 289–90
and administration, 283–6, 288–9,
309, 319
on history, 276–7, 321–4
on industrial classes, 363–6
on industrial society, 284–5, 292–3,
304, 308–16, 318, 357
L'Industrie, 310n, 311n
on justice, 316, 324
on lawyers and metaphysicians,
310–11
and Marx, 276, 280, 288, 303, 307,
311, 315, 319–20, 321–2, 324,
326, 329, 331, 365, 369
on Middle Ages, 304–5, 313–15,
318–19
on moral order, 316–19
on nationalism, 363–6
Nouveau Christianisme, 352n, 358n,
359, 361
Oeuvres de Saint-Simon et d'Enfantin,
283n, 307n, 308n, 309n, 310n,
311n, 315n, 316n, 319n, 352n,
358n
organic view of society, 313–15, 19
L'Organisateur, 284, 304, 307n, 309
on philosophy, 356–7, 360–1
on religion, 355–61
on rights of man, 316, 372
on science, 308–9, 356–7, 359–60
on social change, course of, 277,
302–21
on social order, 312–13, 319–20